GLOBAL
ORDERING

Other volumes planned in the Globalization and Autonomy series:

Renegotiating Community: Interdisciplinary Perspectives, Global Contexts
Edited by Diana Brydon and William D. Coleman

Empires and Autonomy: Moments in the History of Globalization
Edited by Stephen Streeter, John C. Weaver, and William D. Coleman

Unsettled Legitimacy: Political Community, Power, and Authority in a Global Era
Edited by Steven F. Bernstein and William D. Coleman

Property Rights: Struggles over Autonomy in a Global Age
Edited by William D. Coleman and John C. Weaver

Deux Méditerranées: Les voies de la mondialisation et de l'autonomie
Edited by Yassine Essid and William D. Coleman

Indigenous Peoples and Autonomy: Insights for a Global Age
Edited by Mario E. Blaser, Ravindra de Costa, Deborah McGregor, and William D. Coleman

Cultural Autonomy: Frictions and Connections
Edited by Petra Rethmann, Imre Szeman, and William D. Coleman

Globalization and Autonomy: Conversing across Disciplines
Diana Brydon, William D. Coleman, Louis W. Pauly, and John C. Weaver

See also the *Globalization and Autonomy Online Compendium* at
www.globalautonomy.ca.

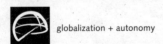

globalization + autonomy

GLOBAL

Institutions and Autonomy in a Changing World

ORDERING

Edited by Louis W. Pauly and William D. Coleman

UBCPress · Vancouver · Toronto

17 16 15 14 13 12 11 10 09 08   5 4 3 2 1

Printed in Canada on ancient-forest-free paper (100% post-consumer recycled) that is
processed chlorine- and acid-free, with vegetable-based inks.

Library and Archives Canada Cataloguing in Publication

    Global ordering: institutions and autonomy in a changing world / edited by Louis W.
Pauly and William D. Coleman.

(Globalization and autonomy, ISSN 1913-7494)
Includes bibliographical references and index.
ISBN 978-0-7748-1433-1 (bound); ISBN 978-0-7748-1434-8 (pbk.)

    1. Globalization–Political aspects. 2. Globalization–Economic aspects. 3. Globalization–
Social aspects. 4. Culture and globalization. 5. Autonomy. I. Pauly, Louis W. II. Coleman,
William D. (William Donald), 1950-III. Series.

JZ1318.G56 2008   303.48'2   C2008-900653-4

Canadä

UBC Press gratefully acknowledges the financial support for our publishing program of
the Government of Canada through the Book Publishing Industry Development Program
(BPIDP), and of the Canada Council for the Arts, and the British Columbia Arts Council.

This book has been published with the help of a grant from the Canadian Federation for
the Humanities and Social Sciences, through the Aid to Scholarly Publications Programme,
using funds provided by the Social Sciences and Humanities Research Council of Canada.
Research for the volume was supported by the Social Sciences and Humanities Research
Council of Canada through its Major Collaborative Research Initiatives Program, Grant No.
412-2001-1000.

UBC Press
The University of British Columbia
2029 West Mall
Vancouver, BC V6T 1Z2
604-822-5959 / Fax: 604-822-6083
www.ubcpress.ca

Contents

Part 2: Regional Variations

Preface

The Globalization and Autonomy Series: Dialectical Relationships in the Contemporary World

THE VOLUMES IN THE Globalization and Autonomy series offer the results from an interdisciplinary Major Collaborative Research Initiative (MCRI) funded by the Social Sciences and Humanities Research Council of Canada (SSHRC). SSHRC set up the MCRI program to provide a vehicle to support larger projects with research objectives requiring collaboration among researchers from different universities and across a range of disciplines. The MCRI on Globalization and Autonomy began in April 2002. The research team involved forty co-investigators from twelve universities across Canada and another twenty academic contributors from outside Canada, including scholars from Australia, Brazil, China, Denmark, France, Germany, Slovenia, Taiwan, the United Kingdom, and the United States. Drawing on additional funding from the International Development Research Centre (IDRC), the project became affiliated with a separate interdisciplinary research team of twenty-eight scholars, the Groupe d'Études et de Recherches Interdisciplinaires sur la Méditerranée (GERIM). GERIM is based in Tunisia and includes members from France, Spain, Jordan, and Lebanon as well. Scholars from the following disciplines participated in the project: anthropology, comparative literature, cultural studies, economics, English literature, geography, history, music, philosophy, political science, and sociology.

The project was conceived, designed, and implemented to carry out interdisciplinary research. We endeavoured to put disciplinary-based theories and conceptual frameworks into dialogue with one another, with a view to developing new theories and understandings of human societies. Four conditions needed to be met if research were to be done in this way. First, we brought humanities and social science disciplines into a relationship of mutual influence, where perspectives were integrated without subordinating one to another. To achieve this integration, the team agreed on a set of core research objectives informed by existing writings on globalization and autonomy. Members developed a number of research questions designed to address these objectives, and a research plan that would permit them to address these questions in a focused, systematic way. Second, team members individually were encouraged to think inside disciplines other than their own and to respect differences across disciplines in terms of how the object of knowledge is constructed. Third, team members were selected to ensure that the research was carried out using multiple methodologies. Finally, faced with researching the complex relationships involved in globalization, an interdisciplinary approach meant that our work would be necessarily pluri-theoretical. We held to the view that theories would be most effective when, in addition to applying ideas rigorously, their proponents acknowledged the limitations of any particular theoretical perspective and consciously set out to cross boundaries and use other, sometimes seemingly incommensurable, perspectives.

To ensure intellectual integration from the start, team members agreed on this approach at the first full meeting of the project and committed to the following core objective: *to investigate the relationship between globalization and the processes of securing and building autonomy.* To this end, we sought to refine understanding of these concepts and of the historical evolution of the processes inherent in both of them, given the contested character of their content, meaning, and symbolic status.

Given that *globalization* is the term currently employed to describe the contemporary moment, we attempted to:

- determine the opportunities globalization might create and the constraints globalization might place on individuals and communities seeking to secure and build autonomy
- evaluate the extent to which individuals and communities might be able to exploit these opportunities and to overcome these constraints
- assess the opportunities for empowerment that globalization might create for individuals and communities seeking to secure and to build autonomy

- determine how the autonomy available to individuals and communities might permit them to contest, reshape, or engage globalization.

In seeking to address the core objectives for the project, we moved our research in three interrelated directions. First, we accepted that globalization and autonomy have deep historical roots. What is happening today in the world is in many ways continuous with what has taken place in the past. Thus, the burden of a contemporary examination of globalization and autonomy is to assess what is new and what has changed. Second, the dynamics of the relationship between globalization and autonomy are related to a series of important changes in the locations of power and authority. Finally, the globalization-autonomy dynamic plays out in the construction and reconstruction of identities, the nature and value of community, and the articulation of autonomy in and through cultures and discrete institutions. In each of these three areas, the team developed and agreed to answer core questions to provide clear direction for the research. The full text of the questions is available at http://globalization.mcmaster.ca/ga/ga81.htm.

Over successive annual meetings of the team, our research coalesced around the following themes: institutions and global ordering; democracy and legitimacy; continuity and rupture in the history of globalization and autonomy; history, property rights, and capitalism; community; culture; the situation and struggles of indigenous peoples; and the Mediterranean region as a microcosm of North-South relations. The researchers addressing these themes tended to be drawn from several disciplines, leading to interdisciplinary dialogue within each thematic group. The themes then crystallized into separate research problems, which came to be addressed by the volumes in the series. While these volumes were taking form, the project team also developed an online publication, the *Globalization and Autonomy Online Compendium* (see next page), which makes our findings available to the general public through research summaries; a glossary of key concepts, organizations, people, events, and places; and a comprehensive bibliography. The ultimate objective of all of these publications is to produce an integrated corpus of outstanding research that provides an in-depth study of the varying relationships between globalization and autonomy.

Globalization and Autonomy Online Compendium

Readers of this volume may also be interested in the *Globalization and Autonomy Online Compendium* (available at www.globalautonomy.ca). The *Compendium* is a collective publication by the team of Canadian and international scholars who have been part of the SSHRC Major Collaborative Research Initiative that gave rise to the volumes in the Globalization and Autonomy series. Through the *Compendium*, the team is making the results of their research available to a wide public audience. Team members have prepared a glossary of hundreds of short articles on relevant persons, places, organizations, events, and key concepts and have compiled an extensive searchable bibliographical database. Short summaries of the chapters in other volumes of the Globalization and Autonomy series can also be found in the *Compendium*, along with position papers and peer-reviewed research articles on globalization and autonomy issues.

Acknowledgments

THE EDITORS WOULD LIKE to express their immense gratitude to Nancy Johnson, the project editor for the MCRI on Globalization and Autonomy, for her excellent work, support, and committed professionalism. We are also grateful to Jennifer Clark, Sara Mayo, and Sonya Zikic for administrative support throughout the project. The editors acknowledge that the research for their contributions to the book was undertaken, in part, thanks to funding from the Canada Research Chairs Program. Finally, the editors and volume authors would like to thank the peer reviewers of this book for their helpful and insightful comments and suggestions.

Global Ordering

chapter 1

Globalization, Autonomy, and Institutional Change

William D. Coleman, Louis W. Pauly, and Diana Brydon

INDIVIDUALS AND COMMUNITIES AROUND the world are becoming ever more deeply connected to one another. For better or for worse, what happens abroad now affects us deeply at home. Nevertheless, whether as individuals or as members of discrete communities, human beings continue to place a high value on their autonomy. They insist on shaping the conditions of their existence to the fullest extent possible. This book, and the series of which it is a part, investigates the relationship between globalization and autonomy.

Personal and collective autonomy are to some degree modern practices, emerging out of the idea of individualism. "The picture of [modern] society is that of individuals who come together to form a political entity against a certain pre-existing moral background and with certain ends in view" (C. Taylor 2004, 3). To a certain extent, this modern idea of society has been globalized over the past three centuries. This process does not mean that it is necessarily acted upon or fully implemented; rather, it implies that some subset of persons in many societies learn and think about such an idea. If it is acted upon, the results are not necessarily the same in all parts of the world. We are, rather, in a condition of "global modernity," where there are conflicting perspectives on the idea of individualism, not just a dominant Eurocentric one. Accordingly, how societies understand individualism, how individuals come together, what autonomy means, and how it is practised vary depending on historical and cultural context (Dirlik 2007). Such a coming together presumes individuals have autonomy and that they form societies that will be self-governing or autonomous. The notion of the sovereignty of the people and related ideas of self-government and self-determination are also implicit in this conception of modern society. In this research project, we refer to this notion as *collective autonomy,* in the sense that it presumes a community or society, a collectivity, that seeks to govern itself.

This book focuses on one aspect of the modernity project — political institutions, specifically those that codify and make routine the creation of a public sphere and arrangements for governing activities within it. Such institutions shifted and changed as, after the eighteenth century, personal autonomy gradually extended beyond a nucleus of men with significant property holdings. Over time, society itself became larger and character-ized by a more complex division of labour or, in sociological terms, more pronounced levels of functional differentiation. For the most part, however, when people today refer to "society" they are thinking of nation-states or state-nations that exercise collective autonomy and that have institutional-ized personal autonomy through practices like citizenship.

We argue that globalization troubles the social imaginary of modernity and the associated notions of personal and collective autonomy in several ways. In doing so, it puts significant pressures on actual political institutions, and creates demands, in some instances, for new global ways of ordering. First, modernity has itself become globalized and, in the process, context-ualized in ways often different from its European roots. As such, the rela-tionships between personal and collective autonomy differ from one place to another. Such differences may complicate finding the consensus needed to build new institutions with more global mandates. Second, globalization gives rise to some particular challenges that cannot be addressed well by individual societies acting alone or even by states acting in cooperation with one another (internationalization). Third, the dominance of a given nation-state society or community in the lives of many diminishes relative to membership in other communities including a "human" one. Personal autonomy thus expands when it comes to defining, living, and working within possible collectivities. Finally, globalization creates openings for new social imaginaries that radicalize individuals' understandings of their personal autonomy and its relationship to the collective autonomy of the society of which they are part. As Appadurai (1996, 31) notes, "the imagin-ation has become an organized field of social practices, a form of work ..., and a form of negotiation between sites of agency (individuals) and globally defined fields of possibility."

This opening chapter offers a framework for thinking about these relationships. The chapters that follow use that framework to describe and analyze changes and developments in important institutions that mediate these relationships. Human beings still separated by boundaries and barriers of various kinds are adapting existing institutions and creating new ones as they seek to bring order to their increasingly complex and increasingly shared lives. The authors of this book come from different scholarly disciplines, but they all begin with a common understanding of key concepts.

Globalization

Globalization is typical of many concepts in the social sciences in that it carries considerable ideological baggage. Its meaning differs depending on whether one listens to protesters on the streets during World Trade Organization (WTO) meetings, or to global bankers talking about market structures, or to government ministers from Australia to Zambia. Some speak of a process that enriches and extends human life, while others describe a pathway to marginalization, impoverishment, and insecurity. Not only does the term *globalization* carry considerable ideological baggage, but it is also a term at the centre of a growing body of social theory that challenges other theories and ways of understanding the world in which we live. Mindful of its ideological as well as social scientific uses, scholars are learning to proceed carefully as they inquire into its causes, consequences, and meanings. Although the authors assembled in this volume recognize that ideologies inform social analysis, they are also interested in rigorous theoretical debate aimed at deepening understanding of what globalization entails and what it means for how human beings change the way they act towards one another in a shared world.

Considerable reflection on globalization has taken place in the social sciences since the early 1990s. After reviewing many of the competing definitions of globalization emerging through that work, Scholte (2005, 59) neatly suggests that globalization involves "the spread of transplanetary — and in recent times also more particularly supraterritorial — connections between people." A political scientist, Scholte emphasizes social connections "that substantially transcend territorial geography" (Scholte 2005, 61). Tomlinson, a sociologist, similarly characterizes this "empirical condition" of supraterritoriality as one of "complex connectivity" — a set of "connections that now bind our practices, our experiences and our political, economic and environmental fates together across the modern world" (J. Tomlinson 1999, 2). For their part, some literary critics see globalization as "a structure of feeling ... that springs from the media-saturated soil of our daily life" (Livingston 2001, 145). Others stress the ideological force of globalization narratives, particularly the ways in which they seem to achieve a levelling around the world, with the result that the inequalities of connections and their critique tend to be ignored (O'Brien and Szeman 2001, 606). The relative importance of physical location is reduced by globalization. Especially characteristic of the current era is that these supraterritorial connections are emerging on a larger scale and at an accelerating rate. In this respect, contemporary globalization is different from the spread of transplanetary connections in the past.

Latham and Sassen amplify this point by commenting on the role played by communication and information technologies in reshaping social space, particularly in terms of its scale. They write:

What has tended to operate or be nested at local scales can now move to global scales, and global relations and domains can now, in turn, more easily become directly articulated with thick local settings. In both types of dynamics, the rescaling can bypass the administrative and institutional apparatus of the national level, still the most developed scalar condition. As a result of the growing presence and use of these technologies, an increasing range of social relations and domains have become de facto transboundary. (2005, 2)

It follows that the building of connections in global spaces means that individuals are conscious of the globality of those spaces. Robertson (1992, 8) refers to "an intensification of consciousness of the world" or increasing globality in many societies, where *globality* refers to the consciousness of the world as one place. As relationships are formed in such global spaces, Appadurai notes a changing role for the imagination. Individuals place themselves in a world context and imagine themselves doing new things in different ways than before.

With these points in mind, the collaborators in this volume begin with the following understanding of globalization. Globalization is the transformative growth of connections among people across the planet. In the contemporary era, many of these connections take a supraterritorial form. In ever more profound ways, globalization ties together what people do, what they experience, how they perceive that experience, and how they reshape their lives. In short, individuals and communities begin to see the world as one place and to imagine new roles for themselves within it.

Supraterritoriality

This definition of globalization suggests that *supraterritoriality* is a distinguishing characteristic of many transplanetary connections being formed in the world today. As such, a growing minority of individuals, still ostensibly rooted in discrete nation-states, now live and work in the space of global flows — of capital, of information, and of unbounded possibilities. In contrast, the vast majority of the world's population continue to live and work in the space of defined places.

When one views globalization as the growth of supraterritorial connections and one makes the linkages between this growth and underlying changes in technology, one can see more clearly how space itself is being reordered. In the space of flows, where elite individuals move relatively freely between the office towers and entertainment venues of global cities, the world is increasingly experienced as one "timeless" place (Castells 1996, chap. 7). This space is not limited to the advanced industrial states that built the cooperative intergovernmental institutions still attempting to regulate it; elites in the relatively more prosperous developing and transition states have increasing access to it as well. But the lucky few who happen to be born in rich countries still appear to benefit disproportionately.

In contrast, the space of places is filled with people who face boundaries that remain difficult to penetrate. These are the boundaries that separate the poor from the wealthy, that restrict movement from one state to another, that force movement from rural areas to urban slums, and that limit access to education and health. This space continues to be shaped by the territorial boundaries of states. To the extent that it is regulated, it is regulated by states; and states therefore remain the principal targets of those seeking the means to break through those boundaries. The space of places remains the predominant space in developing countries; it is matched in developed countries wherever living conditions are in decline.

The chapters in this book suggest that the denser the space of flows, and the greater the challenge of holding the allegiance of super-empowered elites, the more difficult it is to address problems of global order through existing institutions. At a certain point as globalization proceeds, institutional adaptation seems likely to be superseded by the necessity to create new kinds of institutions. The image as well as the reality of supraterritoriality in the very processes that sustain — or endanger — life itself cannot help but force a re-imagining (Sen 1999). That this imagining is difficult is immediately understandable. History, ideology, habit, and vested interest stand in our way. In these respects, autonomy becomes a crucial avenue of investigation.

Autonomy

Autonomy, like globalization, is a controversial and often-contested term. It is commonly used in two general ways. First, it refers to the situations of individual persons and to their capacity to shape the conditions under which they live (Held 1995). In part, their capacity to shape those conditions depends on the kinds of conditions in which they find themselves. As Appiah notes: "To have autonomy, we must have acceptable choices" (2005, 30). In other words, certain conditions and certain institutions will prove more amenable to the exercise of autonomy than others. The term is also used in connection with collective bodies — nation-states, minority groups within states, indigenous peoples, and religious movements being common examples. In this collective sense, autonomy usually means something closer to the Greek roots *autos* (self) and *nomos* (law): the capacity to give oneself laws. Autonomy is the principle that modern thinkers assume ensures individual and collective fulfillment and that enables legitimacy to be realized when it comes to collective decision making within democracies. The extent to which autonomy is a universal value is much debated in contemporary times. As Marilyn Friedman notes, "The ideal of autonomy is a debatable requirement for a good human life" (2003, 189). She finds that some groups explicitly reject this value and others implicitly value collective autonomy while refusing to recognize the need for personal autonomy. Nonetheless, it is difficult to discover an alternative principle on which to base respect for the decisions of others.

Autonomy and Modernity

Many would associate autonomy in these forms with the onset of modernity in Europe. Writing over a century ago, Simmel (1971, 219) argued that the oppressiveness of medieval institutions gave rise to the idea of the pure freedom of the individual based on "natural" equality. This eighteenth-century idea of individualism, he added, came to be complemented by another version of individuality in the nineteenth century, that of the particular and irreplaceable person. Such an idea, rearticulated and developed by philosophers since Simmel's time, has become incorporated into what Charles Taylor (2004, 23) calls the "social imaginary": "the ways people imagine their social existence, how they fit together with others, how things go on between them and their fellows, the expectations that are normally met, and the deeper normative notions and images that underlie these expectations." In the West, such an imaginary is translated into notions related to autonomy: people have "a right to choose for themselves their own pattern of life, to decide in conscience what convictions to espouse, to determine the shape of their lives in a whole host of ways that their ancestors could not control" (C. Taylor 1991, 2). The Western social imaginary, in turn, takes different forms in different societies, both within and outside the West, with the result that the performance of autonomy now varies from one place to another.

Philosophers see the modern view of personal autonomy as complementary to collective autonomy in the sense that, in modern societies, individuals decide upon the rules and the forms through which they will be governed. Originally, the idea of collective autonomy was anchored in personal autonomy. Simmel (1971, 252) added that the larger the collectivity involved, the more personal autonomy is available, at least in theory: "Individuality in being and action generally increases to the degree that the social circle encompassing the individual expands." For larger collectivities, individuals create "forms" or institutions that are based on an increasingly complex, functional division of labour that permits, in turn, the continued freedom of the individual to choose a particular pattern and way of living. Adam Smith, of course, had discussed the institutional structure of the market economy in similar terms in 1776 (Smith 1776/1991).

By the early twentieth century, however, when Simmel was still writing, this fortunate complementarity of personal and collective autonomy seemed increasingly belied by practice. The very institutional forms that were supposed to free the individual had come to operate on the basis of a technical rationality that frequently left the individual in what Weber called an "iron cage." The technologies accompanying these institutions and required for their functioning narrowed and flattened human lives (C. Taylor 1991, 6). Bauman (1998) highlights the advent of a highly consumerist, materialist individualism that leads to a kind of narcissism that is antithetical to concerns about others or the functioning of society. Accompanying this centring on the self is an indifference to participating in self-government,

7

or in the realization of collective autonomy, thus opening the way to a modern form of despotism (C. Taylor 1991, 9). Drawing on Tocqueville, Charles Taylor sees collective autonomy placed in the hands of mild and paternalistic governments, where everything is run by an "immense tutelary power" (ibid., 9).

Globalization is seen by some as a set of processes that intensify the decline of a positive link between personal and collective autonomy. Technology becomes ever more dominant, to the point that Beck (1992, 2006) can plausibly argue that societies the world over are held hostage by the risk of their own disintegration and the calamitous consequences that would follow. For individuals, consumerism and materialism transform basic ways of living, both inside and outside of Europe and America. The "soft" despotism that Tocqueville long ago identified as becoming commonplace appears, in fact, to have hardened even in the wealthier countries of the world. Yet, where some see dark changes, others see new opportunities for the building of global institutions that might change the balance between risk and reward in the continuing development of technology. They see the possibilities for building transnational coalitions to counter despotic practices, and they articulate visions of an alternative world where the narcissistic individualism of modernity is replaced by an outward-looking search for social justice.

Autonomy has traditionally been seen in the West as providing the foundation for the principle of the "examined life." Autonomy requires an individual capacity for self-reflection and self-government and an ability to exercise that capacity within social conditions that enable its flourishing. Autonomy is always a matter of degree, because autonomy (even at the individual level) is a social concept that governs relations within a social world. There can be no absolute autonomy. Although most contemporary understandings of autonomy assume that an autonomous decision cannot be made to undermine autonomy, some of the most interesting recent theoretical work stresses the fundamentally relational nature of the concept (Mackenzie and Stoljar 2000; Nedelsky 2001). Being autonomous grows out of reciprocity, obligations, shared experiences, and cooperation with others. Without the support of such relationships, individual autonomy is inconceivable.

Defining Autonomy

In attempting to define *autonomy*, we are conscious of the need to extend the concept beyond the levels of the individual and the nation-state to global forms of self-government. The notion of individual or personal autonomy again relates to the idea that participation in some form of life without serious arbitrary limitations is "our most basic human interest" (Doyal and Gough 1991, 55). There are two basic needs for such participation to occur: health or physical capacity and mental capacity or autonomy. "To be autonomous in this minimal sense is to have the ability to make informed choices about what should be done and how to go about doing it" (Gough 2003, 8).

Doyal and Gough (1991, 55-9) go on to identify three key factors that shape the degree to which individuals might enjoy autonomy. First, they must have the cognitive and emotional capacity to initiate action. Doyal and Gough suggest (ibid., 180) that across cultures one can identify a common set of disabling symptoms indicating weakness in this regard: hopelessness, indecisiveness, a sense of futility, and a lack of energy. Second, individuals must have cultural understanding that permits them to situate themselves in their culture and to know what is expected of them in their daily living. Such understanding requires teaching and learning, whether in the family, through community practices and ceremonies, or in schools. Finally, they refer to critical capacity, the ability "to compare cultural rules, to reflect upon the rules of one's own culture, to work with others to change them and, *in extremis,* to move to another culture" (ibid., 187). To exercise this critical capacity, Doyal and Gough add, requires some freedom of agency and political freedom. Held (1995, chap. 8) adds to this point by listing some human rights necessary for critical capacity: freedom of thought, freedom of expression, and freedom of association. In sum, individual autonomy means being able to formulate aims and beliefs about how to achieve one's choices, to seek out ways to participate in social life in pursuit of these choices, and to evaluate one's success based on empirical evidence in working towards these aims. If a particular society is structured in such a way as to prevent the pursuit of such choices for members of particular groups — women, for example — then the autonomy of those persons may be constrained or eliminated entirely.

This understanding of individual autonomy, therefore, cannot be divorced from collective autonomy, particularly the autonomy of states. Castoriadis (1991), a French philosopher of Greek origin, reminds us of the root meaning: self law-giving. In this respect, autonomy is the opposite of *heteronomy*, which entails subjection to the power of another. To be collectively autonomous, according to Castoriadis, a society as a whole has to have a place for "politics" and thus the exercise of individual autonomy. To the extent individuals must live in community, there must be public spaces where citizens are able to ask themselves freely the following questions: "Are the rules and the laws under which we exist the right ones?" "Are they just?" "Could they be better?" For Castoriadis, therefore, collective autonomy exists when a society is reflexive and is able to look at itself critically. It exists where its members are free, have access to public spaces, and possess the resources, the understanding, and the education needed to interrogate themselves and their laws.

What is also clear about autonomy in this meaning is that it involves an act of the imagination. Castoriadis terms it the "radical imagination." Individuals and groups are able to imagine different futures, different ways of living, and different arrangements in their own lives. They are able to take an idea, talk about it, imagine how it might work in practice, and then take action to see if they can get it to work. In this respect, collective autonomy depends strongly on escaping the bonds of what Charles Taylor calls "tutelary power" and recovering individual autonomy. And the relationship is dialectical: sustaining individual autonomy requires collective autonomy over the longer term.

Autonomy and Sovereignty

Defined in this way, collective autonomy is conceptually distinguishable from state sovereignty. Following James (1999, 39), *sovereignty* is linked to constitutional independence. It consists of "being constitutionally apart, of not being contained, however loosely, within a wider constitutional scheme." James adds that sovereignty has three features. First, it is a legal condition, "founded on law inasmuch as a constitution is a set of arrangements that has the force of law" (ibid., 40). Second, sovereignty, taken in this strict sense, becomes an absolute condition, either present or absent. It is not possessed in terms of more or less. Finally, sovereignty defined in this fashion is a unitary condition. Within the defined territory, only one authority, the state, is in the position of being formally able to make decisions.

Sovereignty typically implies or advances collective autonomy. The degree to which states can take advantage of this condition depends on certain anterior conditions. Within the given territory there must be a *polity*, an imagined community in whom sovereignty is vested through the constitution. The existence of such a socially integrated community has been problematic for many developing countries because of the haphazard definitions of territory bequeathed to them by departing imperial powers. There must also be a functioning state capable of establishing authority in the territory, backed by a monopoly on the legitimate use of coercion. The state must have a bureaucracy sufficiently effective that it is able to implement laws and policies and to gather resources, particularly taxes. The territory in which the polity exists must have sufficient resources both to maintain state institutions and to provide for the economic and social well-being of the citizens concerned. If globalization makes it more difficult to construct such a polity, to maintain a functioning state, or to sustain an effective bureaucracy, the degree to which sovereignty might advance autonomy is less.

Absolute sovereignty also implies that no external authority structures are active in the territory of a given state. As Krasner (2001a) points out, such a situation has rarely been achieved in the real world, and it is certainly compromised in principle in an increasingly globalized world. States simply find it more difficult to control or regulate the movements of goods, capital, people, and ideas across their borders. In such circumstances, they increasingly contract with other states to establish transnational authority structures in an attempt to find ways to control and regulate such flows. The creation of the WTO and the revised system of international trading rules that accompanied its creation illustrate these processes. Even if we accept James' definition of sovereignty, such actions do not involve "giving up" sovereignty. The states concerned still have constitutional independence in a strict, legal sense. Rather, we might say that states are reducing their respective collective autonomies and pooling their authority to expand their options for giving themselves laws. In doing so, they may be placing themselves in a situation of increased heteronomy. This possibility is examined in more depth in another volume in this series on legitimacy (see Bernstein and Coleman, forthcoming).

Although the attraction of parsimony bids us simply to begin with a strict definition of sovereignty, much recent empirical research reminds us that actual institutions enshrining political and legal authority have changed in complex ways throughout human history. Grande and Pauly (2005, 5), for example, observe that in the contemporary environment a complex and partly contradictory transformation of authority remains centred on the state. They contend that even inside the state "this transformation affects the basic institutions, principles, norms and procedures of contemporary policy-making ... It affects all aspects of public authority, in particular the distribution of political decision-making power across territorial levels; the relation between public and private actors; and the definition of public functions." And even if states remain indispensable in efforts to extend political authority beyond conventional boundaries, this new complexity of sovereignty-in-practice means that states themselves "have gradually become enmeshed in and functionally part of a larger pattern of global transformations and flows" (Held et al. 1999, 7). Such complexity is most evident today in the case of the European Union (EU), where the sharing of sovereign prerogatives in a rapidly evolving system of decision making is both subtle and impossible to dismiss. Chapters 11 and 12 by Ulf Hedetoft and Ian Cooper assess the dimensions of institutional adjustment and compromise currently underway among the members of the EU and outline some of their broader implications. In turn, the idiosyncrasies and perhaps the limits of that case are set into sharp relief by the contrasting chapter by Stephen Clarkson on governance in a North America dominated by the United States.

Even if we accept a protean conception of sovereignty-in-practice, it is reasonable to assert that access to the structures of the state today still creates the surest possibility for any specific community to make a claim to collective autonomy in a full range of areas of life. We see this clearly in Chapter 13 by Natalia Loukacheva, who examines the evolution of arrangements for self-governance among indigenous peoples in Greenland and the Canadian territory of Nunavut. Globalization creates situations where states find themselves pushed to delegate their authority, to share it, and, increasingly, to accept a reduction in the scope of claims to unimpeded action. These situations do not necessarily imply the vitiation of political and social structures aimed at the provision of effective government. Rather, the imperatives of globalization and the insistence on autonomy in its various forms come to exist in deepening tension.

Institutions and Global Ordering

Just such a tension defines the terrain for all of the chapters that follow. Upon that shifting terrain, whether through the state or through other authoritative structures, human beings negotiate trade-offs, and they now often do so collaboratively. To the extent that explicit or implicit negotiations regularize patterns of behaviour and continuous interaction, they constitute institutions. By observing the changing contours of those institutions, we can catch a glimpse of the complex relationship between globalization and autonomy.

Globalization and Internationalization

Some of the following chapters deal with the adaptation of established institutions to new environments, others trace the beginnings of new institutions attempting to provide order in increasingly complicated arenas of human interaction, and still others depict institutional dysfunction in the context of conflicting demands. In order to understand all of these developments, we need first to distinguish between the processes that constitute globalization as defined here and internationalization. *Internationalization* refers to the expansion of transactions and flows of resources of various kinds between countries. In aggregate, it generally depends upon and reaffirms nation-states as the basic actors in the international system (Katzenstein 2005, 17). Globalization can encompass such flows, but it entails a basic transformation in perception, a transformation with wide-ranging impact that accompanies a profound deepening in individual and collective connections. If the planet were a human brain, internationalization would signify an increase in normal functioning through established neural networks. In contrast, globalization would suggest the construction of new networks, innovative ways of thinking, and a reconceptualization of the environment within which those networks exist.

Globalization and internationalization processes have coexisted for several centuries, although their relationship to one another has changed over the same period. They are not mutually exclusive or zero-sum processes in the sense that, as globalization increases, internationalization necessarily decreases, or vice versa. They may complement one another, they may co-occur without necessarily having an impact on one another, or they may contradict one another. Historians of globalization argue that in the seventeenth and eighteenth centuries, globalization and internationalization tended to coexist. Non-national loyalties were seen to complement a sense of nationality; state borders were porous; the transnational corporations of the day, like the British East India Company, linked consumers and producers across continents; and cosmopolitan thinking flourished among intellectuals (Hopkins 2002a, 24-6). O'Brien and Szeman (2001, 604) note that "literature was global ... before it was ever national." Whereas, in the seventeenth century, most territories were subject to multiple systems of

13

rule, the situation changed as nationally sovereign states began to gain "exclusive authority over a given territory and at the same time this territory was constructed as coterminous with that authority, in principle ensuring a similar dynamic in other nation-states" (Sassen 2006, 6).

Beginning in the nineteenth century, the nation-state "imposed its system of more rigidly bound territories, languages, and religious conventions on all international networks" (Bayly 2004, 234). Earlier global links were reconstructed by the system of nation-states and ultimately controlled by them. Hopkins (2002a, 30) adds that the cosmopolitanism that was a marked feature of the preceding two centuries was "corralled, harnessed and domesticated to new national interests." Across the globe, land "was converted to property, property became the foundation of sovereignty; sovereignty, in turn, defined the basis of security" (Hopkins 2002b, 6). In the economic realm, older and looser links of global trading gave way to more formal agreements between states. The growth of transplanetary connections accelerated as dominant states built empires and imposed systems of formal and informal rule.

Globalization scholars do not agree on when the tipping point occurred that saw supraterritorial transplanetary connections become sufficiently important that the historic grip of internationality lessened. Eventually, however, a companion system of rule alongside nation-states became conceivable. Karl Marx's analysis of the inexorability of capitalist growth certainly opened one prominent pathway for thinking about such a development. More recently, Castells (1996) points to an information and technology revolution beginning in the 1970s that combined with the capitalist mode of production to produce a new global capitalism. For her part, Sassen (2006, 17) sees globalization breaking through by the early 1980s. Appadurai (1996) concurs but stresses the combination of digital technologies and of increasingly diverse movements of people as creating new opportunities for the social imagination and the working out of global ties.

Globalization scholars do agree that the unleashing of new globalizing processes was made possible by states and the high level of coordination among them that had evolved as part of internationalization. Sassen (2006, 13) suggests that the very highly developed corporate globalization of today would not have been possible without the use of the sophisticated capabilities of national economies that matured under the arrangements of the post-1945 Western economic system. Castells notes the importance of US state intervention to support technological development, particularly that related to national defence, as a key factor in the information technology revolution hatched in Silicon Valley. Both Castells and especially Sassen stress the importance of the concentration of financial and business services in "global" cities that came with internationalization. They suggest that this phenomenon created the basis for the nodes and material infrastructure for the supraterritorial connections that characterize contemporary globalization. That infrastructure, in turn, has led to new challenges to the role of institutions in mediating personal and collective autonomy.

With internationalization, the realization and securing of collective autonomy became primarily the responsibility of nation-states. The expansion of empires in the nineteenth and the twentieth centuries meant that imperial states controlled to a significant extent the degree to which peoples in many other territories of the globe could exercise collective autonomy. These controls could be direct and formal or indirect and informal. US power in the present era tends to be more indirect and informal. Hedetoft (forthcoming) uses the term *neo-imperial* to refer to "the aggregate capacity to project power and interest beyond one's formal sphere of sovereign authority in such a way that other political units ... are induced or coerced into pursuing choices in keeping with the interests and preferences of the neo-imperial sovereign, accommodating it in multiple ways by adapting to its agenda, and more often than not taking this road because it is viewed to be the lesser evil or the most beneficial way to protect and defend national interests." Katzenstein (2005, 2 and 208) offers the term *imperium* to characterize US rule: it refers to the conjoining of power that has territorial and non-territorial dimensions, with the former being related to internationalization and the latter to globalization. Whatever term is used, the assessment of the degree of presence or absence of collective autonomy becomes more difficult as forms of rule influenced by globalization conflict with traditional patterns of territorially-based empires and states.

The intensification of internationalization in the nineteenth century meant that the degree to which individuals possessed personal autonomy came to depend heavily on the nature of rule in the state within which they were citizens or (imperial) subjects. Other factors were obviously important: relative wealth, gender, access to food, and physical well-being, to name but a few. These factors too were variously available depending on the state to which one belonged. Associated processes of individualization — the spread of private property rights, the expansion of the electoral franchise, and the growth of material consumption — all contributed to transforming the values of autonomy in a direction of individual, and over-whelmingly male, self-reliance.

Over this same period, various globalizing processes challenged the exclusive control of personal autonomy by states: anti-slavery movements; campaigns to remove wealth-based criteria for manhood suffrage; the growth of trade unionism and worker internationalism; the struggle for female suffrage and other rights for women; and the pursuit of self-determination by colonized areas, indigenous peoples, and cultural minorities. The fostering of ideas focused on claims to rights simply on the basis of being human generated similar challenges. These globalizing processes encouraged questioning and ultimately the broadening of claims to collective autonomy, and this questioning challenged the state's monopoly.

Consequently, as the repositories of rules and the mechanisms for establishing order, institutions provide a window on how globalization is shaking up established patterns in the exercise of collective and individual autonomy. As Dunn (2003, 53-60) suggests:

> It remains a question of the keenest interest how far globalization has in practice enhanced the autonomy of different groups of human beings, and how far such gains in autonomy as it has delivered have been applied in practice for the advantage or disadvantage of other human beings ... If we think of autonomy as a metric for social achievement, and ask how far different societies today contrive to maximize it, we can be confident of some of the answers ... But if we ask how far globalization promotes or impedes the maximization of autonomy in different settings, we should expect a somewhat different cartographic pigmentation ... The autonomy of some will be all too evidently a reciprocal of the heteronomy of others.

Accordingly, we allow for the possibility of variable relationships between globalization on the one side and individual and collective autonomy on the other. We also keep in mind that in modern societies individual autonomy and collective autonomy are related to one another in complex, dynamic ways.

Assessing Institutional Change

As a first analytical cut, we might surmise that the scope and novelty of change in institutions should vary depending on whether they are a response to internationalization or globalization. Katzenstein (2005, 20) suggests that the former points to "incremental change" while the latter involves more "transformative change." In principle, distinguishing these two types of change from one another should be relatively straightforward. If we see distinctly new global institutions and processes or if we note fundamental changes to international institutions, we are likely observing globalization. For example, the chapters by Guy Gensey and Gilbert Winham and by William Coleman in this volume demonstrate that the WTO is identifiably different and profoundly global in ways that the loose set of agreements clustered around the General Agreement on Tariffs and Trade (GATT) were not. Correspondingly, the role of the World Heritage Committee of the United Nations Educational, Scientific and Cultural Organization (UNESCO), reviewed by Caren Irr in Chapter 5, exemplifies the evolution of an existing institution consistent with incremental change. On the surface, there seem to be no fundamental reforms afoot, such as those periodically articulated in institutions governing global trade. But, as Irr herself suggests, a deeper look is warranted.

Saskia Sassen emphasizes a second set of globalizing processes, in addition to distinctly novel global institutions and processes, that do not necessarily result in formal institutions of the familiar type. Rather, changes can occur inside defined territories and even within national and international institutions that emerged as part of earlier processes of internationalization. Even though such developments can be lodged in national, if not subnational, institutions, they "are oriented towards global agendas and systems. They are multisided, transboundary networks and formations which can include normative orders; they connect subnational or 'national' processes, institutions and actors, not necessarily through the formal interstate system" (Sassen 2006, 3). Sarah Eaton and Tony Porter in Chapter 7 give us an indication of this kind of globalization in their discussion of the emerging system for regulating the accounting systems of corporations. No conventional institutions are formed in the development of such regulations, but some established practices are changed, and some existing nation-state institutions become linked in novel ways. What emerges is a global network that mixes private and public governance under an increasingly shared set of norms that is no longer controlled or channelled through states. Similarly, Irr describes the path taken by the World Heritage Committee to the point where it could speak of a global cultural "commons" by the end of the 1990s. It had developed a set of global networks and norms such that the destruction of the Bamiyan Buddha statues in Afghanistan could be constructed and perceived as a loss to the "world" in ways inconceivable even some thirty years before.

In short, institutional forms within and across states can appear quite static, but their actual underlying condition may be one of deepening enmeshment in processes that remain open-ended. More than one observer has recently noted that a new global order is today being built on the recognition that addressing many of the most pressing problems of the age — environmental degradation, human security, systemic risks associated with globalizing finance, continuing abuses of human rights — requires systematic interaction and cooperation among political authorities at various levels. Slaughter (2004, 10) echoes many analysts when she notes that what is new is the "scale, scope, and type of transgovernmental ties" now implicated by this requirement. The resulting networks "are driven by many of the multiple factors that drive the hydra-headed phenomenon of globalization itself, leading to the simple need for national officials of all kinds to communicate and negotiate across borders to do business they could once accomplish solely at home" (ibid., 11).

Globalization, in practice, has the effect of disaggregating the state and involving various parts of the state — regulatory agencies, executive ministries, legislatures, judiciaries — in increasingly complex global networks. Ironically, such dynamic change can sometimes help account for the growing ascendancy within states of the executive branch, and particularly the head of government or state, at the expense of legislatures and legislative oversight. In Chapter 2 by Louis Pauly, for example, the extension of executive authority is certainly evident in a halting but stubbornly persistent effort to reform the United Nations, and especially to use it more effectively to address the challenges globalization poses for poor countries. The UN is, in part, a classic intergovernmental organization that still symbolizes a world defined by internationalization. The painful, often contradictory, but persistent struggle to adapt it to a new global context points ultimately to broadly perceived shortcomings in contemporary governance structures.

The difficulties confronted in this attempt are currently stimulating much research on the conception of political legitimacy in a system being reshaped by the myriad pressures of globalization. Some of that work (Clark 2005; Reus-Smit 2004b) suggests the possibility that the nation-state is adapting itself to changing normative understandings of appropriate behaviour in a more integrated world. As it does so, it again disaggregates some of its functions and forms, more often now in collaboration with other actors. This type of process constructs new kinds of global networks. The dilemmas faced by such networks in actually addressing hard policy problems are well exemplified not only in Pauly's chapter, but also in Petra

Rethmann's chapter on the frustrating experience of the International Whaling Commission.

Sometimes complementing and sometimes challenging networks that continue to rely on the political authority of nation-states are newly assertive networks of activists engaged in local actions linked to global struggles and campaigns. New communications technologies make such networks viable beyond the conventional boundaries of nation-states in ways not seen before (Sassen 2004; Appadurai 2002). The institutional and policy outcomes associated with them are likely to vary. Chapter 9 by Michael Webb with Emily Sinclair examines the limits of such networks in the crucial arena of social policy, which has become increasingly prominent as the economic dimension of globalization disrupts traditional social orders around the world.

Nevertheless, it would be a mistake to think too narrowly about the institutional and policy implications of globalization as it is manifesting itself in the contemporary period. Globalization is by now endogenous to nation-states as well as to the international institutions established by them. It is also exogenous to the extent that it forms new global structures and transnational connections unlikely to be broken by any circumstances short of catastrophe. The chapter by Claire Cutler on the development of transnational private law provides a highly suggestive template for examining other institutions that begin to deliver what can accurately be termed *governance,* even to widely dispersed communities of human beings. Read together, the chapters by Eaton and Porter, Cutler, and Webb and Sinclair provide a glimpse of a world beyond the straightforward interdependence characteristic of internationalization, a world characterized by "the actual production of spatial and temporal frames that *simultaneously* inhabit national structures and are distinct from national spatial and temporal frames as these have been historically constructed" (Sassen 2006, 23).

Structure of the Volume

In just such a view, our aim in this volume is to bring evolving compromises and adjustments to light through comparative explorations of change within institutions of global ordering. Most of the chapters in this volume begin with a key state, international, or global institution, that already embodies some imposition of collective rights on the absolute freedom of the individual. But they also concern other embodiments of the principle of collective autonomy, which under conditions of global economic and social transformation challenge both the dominance and the radical independence of the state. Indeed, the common thread pulling the chapters together is the deepening struggle between different expressions of collective identity, and between different sets of collective and individual interests, associated mainly with supraterritorial pressures that privilege the space of flows over the space of places. Each chapter brings a particular element of that struggle to the fore by examining its observable manifestation in unique institutional contexts.

To discipline the analysis across the chapters, each author structured an exploration of a particular established or rapidly evolving institution around the following specific questions:

1 In a given area, how are established institutions with governance/ steering/meaning-generation functions adapting to the dynamic tension between globalization and autonomy? Or, how and why are new institutions, or institutionalized practices, coming into existence to address such a tension?

2 Why are the most significant changes occurring, and how do they bear upon global ordering? What specific conceptions of autonomy are at work underneath those changes, and why are any contests between differing conceptions playing out the way they are?

3 What are the most important implications of institutional changes for the autonomy (explicit or implicit) of the key actors involved? Do these changes force revisions in traditional or conventional understandings of the nature and meaning of those institutions — or of the sense of the efficacy, justice, and fairness implied by their operation?

The first few chapters in the first section look at established international organizations, all of which have lately been struggling to adapt to rapidly changing global conditions. They concern the economic role of the United Nations, aspects of the development of the World Trade Organization, and contemporary developments in UNESCO and the International Whaling Commission. These chapters are followed by others examining the possibilities and limits of new forms of global ordering that arise within and outside the conventional realm of state authority. The second section of the book compares and contrasts experiences with institutional evolution at the regional level in North America, Europe, and the Arctic. Together, the authors of this collaborative work demonstrate the usefulness of the autonomy metric as they examine institutions being moulded and remade by globalization.

Part 1: Systemic Themes

chapter 2

The United Nations, the Bretton Woods Institutions, and the Reconstruction of a Multilateral Order

Louis W. Pauly

THE UNITED NATIONS HAS never played a central role in managing the increasingly interdependent economic relationships of its leading member states. The first secretary-general certainly planned for such a role, even if he soon discovered that the United States and Great Britain preferred to assign key and independent mandates to the two organizations they had previously created at Bretton Woods, New Hampshire — the International Monetary Fund (IMF) and the International Bank for Reconstruction and Development (World Bank). From the outset, moreover, responsibilities for international trade negotiations were deliberately segregated and kept under the loose institutional auspices of the General Agreement on Tariffs and Trade (GATT).

After more than half a century, during which an interdependent economy organized around national markets has evolved to the point where the term "global economy" begins to make sense, multilateral trade talks occur under the auspices of a World Trade Organization (WTO). In fact, as Gensey and Winham demonstrate in Chapter 3, an increasingly robust dispute-settlement system is now evolving within the WTO. At the same time, the mandates and missions of the IMF and the World Bank continue to adjust significantly. These separately constituted intergovernmental organizations today often find themselves competing with many formal organizations, informal forums, and loosely structured networks for the mandates and the resources to govern limited aspects of the global economy.

The United Nations, meanwhile, remains where it has long been — on the margins. In short, what scholars now call "global economic governance" exists without an effective capstone organization (Tabb 2004).

Nevertheless, the economic and social dimension of UN operations has always been prominent and has always rested on the political legitimacy conferred by its charter, by the organization's universal membership, and by a shared aspiration for some form of collective governance in the light of past crises and future systemic challenges. From the inception of the UN, the membership focused its more specific missions on the connections between development, security, and human rights. Although the precise nature of those connections, as well as the conceptual and practical content of its specific missions, has shifted considerably over time, UN members provide the organization with substantial staff and financial resources to pursue its missions. UN members also regularly engage in efforts to reform and expand those missions. Despite sometimes vitriolic debates on shutting the organization down, especially in the US Congress, the missions, the resources, and the reform exercises persist. Why?

To address that question, this chapter examines the broad economic mandate of the United Nations, mainly as it touches on issues that overlap with the mandates of the IMF and World Bank. It locates the main reason for both the shallowness *and* the endurance of that mandate in the deepening tension between globalizing processes and the political need to accommodate persistent variations in the actual autonomy of UN members. By its nature, the game of globalizing capitalism putatively enhances the individual autonomy of the game's winners. Despite widening inequalities, moreover, it is reasonable to argue that the total number of winners expands as the game widens and deepens. But global politics remains centred on a different kind of autonomy, the autonomy of certain kinds of collectivities, namely, nation-states.

Economic globalization arguably enhances the capacity of certain states to define key objectives, mainly in a domestic context and then to craft effective policies to achieve those objectives, even as it reduces the capacity of certain others to do the same. The resulting struggle, the struggle of discrete collectivities to harness globalization for their own purposes — in other words, to seize its freedom-enhancing benefits and limit its freedom-reducing costs — presents the central dilemma. The hope, of course, is that a rising tide will lift all boats, even if the politics surrounding the proliferating agenda of global economic governance still revolves mainly around the practical matter of controlling the floodgates. In this chapter, we shall see how continuing political struggle accounts for an inelegant but persistent process of incremental adaptation within the UN and of deepening cross-organizational collaboration between the UN and the Bretton Woods institutions.

The United Nations in Principle and in Practice

The UN inherited from its hobbled predecessor, the League of Nations, a bureaucratic apparatus capable of building a meaningful mission for itself in the postwar international economy. The seeds were present for a role in what later would be known as multilateral economic surveillance and the constructive national policy coordination potentially flowing from it (Strange 1954; Pauly 1997; Weiss et al. 2005). Aspirations to build a new world order that included all of humanity were surely also there from the beginning. Deep ideological conflict over the precise nature of that order was, of course, embedded in the UN from its inception as well. The fact that the Soviet Union remained in the UN certainly rendered a coherent economic mission more difficult to design. Conversely, the fact that the Soviets declined to join the IMF and the World Bank ostensibly facilitated the early development of these institutions. Nevertheless, the universality of membership and the initial vision of common governance, vague and primitive though it surely was, gave the UN a sense of legitimacy that no other organization had. But from the beginning, that sense would rest more on institutional representativeness than on institutional effectiveness.

Early on, a consensus among the UN's most powerful capitalist member states limited its economic role but simultaneously encouraged it to develop an associated set of political forums and the bureaucratic apparatus to support them. The consequence has never been an entirely happy one, either for UN officials or for member states. If we think about the situation in terms of political underpinnings for the global economy as it gradually evolved, one consequence was the ad hoc but generally useful emergence of various programs targeted specifically at developing countries, most of which were eventually placed under the umbrella of the United Nations Development Programme (UNDP). Another was the desultory expansion of an unwieldy Economic and Social Council (ECOSOC) and the various regional and functional commissions reporting to the General Assembly through its channels and procedures. Supporting ECOSOC and associated work through high-profile conferences are various departments in the Secretariat, especially the Department of Economic and Social Affairs (DESA).

As in the case of UNESCO discussed by Irr in Chapter 5, it is fair to say that the ambition of officials leading ECOSOC and DESA at any particular point in their history has exceeded their actual authority. Despite aspirations embedded in the UN Charter, a practical plan did not emerge until the early 1950s, when the General Assembly voted to establish the Special United Nations Fund for Economic Development. The idea was to combine technical assistance with subsidized financing of infrastructure projects (Weiss, Forsythe, and Coate 2004, 226; Jolly 1995). Despite the fact that developing states had the numbers in the General Assembly to create such a fund, only the United States had the resources to fill it. It refused. Although in later years the United States turned to the IMF and the World Bank for similar purposes, it would exert tight resource and mission constraints on those institutions. During the early stages of the Cold War, moreover, the United States chose to disburse most of its official funding for reconstruction and development directly.

By the mid-1960s, the United States and the advanced countries in the position of creditors to the system acquiesced in the reorganization of technical assistance activities in the UN through a new United Nations Development Program, even as they built up the capital bases of the World Bank and IMF. Their now firmly established preference was to provide the vast bulk of financing for development through revived capital markets. Moreover, the supplementary roles of the UN, the Bank, and the IMF were by then grounded in a permanent contest over organizational authorities and resources.

In the 1970s, that contest erupted into an ideological battle between developing and developed countries over the idea of a New International Economic Order (Krasner 1985). When the battle was over, the idea of radical systemic transformation faded away. By the time the Cold War ended, developing countries commonly moved towards policies favouring freer markets. But they and their counterparts from the advanced capitalist world persisted in more moderate efforts to redefine and reform the UN's economic role and to bring it into productive collaboration with the continuing roles of the IMF and World Bank.

Each succeeding round of negotiations on UN reform in the economic arena still exposes deep divisions among the membership on the question of how to provide a globalizing economy with the kind of solid political foundations promised by the legitimacy that derives from universal representation. To understand the underlying dilemma, the analytical framework proposed in Chapter 1 is useful. A world that requires the existence of an inchoate economic mission for the United Nations but cannot seriously empower the organization reflects an as yet irresolvable tension between globalization (as the supraterritorial expansion of economic and financial flows) and powerful demands for two kinds of autonomy: the autonomy of individuals, prized in principle in the liberal tradition that underpins key democratic member states, and the autonomy of collectivities still mainly defined as nations.

The developments recounted below suggest at most a slowly emerging consensus among UN members. In some, advancing the cause of individual autonomy still mainly involves defending and even expanding the autonomy of a defined collectivity, either the collectivity of the traditional nation-state or, as in the case of Europe, a region comprising states willing to blur the legal and political boundaries once separating them. In others, however, those two objectives can work at cross-purposes. The opportunities globalization provides for selective enrichment can erode a sense of collective identity, expand inequalities, and deepen mass poverty. Globalization can empower predatory governments, and, in the extreme, enhance the ultimate prospect of state failure. Only a few short years ago, it looked like a wave of economic liberalization was unstoppable across much of the developing world. Of late, instability in sub-Saharan Africa and the resurgence of populism across Latin America underline the main point here. The effect of globalization on the autonomy of political collectivities, or more specifically on the ability of political collectivities to harness their power to enhance the life prospects of the decisive majority of their constituents, continues to vary. That variance is reflected in the UN in the political tension between two sets of member states, those at the leading edge of globalization and those caught up in intensifying domestic conflicts associated at least in part with globalization. In short, a diversity of interests in the nature and objectives of global economic governance coincides with an idiosyncratic interaction of pressures for individual and collective autonomy within UN members. Globalization may enhance the autonomy of a widening number of individuals in only some polities, and it may similarly undercut the cause of collective autonomy only in some polities. This continuing diversity helps explain both the fragility of the UN's economic role and the stubborn persistence of attempts to enhance it.

The UN and Economic Globalization

In the 1970s, the UN was at the centre of an acrimonious debate on the political redistribution of the world's economic resources. A broadening ideological commitment to freer markets eventually ended that debate even before its socialist alternative essentially evaporated after the Soviet Union collapsed and China turned decisively towards economic openness. Today the policy language employed by ECOSOC, DESA, and the UNDP seems nearly as market-friendly as the language long associated with the IMF and the World Bank. Not coincidentally, the Bretton Woods twins have proved more willing than they were during the early postwar years to collaborate openly and directly with other agencies within the UN system.

Just prior to the March 2002 Monterrey Conference on Financing for Development and in the joint work programs that followed, the extent of this change became more obvious. Key supporters of the Bretton Woods institutions — the United States and its main industrial partners — publicly supported the framing and promotion of the UN's Millennium Development Goals. They also welcomed the secretary-general's Global Compact initiative to encourage corporate social responsibility in the development process, and they pledged to work with the UN to bridge the "digital divide" between rich and poor nations. Beyond rhetorical expressions of support, several nearly simultaneous decisions by the US president and Congress suggested that the UN had recovered a unique role in the field of economic development: the Americans brought their financial accounts in the UN up-to-date, they rejoined UNESCO (see Chapter 5), and they structured new types of complementary foreign aid programs in what they called the Millennium Challenge Account and the HIV/AIDS Initiative (Brainard 2003; Brainard et al. 2003; Radelet 2003).

Despite this rapprochement, the UN remained at the centre of political storms inside the United States and elsewhere over the future shape of global governance. Investigative reports connected with the Iraqi sanctions mismanaged by UN officials and various UN reform proposals piled up late in Kofi Annan's term as UN secretary-general. A combative and contentious American ambassador appointed for a truncated term in 2005 made matters more difficult, and the UN remained a favourite whipping boy inside the US Congress. Nevertheless, in the arena of economic and financial policy, the underlying story of the UN during the contemporary period has been one of tentative but noteworthy revival. It is the story of a sprawling, untidy institution stretched thin by its members being assigned new tasks without the provision of the resources required to accomplish them. It is the story of institutional adaptation in a turbulent environment.

The puzzle is why an institution at the margins of key economic and financial policy decisions from the time of its inception has not simply been abandoned. After decades characterized by financial crisis in many industrializing countries, by economic backsliding in many of the world's poorest nations, and by unmet promises of aid and policy reform within industrial countries, it would be easy to take a cynical position on the adaptation of the UN's economic functions and about parallel changes in national policies. A determined act of will is required to argue that contemporary changes in the UN's economic mission, its relationship with the Bretton Woods institutions, and limited industrial-country support for UN-advocated development policies mean nothing. Such an argument would also rely on a seductive but unrealistic sense of historical continuity and on a conviction that leading states are incapable of discerning their own long-term self-interest.

The postwar settlement gave rise to functionally specialized international organizations and reflected a confluence of national security and economic policies soon to be reshaped by the Cold War. After 1989, only the most romantic of liberals — liberals of the nineteenth-century laissez-faire variety — might have imagined the dawn of a new era of clarity, enlightenment, and broad global agreement on the common good. The subsequent persistence, revival, and adaptation of the economic organs of the UN suggest something less dramatic or, perhaps, something less grand. They signify the serious deepening in a policy dialogue between leading and following states in a globalizing economy, a dialogue necessarily mediated by international organizations. That dialogue is fundamentally structured by the continuing realities of state power, but its content increasingly concerns policy changes in all market economies that promise to strike a better systemic balance among the objectives of political stability, economic efficiency, and distributive justice. It is this dialogue that has revived and begun slowly to transform the general economic mandate of the UN.

The Legacy of Systemic Crisis

Soon after the end of the Second World War, the economic and financial staff of the UN was relegated to working on economic questions of marginal significance to the leading states, questions mainly having to do with decolonization and the future development of poor countries. To the extent that finance ministers and central bank governors thought about international organizations, their attention inexorably drifted to the IMF, the World Bank, and eventually the Bank for International Settlements. For its part, the UN, and especially ECOSOC, became the domain of ministries of marginal significance to core economic and financial policies in many member states, namely, foreign and development ministries.

It is no surprise, then, that the economic functions of UN headquarters evolved mainly along the line of coordinating for ECOSOC the disparate activities of affiliated commissions and agencies. Over time, even its capacity for serious analytical work had come to be overshadowed by better-funded research departments in the World Bank and the IMF (Weiss et al. 2005, 317-22). It nevertheless maintained a publication program, not only through DESA but also later through the UNDP, the UN Conference on Trade and Development (UNCTAD), and various regional economic commissions. But even before leading states began moving their most prominent multilateral interactions out of classic international organizations altogether, and into more restricted forums like the G-8, it would have been hard to deny that ECOSOC, with its fifty-four member states and its supportive apparatus, was of limited significance (P. Taylor 2000; Hill 1978).

The central economic units within the UN nevertheless persisted. It could be, as public choice analysts might explain, that bureaucracies once established are intrinsically difficult to disestablish. Clever bureaucrats find ways to keep their salaries coming. But it could also be that such an explanation is too facile. Developments in the early years of the twenty-first century, which occurred in the immediate aftermath of a series of financial crises that shook the post-1945 system to its core, pointed to more complicated reasons. The very persistence of multilateral political instruments reflected both the continuing necessity and the continuing fragility of public authority underneath a globalizing economy commonly depicted as a private market-led juggernaut. Forums of more limited membership certainly proliferated; but after every bout of systemic financial instability the world turned back to the more broadly based conference and policy coordination machinery of the UN (Schechter 2001; Cooper, English, and Thakur 2002).

Students of international relations now widely note the resurgence of unilateralism in the United States and elsewhere. They also observe the increasing reliance of the system leader on markets — or at most on political "coalitions of the willing" — to address security issues and manage environmental, health, financial, and other global challenges. Many also point to the continued overshadowing of broadly based multilateral institutions by regional or ad hoc arrangements, like the G-8 and the G-20. In such a context, the revival and expansion of the mandate of the United Nations in the broad field of development finance, and the linkage of that mandate not only with other multilateral institutions but also, as we shall see, with potentially innovative national programs for development assistance, are striking. Especially in a global system now widely taken to be underpinned by the emergence of "private authority," that mandate is worthy of deeper investigation (Rosenau and Czempiel 1992; Cutler, Haufler, and Porter 1999; Hall and Biersteker 2002).

Institutional Adaptation

Long acknowledged by close observers of international organizations is the role of the UN in providing collective legitimation for global projects promoted by its member states (Claude 1966; Hurd 1999; Clark 2005). In studies consistent with this understanding, scholars, intrigued by the subtle changes that can occur even within states as such organizations adapt to changing environments and satisfy new policy demands, analyze change as well as dysfunction within international organizations (Haas 1990; Barnett and Finnemore 2004; Toye and Toye 2004; Murphy 2006). Traditional realists once depicted such organizations and their missions as straightforward reflections of the underlying power and interacting interests of states. More subtle students of the subject now emphasize the circumstances under which they fail to achieve their declared objectives and, conversely, succeed in facilitating complex processes of social learning.

Ernst Haas pioneered research on such processes. His work highlighted in particular the role of supportive expert groups, or epistemic communities. Consensual knowledge developed by such groups and communicated to reflective policy makers, Haas argued, could reshape organizational mandates and promote positive change as long as a blocking coalition of powerful states did not come together. Indeed, the more complex the policy environment, the more epistemic communities and vehicles for collective action seemed required (Kahler 1995). By resisting the notion that conflict and complexity necessarily cut international organizations like the UN and the Bretton Woods institutions out of processes of future policy development, Haas' work was a forerunner of more recent sociological approaches to the study of institutional adaptation.

A compatible body of research depicts post–Second World War international organizations as embodying a process of global socio-cultural structuration. For John Meyer and his colleagues, for example, those organizations constituted a "framework of global organization and legitimation" that both created and assembled "components of an active and influential world society ... The forces working to mobilize and standardize [that society] gain strength through their linkage to and support by the United Nations system and the great panoply of non-governmental organizations around it" (Meyer et al. 1997, 163). However much that system may seem powerless at any given moment, it is in fact an essential part of a macro process through which the nation-state form itself is reconstructed and transmitted, through which state identities are shaped and state behaviour transformed by the universalization of an essentially dominant Western culture. The Second World War ushered in the decisive phase. Afterwards, "rationalized definitions of progress and justice (across an ever broadening front) are rooted in universalistic scientific and professional definitions that have reached a level of deep global institutionalization. Conflict is to be expected, but their authority is likely to prove quite durable" (ibid., 174-5).

Embodying the process through which "world society" is actually rationalized, the adaptation of international organizations would seem necessarily to reflect a politically authorized mechanism for the working out of tensions, for coping with contradictions, and for sustaining the forward movement of societal construction on a global scale. Not by coincidence have such views attracted favourable attention from a new generation of international relations scholars seeking to combine the insights of institutionalism and constructivism.

The prominent liberal institutionalist position on the matter of organizational adaptation does not so much contradict this kind of sociological work as attempt to bring to bear models more clearly borrowed from microeconomics. This approach leads us essentially to expect that organizations, once created, can continually work to lower transaction costs and help directly to clarify and resolve problems of collective action. They become useful instruments for encouraging long-term thinking and exploiting new policy ideas. In such a context, they will tend to persist as long as the problems they seek to address remain in existence (Keohane 1984; Murphy 1994; Vaubel 1986). By their collaborative operation, moreover, they might begin subtly to alter the terrain upon which state interests are recalculated, even in the security arena (Nye 2002). In this view, the process through which they themselves develop is iterative, and it is more likely to be characterized by adaptation than by abrupt change as underlying inter-ests evolve. Scholars advocating a constructivist approach in this field have recently been trying to model this process as either an organic experience of social learning or, when things go awry, of social dysfunction (Barnett and Finnemore 2004). The related work of organizational analysts inspired in part by postmodernism takes this in a more radical direction. While ac-knowledging the reality of adaptive strategies, they contend that the actual avoidance of festering problems calls for intensive critical examination of the core purposes of agencies like the UN and for their structural redesign (Knight 2000, 2001).

By the late 1990s, the UN had accommodated itself to the realities of an increasingly supraterritorial economy, one that implicated all but its poor-est member states. From critical opposition to capitalist orthodoxies in the 1970s, it supported market-centred development in member states, albeit with a definite preference for adjustment "with a human face" (Mehrotra and Jolly 1997). The simultaneous movement of its most powerful member away from the exuberant libertarianism of the immediate post–Cold War period, driven in part by the failures made obvious by the rolling financial crises of the late 1990s, made such an accommodation easier. Still unclear, however, was the trade-off its member states were willing to make between enhancing the autonomy of some or all of their individual citizens, which is the very rationale for an economic system supposedly based on the ideal of personal freedom and opportunity, and the autonomy of the collectivity representing all of those citizens vis-à-vis other collectivities. The tipping point in this regard still seemed obviously to vary.

New Crises, New Opportunities

Thirty years ago, gradually opening capital markets and the volatility of key exchange rates both signified and stimulated a new interstate competi-tion for resources (Emmerij, Jolly, and Weiss 2001). Within the UN, calls for redistribution grew louder, and the World Bank and the IMF, linked to those markets, kept their distance. Today, the Bretton Woods institutions are collaborating more intensively and regularly with the UN, at senior management and staff levels. For them, the UN has become more than an ancillary forum, its leaders more than gadflies. Among other things, the UN now rationalizes and organizes the participation, in intensifying discussions on core IMF and Bank issues, of a widening array of non-governmental organizations (NGOs) and new social actors claiming to speak in the name of "global civil society" (O'Brien et al. 2000; Herman 2002). Into those discussions it brings newly revived relationships with the IMF and the World Bank. Leading states, moreover, are paying attention to its economic work. And, in both leading industrial and developing states, that work has forged new linkages between national ministries long accustomed to keeping themselves at arm's length from one another. None of this means that global economic governance of a systematic nature has suddenly arisen. There are still ideological, strategic, and operational tensions between the UN and the Bretton Woods institutions. But interesting changes are occurring.

Late in 1997, the General Assembly of the UN passed yet another in a long series of resolutions relating to the financial challenges of developing countries (Herman 2002; UNGA 2002). The resolution called for the convening a high-level international conference on financing for development (FfD) by 2001. Because analogous resolutions had been passed regularly, at least since 1991, the casual observer may be forgiven for having ignored the resolution. Surely few would have expected much to come of it, especially as the principal question appeared to be settled in the mid-1970s. The bulk of future financing for development would be delivered by private capital markets, which could increasingly be accessed by the straightforward reform of domestic policies within developing countries themselves. Sound macroeconomic fundamentals plus increased openness were expected to deliver development and prosperity.

As it happened, the UN resolution this time coincided with the onset of a downward spiral in international capital markets, a spiral that would eventually threaten the prospect for economic development and even reawaken memories of global depression. Not only professionally apocalyptic observers but also normally quite sober participants in those markets were very soon thereafter to panic and even to forecast the imminent demise of global capitalism (Soros 1998). In the event, the system did not collapse, but financial policy makers were overwhelmed as severe payments crises spread rapidly from Thailand to Korea, Indonesia, Russia, and Brazil (Blustein 2001). The IMF and the World Bank were quickly swept into the maelstrom; when it ended, their own credibility was hurt. The IMF in particular had been a principal advocate for a world without financial walls. By 1999, it and the Bank were in retreat from crisis-driven efforts to curtail cronyism and statism in indebted developing countries and to open opaque, dysfunctional markets to external competition. But they were not alone in marching backwards. In the fall of 1998, it seems almost embarrassing to recall, the most open and supposedly transparent exemplar of the world of financial globalization undercut the ideological foundation of the then conventionally accepted development agenda, a foundation often referred to as the Washington Consensus. Efficient markets were asserted, and both winners and losers needed to accept the inevitability of adjustment. But even in the United States, during a time of mounting fear, this kind of thinking proved insupportable. In the most spectacular example, instead of letting a highly leveraged hedge fund named Long Term Capital Management fail after its bets were swamped by a financial panic just then rolling in from East Asia and Russia, the Federal Reserve unofficially organized a bailout (Blustein 2001, chap. 11; Pauly 2005). Shortly thereafter, an energetic effort led by Europeans to codify clearer rules to govern more open international capital markets fell into desuetude (Abdelal 2007).

Simple coincidence cannot plausibly account for the fact that desultory discussions just then underway within the UN on the 1997 resolution suddenly attracted new attention. Although it looked like the 2001 deadline for a high-level meeting might slip, momentum began to build on bringing together debates on a range of new issues spawned by two years of global crisis, issues graced with the label "new financial architecture." In the background too was a refocusing of the World Bank's core mandate on poverty reduction. There was also continuing erosion in official development assistance (ODA) commitments on the part of industrial countries, despite a break in their longstanding resistance to providing debt relief to some of the poorest developing countries. Finally, there was movement towards a new round of international trade negotiations intended to take the development challenge seriously (Herman 2002, section 2).

An agenda-setting process on a FfD initiative got underway within the UN, and a preparatory committee suddenly attracted the active participation of the IMF, the World Bank, the International Labour Organization (ILO), the WTO, the Organisation for Economic Co-operation and Development (OECD), the European Union (EU), and the Financial Stability Forum. Unusually, the process engaged UN ambassadors, generally drawn from foreign ministries, with central bankers and officials drawn from trade, development, and finance ministries. As it moved in this direction, the preparatory committee also began to receive input from a wide range of non-governmental organizations. In February 2001, a week-long dialogue opened by the president of the UN General Assembly and the secretary-general attracted a notably wide range of national officials, as well as senior managers from the IMF, the World Bank, and the WTO. (Note that the IMF and the World Bank are officially designated as "specialized agencies of the UN," although they have defended their autonomy within the system since the time of their establishment. The WTO is not formally affiliated with the UN.) The constructiveness of that dialogue was immediately depicted by insiders as an accomplishment. As one participant observed:

> If FfD had ever been construed as a way for the UN to instruct or even give advice to other international organizations, the initiative would have died an immediate death ... The other [organizations] had to see FfD as a serious initiative that was relatively free of the usual negotiating rigidities of the UN ... [and] if not an advantage, then at least no danger in drawing closer to the UN ... Thus diplomats in New York have succeeded in involving all the major "institutional stakeholders" in the FfD process. Some have come warily and some enthusiastically, but all have been engaged one way or another. (Herman 2002, 168)

Working in parallel with officials at this level, separate discussions had commenced at the senior governmental level under the chairmanship of Ernesto Zedillo, past president of Mexico. After these discussions, it was still far from certain what the next step might be. Political transition in the United States, among other things, added a new wrinkle. A commonplace view was that the administration of George W. Bush was decidedly less receptive than his predecessor to using international organizations as forums for addressing global financial matters. But such a view proved wrong, or at least too simplistic. It likely helped that during the early months of the new administration, Mexico offered to host a high-level summit in Monterrey to follow up on the work of the UN preparatory committee (Herman, Pietracci, and Sharma 2001). But insiders say that lobbying by American business associations in Washington was more important. Most prominently, the Business Council for the UN, an affiliate of the United Nations Association of the USA, continued a campaign it had begun during the later years of the Clinton administration to build support for what would become the International Conference on Financing for Development (interview with UN staff, UN, New York, 5 February 2002). To this and other policy arenas, the UN brings its NGO network, which it has officially sanctioned and nourished since its founding. Many NGOs have official status at the UN, are formally empowered to address ECOSOC and other bodies, actually deliver certain UN programs, and play a recognized role in many UN activities.

On 27 January 2002, the preparatory committee completed its consultations with national delegations, with the international organizations, and with recognized NGOs. The result was an agreed draft text for the final communiqué to be debated at the Monterrey conference. Implicitly labelled in such a way as to replace the tattered Washington Consensus, the document was released under the auspices of the General Assembly and spoke of a "Monterrey Consensus." Its main points included expanding trade as an engine for development, mobilizing private financial resources, and enhancing the coherence and consistency of monetary, financial, and trading systems in support of development (UNGA 2002). Even the aficionado would be hard-pressed today to find much that is surprising or controversial here, but the fact remained that this market-friendly approach represented nearly a 180-degree turn from the vitriolic positions associated with the UN three decades earlier. Future historians may look back on the document and see a summary of lessons learned during the crises of the late 1990s.

In March, the extensive preparatory discussions culminated in the Monterrey conference itself, which the presence of fifty heads of state or government transformed into a full-blown global summit meeting. Even more significantly, they were joined by finance, foreign, and development ministers from many more countries, ministers not often happy to meet together in collaborative forums where divergent perspectives and domestic interests were likely to become public and obvious. Behind the scenes, the conference provided a focal point for unusually intense and unusually open collaboration among officials from the UN Secretariat, the World Bank, and the IMF. For their part, IMF officials later explained their interest in going down this path as rooted in three perceptions: (1) that the process would give them a chance to affect the agenda and avoid being blindsided; (2) that it would reinforce concurrent moves to encourage a broad base of member states to "buy-in" to IMF policies; and (3) that the "legitimacy" associated with a well-prepared UN conference would enhance the possibility that borrowing states would "take ownership" of adjustment programs they negotiated with the IMF (interviews with IMF staff, IMF Headquarters, 3 February 2003). Around the time of the Monterrey conference, "streamlining" the scope of the IMF's conditional lending practices had also become the new order of the day.

In historical terms, it seems clear that the UN itself had changed in such a way as to accommodate the views of the World Bank as well as the IMF. Gone, or at least much muted, was the rhetoric of political redistribution linked to the UN in earlier decades. That a concession had been made was clear to senior UN officials from that earlier era. Noted one prominent group, "By seeking consensus with the private sector and OECD and close working relations with the international financial institutions, the value added by the UN in developing an alternative paradigm may be threatened" (Emmerij, Jolly, and Weiss 2001, 144-5).

In the end, the conferees agreed to the text that had been proposed for their final communiqué (UNGA 2002). With a degree of hyperbole, but also with some justification, the text left the distinct impression that both rich industrial countries and poor developing ones were dissatisfied with the conventional wisdom that had dominated the international discourse on development financing during the previous decade. Where the Washington Consensus basically left the challenge of enhancing the collective autonomy of poor countries to their own self-discipline, on the understanding that this would stimulate private capital inflows, the "Monterrey Consensus" reopened the space for the newly energized post-1945 machinery of intergovernmental cooperation to stimulate and redistribute more justly new kinds of private *and* public capital flows. In the years following the conference, joint meetings began routinely to be held between IMF and World Bank executive directors and UN ambassadors, while staff reporting to them sought ways to collaborate more intensively on specific country operations. The UN undersecretary-general in charge of DESA also became a regular participant in the highest policy-making body of the IMF, the International Monetary and Financial Committee.

Towards a Revived Multilateral Order?

Even after memories of the financial crises surrounding the original Monterrey summit had faded, follow-up processes attempted to break some bureaucratic moulds and encourage new habits of consultation. Regular meetings were to occur among national governments and key institutional "stakeholders." On the most important economic and financial challenges confronting developing countries, foreign ministries, development ministries, and finance ministries, both directly and through the international civil service, would have to consult with one another and with their counterparts in other countries on a formal and routine basis. Of all the institutional stakeholders, the UN — where foreign and development ministry officials dominate but are often tested by demands for specialized expertise when dealing with complicated economic issues — would likely be the one most rejuvenated by this process. Despite continuing concerns about its size and the scope of its activities, it is significant that other ministries agreed that the UN had to be useful and would therefore be worth rejuvenating with some expenditure of new resources. In the wake of the financial crises of recent years, and the continuing crisis of underdevelopment in troubled parts of the world, what the UN mainly offered was what it had always represented in principle — a sense of international legitimacy, a good now apparently deemed to be worth putting up with the "inefficiency" of broadly based consultations. Despite all the criticism heaped upon it in recent decades, ECOSOC provided the forum that could engage the broadest range of member states, collaborative intergovernmental institutions, and, not least, burgeoning NGOs (Scholte 1998; Woods 2001, 2006; Buira and Ocampo 2005). By 2005, over 2,500 NGOs had received special consultative status from ECOSOC, which allowed them to participate in council deliberations.

To be sure, ECOSOC simultaneously found itself yet again at the centre of a roiling new debate on UN reform. With a financial scandal in the background, various high-level study groups focused on changing the mandates and modes of operation of the secretariat and of most UN agencies. They tended as usual to focus on the UN's core mission in the security arena. The secretary-general himself convened an expert panel, which weighed in with a more holistic study entitled *A More Secure World* (United Nations 2004). In the section dealing with economic and financial matters, the panel acknowledged directly the fact that "decision-making on international economic matters, particularly in the area of finance and trade, had long left the United Nations and no amount of institutional reform will bring it back" (ibid., 85). ECOSOC had been relegated to the near-impossible task of efficiently coordinating UN funds, programs, and semi-autonomous agencies built up over many decades by member states in response to specific problems of the day. Long-time outside observers had noted that ECOSOC was only a potentially powerful instrument on issues of economic development created over time by the co-location of three functions: integrating specific systemic plans with country-level programs, allocating limited UN financial and personnel resources, and monitoring the performance of UN agencies. Its mission was bound to be difficult, but "doing these three things in the same forum had a multiplier effect on pressure towards system-oriented behavior for policy formulators, resource contributors, and program implementers alike" (P. Taylor 2000, 139). Aiming to adapt just such a three-fold mission to the needs of a new era, the secretary-general's panel advocated three strategies: (1) refocusing ECOSOC on collective security broadly defined through better "normative and analytical leadership" through a new Committee on the Social and Economic Aspects of Security Threats and regular meetings between the presidents of the Security Council and ECOSOC; (2) "measuring key development objectives in an open and transparent manner"; and (3) "transforming ECOSOC into a development cooperation forum" that concentrated on the Millennium Development Goals and received executive direction from both a small committee comprising regional groups and annual meetings with the Bretton Woods institutions (United Nations 2004, 85-6). This section of the report concludes with a tentative endorsement of a Canadian idea for achieving greater "policy coherence." "One way of moving forward may be to transform into a leaders' group the G20 group of finance ministers, which currently brings together States collectively encompassing 80 percent of the world's population and 90 percent of its economic activity, with regular attendance by the IMF, World Bank, WTO and the European Union. In such meetings, we recommend inclusion of the Secretary General of the United Nations and the President of ECOSOC" (ibid., 86; also see United Nations 2005).

Among the many other studies and reports that followed, particularly noteworthy is one commissioned by the US Congress and sponsored by the United States Institute of Peace (Task Force on the United Nations 2005). A bipartisan group led by former speaker of the house Newt Gingrich and former senator George Mitchell tackled ECOSOC directly and bluntly. Agreeing that maintaining and strengthening the United Nations would serve long-term US national interests, the group advocated "reducing the bloated staffing of DESA and ensuring that ECOSOC focuses on useful endeavors rather than, as now, engaging in endless, redundant discourse or pretending that it is the World Trade Organization" (Task Force on the United Nations 2005, 108). The report goes on to endorse verbatim the recommendation of the secretary-general's High-level Panel, with the admixture of strongly supporting the notion of enhancing the "key coordinating" role of the United Nations Development Programme in such a context (ibid., 110-11). In the end, with US corporate practice and the idea of "accountability" very much in mind, the panel agreed on a recommendation to create a chief operating officer to complement the continuing CEO role of the secretary-general and to establish independent external monitoring, presumably by "contributing member-states" (ibid., 107).

In the waning days of Kofi Annan's leadership and in the early days of his successor Ban Ki-moon, it was common to read journalistic accounts of the death of the latest effort to reform the UN. The same kind of pessimism was expressed whenever turbulence engulfed the leadership of the World Bank and the IMF. But the obituaries were premature. Perhaps many observers remain in the shadow cast by the remarkable events surrounding the organization's founding. Perhaps they expect institutional change always to occur smoothly and decisively. They should instead take a longer view and see the UN as a continuation of always difficult efforts begun by the founders of the League of Nations to build a modicum of collective governance in a more interdependent world (McClure 1933; Hill 1946; Pauly 1997; Clavin 2003). They might then be able to discern at least some limited continuity and even progress of the kind Haas and the new sociologists imagined. Certainly in the economic arena, organizational continuity between the League and the UN is hard not to see. And whether UN activities in the wake of the systemic crises of the late 1990s represent significant progress or not will remain a matter of debate. Nevertheless, also now underway are regular annual meetings among high-level officials from the UN, the IMF, the World Bank, the WTO, and UNCTAD on the implementation of policies drawn from the Monterrey Consensus (United Nations 2005). The kind of interorganizational collaboration studiously limited in prior years is now encouraged. Perhaps more significantly, no serious proposal has emerged to take the UN entirely out of the economic and financial arena. As in the past, debate remains focused instead on institutional reform, even in the midst of widely reported organizational identity crises and downturns in staff morale. Still widely if sometimes reluctantly acknowledged is the idea that a global economy requires a broadly based, collaborative, and necessarily political understructure. The alternative notion that informal clubs, limited networks, or public-private partnerships could provide an adequate substitute was subject to significant doubt, especially after financial crises struck in the late 1990s and early twenty-first century.

What else could continuing debate on such issues signify other than a renewed recognition of the need for meaningful authority underneath integrating markets? Certainly it cannot be construed to express a confidence in the automaticity of markets. There was irony in the fact that a radically nationalist administration in the United States, the once and future leader of the post-Monterrey system, signalled a new willingness to work not only with the Bretton Woods institutions but also with central economic organs of the United Nations. That a sense of defensiveness remained apparent did not contradict the reality of states, the United States in particular, being drawn back into legitimate institutional arrangements of a multilateral character. Despite the internal and external difficulties they confront, those arrangements still held the promise of shared and durable prosperity. Of course, doubts remain. Nothing in this policy realm is inevitable, and the dream of a global economy could fade away. Continuing to acknowledge the objective, however, was not a trivial exercise. At the very least, not walking away from the nascent architecture of a stable global order enhanced the legitimacy of the claim by the United States to continued systemic leadership (Pauly 2008). Surely even American nationalists not seriously contemplating pure isolationism must have asked themselves why any other states would follow if promoting and defending the autonomy of Americans, both individually and collectively, was the only goal American policy makers truly sought to achieve.

It is, of course, possible that the post-1945 economic and political order is entering its last stages. Clear evidence of global economic pressures running roughshod over the legal sovereignty of leading states or pushing a critical mass of follower states to revolt against the abridgement of any meaningful degree of political autonomy would suggest one possible future. Conversely, if we witnessed leading states turning decisively against forces that undercut their collective autonomy, or follower states turning clearly in the direction of economic self-sufficiency, that would suggest another. But what we seem to be witnessing instead, certainly in any forum associated with the UN, is the construction and reconstruction of a global society, a society struggling in often contradictory ways to benefit from the opportunities and to limit the constraints presented by globalization.

Certainly for the most powerful, the benefits of economic openness exceeded the costs. The hope remained that eventually the least powerful would face the same situation. Periodic episodes of systemic instability reminded everyone that sustaining just such a hope was key. Signs of intensified collaboration between the UN and the Bretton Woods institutions provide just one mark of a shifting multilateral compromise between the necessity of providing legitimate governance to markets of supraterritorial and cross-regional scope and the insistence of still distinct and still diverse collectivities on the maximum degree of political autonomy feasible in such a context. Surely individuals dominating political life within the leading collectivities, who perhaps prize their own autonomy highly, are not really unhappy either with the continuing economic mandates of the UN and its closer collaborators or with continuing globalization. If so, there is no avoiding their responsibilities for mitigating consequent global risks and for addressing the challenges thereby posed to all those with whom they share a transforming system.

chapter 3   **International Law, Dispute Settlement, and Autonomy**

Guy Gensey and Gilbert R. Winham

ON 1 JANUARY 1995, the World Trade Organization (WTO) came into existence. It was created as part of the results of the Uruguay Round of multilateral trade negotiations conducted under the auspices of the General Agreement on Tariffs and Trade (GATT), which concluded in December 1993. The WTO was confirmed by 124 countries, which also accepted a series of far-reaching trade agreements covering, among other things, agriculture, services, trade rules, industrial tariffs, and intellectual property. These agreements profoundly reshaped trade relationships throughout the world and strengthened substantially the rules-based nature of the trade regime (Vernon 1995). The implications of the WTO flow naturally from the clause that reads: "Each Member shall ensure the conformity of its laws, regulations and administrative procedures with its obligations as provided in the annexed Agreements" (article XVI:4, Marrakesh Agreement). In historical context, this remarkable concession by member states substituted international policy making for unilateral domestic policy making in the important area of international trade.

Along with a deepening of the rules of the trade regime, the WTO agreements also made significant improvements to the dispute settlement system of the GATT. The GATT, negotiated in 1947, was a collection of trade rules that over time gradually became implemented through a customary set of mainly voluntary dispute settlement procedures (Hudec 1991). The WTO agreements formalized these procedures and created a system that was both automatic and compulsory — in other words, a judicial system that looked more like a domestic court than anything previously seen in international law. International trade lawyers have characterized this system as a "legal revolution" (Pauwelyn 2000), one that produced a "paradigm shift" in thinking about international law (Jackson 2005), and one that "requires states to do precisely the opposite of what a sovereignty-based regime would require them to do" (McRae 2000, 30-1). Even if one has no interest in international trade, what has occurred and is occurring in the WTO dispute settlement system is important for what it says about contemporary directions in world politics. In the terms set out in Chapter 1, sovereign states have deliberately used their decision-making authority at the international level to limit the scope of their domestic autonomy in this vital field.

Increased centralization of authority could be read as a gradual emergence of world government, and the WTO agreements do represent significant commitments by member countries. However, the authority of the WTO is not unlimited, even in trade, for if it were, there would be little need for countries to negotiate bilateral or regional trade and investment treaties that respond to specific geographical or regional interests in their respective economies. Bilateral agreements represent a way for countries to pursue key goals with trading partners, often through regional diplomacy, but this does not detract from the WTO process. Such pragmatism is not necessarily a challenge to the authority of the WTO but rather builds upon the structure established by it — a broader, more stable and predictable set of rules governing global trade and investment.

Over time, the WTO has extended governance in the international trade regime through a deepening of trade rules as well as an expansion of the judicial function. There are historical antecedents for both of these actions. Regular trade has always needed rules to ensure that security and property rights were respected (Held et al. 1999, 152), and trade agreements that establish rules are nearly as old as trade itself (Winham 1992). Thus the numerous trade agreements negotiated in the Uruguay Round represented a continuation of form from the past, even if they were a substantial departure in terms of substance. As for the expansion of judicial procedure, it is accepted that the distribution of justice and the formation of courts were among the earliest functions of governance that appeared in the evolution of nation-states (Strayer 1970). The countries that negotiated the WTO may not have been obliged to advance dispute settlement methods as far as they did, but the fact that they felt new rules needed a new system to adjudicate those rules was certainly consistent in some measure with the processes of regime formation in the past.

Despite the historical antecedents for the creation of the WTO dispute settlement system, it still represented a sharp break from the past. One possible explanation lies in the theories of globalization reviewed by Held and his colleagues. These authors elaborate a transformational thesis, in which globalization (understood, inter alia, as a transformation in the spatial organization of social relations and transactions) is responsible for many of the rapid changes that are now occurring in the world. International trade is certainly a place where these changes occur, as they make clear in a table tracing historical forms of trade globalization (Held et al. 1999, 178). It seems very likely that the changes noted in the WTO dispute settlement system are part and parcel of a broader transformation occurring throughout the international trade regime. As Coleman puts it in Chapter 4 in this volume, these changes contributed to a "globalizing moment" in a dynamic process of systemic change.

The broader question now concerns the effect of these changes, which are part of what we call globalization. For example, the WTO legal system could probably be expected to increase the impact of the WTO rules, but how precisely will this affect the nation-states that are members of the WTO and, ultimately, the individuals who are citizens of those nation-states? In any system of law, subjects are expected to obey the law, and they can be punished for disobedience. In what way might the WTO legal system inhibit the juridical autonomy, or even the political sovereignty, of the member countries of the WTO, and how might it affect the concerns of the individuals within those countries? Of all the uncertainties that can be encountered about the WTO legal system, these questions are among the most important for the future of the institution. They go to the heart of the broader question of the degree to which globalization actually affects the autonomy of nation-states and their peoples.

The WTO Dispute Settlement System

Origin of the System

The dispute settlement system in the old GATT developed largely on a customary basis, with very little written down regarding procedures or obligations. When GATT contracting parties had a dispute, a panel of experts was formed to investigate the case and render a report on whether the action in question was consistent with GATT rules. The report was then presented to the (plenary) GATT Council for "adoption," meaning that the report effectively became legally binding on the parties. Consistent with all GATT practice, the decision to adopt was by consensus, including the party that "lost" the case. Even the action to establish a panel in the first instance required consensus. As Hudec (1970, 665) wrote of this system: "The key to understanding the GATT legal system is to recognize that GATT's law has been designed and operated as an instrument of diplomacy." The remarkable thing about this system is that it generally worked very well, even if largely on a voluntary basis.

The Uruguay Round negotiation made the system more formal and less voluntary. The Dispute Settlement Understanding (DSU) became the main WTO agreement on settling disputes. During the negotiation, the parties agreed to certain changes. One change was to give countries the right to establish a panel if they had a complaint against another party. Another change dealt with adoption of the results of a panel. The GATT had required consensus for adoption, meaning that a country could block an unfavourable panel report, but the WTO reversed this principle by requiring that a report be adopted unless the members decided by consensus not to do so. This meant that "dispute resolution decisions will be formally binding on WTO signatory states unless the winner of the case can be persuaded to vote to overrule its own victory" (Shell 1995, 849). Once a panel report was adopted, there was a further obligation to comply with the recommendations of the Dispute Settlement Body (DSB), or sanctions in the form of withdrawal of previous concessions could be authorized for the affected states. These WTO provisions represented a stunning shift from the "pragmatic" conception of GATT/WTO law to a "legalistic" conception, and are probably the most far-reaching of the various changes introduced under the WTO.

Yet another change under the WTO was the establishment of a standing Appellate Body that provided for formal appeals from panel cases. The Appellate Body is a permanent commercial court consisting of seven members who oversee dispute settlement arising in any of the various agreements under the WTO system. The creation of this body was a consequence of the increasing legalism of earlier GATT dispute settlement practice. The Appellate Body was seen by the Uruguay Round negotiators as a safeguard against legal error, and as well an opportunity to build case law that might further promote the development of a rules-based trade regime.

The WTO dispute settlement system represented an enormous step forward for the legal method in international politics, and it is interesting to speculate about why it occurred. One reason has been captured by Robert

Hudec (1991, 365) in the phrase the "momentum of legal development." The GATT was originally established to provide rules to stabilize the various economic and business relations that are essential to permanent trading relations. Once those rules were created, however, it was necessary to implement the rules lest they were to become a mere theoretical exercise without much impact on the practical world.

Therefore, the dispute settlement practices of the GATT gradually evolved in the direction of legal formalism, and even without the Uruguay Round negotiation it is likely that there would have been greater legal rigour in the GATT system. But when the Uruguay Round entered the picture, with its enormous expansion of trade rules in agriculture, services, and so forth, an effective dispute settlement mechanism became necessary so the values provided by the new rules would not be lost. Dispute settlement was seen as necessary to ensure the integrity of the multilateral trade regime that had been built incrementally since the 1940s and expanded sharply with the Uruguay Round in the 1990s.

Operation of the System

Like the GATT before it, the WTO is a contractually based organization. The dispute settlement system operates on the assumption that if a WTO member maintains a trade measure that infringes on WTO rules, this constitutes a "nullification or impairment" of one member's contractual obligations to other (affected) members. In turn, the affected members have a right to bring the matter forward for consultations with the member initiating the measure, and if consultations are not sufficient, affected members may initiate formal dispute settlement procedures (i.e., a panel).

The purpose of these formal panel proceedings is to determine if a measure complained about infringes a WTO agreement. If so, the obvious preferred solution is for the offending member to withdraw the measure. If the member fails to withdraw the measure, affected members can seek redress by suspending concessions that might previously have been negotiated with the offending member. Basically, what WTO dispute settlement does is render a legally binding decision on whether a measure taken by a member is or is not consistent with WTO rules. Beyond that, the WTO leaves it to the affected members themselves to deal with non-compliance, albeit under the rules for retaliation contained in the WTO agreements.

Dispute settlement mechanisms in international law are usually evaluated by the number of cases initiated and addressed within their framework.

On this score the WTO system was an immediate success. In the first three years of its operation, the dispute settlement procedures of the WTO were invoked over 100 times, in comparison to the 207 complaints initiated under the GATT from 1948 through to the end of 1989 (Shoyer 1998, 277). The early activity of the dispute settlement mechanism appeared to justify the claim of Renato Ruggiero, former director-general of the WTO, that dispute settlement was the "central pillar of the multilateral trading system and the WTO's most individual contribution to the stability of the global economy" (quoted in Shoyer 1998, 277).

The WTO system has been in operation for over ten years, and, in the cautious judgment of a former director of the WTO Legal Division, "the system has worked reasonably well" (Davey 2005, 17). Davey bases his judgment on an analysis of 181 cases completed before 1 July 2002. Of these cases, 57 percent were settled at the consultation stage, and an additional 32 percent were settled through formal dispute settlement procedures. Only 5.5 percent of the total 181 cases (or ten cases) proceeded with dispute settlement without arriving at a legally satisfactory resolution. (A final 5.5 percent of the cases were incomplete, for one reason or another.) Considering that the participants in this legal system are sovereign independent countries, these results are encouraging. A further source of encouragement is that developing and transitional country members made increasing use of the dispute settlement mechanism; indeed, in the first five years after the year 2000 they represented a majority of the cases initiated.

There have been many criticisms of the WTO in the first decade of its existence. Some critics argue, for example, that the WTO is deficient in the values of consent, accountability, and equality that are needed to establish legitimacy in an age of liberal democratic government (Howse 2003). Curiously, much of this criticism is directed against the rules and negotiating practices of the WTO itself, and not as much against its dispute settlement mechanism. Where dispute settlement has come under criticism is on its policy of secret proceedings, and on the resistance of panels to accept information not arising with the disputing parties themselves.

Secrecy has been a modus operandi of GATT and WTO panels, in that briefs, hearings, and preliminary reports have not been available to the public. This practice was a holdover from the GATT days, when dispute settlement was conceived more as a diplomatic than a judicial process (Weiler 2001). Disputes under the GATT were perceived mainly as a matter between governments, and, given that confidentiality is the norm in intergovernmental relations, it was normal to extend that confidentiality into investigations of non-performance of GATT contractual obligations. Today this practice is supported mainly by representatives of developing countries, who fear that opening up the judicial process will place their countries under even greater pressure than they already face from large developed countries. Notwithstanding these concerns, the spectre of secret tribunals is not an attractive one in the modern democratic age, and some governments, notably the United States, have taken a principled position against secrecy in dispute settlement proceedings. The practice is apparently changing, as the WTO recently opened panel proceedings in an action by the European Union (EU) to contest continued suspension of concessions by the United States and Canada resulting from the EU ban on imports of beef treated with certain growth hormones.

A related controversial issue is the provision of information to WTO panels, particularly in the form of amicus curiae briefs. Dispute settlement rules give panels and the Appellate Body the right to "seek information" from various sources, which has led the Appellate Body to rule that panels (and itself) could accept unsolicited briefs from non-members of the WTO such as non-governmental organizations (NGOs) like Greenpeace. This ruling was sharply criticized by developing countries on two counts. First, the ruling appeared to give NGOs rights that were not enjoyed by WTO members who were not a party to a case in question. But more important, in a juridical process where information and argumentation equal influence, the right of NGOs to submit amicus briefs increases the power of interest groups, which come mainly from developed countries. For developing countries, the prospect of a court battle against both a developed country government and its well-heeled interest groups is manifestly an unfair encounter.

The amicus issue raises troublesome questions about the interpretation of democracy in the WTO. On the one hand, openness and inclusiveness are important to the democratic process, and the more the WTO can respond to important concerns in society the more it will achieve legitimacy as an international organization. On the other hand, equality and justice are also important democratic concerns, and the more the WTO can do to address the bare fact that it is an organization of a few rich countries and many poorer ones, the more successful it will be in promoting the authority of the multilateral trade regime. The amicus curiae issue raises the question of democratic legitimacy in the dispute settlement process, but it is also an issue that reverberates throughout the entire structure of the WTO regime.

How the DSU Has Operated Respecting Canada

We have stated that the WTO legal system could be expected to increase the impact of WTO rules, but how member states might be affected is not yet clear. Specifically, how might the judicial implementation of WTO rules affect the juridical autonomy, or even the political sovereignty, of member countries? This query could indeed be asked about any of the 150 WTO members. However, as a practical research strategy, we will pursue this question with respect to a representative WTO member. Canada represents a good case study for this purpose. As a middle trading power, Canada has initiated twenty-six complaints under the DSU, making it the most frequent user of dispute settlement after the United States and the European Union (Davey 2005). Canada has not often been a respondent to complaints, although the complaints it has received have led to high-profile cases.

Magazines

The Canadian government has been concerned with protecting national magazines since the 1950s. Until recently, the government had various policies in place to enhance the domestic magazine industry's capacity to produce and distribute distinctly Canadian publications. Canada has argued that magazines are cultural products, part of the national identity, and therefore in need of such protection. In practice, Canada used three main policy tools to protect its industry: quantitative restrictions on "split-run" editions, preferential postal rates for Canadian publications, and an 80 percent tax on advertising contained in split-run editions. ("Split-run" editions are duplicates of the US edition with the same advertising and very little, if any, Canadian editorial content.) In 1996, these policies made it prohibitively expensive for the American magazine *Sports Illustrated* to sell in Canada; consequently, the United States filed a dispute with the WTO.

At issue in this case was whether Canada was justified in protecting cultural products in contravention of its trade commitments in the WTO. The United States argued that the three policies listed above violated WTO law — specifically the GATT prohibition against quantitative restrictions (article XI) and the GATT obligation to extend "national treatment" to foreign products regarding all domestic laws, regulations, and requirements (article III). The United States strengthened its case by arguing that the dispute was not about culture, but competition. It believed that Canada was using the cultural argument to shelter its relatively weaker publishing industries, industries that were surviving on governmental protection, from US competition (*Direct Marketing* 1997). Canada eventually lost this case and was required to change these three policy tools to comply with WTO agreements. In its report, the WTO panel noted that the ability of any member to take measures to protect cultural identity was not at issue in the magazine case; rather the issue was to ensure that Canada's policies did not effectively discriminate against US magazines (WTO 1997).

Pharmaceuticals

The WTO intellectual property agreement Trade-Related Aspects of Intellectual Property Rights (TRIPS) mandates a period of twenty years for patent protection. Canada was allowing its generic drug companies to research copycat drugs, produce them, and stockpile them before the official twenty-year patent expired. These generic drug companies could then begin selling their copies the day the brand-name patent expired, usually at a much lower price. Lax patent rules can mean cheaper drugs for national health care systems and can allow countries like Canada to send affordable generic drugs overseas to combat international health epidemics. The foreign (European) brand-name multinationals wanted the strictest possible rules in place and enforced so as to best protect their intellectual property, development, and research investments. The European Union therefore initiated a WTO case against Canada.

The decision from the WTO came as a partial loss for Canada, which was allowed to continue the early research processes but not allowed to stockpile drugs for ready sale. This raised many social issues about the overall benefit to society of sharing innovative information. As a result of the decision, Canada decided not to participate in exporting cheap drugs to developing countries to treat AIDS and malaria — a decision that has since been reversed as the result of a WTO legal change (Canada 2005).

Canada–United States Auto Pact

This case concerned a challenge to the Auto Pact, which is an agreement for trade in automotive products between Canada and the United States signed in 1965. Under the Auto Pact, Canada agreed to allow certain US manufacturers to import vehicles and parts duty-free with certain conditions, a policy designed to encourage auto manufacturing and the development of the automotive industry in Canada. In particular, the Auto Pact allowed the Big Three manufacturers (General Motors of Canada, Ford of Canada, and Daimler-Chrysler of Canada) to import cars into Canada via their subsidiaries duty-free, while other offshore auto producers had to pay a tariff of up to 6.1 percent. This ultimately meant that the cost to consumers of Big Three automobiles (or their subsidiaries) was relatively cheaper than those of other foreign automobile manufacturers.

In this dispute, the European Union and Japan claimed that Canadian auto policies represented discrimination under GATT article I (most favoured nation treatment) and other provisions of GATT and WTO agreements. The WTO panel and Appellate Body agreed and ruled against Canada. Canada decided to apply to the Big Three the same tariffs it applied to the rest of the industry, equalizing their effect. The major fear in Canada was that the Big Three would lose a portion of their market share to the Japanese and European producers — a problem that never materialized as a result of the changes.

Dairy

The dairy industry in Canada operates within a supply management system that ensures there is sufficient milk production to meet consumer demand. In 1995, the marketing boards established a two-tiered pricing system for milk, whereby excess production was sold on the world market at lower prices to avoid domestic oversupply. Arguably, the system protected the domestic dairy market because farmers used income earned in the domestic market to support processors who exported milk. A WTO case directed at the Canadian dairy industry was initiated in 1997 by the governments of the United States and New Zealand. The WTO agreed that Canada's approach to the export of products made from surplus milk constituted a prohibited export subsidy according to WTO law.

In order to bring its legislation into compliance, Canada undertook various initiatives to fulfill its obligations, including regulatory amendments that suspended various provincial governments and provincial milk marketing boards from any role in the export of milk. Richard Doyle, executive director of the Dairy Farmers of Canada, said, "This is a case of jurisprudence. It very much addresses the issue of how much governments can do in their domestic policies without causing problems for their exports at the WTO" (Jack 2001). Not only did the WTO ruling have immediate implications for the dairy industry, it also had ramifications for the Doha Round of WTO trade negotiations. The WTO ruling essentially redefined export subsidies, which Canada had vowed to eliminate in its negotiating positions.

Regional Aircraft

Two of the key manufacturers in the regional aircraft industry, Canada's Bombardier Inc. and Brazil's Embraer SA, are direct competitors. Both countries used various government-related means to ensure their aircraft companies secured new sales contracts and remained competitive. One way manufacturers can make their product more appealing to airlines is to provide more attractive and affordable financing terms for the purchase of aircraft. When the WTO aircraft dispute was initiated by Canada in 1996 against Brazil, Embraer aircraft typically received generous financing terms offered by Brazil's PROEX program (Sullivan 2002). On the Canadian side, the government maintained a number of subsidies and public support measures to help Bombardier in the production and sale of its regional jets, including agreements with Technology Partnerships Canada, the Canada Account, and Export Development Canada (EDC), a Canadian Crown corporation (Scoffield 1998). As an official export credit agency and agent in all respects for the government of Canada, EDC has a public policy function that it carries out while engaging in commercial transactions. Its financial activities often include those that the government deems to be in the national interest.

Brazil challenged Canada's policies as illegal export subsidies under article 3 of the WTO Agreement on Subsidies. Canada would argue before the WTO that the EDC operated on strict commercial principles and was thus distanced from government action. Canada lost its case before the WTO and was required to bring its financing regimes into compliance. Coincidentally, Brazil was required to do the same, based on a complaint brought by Canada. Both Canada and Brazil worked towards negotiating a resolution to the aircraft dispute that would encompass the Canadian and Brazilian programs (Chase 2002).

Wheat

In order to develop and ensure the quality and availability of wheat in Canada, wheat farmers work closely with the Canadian Wheat Board (CWB). The CWB is a former Canadian Crown corporation with guaranteed financial support from the government of Canada (*International Trade*

Reporter 2003). It controls wheat sales, including pricing, marketing, and shipping policies in order to smooth out market fluctuations (*Globe and Mail* 2003).

The United States filed a WTO claim against Canada, arguing that CWB privileges were not available to foreign exporters. This, they argued, violated the GATT article XVII relating to state trading enterprises that are required to "act in a manner consistent with the principles of nondiscrimination," to act "solely in accordance with commercial considerations," and to afford the enterprises of other WTO members adequate opportunity to compete for such purchases and sales. Canada effectively won this case, as a WTO panel ruled that Canada does not illegally subsidize its wheat exports. Essentially, the legality of the CWB was upheld. However, the panel ruled against Canada on lesser issues related to grain handling and shipping. The requirement that Canada change its grain handling and transportation practices to conform with WTO rules was seen by trade analysts as a much less significant issue.

Common Themes

Three common themes have emerged from the political and legal commentary on the above cases. The first is that the cases have been highly sensitive politically. This has resulted from opposing interpretations of the Canadian government's reasons for creating and defending policies that violate trade rules and of other countries' legal arguments on how those policies infringed WTO law. In the magazines case, for example, one of the key issues was whether Canada was fighting the case to protect its domestic industry's economic position in the face of global media, or was legitimately protecting cultural identity. Some suggested that Canadian magazines should aim to be internationally competitive rather than surviving on protectionism. As a US official noted: "Any protection that has been offered to principally two wealthy Canadian publishing interests ... is purely a commercial issue. This is a difference of opinion over competition and not over culture" (Ditchburn 1999). In the Auto Pact case, political sensitivity was high in southern Ontario, the heartland of the Canadian auto industry. Policy makers in Ottawa were worried that the pact's demise would make investment by the Big Three less attractive in Canada than in the United States. Ottawa had expected to lose the case from the outset, but refused to quit, officials said, in order to give the industry time to adjust to a more open market. The legal wrangling gave the Big Three an extra two years to prepare for head-to-head competition. The aircraft dispute was politically sensitive because Bombardier is based in the province of Quebec, where the preservation of industry and employment was critical for a federal government facing a strong Quebec nationalist presence. In estimating the long-term benefits of easing these economic sectors off government programs, Michael Hart, a Canadian trade policy researcher, noted that "it makes for rough short-term politics ... The political fallout from the WTO rulings could be loud and uncomfortable for the government" (quoted in Baxter 1999, C1).

A second major theme emerging from the cases is that, although Canada actively promotes a rules-based trading system that can benefit all countries, it occasionally fails to abide by the rules itself. The WTO rulings still, however, come as a blow to Canada's protectionist trade policies. Canada lost outright in the magazines, dairy, Auto Pact, and aircraft disputes, and partially lost in the pharmaceuticals case. Because Canadian commerce is export dependent, it will continue to be examined against WTO rules. In the aircraft dispute, the final ruling by the WTO was critical of the way Canada defended its programs in front of the dispute settlement panel. It said that too many details were kept secret under the rules of cabinet confidentiality. It noted: "Canada has failed to explain why such information needs to be protected. In the absence of any such explanation, we are not at all convinced of Canada's reliance on cabinet privilege in the present case" (WTO 1999). As Peter Cook has suggested, "If the EU and Canada really want the world's biggest trader, the Unites States, to be bound by WTO decisions, they should themselves be obeying them scrupulously — not constantly thinking up ways to get around decisions they don't like" (Cook 1999, B2). This is not only a Canadian problem: many WTO members have found it difficult to adjust domestic political considerations to WTO rulings (Sullivan 2002).

A third theme arising out of these cases provides some perspective on the impact that the WTO dispute settlement mechanism has had on the WTO members. It is certainly true that the DSU system of compulsory jurisdiction was an abrupt procedural shift from the more informal methods of the GATT. Like any other WTO member, Canada cannot avoid going to court if another member is determined to take it there. This element of legal obligation lay beneath all six cases reviewed above, where Canada participated as respondent. What should not escape notice, however, is that the rules Canada was accused of breaking were mainly trade rules created in the GATT of 1947, and not the new agreements introduced in the WTO in 1995. In the Auto Pact and magazines cases, Canada fell afoul of GATT articles I and III, which form the basis of the commitments on non-discriminatory treatment that are the very backbone of the GATT. In the aircraft case, the issue was export subsidies on non-agricultural products, on which GATT rules go back to the 1950s; in the wheat case, the question involved the old saw of state trading enterprises. Only in the pharmaceutical patents and dairy cases were the celebrated new rules of the WTO invoked.

Canada's involvement with the DSU suggests that a bit of caution should be introduced into an analysis of the impact of WTO dispute settlement. Rule-oriented behaviour tends to change slowly. It is often easier to enunciate rules than for a collectivity to follow them, as anyone familiar with the struggle for civil rights in the United States could attest to. It is possible, and probably correct, to view the creation of the WTO dispute settlement system as a historic change, and even as a "globalizing moment," but it may take some time for the rules that the system is designed to implement to be completely assimilated into the behaviour of nation-states.

The Impact of the WTO Dispute Settlement System on Autonomy

The DSU with its system of compulsory jurisdiction constituted a substantial change from the way trade rules had been implemented in the earlier GATT regime. These changes surely had important implications for nation-states. Our analysis now turns to an examination of the constraints that globalization, as expressed by the DSU, has placed on nation-state autonomy, as well as the opportunities it may have created for those countries seeking to meet domestic needs by participating in the global economy. Specifically, we will inquire to what extent Canadian policy-making autonomy has been compromised in the wake of its role as a respondent in the six dispute settlement cases examined here. Or, to put it another way, we ask whether a case can be made that there is something to be gained by surrendering some level of autonomy to participate in a global body of rules that exist beyond the nation-state. To address these questions, it is first necessary to establish the key concepts to be used in this analysis.

David Held (1995, 100) defines state autonomy as "the actual power a nation-state possesses to articulate and achieve policy goals independently." Inherent in this definition is that autonomy refers solely to collective as opposed to individual autonomy. We do not reject the argument that individual autonomy and collective autonomy are related to one another. Indeed, a decrease in collective autonomy may very well lead to a reduction in individual autonomy. However, because the WTO is a membership organization composed of nation-states, for the purposes of this chapter our focus is on the collective understanding of autonomy. In order to evaluate the levels of state autonomy lost or gained, it is necessary to determine what is actually lost in the WTO, in contrast to what states can gain by participating in international organizations like the WTO to achieve their goals.

The Canadian Experience

Canada's engagement in the DSU has attracted numerous criticisms of the constraints this system has placed on Canadian autonomy. Analyses of the six cases discussed in this chapter have directed criticism at the changes required by DSU participation that have effectively limited the ability of policy makers to establish economic policies in Canada. After all, in each case, the government of Canada was intimately involved with the industry, both in creating and maintaining the measures that were found to infringe WTO rules.

The effects on policy-making ability can be more clearly understood by employing David Held's conception of disjunctures between the theory of what nation-state sovereignty (autonomy) should entail and the global reality in which it operates (Held 1995, 99). Held defines *disjunctures* as conditions and processes that alter the options open to policy makers. The significance of the disjunctures arising out of participation in the WTO and the DSU is that national policies will have limited effectiveness and will encounter greater resistance if they are not in line with international rules. Hence, it is essential to examine changes in levels of nation-state power and authority that occur as a result of these disjunctures. In the case of power, the question becomes one of who holds it and whether the level of power has changed. In the case of authority, the question becomes, where does it lie? Held (1995, 146) defines *authority* as the ability "to steer behaviour toward outcomes deemed sufficiently just and efficient to be stable under processes for integration and demands for autonomy."

One of the most important effects of these disjunctures is highlighted in the writing of Stephen Clarkson (2004, 153), who refers to the intrusive effects of the WTO on Canada's ability to govern itself as an external constitution or *supraconstitution*. As a manifestation of broader global governance, Clarkson suggests, the WTO enshrines rights and obligations that prescribe acceptable behaviour for states. This includes its norms (such as national treatment), the rights it arguably gives to corporations over citizens, and its strong adjudication and enforcement powers. As we have seen, where Canadian policies were deemed to be inconsistent with WTO rules, the Canadian government altered existing domestic laws and policies. Skogstad (2003) has argued that the impact of WTO judicial decisions serves to undermine legitimate state authority by hampering the ability of governments to deliver policy outcomes. Though governments retain some policy flexibility, their degree of freedom vis-à-vis multinational economic actors is reduced. In the case of WTO norms, Canada was accused of discriminatory treatment against foreign corporations in all cases except the pharmaceuticals case. The consequences of complying with WTO judicial decisions would mean, for example, not being able to protect Canadian magazines at the expense of foreign commercial magazine interests. Arguably, the fact that Canada has had to remove this assistance program has, among other things, created a "diversity deficit" in Canadian media — that is, a "loss of legitimacy of national policies aimed at protecting cultural industries when evaluated against principles of trade" (Drache 2002, 35). Another possible consequence of the removal of such programs is not being able to assist Bombardier in producing and selling aircraft abroad, with the risk that Bombardier becomes uncompetitive.

Another criticism is that agreements like the WTO work to promote the interests of private economic actors at the expense of the broader public interest (Skogstad 2003, 959). In the pharmaceuticals case, for example, Canada was required to observe full-term pharmaceutical patents for generic drug companies. In not observing the full patent term, Canada may have been better placed to provide more affordable medications for the national public health care system, thereby benefiting the Canadian public. Or, given that less-stringent patent requirements may have increased the availability of cheaper AIDS and malaria medications, Canada may have been able to commit to sending life-saving medications to developing countries. These WTO-directed outcomes, critics argue, created a "social deficit" whereby the state's ability to provide more affordable medicines is sacrificed to the protection of corporate intellectual property rights.

Finally, participation in WTO dispute settlement has meant that policies of social and economic importance for Canada, like agricultural marketing boards, are adjudicated by dispute settlement panellists at the WTO.

Citizens do not elect panellists and have no input into the process of the dispute settlement, but they are the ones most affected by these WTO decisions. Skogstad (2003, 960) has questioned whether this reliance on international trade experts is a sufficient source of legitimacy for policy making in modern democratic countries. If it is not, the way the WTO functions in relation to nation-states may be contributing to a "democratic deficit" (Lanoszka 2006).

It should be clear from the results of the cases involving Canada that some level of collective autonomy has been surrendered. The ability of Canada and other WTO members to articulate and achieve economic policy goals independently is reduced on a number of fronts. This, however, seems to be inevitable when a member state decides to accede to the WTO and is involved in dispute settlement. As Slaughter, Tulumello, and Wood (1998, 367) argue, governments now more frequently conduct their foreign relations through more legalized and judicialized international agreements than in the past. In managing globalization, states have been giving up certain levels of autonomy to participate in multilateral agreements, so the capacity of states to rule is changing its form (Held et al. 1999, 495). We argue that this change of capacity represents a *transformation* of state power, which may result in states that are better equipped to fight for their needs.

Canada in the World System

Given such gloomy consequences of WTO participation, why then would countries choose to sign on to such agreements? It is important to recall that all countries that became members of the WTO did so through a legally voluntary act and retain the legal right to leave the WTO at any time. As with much rule-oriented behaviour in society, it is probably the case that the participants in the WTO rules-based system accepted the rules not so much because they themselves wanted to be bound, but because it was distinctly in their national interest to have other participants bound. This calculus is certainly well understood in political theory, and it clearly was at work in the creation of the WTO and all other modern trade agreements.

From the perspective of autonomy, what national governments gave up in a general sense through participation in WTO dispute settlement was the right to define the situation and the right to change their minds. When DSU panels are established, the economic policies of countries that are subject to a dispute are judged in relation to the rules that those countries accepted through WTO membership, and not necessarily through the eyes or needs of national policy makers. Furthermore, when countries are involved in a dispute, they can be legally obliged to obey the rules in practice in the present that they negotiated in principle in the past. Indeed, in most of the WTO cases in which Canadian practices have been challenged, GATT rules negotiated in 1947 were invoked, albeit by an obligatory juridical process in international law that was not put in place until 1995.

General concerns about membership in international organizations are one thing; specific policy concerns such as those raised by the Canadian WTO cases are another. In the six cases under consideration, the Canadian government was prevented from achieving its goals of promoting aircraft production in Quebec, employment in the auto industry in Ontario, less expensive pharmaceuticals, benefits for dairy farmers, and so forth. Is this not a clear indication that the autonomy of the Canadian government has been weakened? The answer is an obvious "Yes": Not only Canada, but all WTO members risk losing some level of autonomy to enact trade-related policies independently if those policies contravene WTO rules. However, in response to the argument that autonomy is extensively weakened by the WTO, there are three arguments that the WTO in fact strengthens autonomy: by reclaiming collective autonomy, by allowing states to better respond to citizens' demands, and by limiting domestic private interests.

First, participating in the WTO serves as a way for nation-states to reassert or reclaim autonomy (Raustiala 2003). Indeed, one reason states join international economic institutions is precisely to lock-in more predictable laws and regulations in order to achieve desired policy outcomes from other countries. International institutions tend to produce outcomes that would otherwise not have happened, and this is their very purpose (ibid., 851). One important outcome is the ability of weaker states to challenge stronger states in a dispute settlement process that, in principle, treats all countries equally. The ability to enter into international agreements and the requirement that states observe such binding rules can increase their autonomy.

The argument that countries lose autonomy upon joining the WTO tends to conceptualize a zero-sum situation whereby power shifted to the organization is power lost completely by its members. However, it is more realistic that the creation of the institution enlarges the depth and scope of collective government power, rather than simply absorbing aspects of pre-existing power possessed by nation-states (Raustiala 2003, 849). In other words, if Canada is told it may not refuse to accord national treatment to foreign imports, in exchange for the autonomy lost by Canada to deny national treatment is the gain it receives in collective autonomy through the act of establishing a legal norm that constrains all countries from engaging in harmful behaviours. It is instructive to note that the more often legal agreements are signed and reap cooperative outcomes, the more often actors will return to this institutional form as a model for future agreements (Goldstein et al. 2000).

Second, in many respects membership in the WTO permits states to respond to and manage more efficiently the effects of international trade. Because states have always operated in an interdependent economic environment, they have never been able to perfectly regulate trade flows across their borders (Krasner 2001b, 234). In effect, states have always been constrained by the dynamism of the international economy. Globalization has created changes in the global economy that have weakened the ability of states to pursue autonomous policies, or at least have markedly raised the costs of doing so. Given a world in which largely irrevocable changes in the global economy have destroyed the ability of states to prosper under autarchy, autonomy no longer consists of the freedom of states to act independently in their perceived self-interest. Rather, membership in good standing in the regimes that make up the substance of international life (i.e., being an active player in the system) is also important. Democratic governance entails responsiveness to growing societal demands. International institutions are now the means by which states satisfy these new and more extensive demands (Raustiala 2003, 862).

Third, the enhancement of autonomy by participating in the WTO entails depoliticizing policy choices, or removing certain policy choices from the state, thereby stripping them away from the rent-seeking private actors that accumulate around state power. Arguably, rent seekers (such as protectionist industries) can dominate and deform the domestic political process, with the result that policy becomes more faithful to popular but perhaps unrepresentative preferences (Raustiala 2003, 863). Petersmann (1995) has argued that trade protectionism represents a constitutional failure, where governments fail to pursue national consumer welfare as the dominant trade policy objective. International trade law, by constraining protectionist policies, can be a solution to this dilemma, and in so doing it can aggrandize rather than limit the autonomy of national governments.

What We Have Learned

The DSU has allowed certain long-standing trade policies to be legally adjudicated in order to bring them into compliance with WTO law. Such cases are often politically sensitive because they determine legal distinctions between how states are used to doing things and the often conflicting requirement to comply with their legal obligations in trade agreements. Adjusting to these realities has been difficult, as it represents a transformation of the traditional understanding of nation-state autonomy. We have found that, while the system does result in some loss of national autonomy, collective autonomy is also gained in other unforeseen ways — ways that may allow the state to better respond to the individual and collective needs of its citizens.

Throughout history, one of the greatest sources of domestic instability in nation-states has been the international system itself. Now, with the globalization of the international economy, national economic security faces even greater risks than in previous decades. The WTO dispute settlement system represents a voluntary reduction of the national autonomy of each member state to avoid an erosion in that security. It is an attempt to apply global rules to a global economy that few members really seem prepared decisively to reverse. The system represents an application of the wisdom of philosophers from Plato to Hayek: without law there is no freedom.

chapter 4　　　　Agricultural Trade and the
World Trade Organization

William D. Coleman

ON 15 APRIL 1994, 124 representatives of nation-states, customs territories, and the European Communities gathered in Marrakesh, Morocco, to sign the Final Act Embodying the Results of the Uruguay Round of Multilateral Trade Negotiations. This series of negotiations on a multilateral legal framework for the international regulation of trade began in September 1986 with a ministerial meeting in Punta del Este, Uruguay. That meeting ended with a declaration of intent to pursue an ambitious and comprehensive revision of the international trade regime. The long, difficult negotiations ended with two surprising results. The first was agreement on the creation of the World Trade Organization (wto), an institution not planned or even anticipated at the beginning of the negotiations. The arrival of the wto realized the longer-standing idea of a major institution governing trade that would complement the International Bank for Reconstruction and Development (ibrd) and the International Monetary Fund (imf), founded at the end of the Second World War.

Some of the wariness about such a major institution could be seen in the us Congress in the late 1940s and early 1950s and came from an unwillingness to countenance liberalized trade for certain agricultural commodities. This unwillingness would come to be shared by the six countries that formed the European Economic Community (eec) in 1957 and then proceeded to draw up a highly protectionist Common Agricultural Policy (cap) in the early 1960s. In subsequent negotiations of trade rules contained in the General Agreement on Tariffs and Trade (gatt), signed in 1948 in the Dillon, Kennedy, and Tokyo Rounds, various coalitions of leading agricultural powers successfully fended off attempts to bring international trade disciplines to the trading of agricultural commodities. The Punta del Este Declaration suggested a return to the charge when it spoke of the "urgent need to bring more discipline and predictability to world agricultural trade" and added that the negotiations to follow should aim "to achieve greater liberalization of trade in agriculture and bring all measures affecting import access and export competition under strengthened and operationally effective GATT rules and disciplines." Three years later in Brussels, the negotiations collapsed because of the inability of the United States and the European Union (EU) to agree on agriculture. All negotiating parties knew that without an agreement on agriculture, there would be no agreement at all.

So if the creation of the WTO was the first surprising result of the Uruguay Round, an Agreement on Agriculture and an accompanying Agreement on Sanitary and Phytosanitary Measures was a second great surprise. When these two agreements came into effect as part of a new World Trade Organization, it was possible to portray the changes as a significant adaptation of the international trade regime to the dynamic tension between globalization and autonomy. When coupled to the institutionalization of the WTO, the agreements intensified political and economic globalization by reshaping the extensity, intensity, and velocity of social relations in the world agricultural economy (Held et al. 1999, 14-16). International economic law became more extensive in binding all of the then 124 governments belonging to the newly created WTO and more intensive in the reshaping of how governments and traders across the world thought about agricultural policy and how they might define policy rules. The velocity of global legal interactions also increased significantly. As a consequence, the economic situation of farmers across the world, the policies that their national governments devised to regulate their activities, and the ways in which states related to one another all changed.

This shift in the legal regime has the potential for changing the distribution of power and authority in the world agricultural economy. If this potential is realized, these changes would involve some rebalancing of the traditional dominance of the United States and western European states belonging to the EU in the world agricultural economy and policy making in favour of increased collective autonomy for some developing countries. They also create opportunities for the expansion of transnational corporate supply chains dominating agricultural production in varying commodities. These chains link businesses that provided the inputs of seeds, chemicals, and machinery used by farmers at the production end to the sales of commodities to consumers at the other. Whereas the autonomy of some developing countries might be enhanced as a result of these global processes, the autonomy of others, usually poorer states, remains weak. The individual autonomy of agricultural producers in all countries is diminished.

I develop these arguments in five steps. First, I discuss briefly some of the key concepts in this chapter. I then examine the pattern of protectionism that dominated agricultural policy throughout the nineteenth and first half of the twentieth century. The third section introduces the GATT, which was signed and came into effect in 1948, and then shows that trade in agricultural commodities remained, for practical purposes, outside the treaty. Next, I describe the Agreement on Agriculture and the powers of the new WTO and show why these institutions helped accelerate economic and political globalization through changes in international economic law. The conclusion then analyzes the implications of the new legal regime for the contemporary distribution of political power and authority.

Studying Global Legal Trade Regimes

The trade of agricultural commodities, like that of other goods, has evolved over the centuries to be a complex mix of legal relationships. For example, when a bale of cotton is traded from a merchant in the southern United States to a textile company in Honduras, the transaction and associated contract are regulated by private international law, including insurance and maritime law, public domestic law such as the national regulatory rules of the United States for exporting and those of Honduras for receiving imports, and international economic law under the auspices of economic institutions like the GATT or a bilateral treaty between the United States and Honduras. Following Benton (2002, 3), we refer to these patterns of structuring multiple authorities as global legal regimes. Prior to the seventeenth century, these regimes would have included very little public domestic law in the form of national regulatory rules or international economic law.

Benton (2002, 11) adds that global legal regimes can take two forms. A *multi-centric* legal order is one where the state is only one among several legal authorities. In contrast, a *state-centric* order is one where states have at least made, if not sustained, a claim to dominance over other legal authorities. Within either of these types of global legal regimes, legal pluralism may vary between strong and weak forms. *Strong legal pluralism* is where significant political attempts have been made to fix the rules between the various legal authorities and forums involved. In contrast, *weak legal pluralism* is characteristic of legal regimes where there is an implicit, usually mutual, recognition of "other" law but no formal model for the structure of the legal order, or where the model that does exist is in formation.

The other two key terms for this chapter are *free trade* and *protectionism*. Both, of course, have a long history in political and economic discourse and have galvanized a wide range of political movements. I follow Irwin (1996, 5) in defining free trade. He writes: "Theoretically speaking, free trade generally means that there are no artificial impediments to the exchange of goods across national markets and therefore the prices faced by domestic producers and consumers are the same as those determined by the world market (allowing for transportation and transactions costs)." The contrasting notion of "protection" became more prominent with the onset of modernity as the nation-state form emerged as the dominant institution organizing territorial space. Derived from mercantilist thinking, protection involves state regulation of trade in ways that promote exports of domestic goods while discouraging imports of goods from other countries. Such protection of domestic industry would ensure, proponents argue, larger increases in aggregate wealth of the given country than would free trade. This protectionist argument was assailed in a systematic way by Henry Martyn in his 1701 publication, *Considerations upon the East India Trade*, later to be followed by the more well-known and comprehensive work by Adam Smith, *The Wealth of Nations* (1776). The debate has continued to the present day in varying forms.

Drawing on these several concepts, the argument in this chapter can be framed in the following way. The creation of the WTO and the signing of the Agreements on Agriculture and on Sanitary and Phytosanitary Measures move the global legal regime in trade away from a state-centric model towards a multi-centric one. They also introduce a stronger form of legal pluralism to the system. These changes in the global legal regime, in turn, reshape the negotiating environment, creating the potential for a modest reversal of long-standing protectionism in agricultural trade towards freer trade in agricultural commodities and foods. The new global legal regime creates options for states and other economic actors to accelerate the economic, political, and cultural globalization of agriculture and food. These globalizing processes enhance the autonomy of transnational agribusiness corporations and provide some potential for enhancing the relative collective autonomy of some developing states, while reducing that of other developing states. Farmers everywhere generally experience a decrease in their personal autonomy.

Free Trade versus Protectionism, 1800-1945

At the end of the eighteenth and early in the nineteenth century, two powerful forces came together in Europe that were to shape the regulation of agriculture in the last two centuries of the second millennium: the theory related to free trade and the increasing institutionalization of the nation-state as the dominant form of governance. By 2000, both this theory and the nation-state were globalized, such that every part of the earth's territory, save Antarctica perhaps, was governed by some state, and, within these states, the advantages and disadvantages of free trade provided the principal axis of debate about the governance of the agricultural economy. In the process, the multi-centric legal order in place since the thirteenth century, involving private commercial law, navigation acts, trade diasporas and entrepôts, and monopolies granted to private trading companies by imperial states, gave way to a state-centric one. Public domestic law and state oversight of private commercial law came to dominate the regulation of trade and commerce, including agricultural commodities and foods.

The most notable early insertion of free trade as an idea into thinking about agriculture came in the Corn Laws debates in Great Britain. The Corn Laws provided for the use of tariffs to protect local farmers against foreign competitors and to ensure that the price of bread did not become exorbitant. These kinds of laws dated back to 1436 in England, suggesting that trade in agriculture had already been viewed as undermining employment, a mercantilist concern (Bairoch 1989; Wolfe 1998, 53). Their renewal at the conclusion of the Napoleonic Wars sparked an intense debate. In 1815, the great British political economist David Ricardo published his *Essay on the Influence of a Low Price of Corn on the Profits of Stock,* where he attacked the Corn Laws as imposing very high costs on the economy as a whole. He founded a Political Economy Club that was to continue promoting the benefits of free trade over the following decade. The mantle was passed on to the Anti-Corn Law League formed in Manchester in 1838. Although the increasingly powerful cotton textiles industry provided important support and political influence to the league, the liberal ideas articulated by John Bright and, in particular, Richard Cobden, were crucial in winning the debate. Robert Peel, the prime minister, had taken a strong interest in political economy. When his government repealed the Corn Laws on 15 May 1846, the free trade era in Great Britain had begun.

The debate over free trade migrated to the Continent in the following fifteen years. Germany had already established an internal customs union in 1834 (the Zollverein) and lowered its external tariff after 1850. Britain and France signed the Cobden-Chevalier Treaty in 1860, which ended French quantitative restrictions on trade and reduced tariffs to modest levels. France, in turn, signed commercial treaties with Belgium, the Zollverein, Italy, Switzerland, and Spain. These treaties contained a most-favoured-nation clause that ensured bilateral liberalization (Maddison 1995, 60; Bairoch 1989, 36). The ideas spread further through imperial ties. For example, Britain ensured that free trade was adopted in India and in other British colonies (but not the self-governing dominions). Similarly, in its informal empire, China, Persia, Thailand, and Turkey, although not colonies, were obliged by treaties to maintain low tariffs. These agreements limited their autonomy in areas of trade and granted extraterritorial rights to foreigners (Maddison 2001, 97).

Great Britain remained committed to free trade until 1931, but most European states did not. European agriculture went into crisis between 1870 and 1890, triggered, in part, by rising imports of cereals from the expanding farm economy in the United States. At the same time, the United States was pursuing a highly protectionist policy overall, limiting the opportunities for industrial exports from Europe. In response, farmers and industrialists in continental Europe developed political alliances in favour of higher tariffs. Pushed by the "rye and iron" alliance, Germany raised its tariff in 1879; other European nations followed suit over the following decade.

The introduction of these tariffs also signalled the strengthening role of the state in "managing" trade. In the last quarter of the nineteenth century, departments of commerce were set up, commercial attachés became more common in foreign embassies, governments encouraged chambers of commerce to set up international branches, and international trade fairs became major events. This strengthened state role was indicated further by the signing of the first international convention whose aim was to manage the production and trade in one product: sugar. Ratified in 1902 by Germany, Austria-Hungary, Belgium, Spain, France, Great Britain, Italy, the Netherlands, and Sweden, the agreement illustrated states' increased readiness to "manage" trade in order to arrest the fall in sugar prices that had begun in 1879 (Bairoch 1989, 71). The idea of "managing trade" through state controls rather than liberalizing trade was to dominate the agricultural policy making of developed countries in the twentieth century. Finally, in this same period, states began to set up departments of agriculture with a charge to put agricultural production on a more "scientific" basis. Experimental farms and extension programs for getting the results of research into the hands of producers became common across Europe, in Japan, and in the United States, Canada, Australia, and New Zealand. The notions of an agricultural "sector" and "agricultural policy" emerged at this time (Wolfe 1998, 54).

These steps towards protectionism led to an international response. An International Institute of Agriculture (IIA) was set up in 1905 by David Labin, an American businessman who believed that farmers could compete better in global markets if they had fuller information on prices and new technologies (Wolfe 1998, 51). Labin also believed that farmers in developing countries could get financial assistance to modernize. The IIA was eventually brought into the economic committees of the League of Nations, but with little effect.[1]

States remained the dominant actors. After the end of the First World War, tariffs remained high, although they were often seen as "bargaining" levels that could be lowered in bilateral negotiations. The force behind trade liberalization in the nineteenth century, Britain, emerged from the war weakened and unable to "enforce" the economic cooperation it had pursued in the century prior to the war. By the end of the 1920s, it became clear that Britain's logical successor, the United States, would not assume this mantle. Campaigning for the presidency in 1928, Herbert Hoover promised to help farmers faced with increased economic problems due to declining agricultural prices (Kindleberger 1989). Early in January 1929, some ten months before the stock market crash, Congress was convened to prepare a tariff bill. The scope of the legislation quickly widened to include industry as well. Every possible interest lined up outside the congressional committee room, with the members eventually being pushed out while lobbyists took over setting the rates. When enacted, the Smoot-Hawley Tariff prompted a swift and angry round of retaliation around the world, precipitating a significant decline in the volume and value of world trade.

The United States had served notice that it was unwilling to follow in Britain's footsteps and take responsibility for world economic stability. For their part, Britain and the Netherlands both ended their commitment to free trade, a commitment that for the Netherlands extended back arguably to the sixteenth century. In subsequent years, nation-states extended their regulatory powers over agriculture, introducing import quotas, price controls, limitations on domestic supply, state trading facilities like the Canadian and Australian Wheat Boards, other government bodies to purchase excess supply like the US Commodity Credit Corporation, and special credit arrangements to farmers. Trade became more tightly "managed" and producers protected.

By the mid-1930s, some American political leaders began to push for a reconsideration of such excessive protection. With the urging of President Franklin D. Roosevelt and his secretary of state, Cordell Hull, Congress passed the Reciprocal Trade Agreements Act in 1934, which transferred authority to enter into trade agreements to the executive branch. Between 1934 and 1945, thirty-two such trade agreements were negotiated and accepted in the United States (Jackson 1969, 37). Winham (1992, 19) describes the legislation as "revolutionary" because it involved implicit acceptance that tariff rates should no longer be a matter of unilateral policy taken by a nation-state, but a matter to be negotiated bilaterally, and hence of international public law. In this respect, the act was an initial step towards postwar reform because many of the clauses in these agreements provided the modalities for an expansion of international economic law after 1945.

Looking back on the chaos and misery of the 1930s, the economist John Condliffe (1941, 394) wrote: "No system of economic or financial co-operation can be effective for long unless it is firmly based on political security, which means, collective security. In assuring collective security, the United States must assume a large share of responsibility and make far-reaching political and military commitments ... If an international system is to be restored, it must be an American-dominated system, based on a Pax Americana."

The General Agreement on Tariffs and Trade

Condliffe's astute analysis and hopes were shortly to be given life as a few political leaders in the United States, having sympathetic contacts in the United Kingdom and France from League of Nations discussions in the 1930s, began thinking ahead about a postwar economic order. Wishing to avoid the "beggar thy neighbour" policies of the 1930s, the United States promoted the idea of international economic institutions to establish rules and norms governing interstate economic relations. At the end of the Bretton Woods Conference in 1944, which drafted a charter for the IMF and IBRD, the states present spoke of the need to "reduce obstacles to international trade and in other ways promote mutually advantageous international commercial relations" (Jackson 1969, 40). Already active on this matter, the US government had been working on proposals for the creation of the International Trade Organization (ITO) as an obvious complement to the IMF and IBRD in building a new liberal economic order.

The ITO was to remain an idea on paper. Its death knell sounded when the US executive announced in December 1950 it would no longer try to secure congressional approval for the idea (Diebold 1952, 7-10). Meanwhile, a General Agreement on Tariffs and Trade for safeguarding tariff negotiations had been drawn up. Negotiated in anticipation of the ITO's creation, the GATT had a strange genesis: it was neither a formally ratified treaty nor an international organization. As a treaty, it didn't come into force (until 1995 and the creation of the WTO) but was always applied "provisionally" based on a Protocol of Provisional Application (Jackson 1998, 12). Anticipated to be a part of the ITO Charter, it was not an organization either. When it came into provisional effect in 1948, the Interim Commission for the International Trade Organization (ICITO) provided administrative support that eventually evolved into the GATT Secretariat. Over the subsequent forty-six years, the GATT gradually became the basis for an important international regime governing trade in most goods except agricultural ones.

The GATT established several key principles in the trading system: internal and external non-discrimination; limitations on quantitative restrictions and other non-tariff barriers; reciprocity; and safeguards in times of economic crisis (Winham 1992, 45-54). So it was perhaps surprising that in the end the GATT was able to achieve "an astonishing amount of world trade liberalization" except in agriculture (Jackson 1998, 13). Here the protectionist measures developed in the interwar period by states remained in force; indeed, they were strengthened.

The US agricultural sector had begun making astonishing progress in productivity in the late 1930s, to be followed by other developing countries immediately after the war. Many of the farmers making these advances in productivity did not want to be undermined by import competition, and they demanded insulation from market forces. Effectively organized and easily mobilized, farmers groups had developed tremendous influence on the US Congress and on parliamentarians in other developed countries. As a result, GATT article XI, section 2(c), permitted import restrictions on any agricultural or fisheries product. At the Havana Conference in 1948, the few developing countries at the negotiations demanded reciprocity. If quantitative restrictions were permitted to keep out their agricultural products, they wanted to be able to introduce such restrictions on industrial products. In making their case for protecting their manufacturing sectors until they could get on their feet and compete internationally, they were invoking a form of the "infant industry" argument articulated by John Stuart Mill in his *Principles of Political Economy* (1848) (Irwin 1996, 116). The United States and other developed countries refused to yield.

Article XI.2(c) permitted quantitative restrictions when they were needed to enforce governmental measures that limit quantities produced or "remove a temporary surplus of the like domestic product." Although this derogation was inspired, in part, by section 22 of the US Agricultural Adjustment Act of 1933, it was inconsistent with the US law. Section 22 permitted the use of import quotas even when there were *no* controls on production. Concerned with this inconsistency, farmers' advocates in the US Congress succeeded in securing the primacy of domestic over international rules by amending the Agricultural Adjustment Act in 1951. The revised legislation stipulated that no trade agreement or other international agreement could be applied in a manner inconsistent with section 22, thereby subjecting international law to domestic law. Congress went on to impose import quotas on a host of products where there were no supply controls.

This violation of GATT rules precipitated a struggle between Congress on the one side and the GATT on the other (Cohn 1993). Congress emerged triumphant in this dispute in 1955, when the United States secured a broad waiver, with no time limit, from its article XI obligations. As Josling, Tangermann, and Warley (1996, 29) observe, the waiver had a "chilling effect on international trade policy." They add that "at a crucial moment in the development of the Agreement [GATT], the United States gave primacy to its national agricultural interests over its international trade obligations." The combination of this waiver and of very few tariffs being bound in agriculture left the door wide open for others to protect their agricultural economies. Certainly, the European Economic Community was able to set up its autarkic CAP with variable import levies with little worry in the early 1960s.

A second important derogation from international trade disciplines came in article XVI (section B). This part of the treaty prohibited export subsidies for manufactured goods, but made an exception for agricultural and other primary products. In 1955, article XVI was amended to read

73

that export subsidies were not to be used to gain "more than an equitable share of world export trade." The meaning of the term "an equitable share" remained vague. The United States in 1958 refused to accept a proposal by other states for a total ban on export subsidies in agriculture. Accordingly, when the CAP was conceived in the 1960s, export "restitutions" joined variable levies as key policy instruments for protecting the common market in agriculture in the EEC.

Developing Countries and Commodity Agreements

In the discussions leading to the draft ITO Charter, a tool of particular interest to developing countries was proposed: agreements to manage trade in commodities. As we have seen, such agreements were not new. A first agreement of this type had been signed to manage trade in sugar in 1902. Chapter 6 of the ill-fated ITO Charter would have allowed for international commodity agreements (ICAs), but only under exceptional circumstances and for a limited time period (Finlayson and Zacher 1988, 28-9). Moreover these agreements were expected to balance the interests of producers and consumers. The developing countries argued strenuously but to no avail that this balance would inevitably tilt in the consumers' favour and offer their producers little protection. An Interim Coordinating Committee for International Commodity Agreements was created in 1948 to promote the implementation of the charter provisions. When the charter collapsed, this committee became a permanent body for the discussion of commodity agreements. It sponsored conferences that led to ICAs for sugar and tin, but it never became an important site of power for mobilizing developing countries in favour of stronger protection.

Developing countries' discontent with the nascent trade regime continued into the 1950s and early 1960s. Part of the discontent arose from the perception that the rules had been developed by the wealthy countries to serve their interests. Jackson (1969, 618) contests this view, arguing that it was not so much that the rules of the GATT discriminated against developing countries but that the wealthy countries did not always follow the rules. Whatever the source of the discontent, developing countries began lobbying the United Nations in the early 1960s for a special conference on trade and development and for a new trade organization in which they could promote and defend their economic interests more effectively. This lobbying led to the first United Nations Conference on Trade and Development (UNCTAD) in Geneva in March 1964. The UN General

Assembly made UNCTAD a permanent institution on 12 December 1964. The hope was that UNCTAD would subsume the GATT and provide an institutional framework for the discussion of commodity issues (Finlayson and Zacher 1988, 32).

The story of UNCTAD is long and complex. Only parts of it are relevant to our discussion of agricultural trade. After it was formed, its membership divided into three groups: the Group of 77 (G77), representing developing countries; Group B, the developed countries; and the Eastern Bloc Communist states. Its emergence led the Group B countries to put more resources into the Organisation for Economic Co-operation and Development (OECD) as a forum for discussion and for preparing common positions. At the first meeting of UNCTAD, the G77 called on developed countries to ensure that domestic agricultural support policies not prevent developing countries from supplying a reasonable part of the domestic markets of developed countries. They also called for a lowering of tariffs and an end of quantitative restrictions in agriculture. The OECD countries ensured that the resolutions were sufficiently weak as to avoid concrete obligations (Finlayson and Zacher 1988, 46).

More generally, the Group B countries resisted the devolution of any of GATT's authority to UNCTAD. Similarly, although UNCTAD took over responsibility for commodity agreements, these agreements never assumed the role in agriculture hoped for by developing countries. UNCTAD never gained the power to make such agreements legally binding; states had to give their acceptance first. Similarly, harkening back to the principles under the defunct ITO Charter, commodity agreements were still expected to distribute votes equally between producer and consumer countries (Finlayson and Zacher 1988, 79).

Summary

Under these conditions at the GATT and UNCTAD, intensifying autarky characterized developed countries' agricultural policy making in the postwar period. The ideas of the dominant "dependent" policy paradigm centred on the need for protected development. According to this paradigm, agriculture was a sector contributing to an important national goal: providing a secure and safe supply of food. But it was also viewed as a sector unable to compete with the non-farm sectors for resources or with agriculture sectors in other countries (Coleman 1998, 636; Coleman, Grant, and Josling 2004, 95). Hence, governments had to provide it with stability by regulating prices and managing imports. Various producer organizations participated in these policy arrangements through corporatist policy networks in most European countries, Japan, and Australia. In the United States, an "iron triangle" involving informal coalitions of producers, the US Department of Agriculture (USDA), and the agriculture committees of Congress tended to control the policy process (Hansen 1991). General farm organizations representing agricultural producers were involved directly in the policy formulation process, and more specialized commodity groups usually worked with public officials in implementing policy. In these closed policy networks, domestic subsidies increased; OECD farmers, particularly large producers, received ever-increasing parts of their income from state support; occasional export subsidy "wars" broke out between the United States and the EEC; and import controls restricting market access became more widespread in many developed countries.

The WTO and Agriculture

Two initially parallel, but gradually interlinked, processes came together to foster institutional adaptation and change in the governance of agricultural trade on 15 April 1994 in Marrakesh, Morocco. On the one side, a crisis in the global agricultural economy opened the door to policy solutions emanating from an epistemic community anchored in the discipline of agricultural economics. Termed a "Farm War" by Wolfe (1998), the crisis involved a struggle between the United States and the European Union over world markets, which visited economic collateral damage on the collective autonomy of most other states involved in the agriculture trading system. Members of the epistemic community helped articulate an alternative policy paradigm anchored in beliefs about the virtues of free trade and liberal markets. On the other side, driven by a host of problems arising out of the increasing globalization of the world economy, the representatives of the 124 states participating in the Uruguay Round of trade negotiations agreed upon the creation of the World Trade Organization, some forty-four years after the International Trade Organization was stillborn. A response to the dynamic tension between globalization and autonomy, this new organization nudged the legal regime governing trade away from a state-centric towards a multi-centric model, featuring strong rather than weak legal pluralism.

Liberalizing Agriculture

In the late 1970s and early 1980s, the problems in the world agricultural economy became more intractable, and an export subsidy war broke out between the United States and the EEC. This struggle was highly costly to the treasuries of the United States and EEC countries, had nefarious spill-over effects on agricultural production in other OECD countries, and caused long-term damage to the agricultural economies of many developing countries. With many of the latter soon to become more active in the trade regime, the EEC-US struggle came to be perceived by most states as a global crisis in agricultural trade. By this point, an epistemic community anchored in the discipline of agricultural economics had begun to develop a new policy-evaluation framework based on neoclassical economics.[2] Key members had developed technical tools that permitted governments to compare levels of protection across the globe despite the dizzying array of different policy instruments in use from one country to another. Other new tools permitted an accurate assessment of the cost to the overall economy of border controls. With members in an increasing number of departments of agriculture in OECD countries, in policy think tanks, and in agricultural colleges in leading universities, the epistemic community was well placed to shape policy discussions at a time of crisis.

Faced with the ever-increasing problems in agricultural trade, the GATT ministers meeting in 1982 set up a Committee of Trade in Agriculture to look into the sector. The work of various experts from the epistemic community came to enjoy considerable influence in this committee (Coleman 2001, 105). Their arguments challenged the basic assumptions of the dependent paradigm. They argued that agriculture could function effectively under normal market conditions and return adequate incomes to farmers. Government policy should be limited to ensuring that the markets worked properly and that there was a safety net available for those farmers facing temporary difficulties. When it came to world markets, governments should work to ensure a "level playing field" and to end any policies at the border that would restrict trade. If domestic protectionism and other price and supply management policies were reformed, the world market would be stable and reliable. This new "competitive" policy paradigm was influential in shaping the language opening the Uruguay Round of negotiations, with its call for the liberalization of trade in agriculture.

The World Trade Organization

Beginning in 1986 and ending in 1994, the Uruguay Round of trade negotiations spanned a period of intense economic and political change. In 1989, the Iron Curtain collapsed, leading to the beginning of the fuller integration of the former Soviet Union and its allied states in eastern Europe into the global capitalist economy. China had begun the process of "economic reform" also designed to enhance its participation in the world economy. In 1991, India introduced a series of liberalizing reforms, signalling its fuller embrace of capitalism. By 1985, China, Hong Kong, South Korea, and Saudi Arabia had joined the list of the top twenty exporters and importers in the world; Brazil and Taiwan were among the top twenty exporters; and Singapore was on the list of the twenty leading importers (Winham 2005). Thus, it is not surprising that in this round developing countries were more represented and active than any previous round. As the world economy globalized, so did the process of negotiating trade rules. Over 120 countries participated in the largest and most complex negotiation in history related to international economics, a far cry from the thirty-three countries that signed the GATT in 1948 (Jackson 1998, 1).

The coming into existence of the WTO on 1 January 1995 marked a significant change in the global legal regime. As Winham (1998, 350) commented: "The WTO is the first international organization of international character to be created following the end of the Cold War, and it completed the third pillar of international economic organization which had begun with the creation of the IMF and the World Bank in 1944. Unlike the GATT, the WTO is invested with a legal personality and organisational presence arguably equivalent to the latter organizations." The overall treaty is called the Final Act Embodying the Results of the Uruguay Round of Multilateral Trade Negotiations. The first element is the Charter of the WTO, which is followed by four annexes that take up most of the treaty's 26,000 pages and all of the substance. The charter clauses deal with procedural and institutional matters.

The WTO's creation accelerated political globalization through legal change. For the first time in history, a globally representative set of nation-states and customs territories had contracted to abide by rules entrenched in international public economic law with regard to trade in goods and services. By 2007, the number of contracting members of the WTO had grown to 150, with over 20 states, including the Russian Federation, in the process of negotiating accession. Gone was the provisional character of the old

GATT. Moreover, the WTO is a "single undertaking" such that all parts of the agreement, whether a newly negotiated GATT, the General Agreement on Services, the Agreement on Trade-Related Aspects of Intellectual Property Rights (TRIPS), or other agreements, are integrated. Of course, this characteristic does not mean that all parts are consistent with one another; such consistency will emerge over time as new negotiations take place and legal decisions interpret relationships across the text. Finally, of crucial significance is the development of the new Dispute Settlement Understanding (DSU) examined by Gensey and Winham in Chapter 3. All of these properties suggest that the global legal regime has moved away from strict dominance by states and weak legal pluralism. It is now characterized by a more multi-centric, rules-based arrangement and by strong legal pluralism in which more states than ever before, as well as private actors and international organizations, are working together to coordinate the governance of trade.

Agriculture

This new legal framework for trade departs significantly from the GATT because it incorporates new rules regulating agriculture. The Agreement on Agriculture signalled an effort to end the protectionism that had governed the sector for the previous two centuries and, in particular, the intensification of non-tariff barriers to trade that occurred in the last two-thirds of the twentieth century. The thinking inherent in the competitive policy paradigm is evident in the agreement. Perhaps the most significant change was tariffication: non-tariff import barriers were ended and replaced by tariffs. When compared to quantitative restrictions and other border measures, tariffs are more transparent, less discriminatory when applied uniformly, and easier to reduce. They impose fewer economic distortions, allowing world price changes to be transmitted into domestic markets (OECD 2002, 225). The contracting parties also agreed to open 3 percent of their domestic markets to imports at minimal tariffs. The agreement imposed restrictions on the use of export subsidies. Finally, drawing again from the expertise of the agricultural economics epistemic community, a system was set up for classifying domestic policies according to their potential to distort trade. Policies were put into "boxes," with the most distorting falling into the Amber Box and the least distorting into the Green Box. Those classified as "amber" were subject to the highest reductions.

The agreement's immediate impact on agricultural markets was small, but the longer term implications are potentially significant. Agriculture became legally an "industry" like other industries. The world markets for agricultural commodities that had developed in exponential fashion over the previous five hundred years were to be treated like other markets for industrial goods and services. Ricardo's lens of comparative advantage was to be applied, with the assumption being that more persons would eat better at lower prices if agricultural commodities were freely traded. Farmers, like industrial workers, would find that their livelihood would be shaped more by shifting developments in those world markets than in the past. The agreement is a politically and economically globalizing one; all members of the WTO are subject to it, and none of their farming population is exempt from it. The implications for countries with huge peasant populations like China and India are only now beginning to be understood.

Conclusion

Assessing the significance of any institutional change is fraught with difficulty under any circumstances. To make such an assessment immediately may be sheer folly. The evidence is mixed. At this very early stage, however, it suggests the importance of the Marrakesh Agreement for changing the scope and form of the regulation of agricultural trade. Representing a globalizing moment, it opened possibilities for deeper globalization. The reformed institutions also rebalanced collective autonomy among states while diminishing the individual autonomy of agricultural producers.

Certainly an argument against the long-term significance of the changes is credible. The agricultural economies of the OECD countries remain highly protected, despite the Agreement on Agriculture. Although many non-tariff barriers to trade such as quantitative restrictions on imports were converted to tariffs under the agreement, many countries bound these tariffs at very high rates. Estimates indicate that agricultural tariffs are about 60 percent on average, while industrial tariffs rarely exceed 10 percent (OECD 2001, 2). The aggregate nature of the formula for tariff reduction gave countries a great deal of flexibility. For example, they were able to trade off large reductions on commodities with already existing low tariff levels against small reductions in commodities with large tariffs. Consequently the *ad valorem* tariffs for sugar in the European Union and the United States are 147 and 129 percent, respectively, the EU tariff on grains is 162 percent, the Canadian tariff on dairy products is 262 percent, and the Japanese tariff on grains is 491 percent (Anderson 2001).

Similarly, the "disciplines" on export subsidies have yet to bite. Export subsidy commitments in the year 1999/2000, five years after the agreement came into effect, amounted to US$5.9 billion, of which 93 percent was contributed by the EU (de Gorter, Ruiz, and Ingco 2004). Export subsidies reduce prices and make it difficult for agricultural exporting countries to compete. When in place for a significant number of years, they put producers of the relevant goods in other countries, particularly developing countries, out of business. Domestic subsidies too remain stubbornly high. In 2001, such support was estimated to be US$311 billion in the OECD countries, roughly equal to the GDP of all the countries in sub-Saharan Africa (Ingco and Nash 2004, 8). Domestic subsidies accounted for 32 percent of total farm receipts in OECD countries, which led to prices received by OECD farmers being 31 percent above world prices (ibid.). With large farmers being by far the principal beneficiaries of these subsidies, it is clear that these farmers remain a potent lobby in the United States and the EU.

In reviewing these changes and taking into account a "Green Box" of support measures deemed acceptable and not distorting of trade, Wolfe (1998, chap. 4) argues that the agreements affecting agriculture are consistent with the long-standing dynamics of Karl Polanyi's double movement. As market forces strengthen, states and other actors move to build institutions and policies that protect those most severely affected while they make necessary adjustments. In this respect, the agreements involved both liberalization and the continuation of forms of protection. Wolfe (2005) adds that legal agreements like these should not be interpreted as final determinants of behaviour. Rather, following constructivist thinking, they provide the framework that shapes the ongoing debates and negotiations about the character of the legal regime. In this view, the Agreement on Agriculture in company with the creation of the WTO are continuous with long-standing dialectical processes of liberalization and protection.

An alternative perspective emphasizes a rupture with the past by placing importance on the creation of new institutions embodying free trade ideas and overseeing a corpus of international economic law. There is some preliminary evidence that these institutions may be important agents of change. In 2003, Brazil lodged a complaint with the dispute settlement body at the WTO about US policies on upland cotton. In a dense, complex document of some 377 pages issued on 8 September 2004, the WTO Panel convened on this complaint firmly supported Brazil's complaint. It ruled that payments made under the 1996 Federal Agriculture Improvement and Reform (FAIR) Act in the United States and direct payments under the Farm Security and Rural Investment (FSRI) Act of 2001 could not be defended under section 13 of the agreement; that various export credit guarantees were export subsidies that contravened US export subsidy commitments under section 10 of the act; and that user marketing payments under the FSRI Act were export subsidies (WTO 2004a). The combination of these policies had brought significant price depression in the world cotton market, constituting serious prejudice to the interests of Brazil.

The United States appealed the panel decision. Perceiving the threat to many of its own subsidy programs, the EU intervened in the appeal as a third party, supporting many of the US arguments. On the other side, Argentina, Australia, Benin and Chad, Canada, China, India, New Zealand, and the Separate Customs Territory of Taiwan, Penghu, Kinmen, and Matsu intervened to support Brazil. In its report, the appellate body upheld virtually all of the panel's rulings and concluded by requesting the United States to bring its policies into conformity with its obligations under the Agreement on Agriculture and the Agreement on Subsidies and Countervailing Measures (WTO 2005a).

In 2003, Australia, Brazil, and Thailand challenged the EU's market policies on sugar. On 15 October 2004, the dispute settlement panel ruled on this complaint, largely supporting the claims made by these three countries (WTO 2004b). It found that the EU had not met its obligations under the Agreement on Agriculture and had exceeded its commitments on export subsidies, which were used to facilitate the sale of the excess sugar into the world market. As in the cotton dispute, the resulting activity depressed world prices while denying a number of countries with highly competitive sugar production access to the EU. Again the decision was appealed, with the appellate body reporting on 28 April 2005 (WTO 2005b). Similar to the appeal of the challenge to US cotton policies, the appellate body upheld the decisions of the panel and requested that the EU change its sugar programs so as to be consistent with obligations under the Agreement on Agriculture.

These decisions provide us with another picture of the importance of the Agreement on Agriculture and its entrenchment in the WTO with its Dispute Settlement Understanding. Decisions by panels and appellate bodies under the DSU are understood to be legally binding on the parties concerned (Jackson 1997, 126; Winham 1998, 352). Sooner rather than later, the United States and the European Union will change their respective policies on cotton and sugar. Markets denied to other members of the WTO will be opened up. These decisions will also be noticed and taken into account by states' agricultural policy makers across the globe; changes will be made in some domestic policies; challenges may emerge to policies related to other commodities, whether grown in the United States, the European Union, or elsewhere; case law will be built; and the political economy of agriculture will change.

Many of the challengers to the United States and to the European countries in these two cases were former colonies, with restricted opportunities to shape their own laws and futures, and thus with little collective autonomy. In the absence of a multi-centric legal regime as has evolved in the area of trade, their autonomy, even as independent countries, might have been highly limited when it comes to US and EU policies on such core commodities as sugar. In the presence of such a regime, however, new levels of collective autonomy appear to be available. Once rules are defined and backed up by compulsory legal jurisdiction, the weaker can call the stronger to account based on those rules. Not all countries are equally able to exercise this autonomy, however. The legal expertise, financial resources, and policy knowledge necessary are not available to many of the poorer developing countries in any systematic way (see Ostry forthcoming). Consequently, the economic and political differences between these poorer countries and other developing countries like Brazil, China, India, and Thailand may widen.

Finally, the Agreement on Agriculture is built on a set of ideas that favour farming practices that can take advantage of export possibilities. These ideas are sometimes contested by those who argue that farming is more than the industrial production of food and is a way of life and a cultural activity producing rural landscapes of considerable charm and beauty. They are also worrisome to countries with large populations like India, which have experienced devastating famines in the past, and give strong precedence to food security. These countries fear that by expanding opportunities for trade, farming will itself change. Thus they contest the intensive "industrial" model of production agriculture based on large-scale farms and built on successive advances in mechanical, chemical, information, and transgenic technologies. They argue that farmers are increasingly stitched into global corporate chains that begin with the corporations supplying the machines, chemicals, and seeds on the one side and end with the food processors, agribusiness trading firms, retail chains, and fast food corporations writing contracts for what is to be produced on the other. The Agreement on Agriculture does offer some avenues for countering these trends. States can use subsidies and other payments that fit the criteria for the Green Box to encourage alternative farming methods such as organic production. A familiar problem still remains. Only the more wealthy states are likely to have the resources to provide these kinds of payments. Farmers in developing countries are less likely to be supported in this way. Accordingly, their individual autonomy, like that of their counterparts in the wealthier countries, is more likely to be reduced over time.

chapter 5

World Heritage Sites and the Culture of the Commons

Caren Irr

DESPITE THE HIGH-PROFILE CULTURE wars of the past few decades, one distinctive but frequently overlooked feature of globalization has been the emergence of international institutions devoted to preserving global cultural heritage. Appearing in the same historical moment as a globally mobile administrative class of "symbolic analysts," the post-1970s international institutions this chapter considers have defined a global heritage and stamped it with their own mark (Reich 1991). The result is a set of world institutions that are semi-autonomous with respect to national and local cultures and strongly characterized by the style of middle management. This chapter will demonstrate how this new global administrative apparatus has used an initially universalist concept of cultural content to produce a moderate and pragmatic vision of the cultural commons. Although the consequences of this vision of a global cultural commons for the collective autonomy traditionally associated with nation-states are highly debatable, international institutions dedicated to world heritage have successfully carved out an exemplary sort of autonomy for themselves. The story of world heritage, then, is not the story of autonomous and sovereign nation-states but of an increasingly autonomous international administrative system.

This system began to develop after 1945. Under the umbrella of the United Nations, a broad group of international governmental organizations arose to implement initiatives addressing a wide spectrum of topics, from health and intellectual property to criminality, sport, and culture, among others (Weiss, Forsythe, and Coate 2004). Although typically organized around international treaties with numerous signatory state parties as members, these institutions reside in host nations that grant them significant legal and operational autonomy, and they have typically developed an administrative logic of their own, as they devise protocols for encouraging and monitoring progress towards treaty goals. Features of this administrative system are recorded in exposés, such as Joseph Stiglitz's bestseller *Globalization and Its Discontents* (2002), which often criticize its ideals and work habits. Although never entirely separate from a broader geopolitical context shaped by influential states, as detailed below and as demonstrated in another arena in Pauly's contribution to this volume (see Chapter 2), international institutions in the UN family have developed a semi-autonomous standing of their own since 1945. This institutional autonomy has changed and solidified over time, reflecting and shaping aspects of global culture. Global governance of this sort may be characterized by harmony as well as tension between international institutions and nation-states.

A crucial feature of contemporary international cultural institutions is their tendency to treat cultural content as a resource to be managed. As George Yúdice has argued, international cultural policy since the 1990s increasingly understands culture in instrumental terms — treating it as a tool for national development, global civil society, minority rights, or urban regeneration. In fact, Yúdice argues that this expedient version of culture is so integral to the contemporary global economy and social justice agendas that it has become the foundation of a new episteme (Yúdice 2003, chap. 1). If Yúdice's persuasive analysis holds, then we can understand international institutions as moving beyond definitions of world culture as either a crystallization of elite values or the expression of a way of life — that is, as high culture or people's culture. Both of these concepts of culture are based on territorial, historical, and/or ethnic foundations. Devoted to the management rather than the origin of culture, international institutions such as the United Nations Educational, Scientific and Cultural Organization (UNESCO) and affiliated programs start from a different premise. Even when they use language that resonates with older culture-concepts, such as "the common heritage of all mankind," such institutions have increasingly modified their terms to suit new purposes. In particular, the administrative resource-management approach has contributed to a denationalization of the culture concept.

To sketch the emergence of this institutional language, this chapter will describe a particularly successful international organization devoted to culture — the World Heritage Committee (WHC). I briefly set the WHC in the context of controversies over the United Nations Educational, Scientific and Cultural Organization (UNESCO) before exploring some of the evolving conflicts within the organization as well as the means of their resolution. This narrative reveals that the concepts of culture the organization has employed have changed along with the organization itself. I conclude that the "culture" protected by the WHC is the product of an unfolding dialectic between the form of the international bureaucracy and local content. Over time, this semi-autonomous organization has not only identified a cultural heritage to protect; it has also defined global culture and made itself integral to that heritage. In turn, the institution's self-concept and organization have changed alongside and together with its changing concept of world culture.

As the WHC has evolved, it has increasingly come to see itself and the culture it defines and protects in terms of the commons. We might say that the institution itself has become an instance of the utopian space of the commons. This may not surprise those who have followed David Harvey's reasoning in *The New Imperialism* (2003), where he argues that the language of the commons necessarily accompanies economic globalization, since the rampant privatization this process involves foregrounds questions of property and enclosure. Harvey calls this dynamic "accumulation by dispossession" and asserts that the language of the commons employed by its opponents reveals the continuity of their struggles with those of earlier periods of dramatic disruption in social life (Harvey 2003, 162). The anti-globalization movement is for Harvey the latest in a long history of revivals of the commons. But, even as we recognize historical precedents, we will also want to recognize that different versions of the commons are possible, not all of which offer the radical critiques Harvey associates with anti-globalization protesters or other internationalist or anti-nationalist positions (e.g., Strati 1991). Within the WHC we find a moderate version of the commons — one that articulates and defends supranational values without addressing the property interests that drive economic globalization. Recognizing and sketching this temperate vision of the commons, rather than offering an assessment or critique of it, is the goal of this chapter.

Intergovernmental Institutions and Culture

The World Heritage program is part of the United Nations and shares several ideals with that organization. Following, as is well known, on the heels of the League of Nations, the UN represented an effort on the part of the

87

participants in the Second World War to ensure that future hostilities did not produce results as horrific as those they had just experienced. In their plan to endorse peace and minimize international discord, the member nations explicitly appealed to human rights, the rule of law, and social progress as means for promoting international harmony. From its founding charter, the UN was thus committed to an expedient view of culture. A common European culture was assumed to exist and to produce common interests and solidarity; a shared culture was thought to create the basis for political internationalism. Culture became the antidote to war for the UN at the same time that it was understood to be one of its causes; the UN's appeal thus lays the groundwork for the sea change in Western intellectual life later known and criticized as the "cultural turn." This phrase refers to modes of thought in which cultural rather than ideological differences explain conflict and provide the means for potential resolution as well.

In the early phase of the cultural turn, during the 1940s, the starting point remained European universalism. Based on the rights-bearing individual striving for freedom, European universalism recognizes no historical and geographical limits and sets itself against the localizing impulses of a medieval world view or the collectivist tendencies of many sacred world views. However, in the 1950s and 1960s, membership in the UN expanded to include many of the former colonies of the European nations that claimed to embody universal culture. The resulting conflicts between rich Western nations and the more numerous but poorer nations of the Third World — conflicts intensified by the Cold War — have been thoroughly documented by historians of the institution and of the twentieth century more generally (e.g., Hobsbawm 1996). The dramatic increase in the number of UN member states during this period (the number has nearly tripled since the 1940s to reach the current high of more than 190) together with the shift from a formal political colonialism on the European model to a neocolonial economy dominated by the United States were arguably the most significant features of the postwar period and as such influenced debates within the organization. Within the UN, the "cultural turn" led directly to disputes resulting from the division between the West and the Third World "non-aligned" coalition.

Disputes over universalism were especially important at UNESCO, the UN organization devoted to culture, education, and science and the parent organization of the World Heritage Committee. UNESCO is a large and multi-functional organization, with ongoing projects in literacy, women's education, media analysis, and many other areas. According to Peter

Lengyel, a long-term editor of UNESCO social scientific publications, leaders of the organization were divided at its inception in the 1940s over its fundamental mission (Lengyel 1986). One group argued that it should be devoted to knowledge production — sponsoring research, collecting and analyzing data, and making policy recommendations on this basis. Others felt it should focus on developing pragmatic social uplift programs and leave substantive research to its national members. Lengyel concludes that this dispute over UNESCO's mission was itself the result of cultural differences among the sponsoring Western nations. He identifies the knowledge-production approach with French politicians and administrators, crediting them as well with a more philosophical and rationalist approach to administrative tasks. The pragmatists were members of the US-Anglo contingent, in Lengyel's view, and they ultimately held sway. If Lengyel is correct, then UNESCO was debating not only its definition of culture, but also the national style of its own operations. This tension between content and form would persist in the organization's subsequent development.

In Lengyel's account, no single nation entirely dominated. He describes, for instance, how the institutional culture of UNESCO has been affected by the physical location of its offices in Paris — currently a rather unfortunate modernist office building in the empty streets behind the École Militaire. And he, like others, attributes significant changes in the organization to its leaders and influential administrators. Since 1946, there have been nine directors-general of UNESCO; they have been citizens of eight different nations (the United Kingdom, Mexico, the United States, Italy, France, Senegal, Spain, and Japan), shifting, over the life of the organization, from primarily western European nations to the East and South. In 1954, the Union of Soviet Socialist Republics joined UNESCO, as did a number of its satellites. According to Lengyel, the Soviet presence was significant but limited, especially in his own social scientific arena. Of greater consequence were conflicts among the goals of the Soviets, the Europeans, the Third World, and the United States. UNESCO's agenda and resources were especially influenced by the United States' pursuit of an overtly ideological interpretation of the relationship between politics and culture during the crisis period of the 1980s.

In 1983, the United States began to criticize UNESCO quite aggressively, and in 1986 it officially withdrew from the organization. Based on a State Department report on purported abuses within the organization — a report that Roger Coate, a political scientist who was an academic observer at UNESCO for several years, has demonstrated significantly misrepresented the views of American advisers — the Reagan administration charged UNESCO with financial excess, irresponsible administration, and the unnecessary "politicization" of culture. After this public criticism and the threat of withdrawal, leaders at UNESCO made rapid reforms in the first two areas, but the United States still withdrew, revealing (in Coate's view) that it was primarily focused on the so-called politicization question and a desire to assert American hegemony in international organizations (Coate 1988). Objecting to the fact that some international disputes were addressed in internal organizational meetings, rather than being confined to the floor of the UN's General Assembly, the United States presented itself as the proponent of neutral, apolitical bureaucratic expertise. It offered administrative universalism as a supplement to the earlier European appeal to cultural universalism.

The Reagan administration was especially concerned that its definition of the free press as necessarily anti-statist and commercial was not endorsed by all UNESCO members. This question was part of a larger controversy over the MacBride Report on cultural imperialism in the media. During the 1980s, as its domestic economy shifted towards the information sector, the United States was actively involved in defending the global expansion of private media and laying the groundwork for a new regime of intellectual property rights. This project is reflected in the UNESCO controversy (Sell 2003). Also, as the largest financial contributor to UNESCO, the United States expected to exercise a correspondingly large influence over policy and did not wish to fund initiatives with which it disagreed.

Contradictions within the US position were noted by many observers. American scientists argued that the United States should remain in UNESCO to retain influence and to demonstrate its support for the overall educational mission of the organization (Colwell and Pramer 1994). The opposition to the "politicization" of culture was disingenuous, said political scientists, when the United States clearly sought to advance its own privatization agenda (Coate 1988; Coate and Weiler 1986). Others suggested that the withdrawal reflected the United States' contradictory approach to a wide range of international issues touching on culture — such as its surprisingly protectionist positions on the traffic in cultural property (Merryman 1986). Regardless, defenders of withdrawal held their ground until 2003, when the United States rejoined UNESCO. In the intervening period, several American administrations concurred with the Reagan-era assumption that administrative expertise can be culturally and politically "neutral" only when it follows American pragmatist and pro-property principles.

American withdrawal from UNESCO resulted in part from a larger ideological and economic shift towards neoliberalism during the 1980s. American criticisms from this point of view produced intense scrutiny of UNESCO and, in the process, inadvertently exposed the interdependence of institutional behaviour and the content of institutionally supported programs devoted to culture. By complaining that its dollars were not buying the political positions on culture that it approved, the United States in effect objected to — and thus revealed the existence within UNESCO of — a recalcitrant international institutional culture, one that produced its own debates, conclusions, and programs on culture. By the mid-1980s, a meaningful alternative to neoliberal development was understood as existing in international institutions of culture. Even if this alternative was not particularly powerful or radical, the Reagan administration at least considered it a worthwhile opponent.

The apparently controversial view that culture could serve as a tool for development appears in numerous UNESCO-sponsored publications. For example, in *The State of the World's Cities* (2004), UN-HABITAT consultants describe culture as an invented tradition, artificially held in place by preservation and also stunted or underdeveloped as a result of colonialism. The book's survey of urban forms is organized by regional categories (Europe, North America, transition economies, etc.) that combine territorial with economic descriptors. Culture on this account reflects underdevelopment and is a commodity that cities can and should use to improve themselves. Descriptions of Sidney, Bilbao, and Singapore are used as examples of the "idea of using culture as a motor of economic growth." At the same time, cultural differences — for instance, between new migrants and settled populations — are understood as requiring planning that treats cultures equally and plans for their perpetuation (UN-HABITAT 2004, 35, 175-6). Evident throughout this report is a commitment to an active and generative concept of culture — one that is not limited to one territory or people or historical moment. The report describes culture as a broadly available resource and as one that can and should be managed by international institutional planners. This view does not mirror the considerably more utopian concept of the cultural commons as the substance of a radical new political subject apparent elsewhere (e.g., Hardt and Negri 2000). Instead, in this UNESCO publication, we find the basic elements of a more social democratic hypothesis that becomes more sharply evident in the documents of the World Heritage Committee.

The World Heritage Committee

Origin and Organization

Among UNESCO initiatives, the World Heritage Convention has been famously successful. Since its beginning in the 1970s, the convention's membership has expanded significantly, as has the number of sites it identifies and protects. The budget of the World Heritage Commission, the body implementing the convention, has steadily increased — although not as rapidly as its responsibilities — and the WHC has had some success in bringing its concerns to the forefront of world news organizations. Most notably, when the Taliban destroyed the Buddhist statues at Bamiyan in 2001, public outcry arose in part because world heritage preservationists had already defined the statues as monuments of world culture and thus deserving of more than merely regional or national special interest. In such cases, the World Heritage Committee has successfully spread its working definition of culture as the proper object of global management.

The World Heritage Convention was adopted in 1972 together with several other international organizations with related purposes. US president Richard Nixon signed the convention almost immediately in 1973, and UNESCO documents credit Americans for initiating the program. This suggests that we could understand the initiative as part of a US-backed effort to counter the Declaration of Economic, Social and Cultural Rights being sponsored by the Soviets in the UN during the same period.

The goal of the World Heritage program, as stated on the UNESCO website, is the conservation of sites of "outstanding universal value" from industrial development and civil unrest, by increasing tourism and improving management of designated sites. Both natural and cultural sites are protected, although the majority are cultural. Although the United States was the first state to ratify the convention, more than 170 others have since become signatories. The WHC began naming sites in 1978 and continues to meet annually for this purpose every July.

The committee's workings assume the formal autonomy of its member states. After state parties ratify the convention, they are eligible for membership. As members, public officials (often those at municipal or provincial levels, but not necessarily those involved in day-to-day site administration; see Ferry 2005) can nominate sites in their own territory for inclusion on the World Heritage List. If the WHC and its advisory organizations approve the nomination, states with sites become eligible for several categories of funding and expert assistance aimed at restoring, preserving, or enhancing worthy sites. Nominations are evaluated by elected members, and restoration and other projects on the sites themselves are supervised by local and international specialists in archaeology, ecology, architecture, and related fields. The WHC also maintains a list of sites that it considers especially endangered by overdevelopment, natural disaster, or war, and it provides extra funds to the relevant states to protect endangered areas, at the state's request. Funds for endangered and unendangered sites alike are dispersed only to states that request them, and the needs of the least developed countries are prioritized. Funds for the World Heritage projects come from voluntary and obligatory state contributions, as well as grants from private foundations and individuals. States that ratify the convention agree to make obligatory contributions to the World Heritage Fund; the contributions amount to 1 percent of each state's contributions to the UN as a whole. In theory, full payment of contributions is required in order for a state to be eligible to nominate sites and to serve as an elected member of the convention. In practice, however, state contributions to the World Heritage projects have often lagged behind formal commitments.

This administrative structure did not emerge without conflict. Since its origin in the 1970s, the World Heritage Committee has passed through four major phases, each of which has been characterized by a particular substantive debate among its members about the politics of world culture. Because international governmental organizations do not exist in a vacuum, these debates reflect the concerns and organization of the committee's parent organization and geopolitical context. In particular, they reveal the effects of post-1980s neoliberalism. But, at the same time, the organization also created its own administrative culture. Its internal debates, as recorded in the committee's reports of its annual sessions, demonstrate the logical evolution of the organization as it has articulated and refined a concept of the global cultural commons.

The 1970s

In its first phase, during the 1970s, the World Heritage Committee was concerned primarily with defining its terms and methods. Its first session was held in 1977 in Paris with representatives from fifteen state parties and a number of relevant non-governmental organizations (NGOs). Participants included representatives from Australia, Canada, Ecuador, Egypt, France, Germany, Ghana, Iran, Iraq, Nigeria, Poland, Senegal, Tunisia, the United

States, and Yugoslavia. With the exception of the African states other than Egypt, most of these early member states have remained active participants throughout the organization's history. In general, membership among richer nations has been more consistent than that of poorer nations, for reasons the committee explored later in its history.

Since the first session, the WHC has routinely interrogated the "whole philosophy" of the World Heritage Convention (WHC 1977a, 3). In particular, members have debated the meaning of the key phrase "outstanding universal value," because it summarizes the criteria for inclusion on the World Heritage List. The full list of criteria for inclusion appears in a separate preparatory document describing operating guidelines. There, heritage is defined as the "priceless and irreplaceable possessions, not only of each nation, but of mankind as a whole," and the economic rhetoric of impoverishment is invoked to describe the loss of such possessions (WHC 1977b, 3). In such descriptions, the committee invokes "value" in a complicated sense — as both measurable and beyond measure, possessed and unpossessed, singular and universal. As scholars of Romanticism have pointed out, this combination reflects an essentially Kantian view of art and culture as the link between material worldliness and the sublime (Woodmansee 1994). It rests on eighteenth-century European aesthetics and universalizes the economic vocabulary of the same era.

The contradictions embedded in this Romantic conception of value are reiterated in the WHC's two crucial modifiers. To be simultaneously "outstanding" and "universal," the works on the list must be exceptional, individual, and remarkable masterpieces whose excellence is nonetheless indisputably evident to all. This suggests that the proper objects of the committee's efforts are those over which there can be no controversy — those that are exceptional by consensus. Aiming for worldwide consensus is of course a very high standard for any international and political organization and leads to innumerable practical and conceptual difficulties. For example, the "outstanding universal value" criterion suggests that, logically speaking, there could be mediocre, undistinguished works of universal value — or outstanding works of merely local value. The latter category is easier to comprehend (and in fact has regularly been used to disqualify nominees from the list), but the former demonstrates a bit more clearly some of the conceptual difficulties that committee members faced when attempting to put some of this high-minded language into practice. In particular, the difficulty involved in deciding when a site has deteriorated (or been destroyed) to such an extent that, while of universal value, it is no longer outstanding has been apparent in several of the committee's discussions.

The criteria for inclusion on the cultural heritage list — the focus of this chapter — make the outstanding versus universal conundrum even more obvious. According to the operational guidelines, to be eligible, sites must:

1 Represent a *unique artistic* or *aesthetic* achievement, a *masterpiece* of the creative genius; or

2 Have exerted considerable *influence,* over a span of time or within a cultural area of the world, *on subsequent developments* in architecture, monumental sculpture, garden or landscape design, related arts, or human settlements; or

3 Be *unique, extremely rare, or of great antiquity;* or

4 Be among the most characteristic examples of a *type* of structure, the type representing an important cultural, social, artistic, scientific, technological, or industrial development; or

5 Be a characteristic example of a significant, *traditional* style of architecture, method of construction, or *human settlement,* that is fragile by nature or has become vulnerable under the impact of irreversible socio-cultural or economic change; or

6 Be most importantly *associated* with ideas or beliefs, with events or with persons, of outstanding historical importance or significance. (WHC 1977b, 3)

These criteria are split between a Western Romantic emphasis on the singular masterpiece that has a place in a linear, recorded, and presumably self-enclosed tradition, on the one hand, and a more anthropological or traditionalist view of culture as collective, anonymous, and holistic, on the other. The appeal in the next section of the guidelines to a standard of authenticity — notoriously difficult to evaluate in a continuously evolving traditional culture — compounds the problem and produces even more awkward dilemmas when applied to natural sites (where it is defined through the analogous category of "integrity"). The document aims to resolve, or at least quiet, these issues by defining "universal" as "highly representative of the culture of which it forms a part" (WHC 1977b, 3). Shifting authorship and singularity to "the culture," this definition of universality uneasily fuses Romantic fixations on singularity with the "characteristic" element important in traditionalist concepts of culture.

This effort to resolve conceptual problems must not have been especially convincing: it disappeared from the committee's discussions almost immediately. In the first general session of the WHC, the operational guidelines were discussed extensively, and many concerns with the criteria for outstanding universal value were raised. Speakers challenged the subjective, Western philosophy of value, as well as the validity of the nature/culture division and the definition of authenticity. These discussions about the limits to universalism persisted for several years. Small revisions to the language of the operational guidelines were proposed, but concrete measures to redefine or eliminate the pseudo-universalism of the convention's language never materialized.

Instead, the question of universalism mutated into what became known as the "balance problem." *Balance* refers in the World Heritage Committee's sessions to the rapidly evident concentration of sites in western Europe, as well as the recurring presence of the same nations on the WHC, as membership increased. By the 1980s, working groups had been formed to find mechanisms to redress "balance." Rather than outline all the legislative details of the committee, I simply wish to point out that the problem of European universalist philosophies being installed as the basis of a supposedly global cultural institution was not so much resolved in this early phase as it was displaced to an administrative issue. By introducing rules requiring the rotation of membership and encouraging the nomination of greater numbers of non-European sites, the WHC recognized the issue without undermining its overall project.

That kind of displacement was not, however, used for all recurring conflicts within the WHC. The problem of the arbitrariness of the nature/culture division, for instance, led eventually to the invention of new mediating categories: "cultural landscapes" that express an ongoing, distinctive human engagement with geography, and "mixed sites" that are significant for both natural and cultural features. Some intractable philosophical problems produced changes to the WHC's basic terms, while other problems moved the committee to reflect on its own processes, rather than its categories. Some issues became moments of institutional self-consciousness. This double response to problem solving in the first period of debate shows the entanglement of the organization's own evolving culture with its conception of the cultural heritage it is assigned to protect. Since the outset, the two have been entwined, and the adoption of new techniques at both levels propelled the committee into its next phase.

The 1980s

In its second major phase, during the 1980s, the WHC survived a certain amount of crisis over its form and content. In 1981, it had 61 state members, but membership had nearly doubled by 1989, reaching 111 (two-thirds of the states who were members of UNESCO). The number and variety of sites the committee was involved in considering and monitoring grew enormously over this period — with roughly twenty-five to thirty sites nominated (and usually accepted) annually. This vast increase in the scale of the WHC's operations, as well as the political and fiscal crisis following the US withdrawal from UNESCO, led to inevitable disputes over the meaning and process of the committee's work.

The organization's major philosophical issue of the decade emerged during the December 1983 session, when questions relating to historic cities were raised. How do historic cities reflect events, ideas, or beliefs, members asked, and what criteria for authenticity apply to a site that is in use and being actively adapted and updated by its current residents? Clearly, a historic city need not be a ghost town to be of outstanding universal value, but what sorts of changes can and should be understood as endangering that value — even to the point of disqualifying the site from World Heritage status? These questions were raised with particular reference to urban vernacular architecture where reconstruction was in process (WHC 1983, 11). The following year, a special report on historic towns reiterated the need for evident architectural interest in each site and the importance of distinguishing between the national and international value of towns (WHC 1984, 3-6), but these reiterations of core principles did not resolve the issue. In fact, these discussions spread to questions about the evolution of "integrity" in rural landscapes and other mixed nature/ culture properties. Both discussions opposed the static conception of value contained in a finished masterpiece and took into account the use-value a particular site might have within an active culture. The challenges raised by the latter more commons-oriented approach were fundamental during this period.

One proposed solution to this dilemma was the designation of a buffer zone around certain sites, protecting them from excessive change. Later this pragmatic strategy would transform into a direct statement of the principle that development and tourism were major threats to heritage. In the 1980s, however, this language was not yet in use, and the issue was displaced by means of an administrative solution. Frequent "monitoring" of listed sites became a major component of the WHC's activities because it involved assessments of changing "value." Gathering, coordinating, and communicating significant information on listed sites became a vital precondition for action on endangered sites, and discussions pertaining to the difficulty of accomplishing systematic monitoring during a fiscal crisis initially substituted for resolution of the philosophical question about what constituted value.

The organization's fiscal crisis during the 1980s clearly related to the US withdrawal, but it was not exclusively the effect of one state's actions. After all, the United States remained a participant and observer at the WHC during the decade and made major financial contributions to its fund even from 1984 to 1986, the height of the crisis. During its ninth session, in 1985, the WHC wrote a special letter to the United States, thanking it for funds, assuring its continued candidacy for the committee, and asking for information on any future contributions. In 1986, the US observer formally expressed interest in and support for WHC activities, in addition to underlining certain legal issues of special concern (WHC 1986, 19). In my assessment, the US withdrawal from UNESCO is important not so much for practical reasons but because it represents a key pragmatic problem for the World Heritage Committee during this period: how to respond productively to international conflicts. The role of international governmental organizations vis-à-vis states, an unresolved issue identified at the first session of the WHC by the director-general of UNESCO, returned insistently during the 1980s. WHC members asked how the committee should respond to explosive international issues, such as which state has the responsibility for protecting Jerusalem's Old City and walls. They inquired how rapid consideration of sites in Lebanon might influence the military actions there in 1983-4. And, somewhat less contentiously, they discussed how the committee could support international programs for cultural preservation (such as an Andean road linking several South American nations or a US-proposed international project on Spanish missions). Throughout the 1980s, the WHC addressed its current and future role in the facilitation of international cooperation.

International cooperation not only involved political crises as the WHC investigated its institutional autonomy; it also raised practical problems to do with coordinating the nomination paperwork. For this reason, the new programs led to a major rethinking of the scale and ambition of the convention. In 1988, at the 12th session in Brasilia, members of the WHC agreed that a global study of world heritage was necessary. After extensive discussion, they chose the following goals for the study: the identification of sites in need of preservation, regardless of state adherence to the convention; regional and national "balance" issues; and thematic issues — mainly related to the town/village matters described above. Funds were then budgeted for the ongoing global study, a key tool by which the WHC subsequently defined itself not only as an agglomeration of specific state interests but also as a semi-autonomous international organization with responsibility for preserving cultural and natural heritage regardless of national politics.

This increase in autonomy with respect to states was accompanied by an expansion of the role of NGOs in the WHC. Although several NGOs had been involved since the organization's inception (namely, the International Centre for the Study and Preservation and Restoration of Cultural Property [ICOMOS] and the International Union for Conservation of Nature and Natural Resources [IUCN]), their number increased during the 1980s. At some annual meetings, the number of NGO observers was equal to the number of member states attending, and environmental NGOs in particular gave influential advice. Some leaders of the WHC moved on to work at major NGOs; for example, Russell Train, a founder of the WHC, later became head of the World Wildlife Fund (WWF). As an established international governmental organization, by the late 1980s, the WHC was part of an international network of interlinked non-state organizations.

The autonomy of this non-state network began to take concrete form in 1989, when the WHC decided to withhold assistance from states that had failed to contribute financially to its fund. In 1990 it also began to issue more directive instructions to states during its annual monitoring of existing sites and evaluation of nominations. The WHC cautioned states against exploitation and destruction of sites and began to define a more assertive role for itself at its twentieth anniversary session in 1992. In the same period, members more frequently reiterated the organization's commitment to prioritizing assistance and training for the least developed countries and regularly considered designating special funds and creating other mechanisms to increase organizational participation from less-developed nations. In these activities, the WHC revealed that it understood its purpose as actively changing relations within and among nation-states.

In short, the World Heritage Committee weathered the crisis period of the 1980s by once again displacing a philosophical dilemma with an administrative mechanism and addressing the philosophical quandary at the heart of a pragmatic problem. During this decade, the organization evolved into a much larger, more comprehensive, and more active international institution. Its conception of cultural heritage in particular became less narrowly attached to a European monumental tradition as it added new categories of heritage and — even though membership was less complete among Asian and eastern European nations — the number of participants grew substantially. By the end of the decade, the organization could credibly claim to represent a global constituency.

The 1990s

In the 1990s, during the WHC's third phase, greater international visibility and ambition brought new quandaries to the organization, but during this period the committee began to develop not only the administrative apparatus of a genuinely global organization but also a vocabulary that gave self-affirming content to that apparatus. During the 1990s, the committee achieved a synthesis around the concept of the commons.

Throughout the 1990s, spokespeople for the committee developed this new theme. Beginning at the 1990 session in Banff, Alberta, committee sessions frequently opened with statements identifying the major threats to world heritage, such as "tourism, urban growth and the degradation of the environment" (WHC 1990, 2). During the 1990s, economic development was frequently mentioned as the enemy of heritage. WHC rhetoric identified social problems — especially those caused by poverty and neoliberal policy — as factors inhibiting its preservation efforts. By 1999, Koïchiro Matsuura, director-general of UNESCO, could address the committee and in the course of his opening remarks, a genre not known for the presentation of highly controversial views, charge that preservation is "a major challenge in the face of economic globalization" (WHC 1999, 2). Matsuura's speech echoed statements made by Russell Train (of the WWF) in 1992, Federico Mayor (director-general of UNESCO) in 1996, and Adnan Badran (deputy director-general of UNESCO) in 1997. Along the same lines, in 1995, the delegate from France drew attention to the danger of the committee's actions contributing to "two-speed" progress, with rich and poor countries accelerating at fundamentally different rates (WHC 1995, 65). This self-consciousness about uneven development, globalization, and the committee's role within it became a recurring theme in the WHC's logic during the 1990s, as it endeavoured to protect the global commons.

As the committee became more explicitly critical of economic development, it also more frequently addressed geopolitical threats to world heritage. It made repeated efforts to safeguard the listed sites endangered by war in the former Yugoslavia — repeatedly cautioning relevant parties and providing significant funding and personnel for the reconstruction of the Old City of Dubrovnik. It also explored sending a mission to Iraq in 1991 (WHC 1991, 8). Members discussed monuments threatened by war in Afghanistan and Bosnia Herzegovina in 1995 and began to explore ways they could protect properties located outside national boundaries — for example, in Antarctica. Even before the high-profile efforts at intervention in the Bamiyan case, the WHC was proactive in international conflicts, in part because it relied on an increasingly coherent philosophy of preservation as a defence of the commons.

The committee had developed criteria for mixed-use properties and cultural landscapes by the mid-1990s. It was working on identifying and protecting new sorts of sites, such as canals, routes, rice terraces, and modern sites of technological interest. It defused some potentially divisive national conflicts by using regional reporting and monitoring strategies. Many of the potentially crippling philosophical dilemmas of earlier years appeared to have been resolved in effect, if not in principle, as the committee expanded its mandate and took on a more active international role.

This more active — even activist — identity was not uncontested. Alternative languages, more compatible with economic globalization and cultural nationalism, surfaced regularly in WHC discussions during the decade. Chronic budget shortfalls routinely led to the discussion of joint projects with private foundations and international economic institutions that were strong proponents of capitalist globalization — the World Bank, in particular. These initiatives culminated in the launch in 2002 of World Heritage PACT, a branch project specifically directed at attracting funding from the private sector to promote sustainable tourism and similar projects. The contributions made by these organizations may in some cases have affected the kinds of projects adopted — for example, in a project devoted to the protection of Nordic culture — as well as the structure of some ongoing projects. Reports frequently refer, for instance, to the need to use experts located in the regions in question, thereby trimming expenses, rather than funding travel for specialists from abroad. Despite the ambitious nature of these new initiatives and the continuing budget problems, though, one finds far fewer references in the reports of the 1990s meetings to asking state parties to follow through on their promised contributions.

The critique of economic globalization seems to have gone hand in hand with acceptance of a certain amount of privatization and the diminishing economic role of nation-states.

Perhaps this reluctance to foreground the responsibilities of states relates to discussions of sovereignty that apparently occupied the General Assembly of the UN during the mid-1990s. Although the vocabulary of sovereignty did not frequently characterize the committee's discussions, it did appear when the WHC began to develop more rigorous standards for monitoring state parties' continuing protection of their heritage. As the WHC asserted its institutional autonomy around the world, the question of whether it was eroding states' autonomy intensified.

Ironically, though, sovereignty, at least in the context of the WHC sessions, was mainly the concern of rich and powerful states, and in this respect it is interesting to note how the terms reversed themselves relative to the 1970s. During the 1970s, the European/North American alliance of wealthy nations claimed universality, and local or regional difference was the concern of less-developed and less-powerful nations. By the late 1990s, however, the vocabulary of the commons was claimed by the poorer and less-powerful nations, while the rich nations sought to assert their exceptional character. In neither moment was nation-state autonomy (and by extension, sovereignty) understood as an absolute good claimed by all. Rather, in these debates over culture, autonomy has been the ideological inverse of the commons; the two concepts enter the discussion together and acquire meaning relative to one another. In my view, it is in this relativistic sense that we should assess some of the claims made on behalf of both autonomy and universalism. Reading the rhetoric of international institutions as multi-layered and evolving debates, rather than as statements of eternal verities, can reveal stakes other than those that might be most immediately apparent.

From this perspective, at least, we can understand why a third sort of challenge to the international administrative logic of the WHC arose at the tail end of the twentieth century. Appearing at roughly the same time, although not quite in the same spirit as the move towards sovereignty and the private sector, representatives of indigenous peoples' groups launched a critique of the committee's version of expertise. During the 2000 session, which took place on land held by traditional owners at Cairns, Australia, a lengthy plea was made for the protection of indigenous peoples' knowledge in and about world heritage areas, and a council of experts in traditional knowledge began to form. The following year, this discussion continued.

Definitions of "indigenous" were debated, and a working group on traditional expertise was established.

While clearly responding to the evident power of ever-expanding bureaucratic systems such as the WHC's nomination and monitoring systems, this kind of critique of the interested character of "expertise" can also be understood as a claim that the project of protecting the commons should or could be taken considerably further. While privatizers contain symbols of the commons within the domain of private property, and defenders of sovereignty treat the commons as an entity that ends at the borders of the nation-state, the proponents of indigenous peoples' expertise urge the recognition and integration of a more holistic version of the cultural commons — one in which people, history, and territory are fused together to produce a management system unified with the site. This approach in effect asks for a more intense and thorough-going synthesis of culture as an object with institutional culture. This theme challenged the WHC to evolve even further and modify its own internal division between cultural content and the experts who manage it. Even though indigenous expertise has not to date become a major component of the committee's operations, this initiative nonetheless reflects an important moment of institutional self-consciousness within the WHC as it has continued to develop means for accomplishing its newly defined mission: the preservation of the global commons.

Conclusion

In the first years of the twenty-first century, the World Heritage Committee has continued to test its muscle as an international institution. Its version of the managed preservation of culture achieved some prominence with the Bamiyan Buddha issue, and, in responding to the crisis of the destruction of the statues, the WHC suggested some future avenues of development. For instance, at the June 2001 meeting of the World Heritage Bureau (a subset of the committee), discussion linked WHC actions to other international treaties devoted to cultural property, as well as considering the legal force of the Taliban's signature on a declaration of protection. Several discussants noted that unrecognized governments, such as the Taliban, revealed the limits of internationalism for the protection of world heritage and international governance generally. Not being a state party in the eyes of the UN, the Taliban not only was ineligible to sign, but also was not bound by treaties like the World Heritage Convention. It was not appropriately subject to the UN's various sanctions and legal tools, such as prosecution in the International Criminal Court, once that organization's authority on cultural property questions became legitimate. For this reason, discussants underlined the need for other tools — such as the intensification of "cultural rights" or the introduction of a category defining a "crime against culture" (UNESCO 2001, 2-5). The concept of a global cultural commons and mechanisms for its enforcement both require further enhancement, the bureau concluded.

In this spirit, the WHC has stressed the role of international governmental organizations in recording and preserving traces of world heritage. Photos of the empty niches left by the Bamiyan statues have regularly appeared in highly visible locations in the organization's publications — such as the cover story on the Silk Road that appeared in the organization's glossy publicity magazine, *World Heritage* (March 2005). Rather than exacerbating interstate antagonisms, though, the World Heritage Committee's tactic has been to foreground its own administrative cosmopolitanism, through projects such as the internationally supported Silk Road collaboration (designed to record the long international route and sites along it on the World Heritage List). In the twenty-first century, the committee clearly identifies a central role for itself in defending world heritage. This role extends beyond negotiating with and between sovereign nation-states, although it is not entirely clear at present how aggressively such a cosmopolitan vision can or will be implemented.

Other issues facing the committee in its fourth decade remain to be defined. Clearly, initiatives to redress "balance" on the World Heritage List will continue, with a special and continuing focus on designating and protecting sites in Africa. Sites endangered by natural disasters such as the 2004 earthquakes and tsunami have inspired major international assistance efforts, while ongoing publicity celebrates successful initiatives, such as the rebuilding of Dubrovnik, as well as new international projects in Nordic regions and sensitive areas such as Israel and the Palestinian territories.

If current trends continue, the WHC will continue to navigate such international questions and perhaps add new areas as well. Internal discussion of the relationship between poverty and heritage has been lively, and UNESCO leaders are concerned that accelerating urbanization and new communications technologies might produce "cultural desertification" and diminish literacy and linguistic diversity (Mayor 2001, 304). Some small new projects recognize the industrial character of global culture. For instance, meetings have taken place with affiliated organization, the International Centre for the Preservation and Restoration of Cultural Property (ICCROM) and the publishers of influential guidebooks, such as Lonely Planet and the Green Guide, to ensure that future volumes will include information on cultural and natural preservation alongside tourist data. Given the turn towards the private sector and partnerships with NGOs and other non-state parties, such projects seem likely to continue.

Whatever the content of the WHC's future projects, it seems certain that the institution's emblem and concepts will continue to circulate and be visible. With the number of world heritage sites reaching 788 in 2005 and encompassing a wide variety of parks, monuments, landscapes, cities, technologies, ruins, fossils, and so on, the World Heritage List includes sites of value to a major portion of the world's people, and its designation is approaching the status of a global brand. This in fact has been a goal of the organization and is a crucial feature of its strategy. The WHC has created a bureaucracy with a global reach to identify and manage world heritage. It has successfully invented an administrative complement to globally mobile capital and the mass migrations and movement of refugees that have constituted a major part of the mobility of labour in this most recent phase of globalization. Like other UN organizations, the WHC extends Weberian rationalization to a global scale — attempting to minimize the effects of war, disaster, unplanned development, and other disruptive forces with representative, proactive, and supra-state administration.

In the end, then, we can understand the WHC's approach to world heritage as a globalized version of the middlebrow ideal epitomized in the United States by the Book-of-the-Month Club (Radway 1997). It promises a moderate, time-saving, practical form of edification, along with the canonization and thus preservation of cultural (and natural) works not necessarily widely known to its audience. Using the authority and power of the annually expanding list, the World Heritage Committee produces through its own quite substantial, even heroic, efforts, a world culture in aggregate, as well as techniques for finding, knowing, and participating in that culture's vitality. Whatever disputes the World Heritage Committee has weathered and will no doubt continue to experience over universalism, the autonomy of national and/or subnational actors, or the nature of the commons, the World Heritage Committee has accomplished this: it has made itself a living archive of a global culture.

Fantasies at the International Whaling Commission: Management, Sustainability, Conservation

Petra Rethmann

FROM THE PERSPECTIVE OF many environmentalists, government representatives, and policy makers, the International Whaling Commission (IWC) has emerged as the epicentre of friction and discord in environmental discourse. Widely reviled for being a "whalers' club," the IWC has long had to fend off a reputation for cronyism and extreme dysfunction. It has even been called a "disaster" by the 1989-93 IWC Commissioner for the United States, John Knauss (2001, viii). Its agendas and rhetoric are often seen as incongruent. On the one hand, environmentalist and animal-rights rhetoric is widely used and accepted within the framework of the IWC, but, on the other hand, considerable disagreement remains on what this rhetoric should produce for humans and animals. As in the story told by Irr about the World Heritage Committee in the preceding chapter, the struggle is on to bend rhetoric for particular — and in this case often contradictory — purposes: "wise use" or conservation, national heritage or animals' autonomy, democratic internationalism or national sovereignty.

This chapter describes the divergent views that exist within the context of the IWC and which make the global management of whales simultaneously a possible and impossible project. In doing so, it offers an analysis of a larger global problem: the protection of nature and the environment. The chapter also examines the contours of the debates around whaling in an attempt to show how nature, specifically in the form of whales, is imagined, described, and remade within one organization where approaches to global governance and the autonomy of people and nature diverge.

Background

I first became interested in looking at the politics of whaling in the summer of 2000 in Anadyr', the capital of the Chukotka region (Chukotkskii Natsionalniy Okrug), when an election candidate freely distributed the meat of a landed bowhead whale in an attempt to win the Native vote. His candidacy failed, but his campaigning technique certainly spoke to the central place of whales on the northeastern Chukotka coast.

I have been doing research in the Kamchatka and Chukotka Peninsulas in the Russian Far East since 1992. This chapter is inspired by insights from this research and is informed by ethnographic fieldwork and archival research in the offices of the International Whaling Commission and at the commission's annual meetings (which I have attended since 2003). Whales, as cetologists and many environmental and animal-rights activists like to point out, are animals of distinction. Not only do they — together with elephants, polar bears, tigers, and certain other species — belong to that charged category of the "charismatic animal" (Freeman and Kreuter 1994, 1), they are also icons of what historian Martin Rudwick (1992) calls "deep time," an unimaginably distant past measured in hundreds of millions of years. For most environmentalists, the question is whether whales, together with other threatened species, will be part of an equally deep future. Struggles proliferate around resource management, use, and conservation. While, for many individuals and nations at the beginning of the twenty-first century, whaling is both literally and metaphorically an unsustainable business, indigenous groups and self-consciously pro-whaling nations such as Norway, Iceland, and Japan continue to argue for the consumptive use of whales. Debates rage between the two antagonistic poles of protection and destruction, and cetaceans themselves have been turned into one of the most powerful tropes of the environmental protection movement (Kalland 1993, 1994; Peterson 1992).

Global demands for biodiversity and species conservation wrestle with particular claims for community history and survival, in which local communities are not only sustained but constituted through whale hunting and harvesting practices (Freeman, Bogoslovskaya, and Caulfield 1998; Brower 2004; Jolles 2002). In this sense, whales are seen as productive of community, although a great deal of scientific and environmental scholarship portrays animals, including whales, as wild, natural beings outside the realm of society. Thus, incompatible suppositions and cultural generalizations shape the debate.

Instead of probing the pros and cons of reasoned argument that, in the case of the IWC, have led to both political and intellectual dead ends (Andresen 1989, 2001), I am interested in tracing the formations as well as effects of arguments that transpire in the context of the IWC. My subject is not the investigation of institutional governmentality or whaling regimes, but the images, narratives, assumptions, frameworks, and conventions of knowing, protecting, or managing that make debates at the IWC so contentious. My focus on "fantasy" — constructions or imaginations of reality — comes at a time when many scholars have become critical of different lobby groups and the IWC and their inability to solve the "whaling problem" (Friedheim 2001; Andresen 2001; DeSombre 2001).

The fantasies I probe here — "management," "sustainability," and "conservation" — are commonplace in the literature on whales and whaling. They are evoked in almost every article I read, but my attention to their construction and imagined effects adds a slightly different emphasis to them. As "fantasies," they are not based on neutral, objective descriptions, but require particular political commitments and imaginations to bring them to life. Yet, for all that I describe them as fantasies, they are no less real in their consequences. Their effects articulate and reproduce themselves in management policies, research programs, and advocacy agendas.

The chapter is divided into three sections, each of which explores one of the three fantasies as a site of political and cultural imagination. I begin by chronicling the institutional history of the IWC, including the values, attitudes, and perceptions that generate the conflicts that so frequently transpire. At the heart of the IWC lies the issue of management, but closely connected are issues of sustainability and conservation. Although ideas about management, sustainability, and conservation inform all aspects of IWC discussions, they come together perhaps most powerfully in relation to indigenous peoples. The section on sustainability looks, in particular, at issues of Aboriginal whaling: it is here that some of the discussions assume their most charged tone. The third section highlights, from a historical perspective, some of the assumptions embedded in the use of the term *conservation*. Conservation is perhaps the most global and unspecified dream at the IWC. Like sustainability, which often doubles as its cousin, conservation is seen as a global issue. But unlike sustainability, the term is more closely associated with the counterculture movement that began to flourish in the mid-1960s, drawing attention to the environmentally fragile state of the globe. This was a time when radical politics translated into environmental critiques; its goal was to raise awareness. In this section, I discuss some of the ideas and actions of Greenpeace, and how they helped to raise aware-ness in conservation biology and science.

At this point, a word on research methodology and writing is in order. Since the strong anti-whaling campaigns during the 1980s at IWC meet-ings, the commission has adopted a policy of extreme secrecy, and its meetings are closed to the public. Formally, the IWC consists of three main committees: scientific, technical, and finance and administration. Standing subcommittees deal with issues related to Aboriginal subsistence whal-ing and to infractions; other ad hoc committees are formed to deal with a wide range of issues as these arise. Scholars cannot attend IWC meet-ings as independent researchers (the only exception are cetologists who are invited by the IWC's office in Cambridge, England, to serve on the Scientific Committee). They can attend the meetings only as part of a national delegation or representatives of non-governmental organizations (NGOs) that hold accredited status with the IWC. One indigenous-rights NGO with which I enjoy long-standing contacts was generous enough to allow me to attend IWC meetings under its auspices. Given the deeply an-tagonistic nature of IWC debates and an official affiliation that was highly visible because of the badge that I, like everybody else, had to wear, it was challenging for me to communicate with representatives of anti-whaling and environmental NGOs and nations at IWC meetings. Yet, in the end, my ability to think about the politics of whaling was aided in large part by individuals on both sides of the divide who were spirited and generous enough to share insights and information with me.

Within international conversations about biodiversity, resource manage-ment, and sustainability, the IWC is notorious for the incommensurability of perspectives expressed within the organization. Governments, scientists, and policy advisers within the IWC are often deeply at odds with each other, rejecting each other's agendas as being outside what each imagines to be good politics. Stories of bribery, political scandal, cultural conflicts, and corruption regularly feature in descriptions of the IWC — in both the academic literature and on the Web. Even among those who imagine discourse in the dispassionate language of "policy" and "reason," there is a great sense of despair and anguish about the future of the whaling industry, the oceans, and whales. I have found it challenging to write about the different perspectives and struggles without being too much caught up in the stark dichotomies that govern the debate. One way to approach this challenge was not to efface the sentiments and conditions that generate analyses marked by a sense of political hopelessness and despair. A second way was to make visible the paradoxes, frictions, and contradictions of the debate and not to hide them in cool analysis. A third way was to use an ethnographic writing style to make the contours of the debate as vivid as possible.

First Fantasy: Management

Whales have been the subject and focus of cultural, political, and economic regimes of management for a long time. Historically, archaeological records tell us that whale species have been hunted at a subsistence level for the last five or six millennia (Slijper 1962). Scholars of whaling and whale use record that commercial whaling, most frequently associated with the invention of the explosive grenade harpoon by Svend Foyn in 1864, started, in fact, as early as the ninth century in the North Sea and the English Channel, and the twelfth century in the Bay of Biscay (Ellis 1991). Whale oil was used for lighting and heating, soap, and paint manufacturing, while baleen provided pliable stiffening for articles such as umbrella ribs, corset stays, and carriage springs. Given the demand for such products, by the first decade of the 1900s many whale stocks were close to depletion (Mackintosh 1965). Until late in the nineteenth century, hunters targeted the relatively slow-swimming species that usually float when dead (e.g., blue whales, bowhead whales). Later, the use of harpoons and factory ships with stern slipways made it possible to haul species that do not float easily (e.g., minke whales) for immediate processing on deck. Parallel with European whaling were Japanese coastal fisheries, possibly dating from before the tenth century for right whales and the sixteenth century for grey whales, which used specific netting techniques and hand-held harpoons. National economies were shaped by whaling. Species diversity that had evolved over millions of years was erased within centuries. Yet, in the last decades of the twentieth century, things began to change as many people came to value whales more as a natural than as an economic asset.

Established by the International Convention for the Regulation of Whaling (ICRW) that was signed in Washington on 2 December 1946 by Argentina, Australia, Brazil, Chile, Denmark, France, the Netherlands, New Zealand, Norway, Peru, the Soviet Union, South Africa, the United Kingdom, and the United States, the International Whaling Commission met for the first time in 1948 to negotiate a manageable whaling regime.[1] By that time, the oceans were all but depleted. In the peak year of 1937-8, thirty-five shore stations and thirty-five floating factory boats with hundreds of catcher vessels took 54,902 whales worldwide (with 46,039 whales, or 84 percent of the total, taken in the Antarctic). Management became a necessity. Today, the IWC has become a full-blown international organization, with fifty-six countries participating in the 2003 meetings.[2]

The right to whaling has emerged as a particularly hot issue at the IWC. Vocal government representatives from Australia, Mexico, Germany, and New Zealand, for example, imagine whales as a resource in need of protection, while indigenous representatives from Chukotka or Alaska argue that whales are for them not only an economic resource but also strongly associated with spirituality, community making, and tradition. Cetologists and conservation biologists also raise important questions about the autonomy of nature in general and whales in particular. Whale researchers such as Robert Payne, Linda Weilgart, and Hal Whitehead have begun to record the singing of whales and to study their social and family relations (Payne 1995). In addition to describing the structure, dynamics, communication systems, and organization of "cetacean societies" (Mann et al. 2000), scientists have added a new dimension to understandings of autonomy and discussions of "rights." They argue that the real issue is not so much the study of whale behaviour and the protection of their habitat, but how the autonomy of whales (in the sense of their independence from humans and their capacity to create society and culture) can be supported and maintained. Yet disparate as they may be, in all of these discussions and conversations *management* emerges as the central tool and trope by which to envision a future for both humans and whales.

As if to defy the presumed clarity of the term, management moves in many directions. The ICRW recognizes "the interests of the nations of the world in safeguarding for future generations the ... whale stocks," but it is also designed to "make possible the orderly development of the whaling industry" (ICRW, 1946). Management, then, is more indefinite, uncertain, and unclear than it at first appears. Pro-whaling lobbies such as the High North Alliance, the Institute of Cetacean Research, and the World Council of Whalers argue that whaling is of particular economic and cultural value, while anti-whaling lobbies look at whaling as a particularly harmful form of resource extraction. Perspectives fragment as groups find themselves aligned with other groups that may have differing interests and methods. Should the IWC adhere to its original interest and charter, as nations such as Japan and Caribbean countries like Dominica argue, or should it take the changing world into consideration? Australian, New Zealand, and western European representatives habitually accuse Japan of exploitation and economic greed.

The Japanese angrily reply with charges of cultural imperialism and insensitivity; apart from economic gain, they argue, cultural values are at stake. Thus, instead of creating openings and possibilities, the rhetoric of management leads to administrative and political deadlocks. Economy and ecology form the disparate positions at the heart of the ICRW, and their imagined incommensurability creates what anthropologist Arjun Appadurai — in a different context — has called "tournaments of value" (Appadurai 1986). How can the "good management" that everybody so desires grow within the context of such incommensurable values? Instead of providing "good measures" for management, the ICRW pits economy and ecology against each other, as if these agendas were mutually exclusive. Instead of political openings and dialogue, bitterness and enmity grow.

Issues around whaling came to a head in the 1970s. Notwithstanding thirty years of whaling regulation, by then the losses in whale species were dramatic, ranging from almost total loss of some species to the endangerment of others. One could unequivocally say that the function of the IWC had been badly compromised, cetacean biodiversity drastically reduced, and the sustainability of whale stock across the world turned into a major problem. As everybody now agrees, until the beginning of the 1970s IWC politics had been based on economic maximization. The most pervasive trope for imagining whales as resources and not as animals was the blue whale unit (BWU). The BWU was conceived as a means of assessing the economic value of whales in terms of average oil yields — that is, one blue whale was equivalent to two fin whales, two and one-half humpback whales, or six sei whales. At its twenty-fourth meeting in 1972, the IWC called for the end of the BWU as a means of regulating whale catches and attempted to find biologically relevant quotas related to species and stocks. Most countries had stopped their whaling operations in the 1960s, but Iceland, Norway, the Soviet Union, and Japan continued whaling. At the beginning of the 1990s, whale stocks, especially baleen whale stocks, had been heavily affected by illegal whaling. For example, in the 1950s and 1960s, the Soviet Union (and most likely other countries too) had falsified catch statistics for its whaling operations in the southern hemisphere (Yablokov 1994; Zemsky et al. 1995). Although the four Soviet factory ships in operation at that time recorded a catch of 152 humpbacks, in fact 7,207 had been taken.

Environmentalism entered the IWC through social movements of the global North. Stirred up by industries' destructive effects on natural and social systems, and by their misguided policies based on misleading slogans of growth, progress, development, and nation building, environmental activism flourished. Between 1960 and 1965, more than 63,000 whales were killed each year, a catch that was justified by inherent economic insecurities in whaling countries. In this context, global options for environmental protest and conservation widened. In 1982 the IWC voted for a global moratorium on commercial whaling to take effect in 1986. Former whaling nations such as New Zealand, Australia, Germany, and the United States shifted the balance within the organization towards environmental awareness. They no longer viewed whales as part of their economic livelihood and came to realize that this once relatively stable natural resource was not only dwindling, precarious, and fragile, but also unique. In this assessment, environmental awareness was supported by science as cetologists in the North developed a language that emphasized the sociality, cultural behaviour, and communicative abilities of whales.

The environmental movement within and outside the institutional borders of the IWC celebrated the moratorium as a victory, but at the same time, as new visions for whales developed, frictions grew. Not everybody was prepared to move from a language of resource management to one of protection and conservation. Norway objected to the moratorium and continued commercial whaling while Japan issued scientific permits to allow the hunting of whales forbidden in commercial operations. Aboriginal peoples charged that resource use was imagined from the perspective of national elites, not local residents. In a parallel point of view, Caribbean countries especially argued that the IWC's newborn environmentalism took a limited form, favouring Northern conservation priorities — "saving tigers," "rescuing elephants," and "protecting biodiversity." Together, whaling and anti-whaling groups argued that the interests of the communities they represented and cared for were sidelined. The environmental dream seemed to place nature and community — or environmental integrity and social justice — in conflict.

Although the overwhelming majority of IWC member states continue to insist on a ban of all commercial (and scientific) whaling, discussions of "management" are still dominated by mathematical assessments of the size of whale populations and "catch limits." On the advice of the Scientific Committee, the IWC responded to the 1972 Stockholm Conference on the Human Environment, sponsored by the United Nations, by embarking on a period of intensified research known as the International Decade of Cetacean Research. Subsequently, the Scientific Committee adopted a new management procedure (NMP), designed to set catch limits at levels no greater than individual stocks could sustain. In the eyes of the IWC, the procedure looked attractive because it seemed to offer a just and fair process for setting appropriate catch limits — in principle. But in practice, great difficulties arose. Precisely because whales are difficult to see and to follow, they are also difficult to count and to study. They spend most of their lives below the ocean's surface, emerge sporadically and for a short time, and range widely. There are no tracks, scats, or nests so that one can easily locate them. All of this makes the management of whales, including the analysis of population and other statistics, challenging.

When, in 1982, the IWC agreed on a global moratorium on commercial whaling, it also agreed that by 1990, at the latest, it would have undertaken a comprehensive assessment of the world's whale stocks. For various reasons, the comprehensive assessment was never completed (although there are now detailed assessments for grey whales in the North Pacific; bowhead whales off Alaska; minke whales in the southern hemisphere, North Atlantic, and western North Pacific; and fin whales in the North Atlantic), and the NMP was supplemented with a revised management procedure (RMP). The stated goal of the RMP is to achieve an acceptable balance between conservation and the exploitation of baleen whales. It provides a highly mathematical model for calculating acceptable catch limits by taking known catch histories, current population estimates, stock size, and production models into consideration. Yet the mathematical and scientific elements of the RMP have been thrown into question by the revised management scheme (RMS) on which anti-whaling countries, perhaps foremost the United Kingdom and the United States, insisted. Issues such as unauthorized ("pirate") whaling, "inhumane killing," illicit trade in whale products, underreporting of catch data, and the effects of environmental degradation are seen by IWC anti-whaling member states as major concerns in discussions about the relaxation of the current moratorium that the RMP would replace.

At the IWC's 2003 meetings in Berlin, Germany's environmental minister Renate Künast introduced the Berlin Initiative on Strengthening the Conservation Agenda of the International Whaling Commission. The initiative focuses on conversation, not management. It places "special emphasis on ... benefits to conservation," and recommends the establishment of a Conservation Committee "to explore how the Commission can coordinate its conservation agenda through greater collaboration with a wider range of organizations and conventions, including *inter alia* CMS, CCALMR, IMO, IUCN, and UNEP."[3] "Nature," said Künast in her opening speech, "is not something that needs to be overcome but a source of preservation." She pointed out that Germany, as a former whaling nation, was keenly aware of the need for whale protection and strongly committed to whale conservation. But declarations such as Künast's raise a number of questions. Just how is nature preserved? Who speaks for nature? And on whose behalf? While heated, discrepant voices issue ostensibly calm proclamations, they also squabble about social justice issues, cultural rights, new forms of eco-imperialism, North-South inequalities, and dreams of harmony for humans and nature. What counts as the "environment" in IWC research initiatives and negotiation is a matter of perspective and is at the heart of the unproductive deadlock that discussions within the context of the IWC have reached. There is no triumph of political globalization here. Rather we find a swirl of acrimonious debate and searing criticisms between nations and pro- and anti-whaling activists as political partialities are forged in dissension, fragmentation, and regional specificity.

Second Fantasy: Sustainability

In the 1970s and in the most intense years of the anti-whaling campaigns in the 1980s, an interesting thing happened in environmental thinking: it "discovered" the "tribe." Environmentalists came to evoke indigenous groups, whom they defined by their cultural differences and nature-based thinking, in discussions of sustainability and care. No matter that the focus on nature ignored other issues of concern to indigenous peoples, such as colonialism, nationalism, state rule, and urbanization. Environmental movements seized on the idea that indigenous peoples were closer to and always in tune with nature. What anthropologists sometimes questioned as romanticization or exoticization, others viewed as embracing the wisdom of an ancient world. Chroniclers (Brown and May 1991; Weyler 2004) describe how the nascent environmental organization that would become known as Greenpeace, for example, drew on a small booklet entitled "Strange and Prophetic Dreams of Indian Peoples." The book *Warriors of the Rainbow* (Willoya and Brown 1963) contains an ancient prophesy told to a young boy by an older woman, Eyes of Fire, which says that when the earth is ravaged, the sea blackened, the streams poisoned, and the deer dead, people will again gain reverence for the earth and come together as Warriors of the Rainbow. The elder's words in this story echo those of similar warnings by, for example, Black Elk of the Lakota nation. In this context, it was not surprising that, in 1973, Paul Watson, a founding member of Greenpeace and the Sea Shepherd Conservation Society represented Greenpeace during the standoff between the American state and the American Indian Movement at Wounded Knee. These are connections that were made in the imagined space of mutual interests and concerns.

After the initial years of environmental and anti-whaling organizing, however, the trajectory of this alliance has almost been reversed. Aboriginal peoples who whale and attend IWC meetings maintain that they know whales not only as a source of spirituality but also as a resource. For example, at the 2004 meetings in Sorrento, Italy, hunters from Point Barrow, Alaska, pointed out that whales, especially bowhead whales, are kin but that Iñupiaq also "love to eat the whale." Such statements are frequently corroborated by documentation that anthropologists and other social scientists produce and that are part of indigenous legitimizing strategies for Aboriginal whaling (Bodenhorn 2003; Jolles 2002). To anti-whaling lobby groups, it often seems as if indigenous peoples do not quite hold up to their imagined promise as allies. Indigenous peoples at IWC meetings are not necessarily the peaceful dwellers of forests and tundras with whom environmentalists frequently claim particular affiliations. These are people who appreciate the endurance and expertness of hunters to make a good kill. Indigenous whaling, vilified on the Web as "blood-in-the-water whaling,"[4] is highly contested. Today, environmentalists and indigenous peoples often find themselves on opposite sides of the controversy. In this debate, "sustainability" has become the trope that is bent to particular, contradictory purposes. Environmental protection and social justice do not coalesce but clash in currents of political challenges and divergent agendas.

The IWC revised its long-standing policy allowing Aboriginal peoples to hunt otherwise protected grey whales. In 1979, recognizing that the commission "lacks expertise as to the needs of aboriginal peoples," the IWC held a meeting of a panel of experts on Aboriginal subsistence whaling. Following this, in 1981 an Ad Hoc Technical Committee Working Group on the Development of Management Principles and Guidelines for Subsistence Catches of Whales by Indigenous (Aboriginal) Peoples met before the IWC meeting and agreed on the definition of Aboriginal subsistence whaling as "whaling for the purpose of local aboriginal consumption carried out by or on behalf of aboriginal, indigenous, or native peoples who share strong community, familial, social, and cultural ties related to a continuing traditional dependence on whaling and on the use of whales" (IWC 1981). In this working definition, *local aboriginal consumption* means the traditional uses of whale products by local Native communities in meeting their nutritional, subsistence, and cultural requirements. The term includes trade in items that are by-products of *subsistence catches* that is, catches of whales by Aboriginal subsistence whaling operations (Donovan 1982; Gambell 1999, 187). Following the recommendations of the standing Aboriginal Subsistence Whaling Subcommittee, established in 1982, most governments, including those on the anti-whaling side, and environmental NGOs recognize the validity of this definition as well as the historical and cultural need for indigenous peoples to whale. Yet at the same time, these definitions are not uncontested. At the 2003 meetings in Berlin, when Aboriginal whaling quotas were set anew, violent debates over the precise definition of subsistence transpired. The Aboriginal director of Whale Watch Kaikoura Ltd., a whale-watching enterprise in New Zealand that is 100 percent Maori owned, spoke out against killing and in favour of whale watching as the best way towards sustainable subsistence. Community strength and sustainability, he said, may be gained from ecotourism and environmental advocacy. These, then, are the two poles around which the subsistence debate revolves: the loss of animal life and the legitimacy of indigenous needs.

Discussions at IWC meetings are not for the squeamish. Talk of primary and secondary killing methods shapes a great deal of discussion around whaling, with the Working Group on Whale Killing Methods and Associated Welfare Issues providing most of the data. In most cases, Japan, Norway, and Iceland use penthrite grenade harpoons as their primary killing method. Fired from a cannon mounted on the prow of a ship, the harpoon enters the whale's body to the depth of about a foot and then detonates, killing the whale either by trauma, laceration, or the generation of shock waves that destroy the brain. Although the majority of IWC member states consider all forms of cetacean killing, including by-catch, as objectionable, they consider this technique as the "most humane" because it results in a relatively quick death. And while all forms of killing are the subject of great controversy within the context of the IWC and beyond, indigenous forms of whaling are especially maligned on animal-welfare grounds. Part of the problem is that, in the eyes of anti-whaling governments and many environmental and animal-rights groups, Aboriginal ways of whale killing are not efficient. Methods used in Aboriginal hunts are often less accurate and quick than those used in commercial whaling operations, and they result in stress and possibly panic and fear both in the target whale and other whales nearby, lower instantaneous death rates, and higher struck and lost rates. In Chukotka, for example, whalers use darting guns with black powder grenades or harpoons. This method can be so ineffective that in 1997 ten floats were required to secure a whale, and then a metal-tipped lance and 600 to 700 bullets were needed to finish the job. In one 1999 hunt, it took over three hours and forty minutes and 180 bullets to kill a single grey whale. Aboriginal hunters who are present at IWC meetings when such charges are laid frequently verify such data but say that they do not understand why those who accuse them do not provide them with better technology so that the kill can be accomplished more efficiently.

Most of the world's Aboriginal whaling is monitored by the IWC.[5] Under current IWC regulations, Aboriginal subsistence whaling is permitted for four specific whaling operations: (1) minke and fin whales in Greenland, (2) humpback whales in the Caribbean (specifically at the island of Bequia in St. Vincent and the Grenadines), (3) bowhead whales and formerly some grey whales in the United States (Alaska), and (4) bowhead and grey whales in the Chukotka Peninsula in the Russian Federation. It is the responsibility of national governments to provide the commission with evidence of the cultural and subsistence needs of Aboriginal peoples, as well as evidence for cultural and economic "needs" in the form "needs assessments." Although most indigenous peoples present at IWC meetings tend to consider this procedure as an unlawful imposition on their communities, they also tend to comply to counter the criticisms of environmentalists and anti-whaling governments. Those who participate in national delegations speak to IWC delegates about the importance of community-based history, subsistence, and conservation. Conflicts are bound to flare up when indigenous groups who are permitted to whale, trade the quotas allotted to them with other Aboriginal groups. The issue came to a head in 1997, when the US government paired its proposal for Makah whaling with one submitted on behalf of Chukchi hunters by the Russian Federation. In 1994, the US government had removed the grey whale from the endangered species list, and the Makah of Neah Bay in the Olympic Peninsula of Washington approached the US government for an annual grey whale quota. Permission, said the government, would be granted if the IWC agreed to the Makah hunt, but, after a long and drawn-out debate, the IWC rejected the proposal. In 1997 the Russian Federation, out of their overall limit of 140 grey whales for each of the years 1998-2002, offered a quota of five grey whales to the Makah. On 17 May 1999 Makah whalers landed a grey whale. Although this has so far been the only whale taken, the deal increased frictions between environmental and indigenous groups within the context of the IWC.

An added problem is that the IWC holds no exact definition of "subsistence." Is it the hand to mouth economy of indigenous peoples, classified as "immediate consumption"? Or does it also include the cash and other benefits that are the result of economic trade and exchange? What if Aboriginal peoples trade whale meat that they also see as commodity and product? The case of Chukotka, once again, has become notorious in the IWC. Environmental and animal rights commissioners and activists at the IWC charge that, while Chukchi women and men living in the village of Lorino (approximately 100 kilometres from the Arctic Circle) are allowed "subsistence hunting" of grey whales, they also use the meat to feed the foxes they raise for fur in the village. Many of Lorino's whalers are employees of this farm as well, and their argument takes advantage of a loophole in IWC regulations that allows Native peoples to "trade in items that are by-products of subsistence whaling." At the meetings, however, Russia insists that the foxes are fed only whale by-products.

To strengthen their status and position, Aboriginal peoples create collaborations not with environmentalists but with pro-whaling NGOs and nations. Pro-whaling NGOs such as the High North Alliance or the World Council of Whalers are international coalitions of indigenous peoples, pro-whaling advocates, and nations; such NGOs insist that they build alliances and do not squash diversity. These coalitions not only converge in the argument that whales are resources and that whaling can be sustainable, but they also agree that whaling supports communities and the customary relations between "whaling people and the whale."[6] These coalitions support the small-type whaling defined by the IWC in 1976 to mean operations using powered vessels with mounted harpoon guns to kill minke, bottlenose, pilot, or killer whales (orcas). Such small-type whaling occurs almost exclusively in four coastal communities in Japan (Abashiri, Ayukawa-hama, Wadaura, and Taiji), which take minke whales within forty-eight kilometres of the shore. The whales obtained from these catches are claimed by these whaling communities and play an important role in the cultural and social cohesion of the community.

Environmentalist groups (e.g., the World Wildlife Fund) have warned indigenous communities that the pro-whaling countries that claim to support Aboriginal whaling are in fact motivated by greed and imperial interests. In addition, some professors of zoology and marine studies (Lavigne, Scheffer, and Kellert 1999, 17) question the motivation of pro-whaling countries such as Japan or Norway in actively supporting Aboriginal whaling, fearing that these countries exploit indigenous peoples' arguments for their own ends. Implied in such criticisms of pro-whaling agendas is the fear that indigenous peoples, just like everybody else, will be motivated by monetary greed and take more whales if their whaling practices are not strictly regulated and defined. Yet indigenous hunters from Point Barrow pointed out that they — using an analogy to models of land use that define the cultures of most IWC member countries — regard the ocean as a plot of land from which one not only subsists but by which one lives. Given such arguments, one can see how proponents on different sides of the debate struggle and clash.

Third Fantasy: Conservation

In his narrative of the *Phyllis Cormack,* a boat chartered by Greenpeace for a protest of American nuclear testing near the Aleutian island of Amchitka in 1970, *Vancouver Sun* journalist Bob Hunter, one of the founders and initial frontmen of Greenpeace, was struck by the magnificence and splendour of whales. At a time when most whale species were thought extinct or close to extinction, the crew encountered several whales: "'There's more! Three ... four! They're sperms ... No! Finbacks! No ... I dunno. Wow! Whales!' ... 'Wal, they're not all extinct,' muttered the skipper" (Hunter 1979, 89). The unexpected surprise of encountering whales at a time when the oceans were thought to be depleted jolts the crew into a rush of political activism and mobilization. Indeed, Greenpeace's anti-whaling campaigns of the 1970s and 1980s became one of the defining markers of environmental organizations, as well as one of the most notorious sites of environmental action.

Together with the protests against nuclear tests in both the northern and southern Pacific, the anti-whaling protests helped make Greenpeace. They are an essential part of the organization's origin narrative, retold repeatedly in personal memoirs and historical representations of the organization (e.g., Weyler 2004). At today's IWC meetings, a plethora of environmental NGOs and organizations draw on this story but also offer arguments of their own. Associations as diverse as the Sea Shepherd Society, the Whale and Dolphin Conservation Society, the Whale Center of New England, the Earth Island International Marine Mammal Project, the World Whale Police, the International Fund for Animal Welfare, the Cetacean Society International, the Friends of the Earth, the Cousteau Society, the Humane Society of the United States, the Pacific Whale Foundation, and the Save the Manatee Club distribute flyers, pamphlets, promotional materials, and brochures. Most infamous among these is *ECO*,[7] a daily release written and published by representatives of non profit environmental and animal-welfare organizations that attend the annual IWC meetings. An issue published at the 2003 Berlin meetings unleashed a scandal of far-reaching proportions. A cartoon depicting Caribbean nations as Japan's black "lap dogs," with a caption reading, "His Excellency the lap dog! Millions of the master's yen buy many votes," sparked charges of racism. The accompanying article accused Japan of buying IWC votes from Caribbean nations in its effort to resume commercial whaling, charging that over a period of thirteen years Japan pumped more than $160 million in fisheries aid for that purpose into Antigua and Barbuda, Dominica, Grenada, St. Lucia, St. Kitts and Nevis, and St. Vincent and the Grenadines. The IWC meeting came to a four-hour halt as the conference chair held an emergency meeting to discuss the newsletter. He called for an apology, but the newsletter's sponsors replied they could not address the issue because the commission "failed to identify even one specific complaint." Moreover, they argued, "It is not the duty of *ECO* or any free press to apologize to any government or international institutions for publishing the truth or honest opinion, however much that may offend." Later, individual groups issued apologies to parties who may have been offended, stressing they were not involved in the newsletter's editorial content. The matter of the cartoon has continued to linger, and at the 2004 meetings stabs taken by the pro-whaling lobby against anti-whaling groups only intensified.

Depending on one's perspective, environmentalism has become the greatest promise or greatest threat at IWC meetings. Yet what is most striking is how alliances have changed. In the 1970s, environmentalists saw "tribal" people as their most authentic allies; today, collaborations between environmentalists and conservation biologists are most powerful and prominent. Sea mammal biologists, including cetologists, have begun to align themselves with environmental and anti-whaling movements and their concerns.[8] Yet for scientists to shift, environmentalism itself had to shift. In its initial phase of organizing at the IWC, one of Greenpeace's preferred methods of raising public awareness was the "mindbomb" — simple images delivered by the media that would "explode in people's minds" and create a new understanding of the world (Weyler 2004, 73). Today, shock value has largely been replaced by disciplinary knowledge and scientific data. Fisheries models — that is, models that did not take into account the fact that whales were mammals and exhibit behavioural forms distinct from those of fish — that were in use until the mid-1980s have been replaced with the analysis of coda dialects and population models that reflect the ways in which whales move through the oceans. Until the 1960s, much of what was known about whales was inferred from dead bodies, although historical records have always played a role. But with the emergence of new research technology and a more holistic vision of the globe, science began to change (Cosgrove 1994). As a particular form of knowledge about nature, cetology is now as concerned with biological research as it is with the preservation of single whale stocks and species, and scientists often make the same inferences as environmentalists about the interests of non-human species. "There is a lot we may never know about the motivation and behaviour of nonhuman organisms," stated one cetologist at the 2004 Sorrento meetings, "but we can imagine that they, like us, want to live."

The question of life (and death) is at the heart of most IWC concerns and discussions. And many biologists have come to argue that their studies are not only part of a culture of biology and science but also an expression of their "love for life" (Wilson 2003). Cetologists' fight for species diversity and life, especially whale life, has taken many forms. One of that fight's most pronounced aspects, which does not happen directly at IWC meetings but takes the public as its forum, is the publication of handsome coffee-table books that are articulations of reverence and respect for the (always assumed) beauty and grandeur of whales (see, e.g., Darling 1999; Stewart 1995). Carrying their arguments beyond the frame of the IWC, conservation biologists engage that most powerful of all arenas: the public.

Fourth Fantasy: The Future

IWC politics is a bundle of incongruities and contradictions. Groups from different cultural, historical, and political backgrounds are pitted against each other; so are humans and animals. The principles of the ICRW are ambiguous. Who is at their centre? Environmentalism, it appears, has come to prevail within the ICW, but not without a challenge. Indigenous representatives charge that non-governmental organizations, environmental advocates, and civil society constitute a transnational governmentality, spreading a new imperial power that reaches deep into the heart of their cultures and seems to negate their autonomy and specificity. At the same time, representatives of national states cannot agree on global management and whose autonomy and perspectives should count. Yet whales are autonomous too, in the sense that they are capable of life without humans.

Whose autonomy, then, should be at the centre of IWC decision making? And are there ways to envision the autonomy of diverse states and groups, as well as humans and animals, as interrelated instead of as antagonistic? To think about such interconnections is no easy task. To recognize the autonomy of both animals and humans in a struggle about life and death requires moving beyond the presumed dualisms of so many debates that happen at the IWC.

Most analysts seem to agree that the debate on whaling has reached a stalemate. Moreover, the global future for animals, especially those that most Western peoples regard as "wild," are frequently described as "apocalyptic." In their darkest scenarios, anti-whaling countries paint the future of the globe as one of annihilation and catastrophe. At stake in these portrayals are questions of management, sustainability, or conservation, but also humans' love of and respect for the autonomy of animals. It is perhaps the recognition that animals are not lesser beings than humans and that all life is deeply connected that has most driven the anti-whaling lobby. And it is in these imaginations that the autonomy of whales is constructed. Autonomy within the global decision-making forum of the IWC, then, moves many ways. While in conventional political imaginations the autonomy of nations trumps the autonomy of whales, a global environmental network has been emerging that challenges such assumptions. In the end, it remains to be seen how the uneasy relations between environmentalists and nations translate into meaningful politics for both humans and animals.

Economic production and environmental resource use are not neutral matters of efficiency, natural capacity, and profit margins. Even whale and/or conservation biologists or ecosystem modellers (think of the NMP, RMP, and RMS) cannot dismantle the politics of whaling constituencies and nations. While cetologists (Samuels and Tyack 2000, 9) argue for a cetacean-centric perspective, and anti-whaling advocates for the intrinsic rights of whales, the echoes of imperialism continue to reverberate in criticisms of whaling rights and environmental protection. Rhetorics of sustainability, on the one hand, and rights, on the other, create frictions between parties. Perhaps the negotiations are so heated and decisions so difficult to achieve precisely because whaling, in the end, is a matter of life or death.

Conventions and agreements such as the ICRW hide, but do not stop, the making and affirming of cultural and political frameworks in all human activities. My contribution to debates around whaling and the IWC has been to draw attention to the antagonistic and frequently mutually exclusive patterning of ideals, rhetoric, and assumptions that transpire within its context. The IWC must contend with changing public perceptions, as well as the historical specificities of those who look at whales as a source of livelihood and as free resources.

chapter 7 — Globalization, Autonomy, and Global Institutions: Accounting for Accounting

Sarah Eaton and Tony Porter

SIGNS THAT ACCOUNTING IS about much more than men in white shirts poring over ledgers in dusty back rooms have been increasingly evident. The collapse of Arthur Andersen, one of the Big Five accounting firms, as a result of its role in the Enron scandal implicated accountancy in the types of creative financial manipulations that we usually associate with the worst excesses of global finance. The tendency of "accountability" to displace "democracy" in discussions of legitimacy internationally is another hint that there is more to accounting than counting. Those who follow accounting more closely will also be aware that the International Accounting Standards Board (IASB) has enjoyed a remarkable upswing in prominence in recent years and has become by far the most successful case of the making and management of rules by an independent private-sector institution at the global level.

Consistent with the focus of this book on the implications for autonomy of globalization, we take this chapter as an opportunity to explore the impact on autonomy of the globalization of bodies of technical knowledge and the institutions, practices, and actors associated with them. Our starting premise is that global accountancy is best conceived broadly as a private international regime, or as "an integrated complex of formal and informal institutions that is a source of governance for an economic issue area as a whole" (Cutler, Haufler, and Porter 1999, 13). The case of accounting, we argue, offers an intriguing twist on the zero-sum conception of the globalization/autonomy dualism that one commonly encounters: our research suggests that the autonomy of some global institutions is actually enhanced by globalization. We focus on three aspects of accountancy that point to the accretion of accountancy's substantial authority and power in virtue of globalization: industrial organization, national regulatory regimes, and global governance capacity. We suggest that, while accounting is a particularly apt demonstration of this phenomenon, the insights of this chapter could be applied to many other types of technical knowledge.

Despite the obvious relevance of autonomy to contemporary life, there remains a serious gap between philosophical approaches, which have provided a great deal of insight into what autonomy implies for individual thought and conduct, and social theories, which seek to understand its relationship to social structures or collective actors such as states or nations. We see bridging this gap as useful because of the relationship between individual and collective autonomy that is discussed in Chapter 1 of this book. Accountancy, as a body of knowledge and a social practice, provides an excellent opportunity for bridging this gap. Not only does it involve individual professionals who must discipline their thinking and conduct with reference to a set of broader technical rules, but, as a profession with a long and now very troubled tradition of self-regulation, it allows us to explore the issues of self-rule that have been central to philosophical thinking about autonomy at a larger social scale. We shall argue that this scale, *between* the individual and global society as a whole in both a size and mediating sense, is increasingly important in our ever more functionally differentiated world. In shifting to this scale, we hope to be able to better understand the conditions today under which the autonomy of some individuals, social groups, and bodies of knowledge can be reconciled with the autonomy of others, and with values other than autonomy. We explore these questions in the context of rapid globalization.

Control at a Distance: The Place of Accounting in Globalizing Processes

The globalizing aspects of accounting are in part connected to its role in capitalism and capitalism's role in globalization. Accounting has always enhanced a type of control that is consistent with capitalism as a form of social organization, including the production of the type of standardized measurement of firms and goods that is needed for market forces to impose their horizontal pressures on firms; the type of performance measures within the firm that allows managers and owners to control employees; and the type of government or national statistics that enable states to shape economic growth and national development but within the context of the fiscal prudence and other limits that ensure that the state supports rather than replaces the market economy. Today public-sector accounting is relatively autonomous from private-sector accounting; in this chapter we focus on the latter.

Accounting made the emergence of joint-stock companies possible by instilling confidence and making accurate allocations among investors, as with the East India Company, chartered in 1600 (Brewster 2003, 35). In the 1850s, the British state began requiring independent examination of a company's financial statements (ibid., 48), reinforcing accounting's autonomy. Accounting practices developed in the railroad companies in the late-nineteenth-century United States played a key role in the emergence of today's multi-unit, professionally managed corporation (Hoskin and Macve 1994, 88). Accounting contributed to the science of production initiated by Frederick Taylor, with its time-motion studies and efforts to maximize efficiency in the daily activities of workers. It was a turning point in the appropriation of knowledge of crafts workers by management, which was associated with the adoption of assembly lines (Miller and O'Leary 1994). In this respect, the increasing autonomy of the abstract knowledge represented by accounting came at the expense of the autonomy of individual craft workers.

Accounting is also thoroughly implicated in a key contemporary feature of economic globalization: capital market integration. Obstfeld and Taylor (2004) suggest that capital markets in the past century have been U-shaped with respect to international integration. Following a period of sustained and deep financial integration in the early part of the twentieth century and a precipitous drop between 1914 and 1945, capital market integration has been steadily on the rise. It is the resurgence of global capital markets more than any other factor that has contributed to the growing power of accountancy. Accounting information is the key means by which far-flung investors and creditors can exercise a measure of control over corporate managers. Indeed, widespread support for the development of international accounting standards is explainable in terms of a common interest in bringing down the cost of capital even further by eradicating the inefficiencies implied by discrepancies between national accounting rule systems (Tweedie and Seidenstein 2005).

The Consolidation of Global Accountancy

Through an analysis of recent developments in global accountancy at the firm, national, and global levels, we suggest that increasing industrial concentration, the Anglo-Americanization of national regulatory regimes, and an increase in the global institutionalization of accounting and auditing are deeply intertwined, and mutually reinforcing, phenomena. For this reason, we see the private international regime of global accountancy as the proper unit of analysis and not, for example, the Big Four accounting firms or the International Accounting Standards Board.

The accounting industry is, however, remarkably concentrated, with the top four accounting firms playing a decisive role in the development of the industry internationally. In part this dominance includes their funding of the IASB, an institution that we explore in the next section. They also exert influence through their connections to the US government and through their ability to claim a unique role in global finance based on their global expertise. By seeking aggressively to expand their own markets, they help create de facto global standards and practices, even if they remain less global in their daily operations than they claim. In recent years, the big accounting firms have increasingly seen their route to profits as involving the provision of consulting services (see Miller-Segarra 2002) to their large corporate clients, even at the risk of losing the trust among investors that comes from independently attesting to the integrity of their clients' financial statements or detecting fraud in their clients' operations. This change has amplified their role in promoting the interests of multinational corporations.

We may interpret the growth of these transnational accounting firms as enhancing the autonomy of accounting from local contexts, a theme we also address in the next section when we examine convergence across national jurisdictions. However, we also can see potential serious conflicts between the attempts of individual firms to enhance their own autonomy at the expense of the autonomy of accounting at large. The damage that resulted, both to individual firms and to the economy as a whole, confirms the link between autonomous accounting and economic growth that we saw in earlier historical periods.

In 2002 the Big Four accounting firms — PricewaterhouseCoopers, KPMG, Deloitte & Touche, and Ernst & Young — had over $47 billion in total global net revenues. They audit over 78 percent of US public companies and 99 percent of public company annual sales (US GAO 2003). Because they have specialized in particular industries, the relevant concentration ratios can be much higher. For instance, the top two firms accounted for 73.8 percent of chemical and allied industry audits, 81.4 percent of industry machinery and equipment, and 86.1 percent of transportation by air (ibid., 2003, appendix IV). Concentration ratios in other jurisdictions are reportedly similar to the United States. The Big Four had over $47 billion in total global net revenues in 2002, and they are responsible for virtually 100 percent of audits of major listed companies in the UK, over 80 percent in Japan, and 90 percent in the Netherlands (ibid., 18). The accounting industry is so unnervingly concentrated in the United States that KPMG may avoid indictment for allegations of tax sheltering because the US government is reportedly concerned that an indictment could lead to the company's collapse and to an even stronger Big Three (*Economist*, 23 June 2005).

A hint of the type of collusion that can result from such a concentrated structure emerged in connection with the 1991 conviction of a bank vice-president who had defrauded the bank that employed him of $6 million over a sixteen-year period. Deloitte & Touche had been the bank's auditor but had not discovered the fraud; once it was discovered, the bank hired KPMG to investigate the adequacy of Deloitte & Touche's auditing. A scathingly critical report was prepared for the bank by a KPMG partner. However, before it reached the bank the general counsel at Deloitte & Touche reportedly called his friend and counterpart at KPMG, and subsequently the report was rewritten and the KPMG partner who had written it was fired (Lavelle 2000). Although the evidence that all this was connected was circumstantial, the relationship seemed questionable. The general counsels of the largest accounting firms meet for lunch in New York about every six weeks and it seems evident that their membership in a common insurance pool gives each a strong incentive not to cause legal problems for the others.

Not surprisingly, the big accounting firms are among the most important sources of campaign funds for politicians in the United States. In the 2004 presidential election, PricewaterhouseCoopers alone was the third-largest source of contributions to the Bush campaign, with $492,350. The industry spent $6.9 million on congressional races in 2004, of which $2,428,871 was spent on Democrats and $4,475,411 on Republicans (http://www.opensecrets.org). The accounting industry's showering of selected influential American politicians with money helps explain the enthusiasm with which the US government promotes the industry's interests in global capital markets. Some of this enthusiasm is evident in the US regulation of its own markets, which themselves constitute a large share of global markets. For instance, the Bush administration appointed industry lawyer Harvey Pitt to head the industry's main regulator, the Securities and Exchange Commission (SEC), replacing Arthur Levitt who, as chair from 1993 to 2001, had been outspoken on the issue of conflict of interest and other problems in the accounting industry. Pitt promised to make the SEC more friendly to the industry, but he resigned in 2002 after missteps suggesting an unwillingness or inability to recognize the severity of the problems of confidence and integrity in the industry. When his successor, William H. Donaldson, former head of the New York Stock Exchange, turned out to be more aggressive in regulating markets than expected, the Bush administration replaced him with Christopher Cox, a Republican congressional representative and former securities and corporate lawyer. He had been one of the most prominent and extreme critics of post-Enron SEC initiatives to regulate the markets. Cox's appointment was widely seen as an effort to bring the SEC back in alignment with the interests of big business.

The industry's aggressiveness in entering foreign markets is revealed by a detailed study by Caramanis (2002) of events associated with reform of the Greek market. The Greek market had been controlled by a monopoly held by a professional association of indigenous auditors until a reform in 1992. As the international accounting firms entered the Greek market, they set up a rival association. When a socialist government elected in 1993 tried to restrict the operations of foreign firms — for instance, by requiring that their staff write examinations to test their knowledge of Greek standards — a powerful US campaign against these restrictions was launched. It was carried out through unilateral pressures by the US Embassy in Athens and aggressive efforts at the Organisation for Economic Co-operation and Development (OECD), a campaign that the European Union (EU) and other governments such as the UK and Canada would join. In the end, the Greek government backed down.

The structural power enjoyed by the accounting industry is also revealed in the case of Trinidad and Tobago (Annisette 2002). In colonial times, accounting in Trinidad and Tobago had been entirely controlled by the leading British accounting association and by white British-born accountants. Following independence and stimulated by an active Black Power movement, the government sought to promote indigenous participation in all industries, including accounting. It made some efforts to build a capacity to train accountants at the University of the West Indies. Ultimately, however, the professionals, black and white, who constituted the local industry, favoured getting their credentials from a private-sector British association. The reason is that globally recognized standards were seen as necessary to attract the business of US and other foreign firms whose direct investments were rapidly becoming the most important part of the economy of Trinidad and Tobago.

The accounting industry has become a major purveyor of corporate values as it has shifted from its former primary function of attesting to the integrity of financial data for corporate leadership and outside investors to assisting corporations to figure out how best to create value, maximize profitability, and enhance their image (Covaleski, Dirsmith, and Rittenberg 2003). This change involved a struggle and transformation in the profession — an effort to recast accountants as global knowledge experts.

Despite the Big Four's habit of claiming, for marketing purposes, to be global firms, nationality still matters in firm operations. A study of the process by which one big firm decided to enter the Soviet and eastern European markets on the eve of their post-communist transformation (D.J. Cooper at al. 1998) found internal conflict that broke down on national lines, with members of the firm characterizing the behaviour of members from other countries as expressive of their nationality. Decisions were made more on the basis of hunches than careful cost-benefit projections, and past international relations among the countries in which the firm's offices were located and the countries whose markets it was considering entering were important. For instance, the German office was eager to enter eastern European markets in which Germany had traditionally been involved, while the Americans were skeptical. Overall the firm operated more like an alliance of national firms than a globally integrated multi-national corporation.

Another example of the enduring relevance of nationality is the difficulty experienced by regulators in obtaining information about Price Waterhouse (as it was then) activities in jurisdictions other than their own (Arnold and Sikka 2001). Under the terms of the 1983 Basle Concordat, international bank regulators from the wealthiest leading industrial countries in the Group of Ten have been responsible for monitoring the worldwide operations of banks headquartered in their jurisdictions. To do so, they have relied upon international accounting firms to validate the consolidated financial statements of banks. When massive fraud led to the closure of the Bank of Credit and Commerce International in 1992, Price

Waterhouse partnerships refused to cooperate with authorities from other countries in which Price Waterhouse was active. Price Waterhouse (USA) argued "Price Waterhouse firms are separate and independent legal entities whose activities are subject to the laws and professional obligations of the country in which they practice" (cited in Arnold and Sikka 2001, 487).

Accounting and Economic Globalization

Overall we can see that the growth of transnational accounting firms has spread a particular type of accounting around the world, even if this spread is not as advanced as the firms' promotional marketing sometimes suggests. In that sense, they have increased the autonomy of accounting from local contexts. We may interpret this autonomy as a form of functional differentiation, where the growth of transnational business demanded within accounting a further specialization in methods and individuals that could operate with ease across different cultures and languages. However, we can also see that accounting's traditional autonomy, which has been the source of its effectiveness, was seriously undermined by the growth strategies of the accounting firms. Conflicts of interest within the firms increased, and the link of accounting to the public interest was weakened by the aggressive attempts of the firms to manipulate public-sector policy and regulatory processes. Ultimately these attempts led to the collapse of Arthur Andersen, the fifth-largest accounting firm, and cast accountancy in general into a crisis that threatened to seriously damage the corporate sector as a whole. This points to the importance of the relationship between the autonomy of different actors in assessing the value of autonomy in general, a point to which we return in subsequent sections.

Another source of accountants' influence in the processes of economic globalization is found in the high degree of institutionalization within the profession. Within countries and increasingly at the global level, professional accountancy bodies and private-sector standard-setting bodies wield considerable power in the global economy as self-regulators, professional gatekeepers, and rule makers for financial reporting practices. As we will see, this institutionalization has strongly contributed to the harmonization of accounting rules and practices around the world.

Private Governance and Authority: Emerging Policy Convergence?

In many countries, the private sector plays a crucial role in the operation of regulatory frameworks that oversee accounting and auditing practices. The influence of the major accountancy firms in the regulatory process tends to vary cross-nationally with such factors as financial structure, legal tradition, and the strength of the profession vis-à-vis the state (Nobes 1992). Generally speaking, in Anglo-American economies, where capital markets play a crucial role in conducting funds from investors and creditors to corporate entities and back, the accountancy industry has tended to be a dominant presence in regulatory regimes. By contrast, in continental Europe, where capital markets have traditionally been less important than banks in the process of financial intermediation, the state's influence in the regulatory process has historically been unrivalled. In recent years, however, the profession appears to have gained ground in many state-based regimes. An overview of recent developments in the regulatory frameworks of five countries with quite different economic and political institutions — the United States, Japan, France, China, and India — suggests that widespread enthusiasm for the Anglo-American model of accounting regulation is a stimulus for change in some *dirigiste* economies.

In the American system — a model that has been replicated around the world in large part because of the strength of the US capital market — the private sector plays a leading role in the formulation of financial reporting rules, though legislative changes in the wake of Enron have substantially curtailed the influence of the accountancy profession in auditing. Since 1973, the US securities regulator has delegated to the Financial Accounting Standards Board (FASB) the task of writing accounting standards, the rules that structure the financial statements public companies are required to publish at regular intervals. The FASB is a private-sector body that is financially independent of the Big Four but remains close to the industry by virtue of its staff, which is composed mainly of former senior executives from the major accountancy firms. Prior to the collapse of Enron in late 2001, the largest professional association in the United States — the American Institute of Certified Public Accountants (AICPA) — managed a system of auditing self-regulation that operated on the basis of peer review. Widespread concerns about laxity in the system, which were raised by Arthur Andersen's highly publicized complicity in Enron and Worldcom's fraudulent activities, led to a major legislative initiative, the Sarbanes-Oxley Act of 2002. This law transferred responsibility for auditing to the

Public Company Accounting Oversight Board (PCAOB), which describes itself as "an independent, nonprofit, non-governmental body to oversee the auditors of public companies" (PCAOB 2003, 4). The establishment of the PCAOB (nicknamed "peekaboo") represents a significant loss of direct influence on the part of the accountancy industry because the five-person board is appointed by, and responsible to, the SEC. It is, though, a testament to the strength of the self-regulatory tradition in the United States that responsibility for auditing was not directly transferred to the SEC but remains in the hands of a formally private-sector body, though one that is certainly more independent from the audit industry than its predecessor and that is directly overseen by the public sector in practice. The SEC's view that the PCAOB should include members with substantial regulatory experience is reflected in its choice of William McDonough as the board's first chair. McDonough served as head of the New York Federal Reserve for ten years and also chaired the public-sector Basel Committee on Banking Supervision. In its first years of operation, the board's efforts to improve the ethical standards of audit practice have earned it the enmity of American big business (*Economist,* 18 February 2006).

Japan's economy has more in common with the German and French systems than it does with either the United States or the United Kingdom. Thus, it is interesting that recent changes to accounting regulation appear to be bringing the system more in line with Anglo-American principles. As in continental Europe, the Japanese economy has traditionally been defined by a high degree of state intervention, and banks have played a leading role in the provision of finance. The close resemblance of the contemporary accounting regulatory framework to the US system in spite of differences in the two countries' financial systems is explained by adaptation to the Anglo-American model in two time periods: in the immediate aftermath of the Second World War and in the current era of the convergence of international accounting standards and practice. As part of the effort to dissolve the powerful *zaibatsu* companies that were seen to have contributed to Japanese militarism, US administrators in Japan as part of the postwar occupying force attempted to transplant the American regulatory system, with its heavy emphasis on full financial disclosure to investors and creditors, an effort that only partially succeeded in displacing prewar institutions (Cooke and Kikuya 1992, 93, cf. Suzuki 2007). One present-day institution that has its origins in the postwar period is the Japanese Institute of Certified Public Accountants (JICPA), which was patterned on the major American professional body described above. As compared to the AICPA, however, the JICPA has traditionally enjoyed far less autonomy in relation to regulatory authorities. Indeed, until quite recently, the Ministry of Finance (MOF) wielded broad powers that included control over accounting standards and the accreditation process for Certified Public Accountants (CPAs) (Cooke and Kikuya 1992, 121). Beginning in 2001, though, major changes in Japan have brought the system much more in line with practices in the United Kingdom and the United States. In that year, responsibility for accounting standard setting was transferred from the MOF to the Accounting Standards Board of Japan (ASBJ), "an independent and private-sector entity" (http://www.asb.or.jp). Audit standard setting remains with an arm of the MOF, but the JICPA also contributes to auditing rules through the issuance of audit practice guidelines. The ASBJ has played a prominent role in international accountancy as a liaison standard setter with the IASB. As of the time of writing, the ASBJ was holding discussions with the IASB on what steps were necessary to achieve convergence between Japanese and international generally accepted accounting principles (GAAP).

In comparison to Japan, the French state-based model of accountancy regulation appears more robust, though the state is under pressure from many French multinationals to become more in-step with Anglo-American conventions. Since 1947, accounting standards have been written by a government agency, the Conseil National de la Comptabilité (CNC). The council is a fifty-eight-member group made up primarily of public servants and includes five trade unionists alongside a number of other non-accounting experts. Standish (2000, 10) has argued that this state-based regulatory structure has strongly limited France's influence over processes of international accounting convergence. He notes also that the disconnect between the CNC and Anglo-American standard setters, in regulatory structure and in substantive priorities, has meant that French and global accounting firms increasingly serve as an "interface" between French standard setters and international bodies premised on Anglo-American values (ibid., 15). French multinationals have a long history of supporting international GAAP: in the early 1970s, even before there was an international accounting standard setter, many firms elected to use US GAAP (the de facto international standards at that time) to draw up their accounts (Touron 2005). It is likely that in the coming years the January 2005 enactment of the European Union's regulation requiring European public companies to use International Financial Reporting Standards (IFRS) will serve as pressure on dirigisme in French accounting regulation.

Accounting convergence is also under way in two of the world's most important emerging markets. Little more than a decade ago, China's accounting system was tailored to the needs of government agencies charged with central planning responsibilities, a system that proved quite ill-suited to the demands for greater corporate financial information that attended the liberalization of Chinese capital markets (Wei-guo 1996). Thus it was that in 1993, close on the heels of the openings of the Shanghai and Shenzhen stock exchanges, the Ministry of Finance (MOF), with financial support from the World Bank, began to develop a comprehensive set of market-friendly accounting standards. At the same time, the Securities Regulatory Commission was created to advise and assist the MOF in matters of financial reporting. As in other parts of the world, the major professional association, in this case the Chinese Institute of Certified Public Accountants, which was established in 1988, plays an important role in promoting the integrity of the CPA designation by administering qualifying exams and monitoring professional conduct. In 2000, the MOF moved China one step closer to harmonization with international accounting standards with the introduction of the market-friendly Enterprise Accounting System (Xiao, Weetman, and Sun 2004).

Owing to the colonial influence of Britain, India has a much longer affiliation with Anglo-American accounting practices, though even here one observer notes that the accounting standard setters — the Institute of Chartered Accountants of India — are "moving fast" to harmonize Indian accounting with prevailing international standards and practices in order to make corporate accounts "more amenable to analysis by foreign investors and analysts" (Iyer 2001).

Private Global Authority

At the global level, private-sector accountancy organizations are accumulating even more authority than their national counterparts. Since 1 January 2005, the International Accounting Standards Board has served, effectively, as standard setter for capital markets in the European Union. On the auditing side, with blessings from all of the leading international financial institutions, the International Federation of Accountants (IFAC) and the International Forum on Accountancy of Development (IFAD) are currently working with national professional accountancy bodies to standardize audit practices around the world.

The Economist (6 March 2004) surmised that Sir David Tweedie, chairman of the IASB, could be the "most important man in capitalism at the moment" because his organization was moving at breakneck speed towards its self-prescribed goal of the worldwide convergence of accounting standards. International Financial Reporting Standards are now binding upon all public companies in the European Union, and international standards have replaced financial accounting codes in dozens of countries around the world, including Australia and Russia. Many other countries, including Canada, permit foreign companies to prepare their accounts in accordance with international standards without reconciliation to national rules. As well, the leading international lending agencies have all incorporated international standards into their processes in one way or another. For example, in the wake of the Asian financial crisis, the IASB's standards began to be enforced via International Monetary Fund (IMF) loan conditionality. Compliance with international standards is also now a key criterion of the World Bank's Reports on the Observance of Standards and Codes.

In view of the importance of the IASB in contemporary global capitalism — the rules they produce set the parameters of the financial information corporations disseminate to investors, creditors, and the wider public — troubling questions have been raised about the appropriateness of the board's private-sector structure to its task. The IASB's constitution requires that board members be selected by a group of trustees solely on the basis of their "technical expertise" in accounting matters; neither geographic representation nor functional diversity is required by the constitution. The technical ability selection criteria were an attempt to prevent standard setting from becoming captive to the short-term interests of particular firms or political actors, but it has proven controversial because of the dominant presence of the accounting industry in the decision-making organs of the IASB. The entire fourteen-member board hails from the private sector, and the vast majority of members have spent most of their professional life in one of the big accounting firms. European Commissioners, among others, have taken exception to the absence of a regulatory presence on the board (see, for example, the letter of comment by the European Commission Internal Market Director-General [ECIMD-G 2004]).

Another source of controversy is the board's funding arrangement. The IASB relies on donations to finance its operations, and while the IMF and the World Bank, in addition to many central banks, have contributed to the IASB's purse, the vast majority of its funding comes from big business. Of these private contributions, by far the most support comes from the Big Four, each of which agreed to supply the board with $1 million annually. The IASB has sought to provide the standard setters in the board some autonomy from the financial backers by giving the formally separate International Accounting Standards Committee Foundation Trustees responsibility for fundraising. The adequacy of this constitutional separation has been called into question by critics who have suggested that IASB board members are in a conflict of interest because they are writing the rules that their financial backers subsequently use in the preparation of their own accounts (e.g., Zeff 2002).

While there is enthusiasm for the IASB's work in many business, regulatory, and political circles, the point has often been made that the harmonization of accounting rules is only a starting point in the effort to converge financial reporting practices worldwide: without scrupulous auditors and effective policing by regulatory agencies working to hold corporate entities to account, a set of global rules amounts to naught (e.g., Hussey 1999). In response to these concerns, IFAC and IFAD — both private-sector, industry-based organizations — have begun programs to harmonize audit and regulatory practices worldwide. Under the auspices of IFAC, the International Auditing and Assurance Standards Board (IAASB) has developed a set of International Standards on Auditing (ISAs) to complement the efforts of the international accounting standard-setters. As of 2004, more than seventy countries have adopted ISAs, and many more have stated that their own audit standards are consistent with international standards (IAASB 2004, 2). In 2003, IFAC also initiated a program to encourage its membership — made up of 157 national professional accountancy associations — to promote compliance with accounting and auditing standards in their own jurisdictions. IFAD's programs have aims largely parallel to IFAC's Compliance Program, though the sights of this newer creation of the global accountancy industry are trained specifically on improving audit and regulatory practices in emerging markets. IFAD's all-encompassing goals are served by its diverse and powerful membership of more than thirty, which includes the IMF, the World Bank, the Basel Committee on Banking Supervision, the Financial Stability Forum (FSF), and the International Organization of Securities Commissions (IOSCO) as well as IFAC and the IASB.

Conceptual Issues: The Dilemmas of Autonomy

So far, we have highlighted the way in which accounting has become increasingly consolidated as an international private regime involving a set of interrelated institutions and rules, mainly private sector, that govern accounting activities around the world. The process has involved globalization, but it has also involved changes in autonomy. Global rules and rule making in accounting have come to structure accounting activity, long regulated by local approaches to authority, as well as some political processes and even, to some degree, the behaviour of individual firms. Standard setting in bodies like the IASB is carried out with regard to technical principles and arguably with some degree of independence and autonomy from local, usually nation-state, rule making. The question is how to think conceptually about the character of this growing autonomy of the international private accounting regime.

Although autonomy has had many shades of meaning, for the purposes of this chapter we define it, following Haworth (1986, 42), as a capacity involving competence, self-control, and independence. In adding *competence* to a literature that often focuses more heavily on self-control and independence, Haworth has provided a way to include a given actor's social condition, much as Amartya Sen's (1999) individual-centred account of development emphasizes "capabilities" and "functioning" (see also Carroll 1972, 589-91). We can bring this social notion of capability or capacity further into our analysis by not restricting the use of autonomy to individuals and applying it to other social actors, such as states (Poulantzas 1974; Nordlinger 1981), nations (Hannum 1990), or even technologies (Ellul 1967; Winner 1977).

The notion of functional differentiation provides a useful way of contextualizing these multiple forms of autonomy in late modernity. An increased differentiation of human societies over history leads, for instance, to the separation into more specialized and autonomous institutions of activities like the economic, child and elder care, education, and governance functions of the family. Similarly, knowledge has become more and more differentiated into autonomous disciplines and subdisciplines. Earlier scholars of functional differentiation such as Parsons (1971) were rightly criticized for apolitical determinism, but scholars more recently have analyzed the role of power in creating differentiated or de-differentiated fields of activity, as well as the reversibility of differentiating trends.

Luhmann provides some especially suggestive ideas about functional differentiation. He identifies a historical tendency for social differentiation based on class to be replaced by differentiation by function. In social systems, humans are linked by communication, and communication is carried on within particular functional subsystems in a self-referential manner. For instance, lawyers must use legal language and references, rather than threats of violence, expressions of physical affection, or economic inducements, in order to function in courts. Luhmann (1984, 64-5) notes:

> Using functional differentiation as a guideline for the self-description of our society does not imply an evaluation as perfection, as the best of all possible worlds, as the outcome of progress or as a system with superior efficiency. As one of the consequences of functional differentiation we even have to expect more or less permanent crises in some of the subsystems. This is the result of structural preconditions which prescribe high autonomy, self-organization, and even self-reproduction of elements *(autopoiesis)* of subsystems and high interdependencies between systems and environments at the same time ... What is good for the individual parts may be a mixed blessing for the total system.

Knorr Cetina (1997, 1) provides an additional insight into the autonomy of objects, including knowledge-intensive objects such as accounting documents as differentiation proceeds. She identifies an "objectualization," which implies that "objects displace human beings as relationship partners and embedding environments, or that they increasingly mediate human relationships, making the latter dependent on the former ... These 'postsocial' developments ... have something to do with the dispersion of knowledge processes and knowledge structures in social life." In other words, competence and independence become ascribed to accounting texts and other objects, supported by various rules and institutions protecting this autonomy. In this respect, we can speak of a field of activity such as accounting becoming autonomous. The autonomy, however, rests on the private authority congealed in the overall international private regime.

How can the benefits of autonomy be maximized while minimizing the negative effects of one actor or institution's autonomy on another's? How can we evaluate variations in the distribution of autonomy across different social settings, especially when one actor's autonomy is dependent upon the loss of another's? In the literature on business associations there is extensive discussion of the advantages and disadvantages of self-regulation, the institutionalization of autonomous private authority. Self-regulation is promoted because of its flexibility, its greater relevance and legitimacy for the regulated business actors, and its cost effectiveness relative to public-sector regulation. If this field of activity becomes too autonomous, however, problems emerge, such as a lack of enforcement capacity, a lack of account-ability to a broader constituency (such as consumers or potential victims of an industry's negligence), the potential it offers for collusive activity among firms, and the view that it is often only a cynical ploy by industry to avoid direct state regulation.

In recent literature on industry self-regulation there is widespread rec-ognition that effective self-regulation rests on the existence of autonomous public institutions. These include the legal system's support for private liti-gation, the referencing of self-regulation in public-sector regulations, the official licensing of a self-regulatory arrangement's members, or the refer-encing of a particular jurisdiction's legal system in self-regulatory codes. At the international level, as mentioned above, the authority and effectiveness of the IASB is enhanced by the incorporation of observance of its standards into the practices of public-sector institutions such as the IMF and World Bank, and by the recognition and acceptance of international account-ing standards by the EU and national governments. Put differently, robust private authority can be enhanced by robust public authority. While com-pliance with accounting standards is elicited to a very important degree by private-sector mechanisms, such as market pressures and private-sector auditors, the public sector can be crucial in strengthening, underwriting, and legitimizing these. More generally, Habermas (1998) has suggested that democratic deliberation plays a unique role in facilitating communication and coordination among types of relatively autonomous functional subsys-tems such as accounting, and that the deliberative and democratic character of public-sector involvement is important for coordination, accountability, and legitimacy of the subsystems. When the forces of globalization help generate an international private regime, however, the vexing question becomes how does one create the public space and foster the democratic deliberation needed to temper and hold to account the self-regulator?

Conclusion

On one hand, the rationalization of accounting and auditing practices worldwide can be seen as contributing to public good. As discussed previ-ously, high quality and truly global accounting and auditing frameworks are a key institutional pillar of globalizing capital markets. It was the Asian Financial Crisis that really signalled the importance of corporate trans-parency to the healthy functioning of capital markets: the events of 1997 and 1998 showed that, without accurate and understandable financial information flowing between managers and investors, financial market bubbles can form and, ultimately, burst. In this light, the globalization of accounting standards and the standardization of audit practices can be seen as contributing to the stability of the global marketplace.

On the other hand, the Anglo-American values enshrined in global accountancy prioritize the interests of OECD-based multinational corporations over valuable social and political goals. The global accounting regime has developed an important degree of autonomy, but not from all actors: the Big Four and the corporations that are their clients are closely involved with developments in the globalization of accounting. Indeed, the autonomy of the accounting regime helps reinforce the autonomy of these firms. However, the accounting regime must also retain a certain degree of autonomy from firms if it is to preserve its effectiveness, as did not happen, for instance, in the period leading up to the accounting crisis that began with Enron's collapse.

In 2003, the IASB mounted its first constitutional review since its inception. One of the major themes to emerge from the public hearings it held on the topic is that the overwhelming dominance of North American, western European, and Australian/New Zealand members at all levels of the IASB ultimately reduces the applicability and efficacy of the standards in areas outside of the North Atlantic. Written submissions from accounting organizations in emerging economies consistently stressed the need for more geographically balanced representation on the board and for standards that reflected the interests of small and medium-sized enterprises (SMEs), which typically account for a much higher proportion of economic activity in developing countries.

IFRS are also focused on capturing only the most immediately market-relevant aspects of business. As a result, the representation of corporate activity that emerges from financial statements excludes other kinds of socially relevant information. Indeed, the IASB's exclusive focus on financial disclosure arguably does a disservice to the twin aims of environmental and social sustainability. Proponents of environmental and social accounting argue that corporations can and should be held accountable for the priced *and* non-priced consequences of their actions.

These failings of the international private regime might reflect the absence of public spaces, a parallel public authority, and thus opportunities for democratic deliberation at the global scale. In this chapter as well as in Cutler's chapter, we see examples of bodies of globalized technical expertise becoming entangled with the power and interests of large multinational corporations, the end result of which may plausibly be labelled private global authority. Other examples may be seen in the relationship of intellectual property lawyers to pharmaceutical and other firms concerned about protecting their patents and copyrights (Sell 1999) and of international tax experts to their client firms (Webb 2004, 794). The autonomy of the private accounting regime has protected and even enhanced to an important degree the autonomy of accountancy firms, their clients, and investors. At first it may seem paradoxical that the autonomy of these last three sets of actors is dependent in the longer run on some degree of autonomy of the standard-setting process from their immediate influence. And all of these in turn depend to some degree for their success on autonomous public-sector institutions, such as the ability of the IMF to promote compliance through conditionality processes, or the ability of public authorities to authorize accounting practices within the territory in which they have jurisdiction and to help enforce professional boundaries that ensure the integrity and autonomy of these practices. The relationships between these increasingly autonomous processes are characteristic of the type of functional differentiation identified by Luhmann (1984), as discussed in the previous section.

In assessing the justice of the autonomy of the international accounting regime, it is not sufficient to evaluate its ability to address the interests of accountancy firms, their clients, and investors — rather it is important also to evaluate its impact on other actors. We have argued that a key criterion in making this evaluation is the relationship of accounting to other subsystems, which include environmental and social practices, as well as specific local economic practices, such as those of small and medium enterprises in developing countries. Even more important is the relationship to subsystems such as legislatures or cognate structures at a global scale because these are responsible for reconciling values across subsystems, creating public spaces for dialogue, and thereby identifying and promoting the public good.

chapter 8   **Transnational Law and Privatized Governance**

A. Claire Cutler

THIS CHAPTER FOCUSES ON the governance roles of transnational commercial law, lawyers, and law firms and makes a case for understanding them as part of a larger transnationalized legal field. It argues that the transnationalized legal field is globalizing legal forms that are creating supraterritorial relations among people (Scholte 2005) by delocalizing and denationalizing the law and removing its creation, interpretation, and application from the constraints of territorial or physical location or place, while simultaneously subjecting local societies and economies to its discipline. This process binds lawyers and other professionals together into a transnational class with an increasingly unified understanding of the world and how it should be governed that is capable of exercising significant autonomy from the state. Similar to the case of evolving accounting regimes explored by Eaton and Porter in Chapter 7, the process has profound implications for the autonomy of discrete communities, for subordinate localities, and for individuals.

Conceptualizing autonomy as self-governance, in keeping with the understanding shared across the chapters of this volume, the autonomy of the transnational legal field operates in relation to the autonomy of local individuals and collectivities by disciplining and, in some cases, displacing or dispossessing them. Indeed, this chapter argues that the institutions of transnational law shape the contours of the contemporary historical bloc. They provide the material conditions, the normative framework, and the organization that govern the global political economy and enable the continued expansion of capitalism.

The transnational legal field forms the infrastructure of what Castells (1996) refers to as the "space of flows" or productive relations that are disconnected from territorial place. Transnational lawyers create delocalized commercial laws and dispute settlement and arbitration procedures that are then globalized through the offices of transnationally organized law firms.[1] They also work with governments and international institutions to create regional and global trade, investment, and financial regimes that impose binding legal obligations on business activities and restrict local autonomy in matters ranging from environmental and safety regulations to labour, property, and cultural rights. These processes, however, are neither unidirectional nor absolute, for the law is subsequently relocalized as the offices of the state and national and local governments are utilized to enforce commercial transactions and awards in courts of law.

To the extent that local enforcement results in granting rights or protections to local individuals and communities, transnational law actually enhances the autonomy of some sectors and individuals. Transnational law, lawyers, and firms form the infrastucture of global capitalism, facilitating its expansionist tendencies, while instantiating tensions between its delocalizing and relocalizing tendencies. In so doing, therefore, the transnational legal field shapes the space of flows in global cities (Sassen 1998), providing the material, ideological, and institutional conditions for the continuing expansion of capitalist productive relations.

The central governance role of private transnational commercial law, lawyers, and law firms is obscured by conventional understandings of governance and law making. Such understandings fail to capture the ways in which private actors and institutions are taking on pivotal governance functions in global economic relations by assisting in disciplining certain local orders according to the logic of transnational capital accumulation. This instance of private authority emerged and grew apace with the global expansion of capitalism and, as such, gives rise to the tensions and contradictions between delocalizing and relocalizing tendencies that inhere in contemporary capitalism. Indeed, a critical understanding of the governance role of transnational legal forms, lawyers, and their firms lies in framing them as crucial mediators of local and global political economies. They are constitutive of a field that is potentially a very fertile site for contesting the subordination of local to global political economies, societies, and laws and for shaping global discipline in ways that enhance the autonomy of some localities. Relocalization may be seen as a terrain of struggle that could open up exciting opportunities for emancipatory politico-legal strategies.

The chapter begins with a discussion of the general obscurity of private law making and the inadequacy of dominant approaches to studying governance and authority. The chapter next analyzes the private governance role of transnational lawyers, law, and firms as a dimension of the global political economy and the contemporary world order. It argues that understanding the private law-making significance of lawyers and law firms is integrally linked to understanding the legal forms they develop, adopt, and transnationalize through their contractual and dispute resolution practices, their increasing concentration through mergers into "mega-firms," and the development of strategic alliances, networks, and other forms of private authority with foreign law firms and service firms, such as accounting firms. It analyzes the services offered by transnational law firms and problematizes their characterization as institutions of "global" governance and law, noting that it is overwhelmingly Anglo-American legal forms, legal norms, and business services that are being transnationalized. This is occurring apace with expansionary tendencies of capital accumulation through the discipline, dispossession, and displacement of some localities and the empowerment of others. The chapter concludes with a consideration of the significance of private transnational law making for the autonomy of governments and societies more generally, suggesting profound implications for public policy formation and the rule of law. It proposes insights from more critical conceptions of law and authority as a means for re-asserting human autonomy and regaining local control over law-making processes.

The Obscurity of Private Law Making

While there is a respected tradition of conceptualizing public international law as a constitutive institution of international society, there is no such tradition of similarly conceptualizing private international law. Hedley Bull (1977), for example, exemplifies the view that public international law is an institution that is fundamentally constitutive of international society: international law articulates the idea of a society of sovereign states as the "fundamental or constitutional principle of world politics in the present era" (Bull 1977, 140; and see Cutler 1991). Bull here is countering dominant realist understandings of international law, which posit the law to be merely epiphenomenal, as a reflection of state interests and power. Indeed, realists challenge that there is any autonomy to public international law, curiously sharing a more general position articulated by many Marxists that law can be seen only as superstructural in nature and operation (Cutler 2003, 94-9). Contemporary "constructivists" have further developed the challenge to dominant understandings by illustrating the existence of a growing body of public international law that both constrains strong states and offers weak states the opportunity to shape political outcomes (Reus-Smit 2004a, 17). According to this approach, public international law is "a central component of the normative structures that are produced by, and constitutive of" international politics (ibid., 23). International politics is thus analyzed as a "rule-governed and rule-constitutive form of reason and action" (ibid.).

Significantly, however, public international law as "a central component of the normative structures that are produced by, and constitutive of, such politics" (ibid.) is conceptualized as a law among sovereigns. The legitimacy of the order is traced to sources that embody state consent (treaties and customary international law), while its very subjects are identified by the doctrine of international legal personality as states or institutions endowed by states with state-like personality. Subject and sources doctrines identify the sovereign state as the repository of international legitimacy, ruling out any law-making authority and subjectivity for individuals, collectivities other than states (such as indigenous peoples), and transnational business corporations and associations, including law firms. Indeed, the dominant conceptions of public international law, as well as related conceptions of law-making processes, reflect hierarchical and formalistic models of authority and rule. Top-down models conceive of law and its creation as a product of sovereign authority, while formalism confines the law and law-making processes to outcomes generated and activities undertaken by formal governmental authorities. Accordingly, law is regarded as a creation of authorities who derive their legitimacy through constitutional doctrines and processes. For public international law (as for domestic law more generally), the legitimacy of the law and law-making processes emanates from the state as an exercise of external (and internal) sovereignty. In the context of domestic law, it is the government that creates the law, judges or arbitrators who apply it, and the coercive arm of the state that enforces it. In this scenario, the lawyer and law firm figure as mere ciphers, technicians, or intermediaries in the process. Their role in a bottom-up process of law creation and innovation simply cannot be reconciled with the hierarchical, formalistic model of rule. This tendency is particularly limiting in the domain of international law, where it is the state that is regarded as the primary subject and source of law. Conventional international legal

thought has great difficulty in accounting for the law-making significance of non-state authorities (Cutler, Haufler, and Porter 1999; Hall and
Biersteker 2002).

While students of domestic law making have widened the ambit of the
law-making process to study the judicial function as a creative and potentially innovative source of law, some, albeit less, attention has been given to
the contribution of lawyers and law firms. Initially focusing upon innovative lawyering in areas of public law, little attention has been given to the
role of lawyers in creating private commercial law. This is due in no small
part to the private/public distinction and liberal theories of government
and political economy that associate public law with politics and the realm
of the government and private law with the putatively apolitical realm of
economics, markets, and individuals transactions. Indeed, in international
law the distinction between public and private law turns very much on
the outward-looking focus of public international law as a law of sovereigns, and the inward-facing anomaly of private international law as a very
technical branch of *domestic conflict of laws* that governs the international
transactions of private individuals (Wai 2001; Paul 1988; Cutler 1997). In
the field of international law, Sigrid Quack (2004, 5) notes that "lawyers
as individuals and law firms as organizations have been ascribed a merely
technical role in drafting the terms of conventions once a balance of political interests has been struck. Partly as a result of this neglect, very little
attention has been given to social conventions and standards as potential
sources of law-making and to the transformation of these social norms
into legal norms."

However, critical socio-legal analyses emphasize the existence of a dis-
juncture between the formal state law and law in practice, or the *living-
law*, as well as a gap between formal international legal status of non-state
actors and their actual law-making significance (Santos 1995). They alert
us to the risks of formalistic analysis and the unquestioned associations
of law with governments and of international law with states. They raise
questions about the ambiguity and indeterminacy of international law and
its making. Indeed, the emerging field of transnational law embodies precisely these indeterminacies and ambiguities, recording specific challenges
posed to international law by postmodernity and late capitalism. While
these challenges are addressed more fully in the next section, it is worth
noting here that there has been an erosion of the private/public distinction
in international law. Private international law is increasingly taking on the
form of international treaties and harmonizing initiatives undertaken by

a mix of private and public actors (Spanogle 1991), while public international law is undergoing extensive privatization as private actors and non-state law increase in significance (Steinhardt 1991).

Transnational law making refers to "legal regulatory activities that span across national borders without essentially having a global dimension" and includes "a variety of different types of actors and different forms of law-making that transcend the scope of nation states without being reducible to interstate law. The term thus encompasses not only private international law-making, but also international and supranational law forms that develop a life as legal institutions beyond interstate treaties from which they arose" (Quack 2004, 2-3). Transnational law comes in different forms: public international law, as in treaties and customary international law; law making by a mixture of government and non-governmental actors, as in many environmental conventions; and private transnational law making, as in international business law and the law governing international commercial arbitration. It thus arises from a number of sources and a multiplicity of governance arrangements, including governance both with and without government. For some, it represents novel forms of governance that are constituting a new public domain: "the complex of more or less formalized bundles of rules, roles, and relationships that define the social practices of state and non-state actors interacting in various issue areas, rather than in formal interstate organizations" (Kennedy 1997, 549n4). For others it involves a "globalization of the mind" by transnational social, cultural, intellectual, and ideological forces that shape elite opinion and structure the legal field (Arthurs 1997). Indeed, as Philip Alston (1997, 435) observes, international lawyers are involved as "handmaidens of globalization": "Whether the focus is on exchange rates, monetary policy, arms control, chemical weapons, land mines, climate change, the ozone layer, endangered species, forest conservation, the rights of minorities, international trade or regional integration," international lawyers facilitate the imposition of constraints on states.

As intermediaries between business and capital (L. Friedman et al. 1988), lawyers are deeply implicated in transnational law making and contribute significantly to the increasing juridification of social relations under late capitalism. *Juridification* involves the framing of political issues and debates in terms of juridical argumentation, the adoption of law-like standards and disciplines, and the proliferation of court-like mechanisms of dispute resolution (Cutler 2005). International lawyers are very much at the centre of these developments, creating law through private contractual practices and creative legal engineering that makes law work for capital (McBarnet 1984; Powell 1993) and then diffusing the law through the practices of transnational law firms and networks of private lawyers' associations and commercial arbitration tribunals. It is the day-to-day practice of law that creates law, at times transforming existing legal forms and in other instances creating innovative legal forms (Powell 1993). For example, US law firms were instrumental in creating and globalizing innovative laws governing mergers and acquisitions and hostile takeovers, such as the "poison pill"[2] and other takeover defences, as well as new contractual forms for venture capital arrangements, financial derivatives, and Internet commerce. Together with lawyers in the United Kingdom, these firms have created new corporate bankruptcy practices that have gained currency throughout the world (see Powell 1993). Lawyers were also instrumental in the reconceptualization of services provision as tradable goods under the Uruguay Round of the multilateral trade negotiations, producing the General Agreement on Trade in Services (GATS), which creates a delocalized legal regime that is revolutionizing local services provision (see Drake and Nicolaides 1992).

Private law making is a practice that has been occurring for over a millennium. Indeed, the history of private international commercial law is bound up with transformations in political economy and governance associated with moves from feudal to capitalist political economies and from medieval to modern political structures. In the feudal period, merchants engaged in long-distance and wholesale trade exercised considerable autonomy in the creation and enforcement of merchant laws, known as the medieval law merchant or *lex mercatoria*. They had their own system of law that was customary in origin in that it was based upon the everyday practices of merchants. Some of the practices were inherited from earlier civilizations and adapted over time as commercial needs and usages changed, including letters of credit, promissory notes, and maritime corporate forms and insurance principles such as partnerships, commenda, and the general average (see Cutler 2003, 113-40). Medieval merchants held their own courts for the settlement of their disputes, and notaries travelled with the merchants, bringing merchant law along with them. These courts operated more like contemporary arbitration tribunals in a significantly delocalized setting in that they were neither subject to the local commercial laws nor enforced by the local political or legal authorities. The medieval law merchant system was thus highly autonomous, although the distinctions between private and public spheres and between domestic and international law were not yet in evidence.

The historical roles played by merchants, merchant law, and merchant courts came to be obscured by emerging distinctions between public and private activity that regard the latter as fundamentally apolitical in character and effect. Their roles were also obscured by the emergence of centralized states, which in the process of state building came to absorb the autonomous law merchant system into their national legal orders, giving rise to the differentiation between domestic and international law. The law merchant was thus reconfigured domestically as private international trade law (Cutler 2003). However, contemporary developments associated with economic globalization and the transnationalization of commercial law and practices are regarded by many as evidence of the emergence of a similarly delocalized modern law merchant. Indeed, the ability of modern merchants to delocalize transactions by choosing non-national bodies of law and procedure to govern their transactions, which are then enforced in similarly delocalized and private international commercial arbitration tribunals, is reminiscent of the medieval law merchant order. Also significant is the central role that merchant customs and practices played historically in shaping and creating merchant law. Today, geographically mobile international lawyers, mega-law firms, and elite networks of lawyers and their business associations work the law and contribute to the diffusion of merchant law throughout the developed world and increasingly into pockets of the developing world. Like their medieval counterparts, contemporary lawyers and law firms are through their practices creating a legal order that is increasingly privatized, denationalized, and delocalized.

Recognizing these privatizing and denationalizing tendencies creates discomfort for conventional analytical and theoretical approaches to international law, for it pushes up against the boundaries of international legal theory, which posits the state as forming the focal point of the legal universe. Gunther Teubner (2002, 199), in developing a conception of the law merchant as a self-regulating system of reflexive law, argues that an autonomous, self-validating, and self-referential *lex mercatoria* "breaks frames" of national law and of private international law. "'Breaking frames' is about the violence that the frame of law and the movement of law exert upon each other. The delimitation of law breaks the law, while the law breaks its delimitations." Teubner (ibid., 206-7) stresses that globalization and privatized rule making break the hierarchical frame of national legal orders and the "historical unity of law and state," resulting in a new heterarchical frame where non-state law is on an equal footing with other forms of "social rule-making." He further notes (ibid., 214) that "breaking frames is the business of social forces and the "objective social reality" of "fragmented globalization." This is neither an inevitable nor an organic process, as some hyperliberals might suggest, but one that turns on human agency and design: "Frames do not break by themselves, it is history that breaks frames, provoking us to build new ones" (ibid., 214).

Whether explicitly or implicitly, international legal scholars recognize that the field is undergoing a transition that is intimately connected to changes in political economy and state-society relations within states and between states, institutions, markets, and peoples. The notion of the *transnationalization of the legal field* has emerged as an analytical optic for capturing these transformations. Drawing on Pierre Bourdieu's conception of social fields (1987), scholars are analyzing new transnational and global transformations in society and political economy that are changing the roles of lawyers, the nature of law practices and operations of law firms, and the national legal fields within which they operate (Dezalay and Garth 1996; Trubek et al. 1994). The legal field is defined as "the ensemble of institutions and practices through which law is produced, interpreted, and incorporated into social decision-making" (Trubek et al. 1994, 411). The transnationalization of law subjects national legal fields to significant reordering and gives rise to tensions between the delocalizing and relocalizing tendencies of late capitalist and postmodern law. In addition, transnational law firms are deepening and intensifying legal disciplines on diverse trade, investment, and financial activities that are clustered around global cities such as London, New York, and Paris.[3] The common element is the central role played by the increasing uniformity of international commercial norms and practices and their diffusion through operations of proliferating transnational law firms and networks of lawyers and related professional groupings. These actors and institutions exhibit significant unity of purpose in developing the legal means for expanding private capital accumulation through the disciplining, and even dispossession and displacement, of local individuals, collectivities, and publics. The autonomy of the transnational legal field thus works against the formation of individual or collective local autonomy. However, the problematic nature of this state of affairs is rendered invisible by the obscurity of the processes by which private interests become sanctified through law. The next section reviews the processes by which private transnational governance has come to form a central place in the contemporary world order.

Private Transnational Governance and the Contemporary Historical Bloc

In addressing how the transnationalization of the legal field is "adapting to the dynamic tension between globalization and autonomy" or "coming into existence to address such a tension," it is important to recall a crucial insight offered by constructivists. This is the notion that law is not just something out there that acts or is acted upon. Rather, law is constitutive of the tension between globalization and autonomy. Indeed, privatized transnational law making emerged apace with and is an integral part of the global expansion of capitalism. As such, it is a constitutive element of the contemporary historical bloc, which is conceptualized as the complex of ideological, material, and institutional forces that form the foundation for world order (Cox with Sinclair 1996; Cutler 2003, 100-4).

A number of developments are typically identified as driving private transnational law making. These range from corporate legal responses to the globalizing business needs of clients or to competitive pressures to maintain or expand market shares posed by the transnationalization of other law firms or the entry of other service providers, such as accountancy firms, into the global provision of legal services; changes in global production patterns; worldwide deregulation and liberalization of trade in services; merger activity; deregulation of capital markets; expansion of global and regional trade; the proliferation of structural adjustment and privatization initiatives; renewed interest in the rule of law; the promotion of democracy through law; and increasing reliance on "soft law" to regulate corporate conduct. Although the influence of these factors is quite diverse, what is common to each is the significance of practice-based, or bottom-up, rule making. As Trubek et al. (1994, 411) illustrate, the key to "understanding global forces" is "legal practice" and how this practice is transforming national legal fields. They note the significance of "the embedded practices of lawyers, judges, and academics. They constitute the legal field as we understand it, whose logics are being transformed directly, and indirectly, by transnational interactions." This is possibly most evident in the way in which the legal regime governing international trade in services is expanding geographically to include most states and is deepening its reach. This expansion is transforming societies by delocalizing and globalizing the regulation of many matters formerly subject to national or local laws, such as the provision of education, health, sanitary, financial, legal, and a whole range of other services (see Drake and Nicolaides 1992).

The emphasis on the transformation of national politico-legal fields is instructive for it highlights the fact that transnationalized legal practice has both a national and a transnational face. This is consistent with the view that transnational law links local and global political economies in complex ways. Possibly even more important, though, is the notion that lawyers both respond to and create transformations in practice; that lawyers, as Teubner suggests, are engaged in reflexive practices. This notion is also consistent with the view that there is a mutuality of influence between human agents, such as lawyers, and politico-economic structures, such as capitalism (Cutler 2003, 2005). Indeed, "probing the links between law and capital also means forging theoretical links between the structures of law and capital and the empirically observed human actions which make them work" (McBarnet 1984, 232). The key players and institutions that appear are private international and transnational lawyers and law firms, commercial international arbitration courts, tribunals and arbitrators, and networks comprising international and transnational professional associations, business service providers, and experts often clustered in global cities. Common to all is the lawyer as practitioner. Significantly, as Doreen McBarnet (1984, 233) noted more than twenty years ago, "the legal profession is an essential element" in a "from-the-ground-up perspective on the relationship of law and capital"; they represent "the underbelly of routine legal practice" where, as "legal entrepreneurs," they routinely make law by establishing legal practice, by modifying existing legal forms by pushing beyond them, creating new ones, or "breaking frames" as Teubner suggests.

> But lawyers are not significant simply for translating factual disputes into clear cut legal terms precisely because there is a second tier to lawyers' work. The lawyer's role is also to work *on the law,* to interpret it, to seek loopholes in it, to *make the law fit the facts* of the client's activities and interests. Lawyers are not just translators but transformers and transcenders of law. (McBarnet 1984, 233)

McBarnet's insightful observation that the law governing capital takes a specifically permissive and facilitative form that is "less a tool than a raw material to be worked upon" (238) highlights the significance of practice and the reflexive dimension of lawyering. It also enables the conceptualization of international law as a form of practice that is deeply connected to the contemporary historical bloc and hegemonic relations, for it suggests that law takes on a form that is specific to the prevailing historical conditions (Cutler 2005; Marx 1976, chap. 1). It directs attention to the way that private international lawyers work the law as organic intellectuals articulating norms that develop a routinely commonsensical appeal as they are diffused through the business world as accepted practices, model contracts and rules, and statements of contractual principles. Relevant, as well, are the legal forms they develop that facilitate transnational capital accumulation by limiting the ability of individuals or local groups to contest their provisions. These include multilateral investment treaties and multilateral and regional trade agreements, such as the World Trade Organization (WTO), North American Free Trade Agreement (NAFTA), and Canada–United States Trade Agreement. Such agreements are entered into by states and form public international law that is directly binding upon states. Their discipline, however, extends beyond states to regulate the activities of private individuals and local communities that have no access to their private and delocalized dispute settlement mechanisms.

Conceiving of international law as a form of practice highlights the centrality of legal institutions and ideologies in the constitution of the hegemonic transnational capitalist class (Robinson 2004). In this regard, it is crucial to note that hegemony is a process through which a class or group establishes the conditions necessary to establish control, not just through force, but through ideologically capturing popular support as the articulator of the public interest or common sense. Law forms are, as Nicos Poulantzas (1978, 88) notes, the mechanism for "cementing together the social formation under the aegis of the dominant class." Law participates in the organization of consent, "including insofar as it masks the state monopolization of physical force, the mechanisms of ideological inculcation" (ibid., 82). Law operates hegemonically through processes of naturalization, rationalization, and universalization (Litowitz 2000). Indeed, today in the fields of international economic and business law the privatization and marketization of regulations governing labour relations, human rights, the environment, corporate ethics, and a variety of other substantive areas is naturalized as the commonsensical and, indeed, the best way to approach legal regulation. Neoliberal economic theories of law are marshalled to establish the inherent efficiency, the organic nature, and hence the economic rationality of private marketized regulation. Private codes of conduct, non-binding statements of principle, and "soft" legal regulations proliferate in both local and global politico-legal orders. Increasingly, economistic, marketized, and commodified criteria for enforcement establish the legal standard.

Once naturalized and rationalized, private legal ordering is then universalized through the operations of multi- and transnational law, tax, accounting, insurance, and financial firms; private business associations; international commercial arbitrators; and international organizations engaged in the unification, harmonization, and globalization of law (Picciotto and Mayne 1999). These firms, associations, and individuals function as the "organic intellectuals" and the *mercatocracy,* or merchant class (Cutler 2003), which transmit the logic of private law making throughout the world as a universal, rational, and natural system of ordering.

The transnational legal field writ large comprises a strikingly diverse variety of actors, institutions, networks, and processes within which legal practices are developed, applied, diffused, legitimated, and enforced. Transnational lawyers, law firms, and their networks and associations constitute a key dimension of the transnational legal field and are the focus of this study. However, significant as well are the practices of international bar associations, international business associations, international commercial arbitrators and their courts and tribunals, as well as national bodies participating in the harmonization and unification of international commercial law. While there is no overarching body that participates in the transnationalization of commercial law — as do, for example, the International Standards Association (ISO) or international accountancy organizations that regulate management standards and accounting practices — it is possible to identify the material, ideological, and institutional foundations of the emerging private transnationalized legal field. These foundations reflect the specific form that global and local political economies take under contemporary conditions of postmodernity and late capitalism.

Materially, postmodernity in law is reflected in legal pluralism, interlegality, and the porosity of law as multiple legal fields operate subnationally, nationally, regionally, and transnationally, cross-secting and overlapping. These fields simultaneously occupy the same space, linking local and domestic political economies and societies through the creation and expansion of legal regimes governing regional and international trade, commerce, banking, insurance, transportation, investment, finance, dispute resolution, human rights, the environment, and criminality (Santos 1987, 1995). Late capitalism in law is reflected in the increasing recourse to law to facilitate the displacement of welfare states by competition states through deregulation and privatized legal codes and procedures, in the intensification and expansion of legal disciplines facilitating transnational capital accumulation, and in the related tendency towards flexible production and "soft law" re-regulation of labour relations, consumer protection, environmental practices, and corporate ethics (Harvey 1990; Robinson 2004). In some places, as in the case of many developing countries, law under late capitalism is working a displacement and dispossession of local production and culture. This process, which Karl Marx (1976, 875) analyzed as "primitive accumulation" — that is, "the historical process of divorcing the producer from the means of production" — is a characteristic feature of late capitalist legal regulation. This is because it is law and increasingly juridified and commodified social relations that create the material reality, the ideological acceptance, and the institutional framework for the privatization of public assets, such as water supplies and industries, throughout the world, as well as the conversion of common and collective property rights to exclusive private property rights, as in the intellectual property regime. As David Harvey (2003, 146) observes, "primitive accumulation, in short, entails appropriation and co-optation of pre-existing cultural and social achievements as well as confrontation and suppression."[4]

Institutionally and ideologically, postmodern and late capitalist formulations of law inform the activities of key international and regional governmental organizations and associations, including the United Nations, the International Monetary Fund, the World Bank and the Organisation for Economic Co-operation and Development, the United Nations Commission on International Trade Law (UNCITRAL), the WTO, NAFTA, and the European Union. These institutions form crucial sites for generating both the material and ideological basis for the continuing expansion of global capitalism. In addition, less visible but increasingly important private associations participate in the constitution of the laws that govern the global political economy. These associations include the International Chamber of Commerce (ICC), the International Law Commission, and the Trilateral Commission; transnational business corporations, cartels, and private business, and accounting, tax, and lawyers' associations (Trubek et al. 1994; Cain and Harrington 1994). These institutions and associations are globalizing a commodified form of law through private regulatory frameworks that assess legality according to criteria of economic efficiency and effective market discipline (Cutler, Haufler, and Porter 1999; Cutler 2005). They contribute to the discursive and ideological significance of international law as the creator of the mythology and common sense understandings that undergird the perceived legitimacy of the contemporary historical bloc. This understanding constitutionalizes neoliberal market discipline and global competitiveness and economic efficiency as the *grundnorms* of an increasingly transnational historical bloc (Gill 2003).

Transnational Law Firms and Privatized Governance

Lawyers and law firms that operate transnationally are increasingly significant participants in the transnationalization of the legal field. Indeed, their geographical expansion through the creation of foreign offices, mergers into mega-law firms located in key hubs and global cities, and the formation of networks and strategic alliances, as well as their expanded scope and reach into societies through the juridification of increasing areas of commerce, industry, and trade all contribute to the extensity and intensity of transnational regulation. Transnational lawyers are moving beyond the international lawyers' realm of "lawyering" into business consulting, risk assessment, management, and dispute resolution through their intimate links to the international commercial arbitration community and large financial institutions, as well as through their deepening associations with accounting, tax, insurance, and other business service providers.

Private transnational rule making thus occurs at multiple levels and links local and global political economies in complex ways. Delocalized commercial norms are generated by lawyers and law firms and then are diffused through their business associations and institutional expansion. Dispute settlement also occurs in delocalized normative and procedural frameworks but, significantly, is relocalized when international commercial arbitration awards are enforced, as they must be, in national courts of law. This process of de- and relocalization is referred to by one scholar as "transnational liftoff and juridical touchdown" (Wai 2001, 29) and forms a dialectic specific to postmodern and late capitalist law (Cutler 2004; Sassen 2002).

Significantly, it is transnational lawyers and their firms that manage this process of de- and relocalization. In fact, transnational law firms, together with the lawyers that constitute them, are among the most significant participants involved in creating the material, ideological, and institutional foundations for the contemporary historical bloc. International commercial lawyers are often described as working at the "edges" of legal rules, bringing their entrepreneurial talents to the development of new contractual forms to meet the changing needs of their clients (Quack 2004, 10). Mega-law firms diffuse new practices and legal forms through transnational mergers,

networks, and strategic alliances, and thus their areas of substantive expertise, location, and organizational form are analytically significant.

While there is no generally accepted definition of a "transnational law
firm," and, as Richard Abel (1994, 739) notes, there is no adequate theory
of how or why law firms grow, firms may be characterized as transnational
in two interrelated ways. Law firms may be transnational in *areas of substantive practice*, specializing, for example, in international trade or investment law, intellectual property law, international commercial arbitration,
international sale of goods, cross-border mergers and acquisitions, hostile
takeovers, joint ventures, capital market transactions, debt restructuring,
privatizations, and the like.[5] Law firms may also be transnational in *organization*, involving both spatial location and organizational form. Indeed,
with regard to spatial organization, it is possible to develop a typology
of law firms on a continuum from domestic at one end to transnational
at the other, with international and multinational organizational forms in
between (Silver 2000). The transnational law firm is characterized by multiple locations often concentrated in major commercial centres, such as
New York, London, Paris, and Brussels. Indeed, the geographical distribution of transnational law firms reveals a heavy concentration in what Saskia
Sassen (1998) refers to as the "global cities" and the major hubs of global
capitalist activity. In contrast, their concentration declines outside of these
hubs, as in the case of the Middle East, and falls off dramatically for Africa.

Law firms may also be transnational in *organizational form*. Again, one
might conceive of a continuum where at one end the "national" law firm
services foreign-based clients from home. At the other end is the "transnational" law firm operating through offices established in multiple foreign
jurisdictions and blending home or national and local legal expertise,
working to delocalize the firm's national identity. The delocalization of
firm identity is achieved by de-emphasizing the firm's home office location and localizing the foreign offices by staffing them with local lawyers
and those with local legal expertise. Baker & McKenzie was the first to
adopt the practice of hiring local lawyers to staff its foreign offices, leading
to criticism that it functioned like a franchise operation, the "McDonald's"
of the legal world, with unreliable quality control. Other firms, however,
such as Skadden, Arps and Clifford Chance have followed suit in an effort
to delocalize their firm identities.

Delocalization of firm identity may also be achieved through mergers with
local firms or firms doing business in foreign jurisdictions (e.g., Linklaters),
or through joint ventures (e.g., Allen & Overy) and looser associations, and

alliances. In some cases, legal consultants, although not legally authorized to practise law in a foreign jurisdiction, are able to offer advice and provide local sensitivity and expertise. The top-ten transnational law firms reveal a rich number of organizational designs, often utilizing all strategies.

The transnational law firm is also characterized by a delocalization of law making through reliance on unified databases, legal forms, and practices, as well as transnational sources of law, forms of law, and dispute settlement norms and procedures, such as those emanating from international institutions such as UNCITRAL, the International Institute for the Unification of Private Law (UNIDROIT), and the ICC (Sassen 2002, 195).

A review of the ten leading law firms reveals that a number of factors have figured in the transnationalization of their substantive legal practices and their organizational design. The major expansion of law firms both geographically and in substantive areas of legal practice occurred since the 1980s and must be seen as part of a larger process of institutional adaptation to changes in global and local political economies associated with the advent of flexible production (Coffey and Bailly 1992) and the geopolitics of what David Harvey (2003) refers to as the "new imperialism." The "hallmark" of flexible production in the service sector is vertical disintegration into a network of small and medium-sized specialist enterprises that supports the activities of the main establishment. The key goal is enhancing the flexibility of the firm to provide services through pliable and fluid labour market structures and an adaptable and a responsive social division of labour creating external economies of scale (Coffey and Bailly 1992, 858). Increasingly, this involves the development of networks among law firms, some of which are created through mergers (e.g., the three leading British firms, Freshfields, Clifford Chance, and Linklaters, merged with German law firms) (Morgan and Quack 2005), while others operate through strategic alliances and "best friends" relationships (e.g., the Big Five accounting firms). As Peter Charlton (2004), the London managing partner for the London-based transnational law firm Clifford Chance, said, globalization "is not about scale, it's about having the right network."

In addition, the geographic expansion has occurred in waves, driven initially by the needs of globalizing clients, and later by competitive pressures to maintain or extend market shares threatened by the geographic and substantive legal expansion of other law firms. American firms led the expansions, at first to service an expanding client base created by the privatization of large industrial works and projects once funded by governments. The wave of privatizations, mergers, and acquisitions throughout eastern Europe and elsewhere provided "new terrains of accumulation," the neoliberal solution to capitalism's chronic problem of overaccumulation (Harvey 2003, 149). The overseas expansion of American law firms transformed the "mode of production of law" by exporting American-style lawyering and large multi-purpose national law firms, referred to as "Cravathist," pioneered in the nineteenth century by Paul Cravath (Trubeck et al. 1994, 423). They were followed by law firms in the United Kingdom and now German law firms (Morgan and Quack 2005).

While there have been efforts to delocalize the identities and operations of transnational law firms, the mega-firms have nevertheless left a pronounced Anglo-American imprint. Indeed, American law firms have been leaders in standard setting, as a result of the dominance of us-based financial institutions and capital markets, as well as American "deal experience," and an entrepreneurial and innovative style of business lawyering (Trubeck et al. 1994). Although some American legal expansion into Europe occurred in the 1960s and 1970s, it was with the neoliberal restructuring of the 1980s and 1990s that the transnational law firm really took shape. The deregulation of capital markets, privatization of industries and sectors, emergence of global production systems, mergers, and acquisitions, European single market, and deepening of trade liberalization in the wto and nafta regimes all generated significant demand for legal services and American corporate know-how. As one observer notes, "American business law has become a kind of global *jus commune* incorporated explicitly or implicitly into transnational contracts and beginning to be incorporated into the case law and even the statutes of many other nations" (Dasgupta 2003).

New York law firms, in particular, played a central role in diffusing American legal practices and innovative legal forms in the areas of financial transactions (e.g., derivatives, securitization, public offerings) and project financing (e.g., debt restructuring and leveraged buyouts) and in defending against hostile takeovers (e.g., "poison pill" and other defences) (Powell 1993; Spar 1997). The leading American law firms (Baker & McKenzie; White & Case; Coudert Brothers) have concentrated in key global cities (particularly London) and have significantly delocalized their identities, constituting "homeless firms" and a transnational elite community (Beaverstock, Smith, and Taylor 2000; Beaverstock 2001).

By the end of the 1990s, American firms were experiencing competition from other service providers, such as the Big Five global accounting firms, which were entering the legal service market. In addition, the leading British firms established their transnational presence, geographically surpassing US firms. This expansion is supported by the importance of London's financial markets and the reliance on English common law and courts as the preferred legal systems for contractual dispute resolution in insurance, shipping, and corporate finance. London's law firms are regarded by British analysts as having a significant competitive advantage "because of the legacy of the British Empire which installed English legal systems around the globe"; the centrality of English law in project financing and privatizations; London's continuing significance as a financial and banking centre and its geographical location and transport links to Europe, the United States, and Asia; the deregulatory climate; and the fact that English is the language of global commerce (Beaverstock, Smith, and Taylor 1999). A mixture of demand and supply factors are associated with the transnationalization of London law firms (e-mail, Internet, electronic document transfer, videoconferencing), including client demand, spreading of risk, competition, merger activity, technological advances, and developments in the European Union, especially the European Monetary Union (ibid.).

Today, quite clearly, the top transnational firms originate from the United Kingdom and the United States and are associated with Anglo-American hegemony in legal forms and practices. These hegemonic legal forms reach deeply into states, conditioning their local productive relations. Possibly the most visible illustration, and one that is increasingly controversial, is the ability of foreign investors to regulate local economic conditions under bilateral investment agreements (BITs) entered into by the governments of the investor and host state and enforced privately by transnational corporations under delocalized law and in delocalized legal proceedings. BITs may well form the central most significant hegemonic transnational legal form.

Private Transnational Law Making and Human Autonomy

Private transnational law making by mega-firms raises important concerns about human autonomy, both individual and collective. Concerns about the "democratic deficit" evident in private transnational law making are increasingly being voiced even by those who see private legal ordering as a valuable and legitimate means of regulation (Wai 2001). As Teubner (2002, 208) argues, private transnational law making requires new forms of democratic legitimacy.

The close association of transnational law firms with capital markets and the major financial institutions raises acute concerns about the hegemony and structural power of transnational capital (Gill and Law 1988, chap. 7). The ability of capital to create and apply laws tailored to meet its specific interests is a form of private-interest government that is difficult to reconcile with the rule of law. It also raises a host of issues concerning the public persona of lawyers and law firms, for lawyers are subject to multiple duties that may well conflict (Arthurs 1999). They have a legal duty to their clients to advance their interests, as well as legal and business responsibilities to their law firms. However, lawyers also have public duties to the state as officers of the court and as guardians of the rule of law. Indeed, it is this public persona that differentiates the legal profession from other professions and is used to legitimize self-regulation by the law profession (Whelan 2001). The blurring of these roles as lawyers operate increasingly in entrepreneurial and business-development capacities, often working in close association with other businesses that do not share similar duties to the public, is deeply problematic and is causing some jurisdictions to rethink and restrict the mergers and associations of law firms with non-legal-service providers, such as accountancy firms.

International arbitration lawyers freely admit that their practices often touch upon matters of public interest and raise the concern that market considerations might outweigh competing public interests (Wai 2001, 222). It is crucial, however, to recognize that while transnational private law making challenges basic understandings of the rule of law and democratic accountability, this is not a necessarily unidirectional process. Indeed, recognizing the dialectical tension between the delocalizing and relocalizing operations of private transnational law directs attention to the conditions of possibility for emancipation through and against law. It raises the emancipatory potential of private international law and local intervention to enhance human autonomy. Highly relevant here is the ability to assert local controls through antitrust and securities legislation that combines private remedies and public purposes, or through tort law, delict, and the laws of contract that engage in social regulation by protecting third-party interests and the interests of consumers or involve environmental protection, collective bargaining, or the protection of weaker parties in economic transactions (Wai 2001; Seck 1999).

Similarly, efforts to assert local autonomy over transnational corporate activity by holding corporations accountable for their commitments to corporate social responsibility in labour, human rights, environmental, and corporate relations become significant (Cutler 2006). Indeed, there is increasing evidence of subordinate groups organizing and expressing their opposition to privatized legal regimes, which may construct an alternative counter-hegemony. The International Labour Rights Fund (ILRF), a Washington-based advocacy organization, used the US Alien Tort Claims Act as the basis for a successful claim by Burmese workers against human rights abuses committed by the transnational oil corporation Unocal. Similar actions have been taken against other transnational oil, gas, and minerals corporations (Cutler 2006). Lawyers are also working with trade unionists, and activists are developing legal strategies to ensure that corporations such as Wal-Mart observe international and local labour standards (Cornish and Stewart 2005). ILRF is presently examining labour practices in Bangladesh, Nicaragua, Indonesia, and China, and Wal-Mart has been taken to court in Canada and the United States to enforce domestic labour standards (ibid.).

Resistance to international intellectual property law is mounting in India, Malaysia, Nepal, Indonesia, Thailand, Sri Lanka, Bangladesh, and the Philippines, as well as in Nigeria, where indigenous peoples are organizing and demanding compensation and remedies for rights dispossessed by transnational mining, logging, pharmaceutical, and oil corporations under BITS and other agreements. Other examples of local resistance to the transnationalization of neoliberal market civilization may also be found in the mobilization of labour in Asia, Latin America, Mexico, and North America; challenges by citizen groups in Canada and the United States to corporate taxation laws and policies that shift tax burdens to individuals; Islamic social movements; opposition to structural adjustment policies in Bangladesh and Zimbabwe; and civil society mobilization in the anti-globalization protests. These are indications of fractures in the discipline of neoliberal economic law. Mark Rupert (2000) cautioned that right-wing populist opposition to neoliberal discipline in the United States has been recognized and is generating *trasformismo* in efforts by world leaders and international organizations to "sustain globalisation" by giving it a "human face." However, he also noted (ibid., 153) that "resistance to globalisation has opened up possibilities for new forms of political practice which are not circumscribed by the territorial state or by the conventional separation of politics from the economy." Indeed, a critical understanding of the transnational legal field highlights the significance of transnational legal forms, transnational lawyers, and transnational law firms in the constitution and potential reconstitution of world order, particularly at the intersection of local and global political economies. Under global capitalism, transnational private law is central to the production and reproduction of commodified and marketized definitions of culture and civilization that reach right into local political economies and frame the conditions of possibility for local autonomy. A critical conception of law highlights the centrality of transnational law firms to the localization of global capitalism. This conception of international law identifies important openings for contestation of this potentially one-dimensional market civilization both through and against law. The distinction is critical and opens up the possibility of practices that, through and against law, can foster human autonomy.

chapter 9

Transnational Actors and Global Social Welfare Policy: The Limits of Private Institutions in Global Governance

Michael Webb with Emily Sinclair

ECONOMIC GLOBALIZATION OFTEN IS blamed for imposing international constraints on national social welfare policies, constraints that allegedly are reinforced by neoliberal ideology and the policy prescriptions of the international financial institutions (IFIS) discussed in Chapter 2. Thus, some critics claim that both the economic and political dimensions of globalization limit the autonomy of the political institutions — national states — that have been primarily responsible for achieving social welfare goals for at least the past century. Recent studies reveal that fears of lost autonomy in social welfare policy were exaggerated in relation to advanced capitalist countries, but that economic and political globalization do impose significant constraints on the ability of developing country governments to sustain social welfare programs (Kaufman and Segura-Ubiergo 2001; Rudra 2002; Genschel 2004).

At the same time, an important non-economic dimension of globalization is the proliferation of transnational non-governmental organizations (NGOS). This trend reflects improvements in communications and transportation across national borders, improvements in education and living standards, and growing global consciousness (Lipschutz 1992; Rosenau 1990; Scholte 2000). These phenomena enhance the autonomy of those individuals who have access to them and enable people to work together at greater distances, giving rise to the potential for new institutions to develop to promote values and interests shared by people in different countries. The result could be to enhance the autonomy of groups based on shared values rather than geographic contiguity. Scholarly and popular attention since the 1990s focused in particular on the growth of NGOs pursuing progressive goals in areas such as human rights, gender issues, and development.

Some argue that the efforts of these actors could offset the erosion of government welfare programs by pressuring governments and inter-governmental organizations (IGOS) to pay greater attention to social welfare, encouraging the spread of cosmopolitan values that encourage states and other actors to focus more attention on social welfare or, more profoundly, developing the capacity to achieve social goals through their own actions (Lipschutz 1992; Wapner 1996; Edwards 1999). In effect, the loss of social policy autonomy by national governments in the face of globalizing pressures could be accompanied by the growing autonomy of non-governmental actors pursuing goals similar to those that states have difficulty pursuing. Thus, the growth of NGOs often is seen as a progressive development by those who distrust governments and IGOS (Falk 2003; Mittelman 2000). While we do not systematically examine either the loss of national government autonomy or the extent to which NGO efforts constitute an effective substitute, we do examine the extent to which NGOS are developing normative autonomy and the ability to influence debates about social welfare policy at the global level.

The possible roles for NGOs in global social welfare policy are best understood in the context of the emergence of networked forms of global governance. In place of the hierarchical, state-centric form of governance that characterized much of the nineteenth and twentieth centuries, theorists such as Manuel Castells ("network society"), Jan Aart Scholte ("polycentric governance"), and James Rosenau ("multicentric world") argue that governance today involves networks linking states, substate and interstate organizations, and non-state actors — networks in which states are no longer as dominant as in the pre-globalization era (Castells 1996; Scholte 2002; Rosenau 1990). Network forms of governance create the potential for non-state actors such as NGOS to have a much greater social impact. As a result, globalization could even have a net positive impact on social justice, as many national governments did little to promote respect for social justice when global economic constraints were looser than they are today. New transnational political forces could pressure governments and IGOS to pay more attention to social welfare or, more profoundly, develop some concrete ability to achieve social welfare goals through their own actions.

This chapter examines whether NGOs actually are developing the ability to shape and even provide social welfare programs at a global level as an example of how new institutions or institutionalized practices are coming into existence to address the tension between market-oriented globalization and state autonomy. Global social policy is understood here to include efforts at levels above that of individual states to alleviate poverty, redistribute the gains from economic activity, and protect vulnerable groups from economic instability. Internationally, global social policy is closely tied to foreign aid and non-commercial private financial transfers from rich to poor countries.

As part of this examination, we consider to what degree NGOs are able to act with autonomy from the same forces that are allegedly constraining the autonomy of states — global market pressures, neoliberal ideology, and intergovernmental organizations committed to economic liberalization. Some critics see NGOs as merely another element of dominant global forces. Mustapha Kamal Pasha and David Blaney (1998, 419), for example, argue that most transnational activism "takes for granted global capitalism as the infrastructure of recent trends." Thus, while such activism "may be a site of possible challenges to the oligarchical organizations of contemporary global political economy," it also represents the continued hegemony of "a narrow band of humanity." From this perspective, NGOs are being incorporated into a neoliberal model of civil society that ultimately sustains rather than challenges dominant approaches to global development (Lipschutz with Rowe 2005; Morris-Suzuki 2000).

In assessing NGOs' autonomy in line with the orientation provided in the opening chapter of this volume, we begin with David Held's understanding of autonomy as connoting "the capacity of human beings to reason self-consciously, to be self-reflective and to be self-determining. It involves the ability to deliberate, judge, choose and act (or not act as the case may be) upon different possible courses of action" (Held 1995, 146). Consequently, we are looking for evidence about whether NGOs involved in global social policy have developed shared understandings of appropriate social welfare policy distinct from the understandings shared by dominant globalizing forces. We label this dimension of autonomy "normative autonomy." But autonomy means more than just a capacity for *self*-reflection and *self*-government; it also involves the ability to act effectively to shape social conditions. In relation to this dimension, we will be looking for evidence that social policy NGOs have the collective ability to influence global patterns in social policy provision. Such influence could be manifest at a number of levels, ranging from that of concrete social conditions in areas in which NGOs run projects, to the policies of individual national governments, to the approaches taken by IGOs. Our focus is on the last of these, on the assumption that policies and norms developed in international forums matter because they shape the concrete actions of IGOs and may exert normative pressure on states to alter their own policies. However, we also consider how funding patterns affect NGOs' ability to take direct action themselves to redistribute resources and protect vulnerable groups from economic instability. The mobilization of independent resources is key to NGOs' ability to offset the erosion of state efforts in the area of social welfare and, thus, also to an assessment of the changing roles of NGOs in global governance.

To speak of "NGO autonomy" is to speak of a form of collective autonomy. As noted in Chapter 1, states were traditionally seen as the key collective actor manifesting autonomy in world politics. Globalizing processes, however, have generated claims for collective autonomy on the part of numerous actors other than states, including economic institutions like transnational corporations, social groups such as indigenous peoples or ethnic groups whose members reside in more than one state, or even IGOs and international law. For NGOs, as with any collective actor, we must also consider the extent to which their values and actions genuinely reflect the views of their members. Power disparities among participants can be substantial, particularly between groups based in the North and those based in the South. Thus, we will also examine whether shared orientations are developed in a fashion that allows for contributions from a wide variety of NGOs.

The autonomy of non-state actors also depends heavily on the ideas and practices of states and IGOs. Improvements in communications and education help create the possibility of transnational activism, but the international political opportunity structure also is crucial (Tarrow 2005; Reimann 2006). International cooperation, regimes, organizations, and meetings matter in a number of ways. IGOs can provide threats that help motivate transnational action (as in the case of structural adjustment programs), but they also create spaces in which geographically dispersed non-state actors can come together to pursue common goals, develop shared understandings, and possibly even develop shared senses of identity. International meetings provide focal points for transnational activism, and the rules and procedures adopted by IGOs can encourage or discourage the participation of non-state actors in international and global political processes. This chapter pays particular attention to how the practices of the UN system influence NGO autonomy.

In order to assess NGOs' normative autonomy and concrete influence, we first examine their participation in the World Summit on Social Development (WSSD) held in Copenhagen in 1995 and the WSSD+5 meeting in Geneva in 2000. UN world conferences like the WSSD are largely about shaping global norms, and they provide NGOs with an opportunity to promote normative change. Such conferences rarely involve the negotiation of concrete, enforceable agreements, though NGOs typically lobby for concrete commitments to which states can subsequently be held accountable (Schechter 2005, 8-9; Friedman, Hochstetler, and Clark 2005). Next, we briefly examine efforts by development NGOs to raise resources from non-government sources. This is crucial to the exercise of NGO autonomy, because funding from government sources always comes with conditions that limit the ability of recipient organizations to decide what programs to pursue. NGOs' private fundraising efforts also help us assess NGOs' success in promoting the development of norms that encourage people to support global social welfare programs.

NGOs at the World Summit on Social Development

The WSSD was one of a number of major world conferences organized by the United Nations in the mid-1990s (Schechter 2005). The decision to convene a summit to address the problems of poverty, unemployment, and social integration reflected the success NGOs had had in raising the profile of social issues after the preoccupation with economic policy and structural adjustment among development policy makers in the 1980s. Several thousand representatives from hundreds of NGOs participated in the conference and the parallel NGO Forum, lobbying diplomats, seeking media attention to put pressure on governments to adopt more generous social policies, and networking with their counterparts from around the world. Even though the actual decision-making processes that produced the conference agreements remained the preserve of states, often working behind closed doors, the WSSD provided NGOs with an important opportunity to raise global consciousness about social policy problems and press for policies guided by social democratic rather than liberal norms.[1]

A starting point for assessing NGO autonomy at the WSSD is to identify the perspectives NGOs brought to the debates and compare these to the perspectives offered by governments and IGOs. Such a comparison provides a basis for assessing the strength of shared NGO understandings about global social policy as distinct from those of the dominant institutions behind economic globalization. To address this issue, we examined NGO, government, and IFI approaches to social welfare policy at the WSSD in relation to liberal and social democratic approaches to social welfare policy (Esping-Andersen 1990; Jessop 2002; Therien 1999). Most NGOs involved in the WSSD shared a social democratic orientation towards social policy.[2] Indeed, the degree of substantive policy agreement among NGOs was quite remarkable despite other differences among them.[3] They were deeply concerned about inequality as well as absolute poverty, believing that all people have a right to a decent, reasonably equal standard of living to be achieved by means of extensive universal social programs. They believe that careful management of market economies is needed to ensure that economic growth is directed towards serving the needs of all citizens. At the international level, social democratic NGOs favour cooperation through strong IGOs based on universal membership (rather than donor-dominated institutions like the World Bank and the International Monetary Fund [IMF]) to manage the international economy, regulate private market actors, and ensure an equitable distribution of the gains from international commerce.

Most states approached social welfare from a predominantly liberal perspective, as did the IFIs (which participated in the WSSD in a consultative capacity). Many EU countries, Canada, and several other states expressed sympathy for some social democratic goals yet usually came down in favour of policy options that were more liberal in orientation. Most Northern states believed that promoting economic growth through market-oriented development strategies was the key solution to poverty, and they favoured targeted social programs to provide basic protections only to those in greatest need. Developing country governments' approaches cannot easily be characterized on the social democratic–liberal continuum, in part because they wanted international deliberations to focus on the international economic environment and believed that the design of domestic social welfare policy fell within the scope of national sovereignty. Many shared the liberal emphasis on economic growth and better access to international markets but tended to see structural adjustment programs as a cause of poverty rather than as a solution to it and argued vehemently for debt relief. As we will see, Southern governments shared the latter views with NGOs, but Southern governments rejected NGO proposals that would have limited Southern governments' social and economic policy autonomy (Friedman, Hochstetler, and Clark 2005, 143-4, and statements cited in endnote 2).

Key Issues for NGOs

On the basis of a reading of NGO statements, WSSD documents, and reports from the International Institute of Sustainable Development (IISD), we can identify four issues that received consistent attention from NGOs at the WSSD: the causes of poverty; the link between economic and social policy in structural adjustment; the need for increased and redistributive funding for social programs; and the role of the UN, the IFIs, and civil society in global social policy. We examine each of these issues in turn, focusing on both dimensions of autonomy identified in the introduction to this chapter: the degree to which NGOs exhibited normative autonomy from governments and other dominant globalizing forces, and the extent to which NGOs were able to exercise influence on the conference outcome.

The Causes of Poverty
Most NGOs have viewed poverty as a structural consequence of the market-oriented economic systems promoted by Northern governments and the IFIs, and their views did have some influence at the summit. The Copenhagen Declaration released by governments at the conclusion of their meetings recognized that while globalization has resulted in economic growth, it has triggered intensified poverty, unemployment, and social disintegration, and it acknowledged that "poverty, lack of productive employment and social disintegration ... [are] a manifestation of ineffectiveness in the functioning of markets" (United Nations 1995, 5-7). However, the declaration identified the causes of poverty in terms of the inability of individuals to access economic opportunities created by market-based economic systems, not as arising from those systems themselves. Many of the solutions, therefore, focused on measures to enable people living in poverty to participate more fully in the market economy rather than on regulating or restructuring the market economy itself (United Nations 1995, 32-6, 41-2; see also Felice 1997).

NGOs, who were highly critical of this and other liberal features of the Copenhagen Declaration, created their own "Copenhagen Alternative Declaration" at the conclusion of the conference. The Alternative Declaration stated that "the over-reliance that the documents place on un-accountable 'open, free-market forces' ... aggravates, rather than alleviates, the current global social crises" (NGO Forum 1995).

Economic Policy, Social Policy, and Structural Adjustment

Many NGOs blamed structural adjustment programs (SAPs) for worsen ing poverty and social exclusion in their preoccupation with economic growth. Consequently these NGOs favoured an integrated approach in which economic policies would directly address social problems rather than simply aim to promote economic growth on the assumption that growth will solve social problems. NGOs and developing country governments succeeded in getting explicit language in conference documents to address the "adverse social consequences of ... SAPs and the need for socially responsive and responsible structural adjustment" (*Earth Negotiations Bulletin* [*ENB*] 10 [36]; see also *ENB* 10 [11]). This was a notable achievement, as it challenged what had been an article of faith in the IFIs and among some Northern governments. Much of the Copenhagen Declaration, in such areas as its strong approval of market-oriented economics and its tendency to propose non-economic policies to address social problems, implicitly accepted the separation between economic and social policy. But other clauses tempered this liberal orientation by proposing to achieve social democratic goals through liberal means. For instance, Commitment Eight pledged to ensure "that when structural adjustment programs are agreed to they include social development goals" (United Nations 1995, 22).

However, the policy solutions suggested in the declaration largely took the form of adding "basic" (i.e., minimal) and "targeted" social protections to the liberal economic model rather than altering the basic model (United Nations 1995, 22, 53). NGOs, in contrast, favoured universal programs to promote solidarity and social justice, and framed anti-poverty, health, and education programs in the language of human rights. In their Alternative Declaration, NGOs "reject[ed] the notion of reducing social policies in developing countries to a 'social safety net,' presented as the human face of structural adjustment policies in the WSSD documents" (NGO Forum 1995). Even so, in the IISD's view, this was the first time developed countries had agreed that "social effects must be addressed in the implementation of SAPs" (*ENB* 10 [36]).

Redistributive Funding for Social Development

Key NGO priorities in the area of funding included concrete commitments to increase foreign aid flows and redistributive measures to mitigate global inequality. They called yet again for the rich countries to commit to spending 0.7 percent of their gross national product on official development assistance (ODA). The International Council on Social Welfare (ICSW), supported by other NGOs, promoted the so-called 20:20 initiative, whereby developed countries would commit to allocating at least 20 percent of their ODA to basic social programs, and developing countries would commit to spending at least 20 percent of their government budgets on such programs (Schechter 2005, 141). However, this initiative was strongly resisted by developing country governments, which viewed it as simply another Northern intrusion on national sovereignty (Friedman, Hochstetler, and Clark 2005, 143-4). More generally, NGOs emphasized the need to reduce inequality by redistributing income and resources, both from rich to poor countries and from wealthy to poor people within countries. However, they had few concrete proposals for achieving redistribution, aside from debt cancellation and the implementation of a Tobin tax on foreign exchange transactions (NGO Forum 1995).

The Copenhagen Declaration acknowledged some of the goals identified by NGOs but included little that would help achieve them. It supported "increasing significantly and/or utilizing more efficiently the resources allocated to social development" (United Nations 1995, 23), but the 0.7 percent ODA target and the 20:20 initiative were identified as desirable goals rather than firm commitments (ibid., 24 and 83). These suggestions were not taken seriously by donor states, most of which cut ODA sharply after 1995. Governments also fell back on the traditional liberal solution: developing countries were encouraged to "implement macroeconomic and micro-economic policies to ensure sustained economic growth ... to support social development" (ibid., 23). Inequality was discussed throughout the declaration as meaning unequal access to resources and opportunities, not the actual unequal distribution of resources. The declaration contains no indication that even basic social services are entitlements or rights that should be provided by the state, as NGOs had argued ("Quality Benchmark" 1994; van Reisen 2000).

In sum, NGO views had a minimal impact on the core issues of funding for social programs and redistribution. The failure of NGO efforts in this area, combined with their inability to develop strong private sources of funding for social development (see below), reveals a persistent reality of civil society: governments are the only actors with the financial capacity to have a real impact, and NGOs are still able only to lobby from the outside. Transnational NGOs may exhibit normative and intellectual autonomy but usually lack the material capacity to put their distinctive social policy ideas into practice.

The Roles of the United Nations, the IFIs, and Civil Society

NGOs at the WSSD had two key demands in relation to institutions dealing with global social policy. First, they wanted the UN, through the Economic and Social Council (ECOSOC), to assume more control over international economic organizations, especially the World Bank and the IMF. The chapter by Pauly in this volume covers some of the relevant history in this regard, but the point is that NGOs continue to view the UN as more sympathetic to strong, direct international action on social policy than are institutions dominated by the advanced capitalist countries, and as much more open to NGO participation than are the IFIs (on the IFIs and civil society, see O'Brien et al., 2000). Second, NGOs wanted the IFIs, ECOSOC, and other IGOs to become more open and transparent and to involve "social movements and citizens' organizations at all stages in the negotiation of agreements, project implementation and monitoring" (NGO Forum 1995). NGOs were very critical of the tendency they saw at the WSSD (and in the IFIs) to portray people living in poverty as victims in need of external intervention rather than as active agents who could meaningfully contribute to poverty eradication (ENB 10 [22]). The NGOs wanted international efforts to empower civil society and to make social development policies more inclusive and more responsive to the views of the intended beneficiaries (see, e.g., Arunachalam 1995). The Copenhagen Alternative Declaration argued that "communities must gain control over the activities of all enterprises that affect their well-being, including transnational corporations" (NGO Forum 1995).

The Copenhagen Declaration did not support NGOs' call for an increased role for the UN in global social policy[4] because the developed donor countries were determined to maintain control of development assistance and advice through the IFIs. However, it did include commitments to improve consultations with civil society, and it adopted the language of "people-centred development" (United Nations 1995, 9). The provisions of the Programme of Action on social integration seek to empower civil society and give "community organizations greater involvement in the design and implementation of local projects" (ibid., 70). The IISD commented that "language on the empowerment of civil society is quite strong" and attributed this to the efforts of the NGOs. (ENB 10 [36]).

The success of NGOs in gaining support for a larger role for civil society in global social policy is significant but needs to be qualified in three respects. First, while most governments were willing to grant NGOs a larger role in helping implement social programs, they were much less open to

granting policy making and monitoring roles to non-governmental actors. Second, the emphasis on empowering individuals and groups is quite
consistent with liberal political philosophy, if not with neoliberal economics as often practised. This consistency with dominant ideological currents
undoubtedly helped secure acceptance of the idea, both at the wssd and
in other un meetings in the 1990s (Reimann 2006). Third, the way in
which these goals are implemented remains critical. The emphasis, especially in the imf, often seems to be on getting recipient governments and
local communities to "take ownership" of structural adjustment programs,
rather than on designing policies on the basis of the goals and perceptions
of local groups.

NGO Autonomy and Institutionalization

The four issues discussed above reveal that most ngos approached questions of global social policy from a more social democratic perspective
than that favoured by most states and the ifis. ngos shared common values and senses of self-identity that collectively united them and set them
apart from states (both Northern and Southern) and the ifis. This was
most apparent in joint position papers such as "The Quality Benchmark
for the Social Summit" signed by a large number of ngos involved in
the preparatory meetings (van Reisen 2000, 37) and ngos' "Copenhagen
Alternative Declaration" (ngo Forum 1995). Their readiness to criticize
dominant institutions demonstrates that ngos have substantial autonomy
from the forces behind market-oriented globalization. Most ngos did
argue for substantial reforms of market-based economic systems rather
than for replacing them with socialist alternatives, as expected by radical
critics. Leaving aside the question of whether socialist alternatives might
be better, it is important to note that reformist views were shared by a large
number of ngos based in the South as well as the North, challenging the
notion that ngos are simply another mechanism of Northern hegemony.
Also significant are the efforts Northern ngos made to challenge dominant Northern perceptions of people living in poverty and to empower
Southern civil society.

The collective normative autonomy demonstrated by ngos at the
wssd reflected a substantial element of reaction against dominant forces,
as emphasized in traditional theoretical understandings of autonomy
(Sylvester 1992, 156-64). Some of the strongest and most consistent ngo
positions were their critiques of free markets and institutions like the World

Bank and IMF, which is consistent with Donatella della Porta and Sidney Tarrow's suggestion that "opposition to neoliberal globalization [may be] an emerging master frame" among transnational activists (della Porta and Tarrow 2005, 11). At the same time, there was a shared consensus around positive proposals for measures needed to achieve shared NGO values, and this consensus emerged through a deliberative process consistent with the feminist concept of relational autonomy (Sylvester 1992, 156-64). The specific concerns of each group gained coherence and strength through their association with related proposals and with the joint adoption of a human rights framing of problems of poverty and social development (van Reisen 2000). Optimistic assessments of contemporary social movements stress their respect for diversity and difference as a source of strength (Gill 2000; Klein 2001), whereas more traditional approaches to interest-group politics tended to associate diversity with disunity that undermines the collective political influence of the groups in question (Tarrow 2005, 176-7). In the WSSD meetings, normative and intellectual diversity did not prevent common NGO efforts to influence governments.

In contrast to their strong normative consensus, NGOs did have some difficulty working with each other and developing institutional mechanisms to help them pursue their shared goals. The large number of NGOs involved in the WSSD process included groups like the ICSW with a long history of involvement with the UN and formal consultative status with ECOSOC as part of the Conference of Non-Governmental Organizations (or CONGO, as this traditional institutional mechanism for NGO coordination and participation at the UN is sometimes labelled). But the early 1990s was a time of rapid growth in NGO mobilization around UN events, and the UN itself was making greater efforts to expand involvement of non-traditional NGOs in its work — especially NGOs from the South. The spread of democracy after the Cold War encouraged the growth of Southern NGOs that wanted to play a larger role in international deliberations (van Reisen 2000, 16-17). The development of the Internet greatly eased communications among far-flung groups and made it easier for a wider range of groups to follow international meetings and provide input. This challenged the special status, as points of entry for civil society into UN processes, of the NGOs that were members of CONGO (ibid., 22-3, 29-33).[5] Many of the newer NGOs were nationally oriented and emphasized grassroots activism, whereas formal consultative status with ECOSOC had been restricted to "international" NGOs — mainly federations of national groups, whose representatives at UN meetings were oriented towards international diplomacy even if the membership of the federation included grassroots activists (as was the case with the ICSW). Activists in the newer groups felt that the CONGO NGOs were too bureaucratic and did not represent popular opinion at the grassroots level (Willetts 2000, 3; van Reisen 2000, 29).

For their part, CONGO NGOs feared that many of the newer groups did not understand how the UN worked, were not prepared to make useful contributions in the necessary spirit of compromise, and made "extravagant claims of representativity" — particularly in comparison to NGOs represented in CONGO with well-established internal procedures for determining group positions (Disney 2000, 17, 13, 18-20). The differences between the CONGO NGOs and the newer national NGOs partly overlapped with differences between Northern and Southern NGOs, as the CONGO NGOs tended to be headquartered in, and led by activists based in, the North. But some CONGO NGOs had strong representation from the South, and there were significant North-South tensions among the newer groups as well (van Reisen 2000). The differences between these two types of groups were apparent at all of the major UN world conferences in the first half of the 1990s, not just the WSSD (Friedman, Hochstetler, and Clark 2005, 59) and marked an important change in patterns of NGO participation in world politics.

Opening up the process to diverse, non-traditional NGOs focused attention on the need for new institutional mechanisms to coordinate NGO input into the intergovernmental negotiating process, which was still closed to NGOs as direct participants. CONGO was concerned that too many disparate voices from NGOs unfamiliar with UN processes could undermine the prospects for civil society influence; it perhaps also feared that the privileged status of the NGOs represented in CONGO was under threat. It proposed to create an International Facilitating Committee involving the CONGO NGOs and new groups to be invited by them, but this was not acceptable to the other groups because it would give the CONGO NGOs too much control (van Reisen 2000, 31-3; Disney 2000, 10). With the failure of this initiative, there was collective disarray among NGOs at the first meeting of the preparatory committee prior to the WSSD summit, though some individual groups were well prepared. IISD observers also noted that many NGOs were ineffective at this meeting because they emphasized rhetoric over practical solutions to poverty eradication, which the IISD attributed to "the total absence of representatives from affected sectors, such as marginalized social groups and the trade union movement" (*ENB* 10 [11]).

After their mixed experience at the first preparatory session, NGOs focused on organizing and sharing ideas to be more effective in future preparatory sessions. The UN helped by providing funding to enable groups from the least-developed countries to travel to the sessions in New York. NGOs grouped themselves into a number of caucuses, of which the "most active and closely engaged with the intergovernmental negotiations" were ICSW, the Development Caucus, and the Women's Caucus (Disney 2000, 10, 12-13; van Reisen 2000, 29, 34-5; *ENB* 10 [22]). Working in informal caucuses enabled NGOs to overcome their inability to reach agreement on institutional mechanisms of coordination and to avoid having their individual views diluted in a common position.

The Dutch development agency Novib played an important role in facilitating coordination among European NGOs and between development NGOs from the North and South, as did the Women's Environment and Development Organization (WEDO) among women's groups (*ENB* 10 [11]; van Reisen 2000). Novib's efforts reveal a particularly self-reflective approach to coalition building in the face of the differences and sources of tension noted above. Working closely with some Latin American groups with which it had prior ties, Novib invited other NGOs from the North and South to meetings which it hosted (this eventually became the Development Caucus), initiated and funded a mechanism for disseminating information to Southern NGOs via the Internet, and developed a position paper through extensive consultations with other groups around the world. The ability to have genuine two-way communications via the Internet was critical in the process of developing a normative consensus among NGOs, a consensus that formed the basis of the "Quality Benchmark" document, which began life as Novib's draft position paper (van Reisen 2000, 35-7).

The work of the Development Caucus reveals how difficult it is to coordinate activities among diverse NGOs. The NGO community lacks institutional mechanisms for choosing leaders, deciding who can participate, and overcoming substantive disagreements.[6] Collective action therefore rested on initiatives taken by groups like Novib and WEDO, which had strong individual leaders and substantial financial resources, but their initiatives often generated resentment and fears of exclusion similar to those generated by CONGO's attempt to perform its traditional coordinating role. Those tensions were overcome only because groups like Novib and WEDO acknowledged the legitimacy of concerns expressed by Southern groups and were willing to share decision-making power over activities they funded. The willingness to compromise also reflected the strong sense of shared values emerging among NGOs and the shared sense of identity in opposition to dominant forces.

Another important factor was UN officials' determination to ensure wide-ranging NGO participation. Conference organizers provided opportunities for NGOs to address plenary sessions, initially insisting that all speakers must represent one of the caucuses, which UN officials saw as a way to ensure broad representation of civil society. However, according to Julian Disney, president of the ICSW,

> some individual organisations which were very actively involved in the process had memberships that were very much larger and more geographically extensive than was the participation in most of the caucuses. Indeed, some of the caucuses ... had no convincing claim to represent more than a few individuals. Without any formal process for selection, the [NGOs] which eventually were allowed to speak usually included the three principal groupings [the ICSW, the Development Caucus, and the Women's Caucus] and a few others who had special personal influence with ... the secretariat or were especially assertive and persistent in their requests. (2000, 10-11)

The absence of credible institutional mechanisms for choosing among the diverse voices claiming to speak for civil society is an important problem that undermines the credibility, legitimacy, and impact of non-governmental actors in international deliberations (Scholte 2002).

The WSSD had a parallel NGO forum, as do many recent global conferences. This structure allowed non-accredited NGOs to participate in some capacity, provided opportunities for networking, and demonstrated the high level of NGO concern about social development. Despite attracting more media attention than did NGOs' lobbying activities (Disney 2000, 12), the forum had little direct impact on the conference outcome. It did facilitate the development of common perspectives and a sense of common identity among NGOs (Electronic-Commons.Net 2003) and likely contributed to their ability to develop stronger institutional mechanisms for collaboration after the summit.

The discussion so far has focused on NGOs at the international level, but NGOs can also seek influence through national governments. One NGO participant felt that the most effective lobbying technique was for NGOs to focus on their national governments, noting that "some of the best opportunities for input were through the few [NGO] representatives who were members of their government's delegation" (Disney 2000, 11). In the case of Canadian NGOs, Elizabeth Riddell-Dixon (2004, 100) found that close collaboration between NGOs and government officials "enabled the NGOs to influence the precise wording proposed by the Canadian government negotiators at the Preparatory Commission meetings." However, the argument that the best way for NGOs to have their ideas heard at the international level is to work through national governments suggests that NGOs do not pose a serious challenge to the traditional, state-centric world of international relations. It is also worth noting that Canadian groups were particularly well organized under the leadership of three umbrella groups with extensive experience at the UN and benefited from strong support (including funds to hire staff) from Minister of Human Resource Development Lloyd Axworthy (ibid., 103-4). And while these groups did help shape Canadian government policy at the WSSD, they had less impact on more concrete Canadian policies. The 1995 federal budget was announced in Ottawa only days before the Copenhagen summit began, and, to the consternation of Canadian social policy NGOs, the budget included sharp cuts to foreign aid spending (20 percent over three years) and domestic social programs (ibid., 108-9).

NGO Institutionalization after the Summit

Despite disappointments on some of their key issues, many NGOs saw the outcome of the Copenhagen summit as a positive step towards achieving their social democratic goals (Disney 2000, 14). In addition to acknowledging NGO concerns about structural adjustment programs and market-oriented economic globalization, the Copenhagen Declaration included ten broad commitments, each accompanied by a long list of more specific measures to be taken at the national and international levels. Although the commitments were voluntary and worded more vaguely than NGOs had wanted, they did provide a focal point for subsequent efforts to pressure states to provide more generous social welfare programs, foreign aid, and debt relief, and to pressure the IFIs to mitigate social problems associated with developing country debt and structural adjustment programs. The existence of these focal points, in combination with opportunities created by the Internet, enabled NGOs to strengthen their collective institutional capacity to perform a traditional function of private actors — that of monitoring governments, expanded here to include the monitoring of IGOs.

Two NGO initiatives are particularly important. The ICSW organized a series of regional and global forums at which participants monitored IGOs' and regional governments' performance against the Copenhagen commitments, almost invariably finding that their performance fell far short of their commitments (reports of these meetings are available at http://www.icsw.org/copenhagen_implementation/wssd.html). The results of these assessments then were used to help the ICSW prepare thorough position papers for the WSSD+5 meeting in Geneva in 2000. The second initiative was the establishment of Social Watch, an Internet-based network designed to enable national NGOs to monitor their governments' fulfillment of international commitments they had made at Copenhagen and the 1995 Women's Conference in Beijing (http://www.socialwatch.org). Social Watch is an interesting example of international networking to strengthen national activism around transnationally shared goals. Building on the work of the Development Caucus, Social Watch was established under the editorial authority of the Third World Institute in Uruguay, with most of its budget in the early years provided by Novib (van Reisen 2000, 38-40; Hessini and Nayar 2000). It provides annual reports on progress (or its absence) towards meeting the Copenhagen commitments based on reports prepared by national groups of NGOs and produces its own analyses of country policies, social conditions, and global trends, all of which helps NGOs prepare more effectively for international meetings.

Space does not permit a detailed analysis of NGO influence at the WSSD+5 meetings in Geneva in 2000, but overall it was much the same as in Copenhagen. As in the earlier meetings, pressure from NGOs helped ensure that the potential negative social effects of market-oriented economic globalization were acknowledged, as was the need to be more responsive to the expressed concerns of poor people and civil society. However, the specific policies recommended to achieve these goals were much closer to the liberal approach of dominant institutions than to the social democratic approach favoured by most transnational NGOs. NGOs were particularly outraged when the UN joined with the IFIs and the Organisation for Economic Co-operation and Development (OECD) in releasing a document at the start of the conference that strongly favoured market-oriented economic policies combined with liberal social welfare measures, thereby pre-empting much of the debate (IMF et al. 2000; "A Better World for All" 2000).

Overall, even though NGOs had increased their institutional capacity and further developed their common values and proposals — both key indicators of collective normative autonomy — their influence on actual government policies remained modest at the Geneva 2000 meeting. Furthermore, although the NGOs involved in the WSSD process were part of an upsurge of activism by progressive elements of global civil society in the 1990s, the decade also witnessed sharp cuts in foreign aid spending by many governments of rich-countries, contradicting the sentiments expressed in the Copenhagen Declaration. These cuts suggest that activists' impact on global norms was modest, despite their success in pushing for greater attention to the social implications of market-oriented globalization and the views of poor people and civil society in developing countries.

Sources of Funds and NGO Autonomy

The volume and source of funding are critical determinants of NGO autonomy (Pinter 2001). Particularly important in relation to this chapter is dependence on states and IGOs for funds. Access to private voluntary funding could free NGOs from their dependence on states and enable them to pursue programs and policies that they determine for themselves, thereby increasing NGO autonomy in relation to the dominant forces behind neo-liberal globalization. The ability to raise funds privately also is crucial to the claim that NGOs are becoming increasingly important actors in global governance, and it provides an indicator of NGO success in transforming social values.

OECD data on private funding for international development NGOs reveal that it is very small in relation to official development assistance. In the fourteen OECD countries for which data is available over a long time period, ODA accounted for 0.29 percent of GDP in 1970-4, while private contributions to development NGOs accounted for only 0.032 percent. The figures for 2000-3 were 0.34 percent and 0.034 percent, respectively (author's calculations using data in OECD, various years). Second, the volume of private funding generally tracks that of official aid flows, and the former fell sharply in the late 1990s — a period of strong economic growth in most developed countries — at the same time that ODA declined in most countries. NGOs and civil society were not able to step up and fill in the social policy gaps allegedly caused by global economic and political constraints on national social welfare policy. Data for Canadian development NGOs show that they have remained consistently reliant on government for 40 to 50 percent of their funds since the 1970s and had limited success in their efforts to attract more private donations to offset the sharp decline in government funding after the budget cuts that began in 1995 (Brodhead and Herbert-Copley 1988, tables 4.1 and 5.2; B. Tomlinson 2003, table 1). All of this suggests that NGOs have not been very successful in their efforts to transform Northern social values in a direction more favourable to those groups' social democratic principles.

Dependence on government funding clearly constrains NGO autonomy, particularly because governments are increasingly using NGOs as public-service contractors to implement projects designed by official development agencies. This reflects, in part, the influence of the ideology of new public management, which suggests that donor governments should create a policy framework conducive to international development while leaving the implementation of development policies to contracting agencies (Stubbs 2003). One consequence is the "projectizing" of social policy, with NGOs focusing on their roles as public service contractor in micro-projects rather than advocacy on macro issues (Tendler 2004, 119; also Stubbs 2003, 329). The ability to access government funding can enhance NGOs' operational capacity, but at the cost of limits on their policy autonomy in relation to dominant forces favouring market-oriented globalization. Paradoxically, most development NGOs are sharply critical of neoliberal ideology, yet their skills and status as non-government actors make them a good fit for the application of this ideology in the field of global social welfare policy (Stubbs 2003, 328; see also Tendler 2004).

Conclusion

The purpose of this chapter has been to examine NGOs' collective capacity to shape global social policy as an example of how new institutions or institutionalized practices may be coming into existence to address the tension between market-oriented globalization and state autonomy. The short answer to the core question is that, while NGOs are increasingly active in global social policy and have considerable normative autonomy from dominant forces favouring market-oriented globalization, they have not developed the institutional ability either to have a major impact on the social policies pursued by dominant institutions or to compensate for eroding state efforts to provide social protections. Thus, globalization is not associated with substantial institutional change in the area of social policy beyond the erosion of state capacity in some developing countries and the growing role of intergovernmental organizations like the World Bank and IMF.

NGOs have been increasingly active as social service providers (often delivering government-funded programs) and as participants in global debates about social policy. In their advocacy work, NGOs demonstrate considerable autonomy from the dominant forces behind neoliberal globalization, particularly in terms of their ability to develop and articulate distinctive arguments and policy positions that reflect their shared social democratic values. These values have been developed and refined through deliberative processes and are expressed by NGOs from the South as well as the North. Groups based in the North are more active at the level of global deliberations, but Southern groups are not subordinate to their Northern counterparts. The views shared by NGOs pose a distinct challenge to those of dominant institutions like the World Bank and IMF, and NGOs often are sharply critical of those institutions — even if not as sharply as radical critics of NGOs would like. Global social policy would look very different if the NGOs examined in this chapter were in charge.

This chapter also shows that NGOs' ability to participate in global governance depends heavily on the environment created by IGOs. The UN actively encouraged NGO participation in the WSSD process, especially NGOs from developing countries that were not part of traditional mechanisms for NGO involvement in the UN's work. International conferences like the WSSD also provide a natural focus for transnational activism and for national activists dealing with issues on the international agenda. Our analysis supports Sidney Tarrow's argument that internationalism — in the sense of increasingly dense networks of institutionalized interaction among multiple levels of government — "both makes the threats of globalization more visible and offers resources, opportunities, and alternative targets for transnational activists to make claims against other domestic and external actors" (2005, 8-9).

The 1990s provided a particularly favourable international environment for NGOs, but there has since been a backlash that has somewhat reduced the opportunities for international activism — even before 9/11. NGOs were very assertive at UN world conferences in the 1990s, and a number of governments (especially some from developing countries that had been criticized by human rights groups) began to resist procedures that would increase NGO access to UN deliberations (Willetts 2000). Even the Canadian government, one of the strongest proponents of a role for NGOs at the WSSD, was taken aback by intense NGO criticism when it cut spending on domestic social programs and foreign aid on the eve of the Copenhagen summit. One consequence was that Ottawa refused to provide funding for Canadian NGO follow-up work after the summit (Riddell-Dixon 2004, 108-9). Despite these and other examples of weakened government enthusiasm for NGO advocacy, many IGOs do continue to support NGO participation — and even if they did not, international meetings would continue to provide important focal points for international NGO activism.

Despite their increased presence in global social policy deliberations, NGOs are not able to have a major impact on global social conditions and policies. This is clearest in relation to their financial capacity; NGOs have had limited success in developing non-governmental sources of funds and remain highly dependent on states to fund the programs they deliver. Among all of the institutions involved in global governance, only states and the IGOs they create have the legitimate authority to raise revenues on the scale needed to make a difference to global social conditions. The limited institutional capacity of non-governmental actors also is apparent in the difficulties NGOs had at the WSSD in coordinating their positions and selecting representatives to speak on behalf of civil society.

NGOs have had an impact on global social policy norms, but again their impact is limited. NGOs were able to put issues on the WSSD agenda even when those issues conflicted with the interests of dominant actors. Moreover, these groups contributed to the shift from orthodox policies to promote economic growth towards a broader concern with the social dimension of economic globalization. Yet data on private funding for NGOs shows that Northern societies have not become significantly more concerned about the problems of Third World poverty and development addressed by NGOs. Since the WSSD, NGOs have built sophisticated institutional mechanisms, most notably Social Watch, to monitor governments and IGOs. They have taken full advantage of the opportunities the Internet provides to build international networks among people who share similar values but not territorial contiguity.

Despite these accomplishments, social policy NGOs had relatively little impact on the policies actually pursued by governments and the IFIs. Most states have never come close to the ODA target identified in the Copenhagen Declaration, and many actually became less generous after the summit. On issue after issue at the WSSD, governments responded to concerns that NGOs had raised from a social democratic perspective with liberal policies inconsistent with NGO values. Virtually all of the policy developments associated with the WSSD took the form of targeted rather than universal programs, aimed to relieve extreme absolute poverty while leaving inequality largely untouched, and retained the core prescriptions of neoliberal development theory. There is a certain irony here; while NGO efforts to promote social democratic welfare policies have achieved little success at the global level, their efforts to bring attention to poverty and other social problems have contributed to the emergence of a stronger emphasis on liberal social welfare policies at the global level.

The key theme of this assessment — NGO success in highlighting issues while IFIs and other dominant forces retain the ability to determine how to respond — also holds true when one looks at NGOs' long-term impact. Issues like poverty and debt relief have gained much greater prominence in recent years because of NGO efforts, but major institutions of global governance continue to address them largely from a liberal perspective — that is, through targeted programs to accompany market-oriented economic restructuring, such as the World Bank's Poverty Strategy Reduction Papers. Little attention has been paid to traditional social democratic priorities such as universal programs to promote social justice, redistribution of income and wealth, and more effective regulation of the global economy to ensure it serves broader social purposes (Deacon et al. 2005).

In this respect, the roles NGOs play in global social policy appear quite traditional — they remain outsiders in relation to governance processes dominated by governments and IGOs, even as they are able (as at the WSSD) to persuade governments to consult more fully with representatives of civil society. In sum, while social policy NGOs demonstrate considerable normative autonomy, and their impact on global norms likely has made important differences to the lives of people living in poverty, they do not signify a fundamental change away from states as the key institutions of global governance.

Part 2: Regional Variations

chapter 10 · **Differentiated Autonomy: North America's Model of Transborder Governance**

Stephen Clarkson

NORTH AMERICA IS SURELY an unusual candidate for inclusion in this volume, because none of its three constituent states would necessarily come to the mind of a scholar wanting to examine the dynamic dialectic linking globalization with autonomy. After all, the United States is commonly seen not as the object of globalization but as its subject, the agent that generated its hallmark forces — whether satellite-based information technologies, globally reaching transnational corporations (TNCs), or the political muscle and the neoconservative ideology that generated such prime institutions of global governance as the World Trade Organization (WTO). Canada, as a principal follower state, had become so highly integrated with the United States through myriad market, cultural, and social forces that it was invoked decades ago as an anti-model by other countries fearing the loss of their autonomy. In other words, it was a state that had already experienced the deep integration now associated with globalization. As for Mexico, for decades it had been an outrider at the opposite extreme of the global hierarchy — so jealous of its autonomy, so nationalist in its confrontation with *el tio Sam,* so disconnected from global society that it would not even align itself with the non-aligned powers during the long Cold War standoff between East and West.

These considerations notwithstanding, this chapter is based on the following assumptions. First, *because* the United States is generally viewed as the chief driver of globalization (having played the role of the independent, not the dependent, variable in most globalization studies), its behaviour in balancing common interests with its geographical periphery has much to tell us about the various ways in which national autonomy is being reasserted and where, as a result, the global order is heading. Second, *because* Canada has long functioned as a distant warning system for the early onset of deep integration's characteristics — external intervention in its domestic policies, mediatized forces of cultural assimilation, intense communications interlinkages — that are now equated with globalization, its experience with governance mechanisms for steering the transborder resolution of bilateral problems makes it worthy of continued observation. Third, *because* the government of Mexico executed a radical rejection of its commitment to autonomy in order to join the new world order so enthusiastically over the past quarter century — largely through aspiring to unrestricted integration with the US economy — while its public remained fiercely nationalist, it has become a case to watch for countries of the South.

This chapter does not address the questions posed to the world as a whole by the United States, whether seen as benevolent hegemon or rogue empire. Rather, it focuses on its role in its own continent and the resulting transborder governance that links North America's powerhouse with its two nominally sovereign but highly dependent neighbours.

The changes in transborder North American governance that connect with various tensions associated with globalization processes fall into three institutional categories:

1 In response to the demand by American transnational corporations for a mode of regulation appropriate to their regulatory needs for operating in a globalized financing, production, and marketing space, a new form of economic governance was put in place continentally (North American Free Trade Agreement [NAFTA], 1994) in parallel with the one that was being established globally (World Trade Organization [WTO], 1995). Although an apparently significant change, NAFTA turned out to be less impressive than first met the eye.

2 Alongside these institutionalized manifestations of US hegemony, market-based governance characterized many industries in North America as they responded to competitive pressures at home and from abroad. Invisible to most observers, many of these informal practices were considerably more substantial than met the eye.

3 Following 11 September 2001, the US government's reaction to terrorism sparked a reversion to government-led policy making centred

on a reinstitutionalization of the coercive forces of North America's three states. The resulting changes in existing governmental institutions were just what they seemed: a restriction of national autonomy in the periphery, which responded to the global hegemon shifting from an economic to a security paradigm.

Less Than Meets the Eye: Formal Structures of North American Governance

The signature institutions distinguishing the economic thrust of planetary integration have evolved on two levels. First come the regional groupings established by intergovernmentally negotiated treaties led by the European Union, which, as Hedetoft and Cooper remind us in the next two chapters, set the standard for augmenting its member states' policy capacity by integrating them in a carefully institutionalized economic project. Second comes the remarkably powerful WTO, which has already survived a decade of contestation. In using North America as a laboratory for observing how the tension between globalization and autonomy plays out in the actual marketplace, we must not ignore how its institutionalized practices have also evolved at arm's length from these new expressions of economic governance.

The institutional weakness of North America's formal governance structures can best be understood by noting how the United States responded — as the socialist threat to its military dominance petered out — to the threat to its economic dominance, which it identified with the excessively interventionist autonomy of its capitalist competitors. Deeply worried in the 1980s about its apparent hegemonic decline, the United States launched a three-fold strategy to change the rules by which its economic rivals favoured their corporate champions. First, unilateral arm twisting with competitors used the denial of access to the US market to lever reductions in their discriminatory practices, but they failed to decapitate this multi-headed hydra. Second, multilateral negotiations starting in 1986 under the aegis of the General Agreement on Tariffs and Trade (GATT) was the ideal formula for getting new rules favouring US interests, but the Uruguay Round's progress was agonizingly slow, due to the desire of the other major players (the European Union, Japan, Brazil, and India) to nurture their economic autonomy. Finally, bilateral negotiation of comprehensive agreements with compliant neighbours might yield important precedents for the government-constraining rules that Washington wanted to universalize in order to reduce the autonomy of its state competitors and increase that of its own corporate champions on a globally levelled playing field.

Successful negotiation of a Canada–United States Free Trade Agreement (CUFTA, 1989) marked the breakthrough in this US drive to write a new economic rule book for the world, because it radically extended the notion of "free trade" to deepen rights for foreign investors and to include the huge domain of services. By 1993, when Washington was tightening CUFTA's disciplines and extending them to its southern neighbour, Mexico, the competitive spectre posed by a Fortress America caused its interlocutors from overseas to abandon their resistance in the Uruguay Round and sign on to the fundamental reordering of the world's economic norms now known around the world as the WTO.

NAFTA redefined the meaning of North America as a new regional political economy with its own system of governance. This section will first look down "from above" at the institutional forms of the new continental governance in order then to look up "from below" at its civil society engagement in North America's transborder governance.

Looking Down

To a large extent, NAFTA did what the US trade negotiators intended. Its rules "locked in" neoconservative principles in their periphery by entrenching a supraconstitution in Mexico and Canada (Clarkson 2002). But its institutions proved to be insubstantial sites for any continuing cross-border governance. This was not by accident. As the official manifestation of transborder economic integration, NAFTA was distinguished by each partner's reluctance to institutionalize a continuing relationship. Understandably, the global hegemon had little interest in tying its hands with institutions that might concede some decision-making parity to its two geographical neighbours.

For equal but opposite reasons that had to do with its politicians' desire to claim formal political autonomy in the face of the country's considerable economic and cultural integration within US-driven systems (Redekop 1976), Canada had long resisted becoming involved in formalized transnational governance. Even when it negotiated CUFTA, Ottawa's main, if self-contradictory, negotiating aim was to avoid institutional entanglements while putting limits on the American government's ability to harass Canadian exporters by its unilateral acts of trade protectionism.

After President Vicente Fox's election in 2000, Mexico became the most articulate advocate of European Union type institutions that would necessarily constrain the independent policy making of the United States, but during the NAFTA negotiations in the early 1990s, President Salinas de Gortari had accepted CUFTA's weak-institution model as the organizational premise for his trade talks.

The lowest common denominator of the three states' differing motivations for buying into continental economic integration was a formal institutional structure of almost laughable vacuity. The NAFTA Free Trade Commission (FTC) had neither secretariat, address, nor office, since it consisted of little more than the sporadic meetings of the member countries' cabinet-level trade representatives. The power of the FTC remains minimal — compliance with its "recommendations" is suggested, not required, by member governments.

Given its legislative incapacity to build on or amend its rule book without its three signatories formally negotiating new agreements and having them ratified by their legislatures, NAFTA was doomed in the longer run to be superseded by other agreements. In the short run, its frail bureaucratic structure — some thirty committees and working groups established by the agreement's various chapters to oversee the implementation of their provisions — was unable to provide any meaningfully trilateral administration. In one case (tariff reduction), the working group did its job by accelerating the process and subsequently becoming dormant. In another instance (financial services), the periodic meetings of the three countries' delegated civil servants provided a means for the Mexicans to be kept informed of their neighbours' latest banking regulations, although the American and Canadian participants considered the committee's meeting a mere formality. NAFTA's implementation under the supervision of these working groups was meant to reduce the asymmetry inherent in the continent's power relations while simultaneously depoliticizing the manner in which conflicts were resolved between member governments. Because the three countries often had conflicting objectives, mid-level civil servants' ability to carry out the working groups' apolitical mandate was severely circumscribed (Clarkson et al. 2005).

The capacity of NAFTA's three main judicial institutions to resolve disputes arising out of conflicting interpretations of the agreement's hundreds of rules was weak. The binational panels provided for under chapter 20 to deal with general disputes over the implementation of NAFTA's various provisions turned out to be ineffective mainly because their rulings are not binding, as was most clearly illustrated by the trucking dispute between the United States and Mexico. The chapter 20 panel's initial ruling that Washington was at fault and its recommendation that the US moratorium on Mexican trucks be lifted played a negligible role in the issue's ultimate resolution, which was the product of personal negotiation between Presidents Fox and Bush. As a result of this kind of experience, the three states have resorted less and less to chapter 20 in resolving their differences, as it provides no genuinely depoliticized alternative to the US-dominated power politics that had previously characterized bilateral relations in North America.

Designed to guard against the unfair application of countervailing (CVD) and anti-dumping (AD) duties, chapter 19 has had very different effects in each member country. Canadian trade agencies have become more accommodating to American interpretations of the standards they apply in AD or CVD determinations, because American legal professionals participate in the panels' deliberations. NAFTA required Mexico to create a completely new trade remedy system. All the more extraordinary because of its civil law tradition, Mexico agreed to create from scratch common law judicial procedures to ensure that American or Canadian companies would be treated the same way in challenging its protectionist measures as they would be in their own systems.

With the hegemon, the chapter 19 story has been very different. The United States has complied with chapter 19 panel decisions in cases where accepting remands does not face strong resistance from domestic lobby groups. But disciplining the United States' behaviour on issues of major policy importance is another matter. For example, when the US CVD action against Canadian softwood lumber exports was remanded for incorrectly applying the notion of subsidy as defined in US law, Congress quickly changed the relevant legislation in order to define the targeted Canadian policies as illegitimate subsidies. The softwood lumber case highlights NAFTA's legal asymmetry: demands by powerful protectionist interests in the hegemon can trump the putatively binding new norms of continental governance.

The exception to NAFTA's judicial flaccidity was chapter 11's investor-state dispute settlement provisions, which significantly bolstered the autonomy of TNCs while, in a zero-sum exchange, significantly undermining that of the three countries' governments. By extending the private authority of international corporate arbitration to binding jurisdiction over domestic policy making, chapter 11 moved North America along the path of outsourcing government functions to public-private sites beyond the reach of domestic judicial and legislative processes. This phenomenon, which parallels the processes discussed by Claire Cutler in Chapter 8, can be seen most clearly in two major chapter 11 cases that invalidated specific governmental measures: the successful arbitrations launched by Metalclad Corporation (against a ban on the operation of a ground-water-polluting waste disposal plant it had purchased in the state of San Luis Potosí) and that of S.D. Myers (against Ottawa's regulation, passed in accordance with the Basel Convention banning the export of hazardous wastes, that disallowed the export of highly toxic PCBs). Apart from its effect on the parties' sovereignty, this support by regional governance for corporate objections to government actions has serious consequences concerning the domestic capacity for environmental regulation, over which a chill has been cast.

Resistance to a governance regime that necessarily reduced national autonomy varied from country to country. Once the initial struggle by civil society organizations against CUFTA had been lost in the 1988 federal election, popular resistance to NAFTA in Canada fell dramatically. Except for the dismay among environmentalists and nationalists to chapter 11's investor-state dispute rulings, Canadian elites enthusiastically supported an institution that they credited for a massive increase in the country's export figures, even though the rate of productivity growth had declined and real wages had stagnated.

In Mexico, which had made the most wrenching commitments in NAFTA, resistance was highest among the public, whose anger was seen by the world community when thousands of campesinos demonstrated in Cancún during the WTO's biennial ministerial meeting of September 2003. Shaken by the disturbing economic results — a massive increase in foreign takeovers of Mexican companies without increasing economic productivity, a continuing flight of labour from the land to the city and from Mexico to the United States, a fall in real wages, and a growth in both income and regional disparities — the Mexican government nevertheless stuck to its ideological guns in the hope that liberalization would ultimately bring economic salvation.

Public resistance was lowest in the United States, but governmental resistance was highest, actually taking the form of institutional sabotage. The Byrd Amendment, which transferred anti-dumping and countervailing duties to the hands of the protectionist interests that launched these trade-harassing actions, violated the free-trade spirit of NAFTA, as did a prolonged but dubiously justified ban on Canadian beef exports.

Looking Up

Despite high levels of civil society's continental integration at the individual level during two centuries of migration across a porous Canadian-American border and following several decades of very high emigration rates from Mexico into the United States, transborder governance is remarkable by its absence in civil society largely because NAFTA has few institutions where non-governmental organizations can plead their causes. For instance, although First Nations communicate with each other across the national boundaries, they have no common, transborder political activity, as their relevant decision-making bodies are federal, provincial/state, or municipal. NAFTA has no direct salience for them.

Where Canada worked out an intergovernmental arrangement with Mexico to import temporary agricultural labour, a seasonal, unrooted diaspora enjoys only tentative rights. Civil society involvement in the governance of migrant farm workers is at a level much lower than is normal within Canada, because non-citizen Mexicans have little purchase as far as getting social services and enjoying labour rights.

Environmental issues received nominal recognition through NAFTA's linking them with its basic trade-promotion mandate. A societal interest in environmental sustainability was incorporated rhetorically in the agreement's preamble, which claimed to reconcile trade and environmental issues. Heralded as an innovation, the treaty allowed environmental concerns to be considered under the general dispute provisions of chapter 20, but this provision has still not been invoked.

More apparently consequential was the creation of NAFTA's North American Commission for Environmental Cooperation (NACEC), to connect the environment institutionally with trade issues at the continental level. Its political importance lies in the support it has offered to networks of NGOs and other informal transnational bodies, particularly helping Mexican environmentalists to gain legitimacy and to increase their effectiveness within their own polity. However, the NACEC was constrained from the moment of its inception by its three progenitors, who never intended to give it autonomy or political heft. This environmental defender was further undermined by NAFTA's investor-state dispute settlement mechanism whose rules prohibit the participation of environmental NGOs in its judicial proceedings. In a crunch, NAFTA provisions promoting trade and investment trump those defending the environment.

Parallel with American environmentalists' fears that NAFTA would foster ecological disasters from uncontrolled maquiladora production along the Mexican border, American trade unions' concerns about job losses and a "race to the bottom" resulting from free trade led to the creation of the North American Commission for Labour Cooperation (NACLC) with a mandate to defend labour rights continentally. Although it did not establish supranational standards, it required member countries to comply with and effectively enforce their respective labour laws (Macdonald 2003).

In practice, the NACLC's eleven labour rights were only as significant as their means of enforcement, and none of the eight standards prescribing trade union rights was enforceable through dispute settlement. Only three technical labour standards — protection for youth or children, health and safety, and minimum wages — were theoretically enforceable, but the dispute procedures were designed to make it virtually impossible for an NGO to win a case. Complaints filed with a national administrative office (NAO) rarely reach the stage of arbitration, which is based on an "informal" rather than an "adversarial" system. Furthermore, penalties are minor. Not only did the NACLC fail to make its members enforce their own labour standards, it did not even prevent member governments from exercising their autonomy by *lowering* their statutory protections for workers, as happened in Ontario in the late 1990s and in Mexico under President Fox.

NAFTA's weakness in addressing environmental crises and labour rights abuses has meant that effective cooperative strategies among NGOs have developed outside its formal framework. In this respect, the NACLC and the NACEC inadvertently generated a modest, informal, if spasmodic solidarity at the grassroots, notably occasional trinational labour alliances to confront common, continentally structured employers. This occasional solidarity has also generated linkages around specific problems such as broad-based environmental lobbying and mobilization coalitions.

Brought into existence to address the three North American states' needs to become more competitive in the face of pressure from rival regions in Europe and Asia, NAFTA served the United States' interests by constraining Canada's already low degree of autonomy and Mexico's very substantial autonomy without Washington having to make serious concessions of its own.

In Canada's case, US firms made significant breakthroughs into some sectors such as furniture and steel while gaining greater efficiency by closing down tariff-protected branch plants and serving the local market from US and Mexican manufacturing sites. Because Canada's governmental autonomy was reduced in the energy sector, its petroleum industry's freedom to sell as much of Alberta's oil and natural gas reserves as it could pump was greatly enhanced.

In supporting Mexico's abrupt shift from an autonomous industrial development path to maximum continental integration, NAFTA did not sacrifice any autonomy that the neoconservative Partido Revolucionario Institucional (PRI) rulers were not determined to abandon. But for Mexican citizens still loyal to the nationalist values enshrined in their constitution, NAFTA represented a capitulation that further harmed not just campesinos who could not compete against imports of US-subsidized corn but the middle and lower-middle class whose small enterprises could not compete with the local operations of McDonald's, Wal-Mart, or General Electric.

While NAFTA appeared to constitute a regional governance regime that would create a more integrated playing field among North America's three economies, it deepened the asymmetries between them without greatly inhibiting the United States' autonomous capacity to revise the rules in its favour. These changes may have made the North American economy more efficient, but they have not made its governance more stable. On the contrary, because the general public in the continental periphery has not experienced the gains in well-being it had been led to expect, because the playing field seemed to be tilted in favour of foreign TNCs, and because labour unions and environmental NGOs have written off its side agreements, NAFTA is incubating a legitimacy deficit that augurs badly for its future vitality, let alone its stability. The official win-win-win rhetoric concerning regional governance in North America is liable to be replaced by a more selective sense of they-won-but-we-lost.

More Than Meets the Eye: Informal Structures of North American Governance

In the light of NAFTA's weak governance, the extraordinary feature of the North American marketplace is the extent to which its many sectors have increased their cross-border integration without the three states' establishing overarching institutions to manage these economic subsystems. Institutionalized practices have emerged, to be sure, but in response to specific problems and, generally, at arm's length from the formal structures of global and continental economic governance. Typically, these institutions are not visible to the citizenry, as they are not overtly connected to the WTO or NAFTA but are embedded in US-dominated market processes that are only occasionally and incompletely glimpsed through news reports.

Institutionalized processes in the transborder marketplace are as varied as are its different economic sectors, some of which appear continentally oriented, while others are more connected to global governance.

Automobiles

Exceptional in this regard is the automobile industry, which, in the Canadian case, was structured by a formal agreement negotiated between the Canadian and American governments, the (then) Big Four companies' head offices in Detroit, and their Canadian subsidiaries. The Auto Pact of 1965 established the parameters for the Canadian car-assembly and auto-parts sectors until its provisions were dismantled under "free trade." NAFTA's rules of origin, which specified only how much North American — as opposed to Canadian — content was required in every car assembled, deprived Canadian governments of the legal clout that the Auto Pact had once provided them in order to persuade the automobile TNCs to locate more assembly activities north of the border. With the Auto Pact's remaining protections dismantled following a ruling by the WTO in 2000, the institutional framework established for Canada's industry disintegrated. As a result, the continental auto market is structured by the TNCs themselves in response to their continental and global competitive challenges.

Textiles

NAFTA's rules of origin also created a more regionally focused thinking in the textile and apparel industry, which has been invisibly restructured through free trade. NAFTA's rules of origin effectively protected the major American textile corporations while providing limited access to the American market for Canadian high-end apparel companies and much greater markets for low-end maquila producers in Mexico. Canada and the United States became each other's largest export markets, while Mexican exports soared, albeit at the expense of Caribbean producers. Post-NAFTA, Mexico became the base of operations for North American firms seeking to reduce costs through lower wages and taxes.

While larger US or Canadian manufacturers invested directly in Mexico, some mid-sized firms entered joint ventures there as a means of capitalizing on Mexico's competitive advantage in labour without the outlay required to set up their own factories. The size of the American industry, and greater mutual trade between the superpower and its northern neighbour, promoted the consolidation of a US-centred textile and apparel industry with a strong southern periphery.

Capital Markets

The three countries' separate stock exchanges demonstrate a more market-driven institutionalization. For over a century prior to NAFTA, the US capital market dominated those of its northern and southern neighbours even in their early, unregulated form. Institutionalization in this sector can be seen in the degree to which corporations in the two peripheries seek to list their shares in the American stock exchanges and US transnational corporations raise capital in the markets where their branch plants operate.

Continuing continentalization can be seen when the influence of the American exchanges causes Canadian and Mexican exchanges pre-emptively to harmonize their regulations with US standards. Much more autonomous in its formal sovereignty, the Mexican stock exchange has suffered from an even higher incidence of Mexican corporations raising capital in the American market. Cross-listing by US-based TNCs in Canadian stock exchanges and Canadian-based corporations in US exchanges makes the Canadian sector, like Mexico's, a territorial extension of the vibrant American capital market.

In the face of the US exchanges' competitive advantage, formal institutions in the periphery are attempting to bolster themselves. In Canada, efforts are being made to replace the provinces' separate regulatory regimes with a single exchange for the domestic market. In Mexico, where the government both manages and controls the stock market, strong steps are being taken to sustain a domestic capital market within a globalized system by instituting rules that impose transparency obligations on the traditionally family-run corporation.

The current phase of this continental dynamic was brought into high relief following massive failures of US firms in 2003. Regulatory reform of corporate governance and accounting rules, which was sponsored by the US government and the American stock exchanges, caused Canada and Mexico to administer similar cures even if they had not suffered from the same disease.

Steel

NAFTA's failure to create genuine free trade by eliminating the application of anti-dumping and countervailing duties to member states' exports had unique structuring effects in the steel sector. This was particularly notice-able in the Canadian industry, whose exports continued to be subjected to its rivals' trade harassment. As an avoidance strategy, new investments by Canadian steel manufacturers were made principally in the United States, where they became active members in the main lobby organization, the American Iron and Steel Institute (AISI). The resulting Americanization of the Canadian steel sector has created a more US-weighted continental industry in which Canadian and, more recently, some Mexican firms par-ticipate from their new niches in the United States.

As a result, the AISI supported Canada's and Mexico's exemptions from the Bush administration's safeguard actions against foreign steel imports, and the three governments have worked with their respective steel in-dustries to adopt a common North American position prior to interna-tional discussions at the Organisation for Economic Co-operation and Development (OECD) and negotiations at the WTO. Nevertheless, new investments in the US market by Brazilian, Indian, and Russian steel com-panies and the takeover of Canadian steel companies by overseas firms are breaking down the short-lived coherence of North America as a produc-tion area with a common interest in defending itself against competition from other regions.

Biotechnology

Whereas steel showed a process of hegemonification taking place inside the US marketplace, continent-wide, public-private governance driven by US-based TNCs can also be observed operating independently within the three domestic economies. One striking example is the failure of con-sumer activism to achieve legislation requiring genetically modified (GM) foodstuffs to be labelled as such. Monsanto, the leading US practitioner of bioengineering, has fought off labelling attempts in states such as Oregon and in the US Congress. More interesting for our purposes is the replay of this drama in Canada, where certain farmers' organizations in conjunc-tion with the federal Department of Agriculture, and pushed strongly by Monsanto's Canadian operation, successfully kept GM food labelling off the political agenda. In Mexico, a combination of the US and Canadian embassies with US industry prevailed over a PRI-launched congressional initiative to require that GM food be labelled. The story is one of corporate autonomy trumping citizen power in each country but under the unobtrusive, decentralized, yet hegemonic leadership of US industry.

Energy

Some transborder market governance is skewed, thanks to different NAFTA rules governing the bilateral relationships. Whereas the government of Canada acquiesced to US demands that CUFTA defang its capacity to shape the petroleum industry in the national interest through pricing policies and export controls, the government of Mexico insisted that NAFTA respect its constitution's article 27, which entrenches national sovereignty over energy resources and their exploitation.

Although the Canadian petroleum industry is largely self-regulated now, it still operates within the framework created by globally established prices, by CUFTA's prohibition of Ottawa's interventionism, and by each country's tax policies, policies, standards, subsidies, and resource-management programs. Within the framework of hands-off government policy, the Canadian oil and natural gas industry has integrated fully with its American counterpart under the aegis of US-dominated corporate capital. In Mexico, constitutionally entrenched nationalization has restrained the integration that would otherwise have resulted from the persistently high US demand for petroleum. Oil and natural gas are almost entirely owned and controlled by the state corporation, Pemex, which is the country's largest single exporter.

One of the few examples of some trilateral governance-in-the-making results from the Bush administration's drive to buttress its energy security. In the spirit of the Cheney Report, which recommended augmenting its supplies from Canada and Mexico, Washington pushed its neighbours to intensify their collaboration. In the hope of breaking down Mexico's stubborn autonomy in all energy forms and of integrating Canada's provincial electricity utilities in US grids, at the Summit of the Americas in 2001, Bush prevailed on his two counterparts to collaborate continentally with a view to developing an integrated continental market. Even though NAFTA contained a complex energy chapter, *los tres amigos* set up a North America Energy Working Group staffed by officials and energy experts as a separate entity, confirming NAFTA's marginal significance as an institution.

Banking

While governance in steel, automobiles, textiles, and energy displays genuinely continental characteristics because North America constitutes a meaningful production and marketing zone in these fields, other economic sectors in North America are more connected to global than regional governance. For instance, although CUFTA and NAFTA had separate chapters on financial institutions, the internationalization of both Canada's and Mexico's banking markets has been driven more by European than by American banks. With banking in North America being globally rather than continentally integrated, the three states' regulatory systems for banking have become harmonized through the global forum of the Bank of International Settlements, where regulators from all countries formulate standards for their domestic industries. In this situation, the norms incorporated in CUFTA and NAFTA have proven to be of minor importance in the three countries' banking governance.

Pharmaceuticals

An analogous situation pits NAFTA's chapter 17 — which, for the first time, introduced into a trade agreement strong rules strengthening corporate intellectual property (IP) rights — against the WTO's virtually identical agreement on Trade-Related Aspects of Intellectual Property Rights (TRIPS). Even though the US pharmaceutical industry had held the pen when NAFTA's IP rights were written, it has preferred to invoke TRIPS rather than chapter 17 when having Washington enforce these rights in Canada on its behalf, because the WTO's dispute settlement is stronger that NAFTA's (see Chapter 3 in this volume). Transborder governance in North America's pharmaceutical sector is thus more global than continental, showing that the autonomy of American TNCs seeking to enhance their corporate clout in their backyard can in some cases be better promoted — and Canadian or Mexican national autonomy can ipso facto be more effectively constrained — by institutions of global rather than of regional governance.

In sum, highly varied, informally institutionalized processes in the continent's marketplace have emerged as the salient reality of North America's governance, overshadowing in their practical significance the more formalized institutions, arbitration processes, and working groups provided for in NAFTA. Market-led solutions are, by neoconservative logic, ipso facto efficient. Vulnerable to changes in global power relations, they are also necessarily unstable. As for their equity, they are more likely to produce justice for the rich than for the poor, for the strong state than the weak.

Just What It Seems: Transborder Governance after Bin Laden

The process of George W. Bush's administration declaring its independence from the continental and global governance systems that the United States had itself created in the 1990s moved to a higher level when, following a key moment in the chronicle of recent globalization — al Qaeda's attacks of 11 September 2001— Bush made his unilateral declaration of war against terrorism.

Border Security

North American governance, which had been characterized by border-weakening forms of market-steered continental restructuring, suddenly became transformed by the border-strengthening imperatives of government-led continental security that "smartened" the United States' two land borders and promoted a security perimeter for the whole of North America. The elaboration of smart border plans provoked a new level of intergovernmental coordination on the continent in which the two peripheries responded to Washington's requirements that its security be as absolute as humanly and technologically possible. In all cases, security responses since September 2001 have bolstered intergovernmental institutionalization in the continent.

The 30-Point Smart Border Plan was signed by the Canadian and US governments in December 2001 but was largely written under dictation from various Canadian and US business coalitions desperately concerned to keep the Canada-United States border open for trade while secure enough against saboteurs to satisfy Washington. The 22-Point Smart Border Plan signed by the Mexican and US governments in February 2002 was dictated more by pressure from Washington than from interested business. Both programs represented the reassertion of government autonomy in a concerted crusade to defend against the terror of jihad. Although business played a role in pressing for action, implementation of the border plan was by old-style, public-sector government using its coercive powers, with few genuflections made before the altar of public-private governance.

Willing or forced, these measures were accompanied by Ottawa's further harmonizing its visa and immigration policies to tough new US standards Security cooperation between Mexico and the United States derives from the struggle against narco-traffic and the resulting transborder cooperation between adjacent municipalities and states. Since 2001 Mexico City has been drawn into closer integration with Washington's new policy paradigm, which declares that its Mexican border must be as impenetrable to hostile agents and their weaponry as its northern border.

The peripheral states have thus enhanced their coercive capacity in sync with and under pressure from their hegemon. To the extent that combating terrorism was a norm embraced by Ottawa and the bulk of the Canadian public, increased border security could be seen as a further example of hegemonification — strengthening US power but with Canadian consent. But to the extent that US concerns were seen in Mexico as paranoid if not protectionist, Mexican responses to US pressure for border tightening were reluctant concessions to empire by elites in the periphery who knew that, if they did not comply with the centre's demands, their economic access to its market would suffer.

Military Defence

Given the United States' shift from hegemonic/consensual leadership to imperial/coercive global policy, North America's military governance reverted to the two skewed bilateral relationships — intimate dependence and wary autonomy — that it had demonstrated during the first four decades following the Second World War.

Achieving greater continental security was the Pentagon's goal in reconstituting its domestic armed forces in a Northern Command (Northcom) with responsibility for the whole of North America and the Caribbean. Faced by requests that its armed forces cooperate with Northcom and that it even endorse the Ballistic Missile Defense (BMD) program, Ottawa found itself facing the old Cold War dilemma known as "defence against help": either Canadians would defend themselves according to US specifications or the Pentagon would take over their defence according to its own lights. The government of Canada's response was characteristically ambivalent. On the one hand, it made a show of autonomy by refusing to endorse BMD. On the other, it agreed to expand the scope of the North American Aerospace Defense Command, whose satellite-based warning systems will be needed by BMD.

The US-Mexican defence relationship has seen few similar initiatives at integration. With minimal military cooperation in the past, a constitution strictly forbidding the movement of troops abroad, national resistance to integrative initiatives, and resistance from its military leaders, Mexico seems unlikely to play an active part in Northcom and has adopted a stance of delaying and stalling.

In a nutshell, if economic globalization had turned governments into passengers, terrorist globalization put governments back in the driver's seat. Under these renewed military imperatives, historically inscribed political cultures reasserted themselves in North America. The United States psyched itself onto a war footing against a terrifying foe. Canada supported Uncle Sam on most issues, while demurring enough to assert its symbolic autonomy. Mexico reverted to its deeply rooted military nonalignment.

Middle East Diplomacy

Given the powerful pressures of hegemonification that had driven North America's formal and informal governance processes for a decade, it was even more striking that the US war on Iraq was greeted not just by the abstention of Mexico and Canada but by their active diplomatic efforts to prevent Washington from initiating hostilities. Although the United States was exerting its autonomy by imposing its strategy globally, this exercise of power was resisted in its own continent when the differences between the centre's fundamentalist conservatism and the periphery's more social democratic values became starkly visible. With Washington trying to reorder the global hierarchy in a united attack on an enemy whom its economic partners found unthreatening, even its most dependent neighbours found their interests threatened more by Washington than by Bin Laden.

While the Pentagon's plans for continental defence brought Canada and Mexico back to their earlier Cold War relationships with Uncle Sam, its ambitions for militarily imposed regime change in the Middle East in the short term and for the control of space in the long term revealed that any hope for a common North American foreign and security policy along European Union lines was pure fantasy. Battered by systematic expressions of US autonomy, the cause of transborder governance in North America had reached its nadir, showing thereby that the prophets of an irreversible globalization had been disproven by the very superpower that had once provided the chief evidence for their analysis.

Conclusion

The challenge to understanding how the globalization-autonomy dynamic affects governance processes in North America is appreciating that the United States, as their driving force, has a valence simultaneously and interconnectedly at the global, continental, transborder, and domestic levels.

Global Order

The most pregnant US-generated changes in the past fifteen years at a global scale but with North American impact are two-fold. First is the triumph of economic liberalization under an expansive US hegemony (with powerful consequences for reducing domestic but increasing corporate autonomy). Second is the partial negation of this process by four years of global political restructuring under an aggressive/defensive US empire (in which raising national borders in the name of security trumped lowering them in the name of commerce).

When considering their two countries' positions vis-à-vis the United States, nationalists in Canada and Mexico see a relationship of domination: power asymmetries between the hub and its spokes force the latter into a pattern of continual compliance. Nationalism inspires some resistance in the periphery, particularly among Canadians for certain highly symbolic issues such as US wars of empire, or among Mexicans for threats to their constitution's sacrosanct article 27.

But looking at the US periphery from a broader vantage point shows the same two peripheries to be complicit in their own dependence. Their governments eagerly negotiated their way into economic globalization through multiple channels. They sustain their own relationships of domination with weaker economic partners by signing free trade agreements: in Mexico's case, with Central America and, in Ottawa's case, imposing the same state-autonomy-reducing, TNC-enhancing, investor-state dispute arbitration on South Africa that Canadians had objected to in NAFTA's chapter 11 (Schneiderman 2000). These two countries' powerful corporations in petroleum and the information media participate in world TNC networks, and their elites — including their academics and NGO leaders — circulate globally in their own specialized groupings.

Even if the Mexican and Canadian governments resisted joining Washington in its Iraq crusade, they have also resisted building their own bilateral axis in solidarity against Washington. They may declaim against

Yankee perfidies, but the context for their ire is as likely to be the desire for greater access to the US market than Washington will permit as dismay about US demands that they change their own policies.

Continental Domain

North America's apparent participation in globalization's trend towards regional governance turns out to be misleading. A space that generates both integration and fragmentation internationally, North America has itself no separate political centre, no locus equivalent to that played by Brussels for the European Union, as sketched by Hedetoft in the next chapter. The institutional matrix located in Washington's imperially columned palaces enfranchises US citizens just as starkly as it disenfranchises Mexicans and Canadians, whose fates it determines almost as directly.

Designed on the Canadian and Mexican side by negotiators who were ideologically committed to the view that governments should reduce their control of the economy, NAFTA's institutions were too weak to give the periphery any meaningful role in a new kind of continental governance, let alone prevent the centre from violating its rules when it saw fit. This makes the prospects for transborder cooperation contingent on the Americans' perception of the problem, a perception that may be influenced by the periphery's concerns only if they are amplified through the regular channels of US politics.

Transborder Governance

The dynamic interaction between the United States and its periphery has been supplemented by legions of non-state actors in the marketplace and civil society, with business mainly promoting and NGOs partially resisting the multifarious processes of transborder continental governance. Surprisingly more meaningful for governance practices in some reinstitutionalized North American markets are global institutions such as the WTO's TRIPS and the Bank of International Settlements, whose norms have generated new practices in sectors such as big pharma and banking, respectively.

Bereft as it is of structured supranational governance forms, North America has neither a single hierarchical framework nor a separate mode of regulation for its continental accumulation systems. Rather, as our examples have suggested, it presents a multiplicity of informally institutionalized and overlapping networks of information, finance, production, distribution, communication, and marketing.

Domestic Autonomy

The extraordinary sight of the United States resisting the erosion of its own autonomy in the name of its messianically unique mission, but in violation of normative regimes of its own creation, has necessarily affected the periphery. There, assertions of US autonomy have come at the cost of reduced Mexican or Canadian capacity to solve problems caused by US-generated externalities in areas such as water diversion or air pollution. From this we see that, in a dominant state, established institutions that are anchored in constitutional and democratic legitimacy still control how adaptations are made to globalization, whether these be in the name of economic prosperity or anti-terrorist security.

Evidence of some independence in Mexico's and Canada's diplomacy does not mean that these middle-sized powers can recapture their autonomy over domestic policy as easily as can Washington. On the contrary, the structural changes in the periphery resulting from deepened integration make it extremely difficult to turn back the clock. Efforts to re-establish control over the agricultural or petroleum industries in Canada would encounter massive resistance from the interests that have become dependent on intercourse with their American partners. Massive urbanization accelerated by the devastation of the Mexican corn economy cannot be reversed by re-establishing the tariff on corn.

Efficiency, Justice, and Stability

Returning to the broader normative themes of this volume, the analysis presented in this chapter permits three additional observations, even if evaluating the outcome of these complex changes in terms of this volume's socio-economic criteria is not easily accomplished. Efficiencies gained by corporate consolidation at the continental scale and measured by profit levels, executive salaries, or stock market valuations are difficult to weigh against increased income disparities, the loss of middle- and working-class jobs, falling levels of well-being, and lowered rates of productivity growth — all features of recent economic trends.

As for justice, the arbitral processes of global economic governance are notorious for favouring corporate over governmental power and for not reining in the United States' proclivity for breaking its own rules. That Mexico's poor having become poorer and its rich richer is but one index of the injustice that governance in North America seems incapable of rectifying.

There is so little evidence of stability in any of the domains that we have reviewed — other than the US political process's enduring preoccupation with its own autonomy — that it would be foolish to talk about globalization having reached some plateau in its evolution. Alas, watching the spectacle of the recent evolution of governance in North America — which is less than meets the eye as far as NAFTA is concerned, more than meets the eye at the level of market governance, and just what one sees in the reborn security state — does not prepare the observer for anything less than to expect continued turbulence between North America's centre and its periphery.

Observers who interpret the trend towards the consolidation of multistate regional groupings as an institutional response to the dynamic tension between globalization and autonomy must pause when they come to North America. On the one hand, they can find support for their thesis in the fact that NAFTA was negotiated as a response to economic elites in the three states' fear of competitive pressures from overseas. This evidence was buttressed in March 2005 when the three heads of government committed themselves to promote a new Security and Prosperity Partnership for North America and in March 2006 when they institutionalized big business' participation in trilateral governance by giving the new North America Competitiveness Council regular access to the cabinets of the three governments. On the other hand, NAFTA's institutions are patently incapable of generating a continental mode of regulation. The global hegemon's rhetorical commitment to the spirit of regional economic integration is continually contradicted by its proclivity for unilateral and protectionist action. Mexico's call for strengthening NAFTA's institutions along EU lines fell on deaf ears. For its part, Canada has continued to promote transborder cooperation while complaining loudly about American protectionism. In civil society, trinational continental activism is rare. Only in the marketplace does North America appear to exist as a meaningful production and marketing zone, although it is actually more integrated in a global economy than part of an emerging, identifiably continental regime of accumulation. In short, there is much transborder governance in North America but precious little governance of North America.

Although the European Community was seen by many to be the prototype for the new regionalism of the late twentieth century, North America's differentiated autonomy may set the standard for the regionalism emerging in the twenty-first in other areas: few institutional constraints on a largely autonomous hegemon, decreased autonomy for its partners, increased autonomy for transnational business, and diminished access for a polarized civil society to these increasingly dispersed centres of power.

chapter 11　　　　　Sovereignty Revisited:
European Reconfigurations,
Global Challenges, and
Implications for Small States

Ulf Hedetoft

SOVEREIGNTY, A KEY EXPRESSION of the ideal of collective autonomy examined throughout this volume, is the product of European modernity and the attendant monopolization of power, ultimate control, and rights of enforcement by states ruling territorially delimited peoples, exercising power with their consent, and recognized as sovereign by comparable units in the international system (Bartelson 1995; Onuf 1991). Westphalian sovereignty is predicated on this co-extensiveness of nation, territory, culture, and state. This political geometry is real to the extent that ultimate authority is concentrated in one political locus, but imaginary because conditions and possibilities of exercising sovereign powers are based on increasingly complex forms of (inter)dependence and hierarchical relations (Grande and Pauly 2005; Lake 2003).

Sovereignty is defined by the dynamics between international recognition and the relative autonomy of a state in relation to its society. In David Lake's words, "domestic hierarchy and international anarchy are flip sides of the same coin ... Sovereignty is, therefore, an *attribute* of units which, depending on the referent, entails *relationships* of both hierarchy and anarchy" (Lake 2003, 305). Sovereignty exists in the interstices between territoriality and extra-territoriality, rights and power — more and more uneasily as the world is globalized and the regional integration process in Europe challenges the divide between domestic and foreign-policy domains.

These developments represent the most recent stages in a longer transformation process. Since the early 1970s, the notion of sovereignty has been affected by "interdependence" and new institutional means of influencing other states. "Sovereignty is not virginity, which you either have or you don't," as former UK Foreign Secretary Sir Geoffrey Howe argued at the point when the Cold War was coming to a close (G. Howe 1990, 678).

In this spirit, Robert Keohane, among others, has discussed sovereignty as "less a territorially defined barrier than a bargaining resource for a politics characterized by complex transnational networks" (Keohane 1994, 177). If this "resource approach" is applied to Europe, sovereignty appears as a malleable instrument for the pursuit of state interests in the extra-national but intra-EU space. European Union institutions as well as processes of informal governance, networking, or open methods of coordination allow political actors from all member states to influence decision-making and legislative processes in the partner countries. This happens on a formally recognized and mutually agreed-upon basis, by means of external constraints and frameworks (rule making) and opportunity structures leading to voluntary normative alignment (co-optation). This regime further implies that all member states wield more power and influence in the world external to the EU than they could have done within the orthodox framework of Westphalian-type sovereignty and that they can take advantage of the European Union as a buffer against globalizing pressures. In this way, the EU facilitates the process of adapting to and cushioning the impact of globalization (viz. the Common Agricultural Policy [CAP], external trade regulations, common asylum policies, and agreements in other areas such as environmental protection and media and communication). The price member states have to pay for this widening of their autonomous space in pursuit of state preferences is the endogenous abandonment of sovereignty.

The "resource" or "ticket" argument represents a new configuration of national interest and regional integration (Buzan, Jones, and Little 1993; Goldmann 1994). Whereas liberal institutionalism and cooperative behaviour are traditionally linked, changes in the regional environment in Europe have produced a nexus between realism and a new European governance regime involving a super-added layer of "systemic sovereignty." In this view, the political actors on the EU stage seem to have effected a reinterpretation of sovereignty based on the logic that loss of internal sovereignty is (more than) compensated by the increase of external influence and flexibility of action (Hedetoft 1994).

More and more frequently, such a pragmatic redefinition is articulated by political proponents of integration. In the run-up to the Danish referendum on the Euro in September 2000, for instance, chairperson of the

Social Liberal Party (Det Radikale Venstre) in Denmark, Marianne Jelved, argued that Danish sovereignty does not consist of a romantic illusion of what we can "do alone," but in pursuing policy preferences "with others" (Jelved 2000). In return for ceding sovereignty, "Copenhagen" would gain more "power in Brussels." To this way of thinking, sovereignty has transformed into an instrument rather than the essence it is often imagined to be, and standing firm on its essential/formal aspects implies waving goodbye to political influence. Sovereignty and power have parted ways, in spite of the fact that this is not the way things present themselves to the mind of this political actor (the op-ed was, after all, titled "Sovereign Denmark"). For this political actor, sovereignty is seen to have been strengthened by being reconfigured, simultaneously serving as the entrance card to and the chips in a differently configured poker game of international politics.

The remainder of this chapter will suggest an alternative way of conceptualizing such transformations of sovereignty, aligning itself with Ernst Haas' argument that European integration "is concerned with how and why states cease to be wholly sovereign" (Haas 1971, 6), while attempting to explain the structural dynamics of the process as it relates to the globalization/autonomy nexus outlined in Chapter 1. The core argument is that sovereignty in Europe is best analyzed as a three-tiered structure, each tier representing different qualities and gradations of sovereignty, and the three tiers interlocking in different ways for nation-states located at different points on the international power continuum. The main, though not the exclusive, emphasis will be placed on the consequences of the transformation process of sovereignty for small states in Europe.

Tier 1: The Internal Perspective

Ole Wæver (1995) has proposed a way to "solve the sovereignty puzzle in Europe" that will serve well as a point of departure. His analysis posits the European Union as a post-sovereign, postmodern order, which at the same time is attempting to embrace both a traditional modern and an alternative post-modern position. The state has survived and is still sovereign (ibid., 405), but the European order, without itself having assumed the qualities of a new sovereign statehood, represents "systemic post-sovereignty," developing according to its own political logic and representing a dynamic that orthodox international relations theory is unable to capture. The system has transcended sovereignty, but "there is no post-sovereignty at the unit level" (ibid., 430).

The problem with this solution is that it articulates a logical impossibility rather than a paradoxical reality. If the EU order is post-sovereign, then the units cannot be sovereign in their relation to that order, because sovereignty is both an endogenous "unit attribute" and a relational phenomenon and with respect to recognition, comparison, interaction, diplomacy, alliance building). And if the units *were* actually sovereign, then the system cannot be post-sovereign, if it relies on and is unthinkable without the units, and if systemic features are, as Wæver concedes, an integral part of the units and their mode of functioning.

The key to the paradox can be found in the widely shared presumption that "if a state loses sovereignty, it has not survived as a state" (ibid., 405). And because the member states of the EU have clearly survived as states, it apparently follows that they have also been successful in retaining sovereignty. This axiomatic rather than argued assumption misses the key point that the European Union can be instrumentalized by member states and state interests only on condition that sovereignty is no longer an attribute of nation-states in their form as member states of the European Union. There is a trade-off between sovereignty and influence, power and interest construction in a post-sovereign context, which in crucial policy areas takes precedence over national law and follows forms of decision making and governance that defy sovereign national logic. It is not a question of sharing, pooling, dividing, shrinking, or expanding sovereignty, nor of acquiring more real, in exchange for less, formal sovereignty, but of sovereignty not being an operative norm in the conduct of political business in the endogenous European context. Here, nation-states are no longer the sole, highest, or ultimate arbiters of authority. Boundaries are permeable, problems are solved in negotiating networks rather than belligerently "by other means," and balance-of-power politics is not a functional principle.

This does not mean that nation-states no longer exist, only that they exist, in the European Union, in a format whereby national interests (in terms, for example, of security, trade, and foreign relations) have become divorced from national sovereignty. EU member states are autonomous, but are not sovereign units of governance. "Autonomy" is here taken to imply the freedom and space to govern, manage, and act in conditions largely determined by extraneous and dominant agencies. Rule making in these conditions takes place in the external political space, although "domestic" actors can participate in or be consulted regarding rule making, legislation, and practical implementation/enforcement. Recognition — a central parameter of sovereignty — no longer assumes direct, lateral, interstate forms, but takes a detour via EU institutions and multi-level governance structures, which are independent of neither the member states nor the "system." Selected manifestations of these processes are: ongoing debates about the best "sharing of competencies" in different policy areas (on the subsidiarity question, see Chapter 12 in this volume); the complicated voting procedures in the European Council; the mutual imbrication of EU law and national legislation; the intricacies of single market regulations (effectively beyond the control of member states); the steady process of transferring policy areas to the first, "supranational" pillar of the Maastricht Treaty; open methods of coordination; the communitarization of immigration and border controls; the salience of the European Court of Human Rights; and the European Central Bank and the common currency regime, which bar member states from conducting independent fiscal policies and impose considerable budgetary constraints.

Member states (as well as factual and potential accession countries) accept these limitations, constraints, and erosions of their sovereignty because they perceive them to be necessary and desirable from the point of view of pursuing national preferences, internally in the European space as well as externally as regards global challenges. Specific motivations differ on a country-to-country basis (Keohane and Hoffmann 1991), depending on historical factors and political cultures: some are primarily economic, others political (e.g., the strengthening of democracy), and still others security related. The common element is that sovereignty transmutes into autonomy (of planning, action, influence, regulation), traditional government (with its monopoly of the means of violence and enforcement) into soft forms of (multi-level) governance, and territory/borders into policies of space and the management of supraterritorial flows. This is the world of complex sovereignty (Grande and Pauly 2005) — or rather, the complexities of sovereignty in a process of transforming into something else. Member states may still be the "enforcers" of law, but *what* they enforce and *on what legal basis,* is no longer their own sovereign decision — approximately 80 percent of all trade law in Europe, for instance, now originates in EU institutions rather than national capitals.

Three objections could be raised against this reading. Objection 1 is in line with one of Wæver's arguments. In his words, "nothing at present prevents member states from preserving their sovereign quality, as long as they are willing to continue limiting its scope" (1995, 418). States are not per se without sovereignty because certain conditions of that sovereignty are not the property of the state, or because there are cultural or social areas that do not belong within its sphere of sovereign control (e.g., religion). In this view, the relationship between member states and the EU is largely one in which some areas of internal sovereignty have been removed from the nation-state circumference and have reappeared as EU competencies, though it is granted that problems may arise when member states and the EU lay claim to supremacy over identical policy areas/issues.

However, we are no longer facing a clear-cut problem of distinguishing between the form (identical) and the substance (changing) of sovereign authority, but a situation in which the form itself is in a state of transformation. And second, the substantive scope of sovereignty is not completely irrelevant to sovereignty, which is clearly a form, a quality, but one that is ultimately predicated on the presence of certain resources, certain "quantities" of power, people, and production. In other words, there are limits to how few de facto areas of sovereign authority can remain without its legal and political substance being affected too.

Objection 2 is that sovereignty as an idea is still very potent. It may not be what it was, but this is rarely the way things appear to the national mind. Sovereignty permeates our vocabulary and our fundamental approach to social questions, including the "methodological nationalism" of social science (Beck 2002); our mental horizons are configured in terms of living within cultural, geographical, and political boundaries staked out by sovereign units of final authority (Inayatullah and Blaney 1995; Walker 1993). Further, it seems that the more sovereignty is challenged by regional and global processes, the more it tends to gain in importance on the level of political symbolism. Such culturally steeped reactions are especially pervasive in the case of small, vulnerable nation-states, which acutely experience the limitations of their de facto sovereignty.

In turn, such images of sovereignty (produced in a context of real loss) can emerge as anti-EU rhetoric and policies. From the Danish rejection of Maastricht in 1992 to the Irish rejection of the Nice Treaty in 2001, and the 'No' of the Dutch and French electorates to the EU Constitution in spring 2005, there is a direct line following this pattern. In the same vein, the Amsterdam Treaty, 1998, expressed more recognition of national cultural peculiarities than did the Treaty of European Union, 1993, and the draft Constitutional Treaty reaffirms this respect for the "rich cultural and linguistic diversity" of contemporary Europe (European Convention 2004, part I, title I, article 3, 3).

Formulations such as these demonstrate the hold that the idea of sovereignty has on the mental horizon of elites as well as the masses, and because ideas can affect social reality (Giddens 1984; Goldstein and Keohane 1993; P. Hall 1989), it might lead us to conclude that this particular idea is forceful enough to pre-empt a post-sovereign order in Europe. The ideational role might possibly be credited with some short-term constraining effect. (A case in point is the 1994 judgment of the German Constitutional Court [Bundesverfassungsgericht] on the question of "Kompetenzkompetenz" — that is, who has the competence to determine where competencies reside [Hedegaard 2002; Weiler 1999].) But there is little in the historical dynamics of the European Union to support an argument that it can fundamentally alter the course of events. Rather, what we are witnessing is a pattern of asynchronicity between "material" and "ideational" developments, through which notions of sovereignty are adapted to a new context.

Objection 3 argues that member states are still members of international organizations like the United Nations (UN) and hence enjoy sovereign recognition in these institutional contexts. This is a valid point, the implications of which will be addressed in the following section.

Tiers 2 and 3: The External Perspective

The argument to this point has concerned the internal transformation of sovereignty to something qualitatively different. Because the European (and global) context decouples national interests from national sovereignty, the system is no longer effectively based on sovereignty. It is true, as Hendrik Spruyt has argued (1994, 191), that "the EC is not just an extension of state interests" and "has diminished the sovereign state as a locus of decision making," but the link between interests and sovereignty should be reformulated. It is precisely because states are seeking to maximize their interests that they have had to both relinquish sovereignty as an operative principle and enter into new institutional arrangements. For the same reason, relations between member states are not a zero-sum game, the difference between small and big, weak and powerful, states has been considerably modified, and common interests have emerged within the EU — precisely *because* all member states are concerned with their own survival and interests as nation-states (Milward 1992).

Nevertheless, this analysis pertains only to endogenous EU relations. As regards externalities, things work more according to the old template, though here also significant changes have taken place. The external question subdivides into two separate but interdependent tiers.

Tier 2: Orthodox Sovereignty Retained

Here I return to objection 3. International institutions, notably the UN, as well as extra-EU state actors recognize member states, not the EU itself, as sovereign. France, not the European Union, is a permanent member of the Security Council. Denmark can make bilateral trade agreements with China that are based on the mutual recognition of political and legal sovereignty. Germany can oppose US intervention and war in Iraq, while Britain and Poland can support it. Membership in the North Atlantic Treaty Organization (NATO) is national, not communitarian. And all member states have independent diplomatic representations in other countries in order to represent their sovereign will and interests (they do in EU member states too, but these should be analyzed differently in accordance with tier 1).

Also in the external area, the EU occasionally represents, or is simultaneously present in negotiations alongside, member states, especially regarding trade policy and environmental policy, and increasingly foreign policy and security issues too. But the range of areas where this participation applies is still limited; moreover, the European Union, even here, is not viewed as a sovereign entity but pragmatically as a representative of national interests, a collective bargainer. In sovereignty terms, member states have given away their bargaining right in those areas and thus some de facto external sovereignty, but this does not affect their de jure sovereignty. The substantive scope of sovereignty — the number of policy areas it encompasses — has been modified, not its quality. The EU, on the other hand, has assumed some factual external "personality" (actorhood) but no legal sovereign existence. It is in this space of EU/member state interaction that relations to global pressures should be situated and the functionality of the EU for national accommodation to globalization be understood.

Nevertheless, member states appear on the external political stage largely as sovereign units taking their place in the normal workings of the international order. We are faced, therefore, with an anomalous double bind: internally in the European Union, the units have basically lost or abandoned their sovereign quality; externally, their sovereignty is retained, though modified in scope and strengthened in influence because of the EU's protective shield. Thus, sovereignty conforms simultaneously to a modern and a postmodern template. This conclusion is not as illogical as it may seem. Sovereignty is a qualitative relation, not an essence, and that relation can exist in some respects and areas and not in others. The situation is further compounded by the existence of tier 3.

Tier 3: Licensed Sovereignty

The main point here is that the aggregate effect of different globalization processes tends to undermine traditional conditionalities of national sovereignty. Whereas the *international order* recognizes national states as the principal and proactive units of the system, the emerging *global order* subordinates nation-states to its own objectives, turning them into local, reactive units of regulatory governance (Cox 1994).

Licensed sovereignty describes a form of national independence and self-determination where the substantial instruments of ultimate political control reside outside the national context, and where domestic law and order as well as external influence are exercised within a political franchise system that recognizes "sovereignty" in return for compliance with the values and interests of global hegemonic power constellations (Hedetoft 2003a). This is part and parcel of the process through which states are being re-functionalized to assume new roles in a global order implying a more clear-cut differentiation between cores and peripheries, weak and strong states (Bauman 1998).

The case of Iraq — where the United States, while keeping its troops in the country and remaining in control of "the state of exception" (Schmitt 1934/1996), supposedly "handed back sovereignty" on 28 May 2004 to politicians carefully selected for their pro-US sympathies — illustrates the paradoxes of licensed sovereignty. Whereas the formal skeleton of authority, legally and politically, is now represented by persons with Iraqi names and thus legitimate credentials, real power (including the option to overrule by force any decisions running counter to American interests) remains in US hands. The exceptional nature of this case resides in the fact that American rule has been and to some extent still is "formal" and "territorial," where the general preference of American hegemony is to keep it as informal as possible (S. Howe 2003). Thus, through transformative processes being enacted in full public view and within a short time span, the Iraqi case teaches us the inherent connectedness between formal and informal empire and some of the permutations of autonomy and sovereignty that go with this distinction in the era of globalization.

Processes of this nature bear witness to the disempowerment of the traditional core unit of international relations and its new structural embeddedness in the global order (Camilleri and Falk 1992; Holsti 2004; Walker and Mendlovitz 1990). The contribution of globalization consists in the qualitative transformation of resources, processes, and distributive power structures on which sovereign authority is predicated. The success of states depends on abandoning old fashioned claims to ultimate control and accepting that they possess only its formal container. Sovereignty is a right held on condition that certain political preferences, normative standards, and economic policies are maintained. Hence, recognition can be withdrawn and sovereignty is a conditional relationship, which does not guarantee security or stability. To that end, other resources and networks must be activated.

Therefore it is both true and not true that EU states retain external sovereignty in extra-EU relations. International relations and institutions still exist. Globalization, particularly in regard to its synergy with American neo-imperial power and its normative preferences for pre-emptive intervention, constitutes an additional and increasingly forceful systemic overlay. As I argue in Hedetoft (forthcoming), present-day global structures must be analyzed primarily as results of political engineering by representatives of American political preferences, which have consistently been aimed towards harnessing, shaping, and reconstituting the international order for their own neo-imperial purposes. For that reason, globalization today — its institutions, processes, and normative underpinnings — bears the imprint of the American imperial steamroller of the twentieth century, being predominantly the product of more or less liberal ideologies, preferences, and practices on the part of the United States, with all the paradoxes and contradictions this entails. But American power has not totally superseded internationality. The problems that these frequently conflictual forces present to European states, in the area of security politics, were sharply reflected in the divisions within the EU in response to the American decision to intervene in Iraq without the consent of the UN.

The way to navigate in such dangerous waters, particularly for small states, is to be very "pragmatic" about sovereignty and open to alternative ways of pursuing state interests. This is in some ways reminiscent of the European Union itself as a systemic transformation of sovereignty. But as regards the *relationship* between the endogenous transformation of sovereignty in the EU and the exogenous but precarious maintenance of sovereignty in the international system globally, a peculiar dialectic is at work. The existence of the EU and membership therein contributes to enhancing the endogenous sovereign status of EU nation-states in the external world by equipping even small, vulnerable states with both collective and individual power resources and international competences and recognition they would otherwise not have. Thus the regional, post-sovereign partnership, which has eroded sovereignty as an operative principle and norm in its internal affairs, helps to maintain and strengthen sovereignty for its constituent units externally.

It may seem as if there is no significant difference between the practical annulment of sovereignty as an operative principle in endogenous EU relations and the licensing of sovereignty in the global order. Admittedly, there is a significant amount of overlap between the two processes in terms of political outcomes. Nevertheless, important differences remain. In the case of EU relations, the factual neutralization of sovereignty is effected by means of direct bargaining and codified in treaties and institutional mechanisms for interest maximization. There is a quid pro quo at work: interests for sovereignty. Hence, the internal empire of EU integration conforms badly to orthodox power relations between cores and peripheries. In the case of globalization, no such inverse relations hold. Sovereignty is maintained on conditions of political and economic adaptation to centripetal political forces. In other words, in Europe de facto sovereignty transmutes into mechanisms for the strengthening of national interests, but in forms that belie clear-cut boundaries and de jure sovereignty. In the global order, the opposite is happening: de facto sovereignty is weakened, de jure granted, though in most cases this seeming permanence of the sovereignty principle holds out false promises.

Sovereignty and Collective Autonomy in Small European States

A number of salient points about small states in relation to sovereignty and the European integration process have already been made in passing. Key operative notions are vulnerability, openness, the need for security, limited power resources, and adaptability. Due to the exposed position of small states in terms of economic resources and hard power, disjunctures between national interests and real sovereignty are always imminent. In conditions of globalization wedded to the concrete context of European integration, the dichotomy between real and formal sovereignty translates into a choice between abandoning sovereignty and retaining some measure of autonomy while gaining more external influence, or maintaining the constitutional and formal trappings of sovereignty but losing or conceding autonomy and influence (see the comparison between Denmark and Norway below, and Stephen Clarkson's comments on Canada in Chapter 10 of this volume). Hence the answer to the key question of whether globalization is constraining or widening the space for manoeuvre and flexible adaptation of small states is: both, depending on political choices regarding sovereignty, on the nature and complexity of transnational alliance building, and on geopolitical positioning. Whether a nation-state is a member of the EU — and, if so, how and when it joined — makes a difference, but so does the structure of macroeconomic relations, mass/elite interaction, institutional structures, and historical path dependencies.

For all small and middle-sized powers, the issue is handling different states of dependence and exposure within a context of formally symmetrical sovereignties but real hierarchies of power. Traditional ways of coming to terms with dependence on outside forces — and turning these into an advantage rather than a liability — have been conditioned and facilitated by flexible combinations of openness and closure, liberal and exclusionary policies. These includee adapting to economic constraints by embracing policies of openness while wedding them to domestic political consensus, often corporatist decision-making processes, high degrees of economic redistribution across social classes, and extensive political trust building on perceived cultural homogeneity (Katzenstein 1985) — in other words, on confidence among the "ethno-national core" (Brubaker 1996) of highly developed welfare states that their national sovereignty is politically and culturally intact, that elected political leaders do their best to preserve it, and that their choices make a real difference.

Intensified globalization, now politically orchestrated and harnessed to superpower interests, tends to undermine these assumptions. Taking care of national interests in a globally and regionally integrated political economy is bought at the expense of institutionalized dependence, conspicuous and growing asymmetries, and the licensing of sovereignty, or, differently expressed, its virtual abandonment in the European Union. These small- or medium-sized states increasingly "govern under stress," to borrow Marjorie Cohen and Stephen Clarkson's term (2004). This stress creates discontent and identity anxieties, places strains on the national consensus that used to be the chief instrument of flexible adaptation, and is enhanced by migratory inflows that question the traditional cultural compact and national cohesion and that expose the limits of multicultural policy solutions. Conversely, global dependence also breeds dependability of sorts — by holding out a promise of a quasi-feudal, neo-imperial quid pro quo between servant and master, periphery and core (Arrighi 1997; Wallerstein 1995): a new system of uneven recognition entailing possibilities of continued, even growing autonomy on condition that sovereignty is treated as a thing of the past. It is at this point that relations with the European

Union emerge as a way of both securing dependability and containing dependence: a regional shield against global turbulence (Rosenau 1990), and at the same time an institutional form that promises both internal gains and external influence. Different states handle in different ways such problems of sovereignty and autonomy, of putting in place "strategies of societal protection in the face of diminished sovereignty and the growing power of the institutions of global capitalism" (Brodie 2004, 13). Let me exemplify this contention through a contrastive look at the cases of Denmark and Norway.

In spite of the many similarities between these two north European nation-states, their adaptation to the transformative forces impinging on their sovereign quality differs on a number of points. This reflects divergent geopolitical positions; varying economic structures, strategies, and preferences; different underpinnings of social cohesion and political trust; and different security policies — including variations in strategies of balancing between Europe and the United States.

The two positions can be summarized as pragmatic bargaining ("sovereignty can be traded bit by bit") in the case of Denmark and symbolic-constitutional nationalism ("sovereignty is sacrosanct") in that of Norway. However, these summaries conceal intricate configurations and choices of identity and interest, territorial integrity, and pragmatic security.

Possibly the most important element accounting for the different perspectives is that Second World War experiences related to geopolitical position conditioned perceptions and approaches to sovereignty very differently in the two countries. Denmark is contiguous with Germany and was negatively affected by the Second World War but far less dramatically in terms of human suffering, material losses, and economic devastation than many other European countries (e.g., the Benelux region). Denmark was occupied but was never a battleground. It was allowed, because of pragmatic-collaborationist policies, some measure of (Nazi-monitored) self-governance for the major part of the war. The economy, which was in many ways made functional for the German war effort, was relatively intact by the end of the war. The return to "sovereign normality" and the initial phases of the postwar welfare state — barring certain economic austerity measures during the first half-decade or so — was therefore relatively swift (Branner 1992). Nonetheless the war had exposed Denmark's vulnerability and inability to defend itself, and it was clear to the elites that the old policy of neutrality would no longer work. Hence the burning issue was the country's future in terms of international alliances and commitments, and how best to adapt flexibly and successfully both to Cold War conditions and to the European Coal and Steel Community — and later the European Economic Community (EEC). As far as security was concerned, Denmark opted for (or was in many ways pressured into) NATO membership, after some hesitation and a period of toying with the alternative possibility of a Nordic defence community. As regards the first stages of the European integration process, Denmark's geopolitical position and preferences less obviously lent themselves to unconditional participation than was the case in, for example, the Netherlands: the Danish war experience had been less traumatic, national identity and sovereignty issues played a more prominent role for both elites and the popular masses, and the structure of the economy was tilted in the direction of Anglo-Danish trade relations (only gradually to become more strongly "germanized" as the "economic miracle" south of the border started to take off).

Hence, Denmark's international pragmatism was from the outset configured as a balancing act between Europe/Germany and the Anglo-American world — and, in a cultural sense, the other Nordic countries too (Hedetoft 1998). As regards the sovereignty question, balancing in this manner between a strong sense of homogeneous nationalism, an open and flexible economy, and various cultural and security-related alliances and commitments has implied a dichotomization of the issue. On the one hand, sovereignty has been invested with strong identity-related connotations, a tendency that has been pronounced particularly since the first Danish referendum on the European Community (EC) in 1972 — with sovereignty and national identity becoming conflated and sovereignty entering into the symbolic politics of Danish nationalism. On the other, and especially among political elites, the question has been regarded in extremely pragmatic terms (see the discussion of Marianne Jelved's position above), as something that could be and probably would have to be ceded, not in one fell swoop, but gradually in light of changing circumstances.

One of the significant amendments made to the Danish Constitution as far back as 1953 was the addition of article 20, stipulating that sovereignty can be ceded in clearly specified areas either following a referendum or on condition that five-sixths of the members of the Danish parliament support the proposal (Hedegaard 2002; Zahle 1998). This article has constituted the legal basis for all but one of the Danish EU referenda. It has thus paved the way for a separate institution of political culture in Denmark: the politics of gradually surrendering sovereignty, divorcing its political from its cultural-symbolic component, and thus securing autonomy and flexibility of action while maintaining — even when this has to be bought at the expense of exceptions, opt-outs, popular scepticism, and anti-immigrant sentiments (Hedetoft 2003b) — a belief in the continued uniqueness, success, and homogeneous character of Danish identity (Campbell, Hall, and Pedersen 2006). Sovereignty in Denmark is squarely positioned between the symbolism of identity and the pragmatics of adaptation to shifting European contexts and global constraints. And successful political actors need to master this complex balancing act in order to effect the factual erosion of sovereignty (and the concomitant widening of the scope for autonomous action) with the consent of the population.

Norway is different, although it shares the conflation of national pride and political sovereignty. Its experience during the Second World War was more conflictual and violent. By offering active resistance against the Nazi occupation forces, its national identity and pride were vindicated in the process. Both of these factors, combined with the fact that Norway did not gain full national sovereignty until 1905, have led to greater unwillingness in Norway — particularly in wide sections of the population — to let go of the formal trappings of sovereign existence. For this reason, this nation-state is not a full-fledged member of the European Union, elite preferences of this nature having twice been blocked by popular 'No' votes in referenda, and it is a NATO member only with wide-ranging reservations. At the same time, it wants to project itself as a global nation assuming and representing extensive humanitarian and ethical responsibilities, acting as a peace broker, and spearheading aid to developing countries (witness major initiatives such as the Brundtland Report, the Middle East Oslo Accords, the Nobel Peace Prize, the role in aid of victims of the Asian Tsunami, and an immigration discourse steeped in tolerance and decency). In Øyvind Østerud's formulation, "these political compromises ... betray the country's peculiarities: the political need to balance internationalism and nationalism — idealist as well as pragmatic participation, on the one hand, and the protection of sovereignty, on the other" (2004, 40). As regards the European Union, this translates into the anomaly of Norway, by means of the European Economic Area (EEA) association treaty, being an "integrated non-member" (ibid.), formally outside the EU but de facto as dependent on EU legislation and decision making as the bona fide members. In fact, it can be argued that Norway is even more dependent: it has no place at the negotiating table, cannot systematically use informal channels of influence (Christiansen and Piattoni 2004), and must simply accept and convert into national law any rules and directives emanating from Brussels. In addition, it is more vulnerable than full-fledged members due to the normative constraints that often regulate the the behaviour of associated or co opted members of organizations, eager to demonstrate their eligibility by adhering more faithfully to rules and decisions than the members themselves. The Norwegian adaptation strategy vis-à-vis the European Union is a compromise between loss of de facto sovereignty and its symbolic maintenance, between legal integration and constitutional sovereignty, and between near-total dependence and the idea of self-determination (cf. Clarkson's analysis of Canada's position within North America in Chapter 10).

This attempt to strike a balance between symbolic and pragmatic considerations has engendered an unusual form of political asymmetry, buying formal sovereignty at the expense of real autonomy and influence, and forcing the country to adapt docilely to economic and foreign policy externalities not of its own making. Membership of the EEA does, of course, allow Norwegian business unfettered access to the single market on equal terms, but it also transforms the Norwegian government into anything but a sovereign rule-making body and allows market mechanisms — whether of EU provenance or deriving from neoliberal processes of globalization — to invade and determine policy areas that were formerly under tight state control (Claes and Tranøy 1999). In many ways, therefore, one cannot, in the Norwegian case, argue that old-style sovereign government is being replaced by a postmodern kind of governance (Rosenau and Czempiel 1992), which would allow new forms of autonomy and manoeuvre through formal or informal co-decision-making at the supranational level. The current compromise is possible solely because of the social affluence and political safety net deriving primarily from petroleum riches and their derivative, the national Petroleum Fund, and because the anomalous constraints of tier 1 relations (Europe) can be partly offset through the freedom of sovereign manoeuvre at tier 2 — the practice of sovereignty and the visibility of the country in EEA-external relations and international forums. Arguably, however, growing asymmetries in the global system (tier 3) will narrow this window of opportunity too.

Sovereignty and Autonomy in Larger States

A brief reflection on the applicability of the model to larger member states is in order. Logic of the realist kind would indicate that if the European Union were beneficial for small states, it would be a disadvantage for the more powerful ones. Challenged by the analysis above, a distinguished historian, prompted no doubt by this logic, recently asked what would possibly keep Germany from reverting to the classic nation-state logic and "retak[ing] Strasbourg"? My response is built on five assumptions:

1 The EU compact normatively excludes the possibility of such unilateral action, and resorting to it would nullify the basis of the European Union.

2 Channels of influence in the EU have been reconstructed in and through the institutional means at the disposal of member states, regions, corporate interests, non-governmental organizations (NGOs), and private citizens: this is where the separation of autonomy and sovereignty manifests itself in a practical sense and at multiple social levels.

3 Because of this reconstruction of channels of influence, not only have the structure and substance of "national interests" been reconfigured, but European politics is no longer a negative-sum game.

4 Influence and domination are no longer based on territorial conquest and possession for at least three reasons: the colonial experience was costly and bloody; the Americans would not allow a return to formal empire; and globalization makes other forms of expansionist projects more attractive and more efficient.

5 No state has absorbed all these historical lessons better than the German state, which has realized that "normalization" does not require a revival of the sovereign practices of the long nineteenth century (Hedetoft 2003a, chap. 6).

Do these reflections apply to the anomalous case of the United Kingdom? Clearly Britain has been a reluctant member of the EU from the start (S. George 1990) — a fact reflecting that the costs of non-membership even in the 1960s and early 1970s exceeded the benefits of retaining old-style sovereignty. Britain is still in some ways the odd one out (outside the Euro-zone, the Schengen Agreements, and key parts of the Justice and Home Affairs pillar, and deeply dissatisfied with the CAP), although New Labour's European policies have shown more commitment and a more steadfast determination to stay the course. In Blairite discourse, this course is often construed as a wish to become a key power in EU affairs alongside Germany and France. This goal has no doubt been prompted by greater economic interdependence between Britain and the continental countries than previously (involving serious consideration of membership in the Euro-zone and dedicated participation in the Constitutional Convention), but also by a realization that the traditional transatlantic "special relationship" is not strong enough to carry Britain's ambitions forward. Admittedly, Britain's high priority is still to balance between the European Union and the United States in security-related and military policy areas (viz. the war in Iraq and the war on terror), but Britain's active engagement in efforts to build up an independent military capacity at the EU level has nonetheless been considerable in recent years. Euroskepticism is still evident in the United Kingdom but is mostly a popular phenomenon not widely shared by political and business elites, who have realized the economic and political benefits of membership and increasingly seem to agree with Geoffrey Howe that "sovereignty is not virginity which you either have or you don't" (Howe 1990, 678).

The salient difference between the United Kingdom and more vulnerable member states — and the reason why the United Kingdom can permit itself to have a number of opt-outs in different areas — is that the UK is one of the world's key financial centres (London is the only serious rival to Frankfurt and the European Central Bank in Europe) and a nuclear power, permanent member of the UN Security Council, and a member of the G-8; consequently it is better situated to forge a unique configuration of tiers 1-3 for itself. Tier 1, the endogenous abandonment of sovereignty, is modified by opt-outs; tier 2 (the maintenance of traditional, de jure sovereignty externally) is more prominent; and tier 3 (the licensing of sovereignty as a result of neo-imperial globalization) can be proactively affected, because the United Kingdom enjoys a modicum of direct influence on the leading world power, in former colonies, and in key global institutions. Together these factors mean not that the gravitational pull of EU forces can be ignored, but rather that the autonomy and manoeuvre allowed by this configuration requires a delicate balancing act on the part of British political leaders in order to optimize British interests in shifting contexts.

Hence, small as well as more powerful member states benefit from regional integration, and all have to face the costs in terms of a reduction of sovereign status. Unlike the case of North America, the European region generally works as a cushion against global pressures and as a new autonomous space for the pursuit of economic and political interests. On the other hand, only fools do not dread historical determinism; a departure from Europe's internal Kantian peace cannot be excluded, however hard it may be to imagine. Should such a new condition develop, it is beyond doubt that it would also involve a dissolution of the European Union. Sovereign behaviour and EU integration are incommensurable — it is one or the other, not both at the same time.

Conclusion

Four main conclusions can be extracted from the above analysis.

First, the sovereignty question in the European Union must be conceived as a three-tiered structure, where nation-state sovereignty is no longer an operative or helpful analytical concept internally — except as regards political symbolism and the politics of identity — because the interaction between member states and EU institutions/governance has assumed post-sovereign characteristics. Externally, member states both retain sovereignty qualities and see them challenged by global processes. The international system is overlaid by a global one that works according to other political, normative, and structural assumptions.

Second, we must conceptualize member states as both sovereign and not. Sovereignty is relational: different relations mean different qualities and competences in different settings. This does not mean that sovereignty is nothing but a resource, an invitation to the banquet that can be swapped for a bit of influence and yet still be retained. The most important challenge, however, is that, as regards the European Union and its internal configuration, we need to conceive of nation-states where the sovereignty concept no longer explains state behaviour. The conduit of state business, the pursuit of national interests, has taken leave of sovereignty.

Third, small states inside the European Union stand to gain considerably from this restructuring of the landscape of sovereignty. This gain is to be had both within and outside the EU. Inside the EU, the trade-off between sovereignty and political clout, the attendant obfuscation between domestic and foreign politics, and the culture of negotiation and informal governance optimize conditions for achieving national results, minimize risks of confrontation, reduce effects of peripheral status, increase security, and generally create a more peaceful, orderly, and dependable political and economic environment. Externally, the EU enhances the sovereign qualities of vulnerable member states and their visibility in foreign policy debates, and — more pragmatically — it acts as a buffer against the turbulence and unpredictability of global challenges.

States like Norway and Switzerland, and until recently Romania and Bulgaria, are in a more precarious position: the functionalization of dependence is more complicated, the cost of maintaining formal sovereignty is high, and the compensations are probably inadequate and certainly impossible to calculate. The EU continuously determines conditionalities of adaptation over which these states have almost no influence. They are simultaneously being exposed to global forces without enjoying the full protective shield and diplomatic advantages of membership. Hence the question of joining the EU cannot be put to rest and is always one of when, not whether.

Finally, although the EU may be said to have some of the formal trappings of a sovereign unit, it is nevertheless not recognized in those terms. Internally, this is the case because it would require member states to recognize EU institutions and actors as supreme and sovereign, to fully transfer all means of legal-political enforcement to the EU centre, and to abandon all symbolic gestures and discourses of national sovereignty. The fact that sovereignty has evaporated at the "unit" level does not mean that it has reappeared at the level of the "system." The EU has a personality (or several), an important degree of actorhood, but no sovereign existence. As for externalities, the same holds true, but with the difference that here member states *as nation-states* are recognized and behave as sovereign entities. In contrast, the EU, whenever present at international meetings or negotiations, most often appears as a 1+ actor — an extra participant, as at G-8 meetings, a personality with no independent powers or authority but a representative of the regional institutional setting that gives additional weight to the interests and arguments of its member states. This may be in for a change should the European Union gain increasing internal recognition as the supreme provider of security and foreign policy identity of all its members (Bowley 2005). Yet, as both the Iraq conflict and the debates over the Constitutional Treaty have shown, there is still some way to go before such ideas can be transformed into political practice.

chapter 12   **Subsidiarity and Autonomy in the European Union**

Ian Cooper

THE DYNAMIC TENSION BETWEEN globalization and autonomy is particularly acute in the European Union (EU). With its extensive governance functions, and certainly in comparison with other international institutions, the EU has an unusually potent capability to intrude upon the autonomy of its member states. More than a half-century of European integration, part of the broader globalization process, has endowed the EU with a unique transnational legislative and legal system, including a supranational parliament and court. The European Union's powers are both broad and deep. It is an active legislator across a broad array of policy areas — enacting about 2,000 new legal measures each year. Its laws, moreover, are directly effective within national jurisdictions and supreme over conflicting national statutes, even in cases where a member state had opposed final passage. Accordingly, compared to other international institutions, the EU is unusually effective both in its ability to promulgate rules and to obtain the compliance of its member states with those rules. This effectiveness has come at a price, in the form of a popular backlash from those who believe that the EU frequently oversteps the bounds of its legitimate authority. As Hedetoft suggests in the preceding chapter, in response to conflicting pressures the EU has been forced to devise systematic and principled ways to balance the imperative of the uniformity of transnational rules against that of the preservation of national autonomy. I argue in this chapter that the key principle employed to strike this balance is the principle of *subsidiarity*.

In general terms, subsidiarity requires that small social groups be protected against interference by larger social groups, on the logic that central authority is (or ought to be) subsidiary to local authority. Since the early 1990s, European leaders have established a number of institutionalized practices intended to make EU governance conform to this principle. Specifically, subsidiarity requires that in policy areas where competence is shared between the EU and its member states, the European Union must refrain from taking action in circumstances where action at the national level would be more appropriate. Furthermore, the complementary principle of proportionality requires that in all policy areas, when the EU does take action, it should employ the least burdensome means that are sufficient for the purpose. These two principles, codified in general terms in the Maastricht Treaty (1992), were in subsequent years elaborated into detailed guidelines that were eventually inscribed in a protocol appended to the Amsterdam Treaty (1997). The guidelines require, in effect, that the European Union's three main political institutions — the Commission, the European Parliament, and the Council of Ministers — take subsidiarity and proportionality into account at each step in the legislative process. This chapter examines how these institutionalized practices were put into effect, and assesses whether or not they have actually succeeded in changing the way the EU is governed. Before we turn to these matters, we should first examine the philosophical heritage of the concept of subsidiarity and the richly nuanced notion of autonomy that it entails.

Subsidiarity and Autonomy

Although it has roots that extend back to ancient and medieval thinkers such as Aristotle and Thomas Aquinas (Millon-Delsol 1992), subsidiarity is most closely associated with the early-twentieth-century social philosophy of the Roman Catholic Church. This philosophy emphasizes the essential interconnection between individual and collective autonomy. It presupposes an organically structured society, in which each person is embedded in a complex network of social groups, ranging in size from the largest (civil society as a whole) down to the smallest (the family), all of which aid in his or her development as an autonomous individual. Subsidiarity is the political principle that specifies the role of the state within this broader social order. This role is subsidiary to these social groups, which have the primary role in the development of autonomous individuals. Subsidiarity requires that the state must govern in a limited manner, recognizing and

235

respecting the autonomy of the social groups that make up civil society, and never acting in a way that would destroy or absorb them. From this perspective, even though the development of individual autonomy may be the paramount policy goal, the best way for the state to advance it is through the recognition of collective autonomy rather than direct intervention into the lives of individuals. This philosophy has much common ground with communitarianism, which — unlike liberalism, which generally posits that the individual is ontologically prior to the group — presupposes that individual and group identity are in fact mutually constitutive (see my chapter in Bernstein and Coleman, forthcoming). By this logic, collective autonomy could be said to have an inherent value that is not reducible to the autonomy of the individuals who make up the group.

The most important aspects of this subsidiarity principle remained intact even as it was transposed into an entirely new context, from early-twentieth-century Catholic social thought into contemporary EU politics. The essence of subsidiarity is the normative requirement that central authority govern in a manner that respects the autonomy of local authority. The basic philosophy of how higher authority should relate to lower authority remains the same, even though the identity of these authorities has changed: whereas originally subsidiarity had required the state to act in a manner that respects the autonomy of subnational groups, it now requires a supranational entity, the European Union, to act in a manner that respects the autonomy of states. In this context, subsidiarity retains the notion that collective autonomy has an inherent value that must be respected, not just as a matter of efficiency but of morality. Moreover, it is a dynamic principle: it is not so concerned with how to allocate powers between central and local authority as how central authority ought to act in relation to local authority. Finally, subsidiarity is based on a notion of collective autonomy that is subject to incremental variation. This variability makes it a much more subtle principle than sovereignty, which is generally thought of as an absolute condition that is either present or absent (James 1999). Subsidiarity is meant to police the actions of the EU when it is operating on the frontier between EU and national competence: because most EU activity is in areas of shared competence, every European Union action is a potential encroachment on the autonomy of the member states. This autonomy is affected not only by the initial large decision to confer a power on the European Union, but even more so by the numerous small decisions concerning when and how that power should be exercised that make up the day-to-day business of EU governance. Subsidiarity is intended to arrest or reverse the tendency of this governance activity to drift ever-upwards to the European level and the parallel tendency of the European Union's authority to expand into an ever-greater number of policy areas.

What this means is that the analyst who wishes to ascertain whether the European Union's subsidiarity policy has succeeded must be willing to critically engage with the minutiae of EU governance. To know whether, in its day-to-day workings, it is adhering to or defecting from the norm of subsidiarity — that is, respecting or violating national autonomy — one must put EU governance under a microscope. That is the rationale for the empirical analysis to be undertaken below. For example, a question that at first glance might seem to be largely technical — such as which legislative instrument, the regulation or the directive, should be employed in a particular circumstance — actually has a moral principle at stake, because the directive allows national governments a greater degree of policy discretion than the regulation. The basic thrust of this chapter is to examine the nuts and bolts of EU governance and draw some conclusions from an analysis of how the overall size and makeup of the European Union's legislative output has changed in the years since Maastricht. Although each small decision on its own might seem technical or inconsequential, in aggregate they display patterns that reveal changes in the conduct of EU governance with respect to autonomy.

The Development and Implementation of the Subsidiarity Policy

According to most observers, the prospects for the success of the European Union's subsidiarity policy were inauspicious. Subsidiarity was judged to be a principle that was appealing in theory but unworkable in practice, too vague and too subject to radically different interpretations to be operationalized as a significant check on the expansion of EU activities (Føllesdal 1998; Van Kersbergen and Verbeek 1994). Furthermore, the policy seemed toothless because it lacked effective enforcement powers. Although subsidiarity is codified in the Maastricht Treaty, and is thus in theory justiciable, in practice it has not acted as an effective legal check on the European Union's exercise of its competences: to date, not one act of the EU has been annulled by the European Court of Justice (ECJ) for violating the principle of subsidiarity (Estella 2002; Bermann 1994; De Búrca 1998, 1999). Moreover, the policy has not entailed the repatriation of competences back to the member states; in fact, the number of policy areas in which the EU may exercise competence has risen, through various treaty amendments, in the years since Maastricht. Rather, the general approach of EU subsidiarity policy has been normative, setting out procedural and substantive guidelines for the political institutions of the EU — the Commission, the Council of Ministers, and the European Parliament — to follow when deciding when and how to legislate. The effort has been to create a "new legislative culture" in the EU by internalizing a norm of self-limiting governance — subsidiarity and proportionality together — into the European Union's legislative system.

The internalization of subsidiarity into the European Union's legislative culture began in earnest in the tumultuous period in 1992-3 after the Maastricht Treaty was signed but before it had been ratified into law by all member states. Despite subsidiarity's long intellectual pedigree, it actually entered the EU lexicon only in the 1970s and EU law in the 1990s, when it was codified in rather vague terms in the Maastricht Treaty. After the Danish electorate, in a June 1992 referendum, narrowly voted "no" to its ratification, European leaders seized on subsidiarity as a means to demonstrate that the Maastricht Treaty would not create a European superstate. (The Danes voted "yes" to its ratification in a second referendum in May 1993.) To this end, they crafted a set of guidelines for the European Union's political institutions to follow to ensure that future legislation would comply with the principles of subsidiarity and proportionality. The key documents in the development of this policy were a Commission Communication of October 1992, the conclusions of the Edinburgh European Council in December 1992, and an Interinstitutional Agreement in October 1993. The last of these is important because it indicates that this approach to subsidiarity was the unanimous policy of the EU's three main political institutions — the Commission, the European Parliament, and the Council of Ministers. Eventually these guidelines were inscribed in a protocol appended to the Amsterdam Treaty, which was signed in 1997 and became law in 1999. But as this protocol merely gave retroactive legal effect to an already existing set of practices, 1992-3 marks the correct start date of the subsidiarity policy. Of course, cultural change is not instantaneous, and so we should not necessarily expect there to be a sudden change in the European Union's legislative output. As the norm of subsidiarity was progressively embedded into the EU's legislative culture throughout the 1990s, during that period we should expect to see a gradual decline in EU legislative activity.

The key reference in the Maastricht Treaty is article 3b, which in three paragraphs sets out three fundamental principles of EU governance — conferral, subsidiarity, and proportionality:

The Community shall act within the limits of the powers conferred upon it by this Treaty and of the objectives assigned to it therein.

In areas which do not fall within its exclusive competence, the Community shall take action, in accordance with the principle of subsidiarity, only if and in so far as the objectives of the proposed action cannot be sufficiently achieved by the Member States and can therefore, by reason of scale or effects of the proposed action, be better achieved by the Community.

Any action by the Community shall not go beyond what is necessary to achieve the objectives of this Treaty. (Art. 3b TEC)

The first paragraph states simply that the European Union (or, strictly speaking, the "Community") must act within the limits of its legally conferred powers. The latter two paragraphs are different in kind in that they impose normative limits on the actions of the EU even in those areas where it has the legal power to act. Subsidiarity requires that (in areas of "non-exclusive" — i.e., shared — competence) the European Union refrain from acting when action at the national level is more appropriate, and proportionality requires that (in all areas) the EU choose the least burdensome means to achieve the purpose. In theory, the principles require EU legislation to pass three consecutive tests: (1) Does the European Union have the legally conferred power to act? (2) If so, is action appropriate under the circumstances? (3) If so, are the means chosen proportionate to the intended ends?

The Maastricht language may be faulted on a number of grounds. First, it relies on a distinction between exclusive and non-exclusive EU competence that is not defined elsewhere in the treaty; I will return to this problem below, when assessing the empirical record. More to the point for now, the above text is vague in both substantive and procedural terms. Substantively, it does little to indicate how to assess whether a contemplated or proposed measure complies with subsidiarity and proportionality. A parsing of the second paragraph reveals two separate tests, one of *necessity* (the action of member states acting alone is insufficient) and the other of *comparative efficiency* (the objectives can be better achieved by action at the EU level), but these still leave much to the discretion of the EU legislator in deciding whether the European Union should "take action." Similarly, the third paragraph says only in vague terms that any EU action "shall not go beyond what is necessary to achieve the objectives of this Treaty," without mention of what kinds of measures are preferable. Procedurally, the Maastricht text does not indicate exactly whose responsibility it is to ensure compliance with subsidiarity and proportionality, or what procedures they should follow in doing so.

The post-Maastricht subsidiarity policy, which found its definitive expression in the Amsterdam Protocol, was intended to rectify these shortcomings. To begin with, the document makes clear that subsidiarity does not alter the EU's existing constitutional structure: it does not affect the *acquis communautaire,* the institutional balance, or the "principles developed by the Court of Justice regarding the relationship between national and Community law" (art. 2), nor does it "call into question the powers conferred on the European Community by the Treaty" (art. 3). Instead, it is intended to ensure compliance with subsidiarity and proportionality by internalizing these principles into the European Union's legislative culture. To this end, the Amsterdam Protocol sets out substantive and procedural guidelines for their application. Unfortunately, the substantive guidelines for the application of subsidiarity elaborate upon the Maastricht text without providing real clarity. This lack of clarity is, perhaps, due to an inherent vagueness in the concept of subsidiarity itself. Reasonable people may disagree as to whether EU action meets the tests of necessity and comparative efficiency in a given circumstance, and this leaves a large margin of discretion in the hands of those who will decide whether to act. As for proportionality, it should be said that the substantive guidelines are more successful at least insofar as they are specific about which legislative instruments should be chosen so that EU action may be made less burdensome: "Other things being equal, directives should be preferred to regulations and framework directives to detailed measures" (art. 6).

The Amsterdam Protocol makes up for this substantive vagueness by providing detailed procedural guidelines that require the main political institutions of the EU to take steps to ensure that each new legislative measure complies with subsidiarity and proportionality. The procedural requirements are greatest for the Commission, the institution that has the power to formally propose legislation, which must do four things: it must consult widely before proposing legislation, justify the relevance of its proposals with regard to subsidiarity, minimize the financial and administrative burdens of legislation, and submit an annual report to the other institutions on the implementation of article 3b (art. 9). The necessity of new EU action in a given circumstance must be substantiated with explicit reference to the demands of subsidiarity and proportionality:

> For any proposed Community legislation, the reasons on which it is based shall be stated with a view to justifying that it complies with the principles of subsidiarity and proportionality; the reasons for concluding that a Community objective can be better achieved by the Community must be substantiated by qualitative or, whenever possible, quantitative indicators. (art. 4)

For their part, the European Parliament and the Council of Ministers are required, "as an integral part of the overall examination of Commission proposals," to consider their compliance with subsidiarity and proportionality, and to do the same for any proposed or contemplated amendments to the proposal (art. 11).

Since the inception of the subsidiarity policy, these procedural guidelines have become a routine aspect of the European Union's legislative process. Generally, each EU legislative measure is now dutifully accompanied by a statement of reasons that explicitly attests its fidelity to the principles of subsidiarity and proportionality. The official EU position on the question, as expressed in the Commission's annual *Better Lawmaking* reports — to be further discussed below — is that the implementation of the principles of subsidiarity and proportionality has been a success (Azzi 1998; Von Borries and Hauschild 1999). But has there in fact been a substantive change in EU legislation, or are the institutions merely paying lip service to these principles? Is the policy merely an instance of "organized hypocrisy" (Krasner 1999) in which the relevant actors accept the validity of a norm — in this case, subsidiarity — but nevertheless continue to routinely violate it? To be certain of subsidiarity's substantive influence on EU legislation, we must look for empirical confirmation beyond official reassurances. Among the few scholars who have looked at the question, there is no consensus as to whether the subsidiarity policy has actually worked. In fact, there is no consensus even as to what might count as evidence for its success or failure. A large part of the problem is that changes in the "legislative culture" of the European Union are necessarily difficult to measure. A few scholars have attempted to assess subsidiarity's impact on various institutions (Van Hacke 2003) or across various policy areas (Van Kersbergen and Verbeek 2004), but the results have been inconclusive.

One obvious place to look for evidence of the impact of subsidiarity is in the Commission's annual reports on the application of the principles of subsidiarity and proportionality, which have been published since 1993. The *Better Lawmaking* reports set out what steps have been taken in a given year to ensure the correct application of subsidiarity and proportionality. These include both specific instances drawn from the current legislative record and broad initiatives aimed at reforming the European Union's style of governance. Although demonstrating subsidiarity's impact in a particular circumstance is difficult, the Commission points to instances in a given year when legislative proposals were withdrawn or legislation in a particular field was scaled back or discontinued. For example, in its 2004 report, the Commission decided (after carrying out "a series of analyses, studies, and stakeholder consultations") that a system of harmonized "pre-packaging sizes" for certain products, in place since the 1970s, could be substantially repealed, and made a proposal to that effect (Commission of the European Communities 2005, 22). Demonstrating the effect of proportionality is somewhat easier, in that the Commission may point to instances where many legislative options were considered and the least burdensome one was chosen. In 2004, considering how to regulate certain "unfair commercial practices," the Commission decided (after having "assessed several options in its impact assessment") that a framework directive, harmonizing certain aspects of marketing law but also leaving room for voluntary codes of conduct, would suffice (ibid., 23). Since 2002, the reports have also taken note of the other EU legislative institutions' actions with regard to subsidiarity. In general, the European Parliament favours an interpretation of subsidiarity that is relatively permissive of EU action, whereas the Council of Ministers favours a more restrictive interpretation. The Commission notes certain instances where competing interpretations were put forth and how they were resolved. Of course, all of these examples are merely anecdotal evidence of the impact of subsidiarity and proportionality on EU legislation.

Looking at these reports, we must be aware of an essential evidentiary difficulty in trying to prove the effect of subsidiarity, as distinct from proportionality. Complying with subsidiarity consists of taking no action in circumstances in which action at the national level is more appropriate; therefore, the Commission cannot easily point to EU *actions* taken in a given year out of respect for subsidiarity, because the primary evidence of subsidiarity's impact will be those actions *not* taken. This "missing" legislation falls into three categories. First, there are measures that were formally proposed but never enacted. These include those proposed measures that were decisively rejected by the European Parliament or the Council of

Ministers, measures withdrawn by the Commission in the face of opposition, or proposals that have not yet been taken up for consideration by the EU legislator. Second, there are measures that were contemplated but never formally proposed. These are ideas for new legislation that were considered by the Commission in the pre-proposal consultative phase of the legislative process but were subsequently shelved. Finally, there are those measures that were never contemplated. The last category is hypothetical, in that it captures the measures that would have been considered, and perhaps formally proposed and enacted, if subsidiarity had not been internalized into the EU's legislative culture. Although measures in the first two categories may at least be documented — in the chronicles of the European Union's legislative process, and the Commission's consultative documents — those in the third will necessarily leave no paper trail. The size of the last category can only be estimated by looking at how the European Union's aggregate legislative activity has changed since the inception of the subsidiarity policy.

The *Better Lawmaking* reports feature one very suggestive statistical measure that does indicate an overall change in the volume of EU legislation: the number of new legislative proposals produced annually by the Commission fell almost by half in the 1990s. The 2004 report demonstrates graphically that the number of Commission proposals (for regulations, directives, decisions, and recommendations) transmitted to the other EU institutions fell steadily from 787 in 1990 to 404 in 1999, then levelled off at a rate of about 500 per year in the early 2000s (Commission of the European Communities 2005, 28). This finding goes beyond anecdotal evidence in that it seems to indicate that the actual volume of EU legislation has decreased since the inception of the subsidiarity policy. However, the Commission's analysis in this regard is less than perfect. For one thing, it reports only the total number of legislative proposals, without breaking them down according to the type of legislative instrument proposed. Furthermore, it does not distinguish between proposals in areas of exclusive and non-exclusive competence, even though subsidiarity is applicable only in the latter. But the most basic problem with the Commission's numbers is that they measure the annual volume of legislative *proposals*. A more direct way of assessing the effectiveness of the subsidiarity policy would be to measure the annual volume of *enacted* legislation. That would indicate whether subsidiarity has significantly altered the legislative culture of the European Union as a whole.

The Empirical Record: Changes in European Union Legislation after Maastricht

The fundamental problem in assessing whether or not the subsidiarity policy has worked is this: when subsidiarity is effective, the EU declines to act in a circumstance in which it otherwise would take action. Nothing happens. In other words, the particular effect for which subsidiarity is the cause is a non-event, like the proverbial dog that did not bark. For this reason, it is very difficult to provide direct empirical evidence of subsidiarity's effectiveness. Yet it is still possible to provide indirect evidence. Over time, subsidiarity should produce many such non-events, which would presumably cause a change in the EU's aggregate legislative activity. Specifically, if the overall annual legislative output of the European Union has declined in the years since Maastricht, then we can posit that subsidiarity was the cause of this decline. This assumes, in effect, that the legislative output of the EU would have stayed the same if the subsidiarity policy had not been adopted. At a minimum, we can assert that if such a decline is proven to have occurred in the years since Maastricht, subsidiarity provides the best available explanation for this empirical finding.

Thus, here we set out to assess the impact of the subsidiarity policy by analyzing changes over time in the aggregate annual legislative output of the EU. This type of study has rarely been undertaken, and those few authors who have done so have reached quite different conclusions from mine (Pollack 2000; Alesina, Angeloni, and Schuknecht 2005). We may hypothesize that if subsidiarity has had an effect, we should see a marked decrease in the EU's legislative activity since the early 1990s, when the idea began to take hold. Furthermore, we may hypothesize that if proportionality has had an effect, then those legislative instruments that are less burdensome in character would make up an ever-larger portion of the EU's legislative activity over the same period. In that period the European Union has adopted on average more than 2,000 measures per year, employing a variety of legislative instruments. These must be sifted with care, with an eye to three important distinctions: binding versus non-binding acts; acts that are essentially legislative (law making) versus those that are administrative (law enforcing) in character; and acts taken in areas of exclusive EU competence versus acts taken in areas where competence is shared with the member states. The first two are important because, in order to assess the relative impact of subsidiarity and proportionality, we must be clear about what it means for the EU to "take action." The third distinction matters for assessing the impact of subsidiarity, which governs EU action only in areas of shared competence.

It is attention to the second of these distinctions that yields the most important conclusion: while the number of binding acts (regulations, directives, and decisions) adopted annually has declined only slightly since the early 1990s, this apparent stability masks two parallel but distinct trends: the number of acts that are essentially *legislative* (regulations and directives) has fallen dramatically while the number of those that are basically *administrative* (decisions) has risen dramatically.[1] I interpret this to mean that even as the European Union's administrative activity has increased steadily with its expanding regulatory responsibilities, there has been a little-noticed drop in its tendency to make new law. Moreover, while the number of directives — which are less burdensome than regulations — has remained relatively constant, their share in the total number of legislative acts (regulations and directives combined) has increased as the number of regulations has fallen. Thus, while on the surface the data do not indicate much change over time, when interpreted correctly they in fact demonstrate both that EU legislative activity has decreased dramatically since the early 1990s and that the portion of that activity employing less burdensome legislative means has significantly increased, providing prima facie evidence of the substantial effects of subsidiarity and proportionality.

By plumbing the various databases of EU law (Pre-Lex, Celex, and Eur-Lex), it is possible to obtain a complex portrait of the annual legislative output of the European Union, broken down according to type of legislative instrument and policy field. This breakdown can provide some answers as to the effects of the principles of subsidiarity and proportionality over the period since the Maastricht Treaty. The effects of the two principles must be assessed in different ways; whereas subsidiarity may be assessed quantitatively, proportionality requires a more qualitative assessment. If subsidiarity has been effective, then we should see a decrease over time in the volume of EU legislation in areas of shared competence. If proportionality has been effective, then we should see, in all areas, an increase in the use of legislative instruments that impose less of a burden on the autonomy of the member states. Proportionality requires, as the Amsterdam Protocol states, that "Other things being equal, directives should be preferred to regulations and framework directives to detailed measures." Although existing databases do not distinguish "framework directives" from "detailed measures," they do distinguish between regulations and directives. By looking at changes in the relative frequency with which these legislative instruments have been employed, we have at least one indicator of the effectiveness of proportionality over time.

In order to determine the effect of the subsidiarity policy, we must ascertain the exact number of legislative acts adopted each year since the policy began. This is more difficult than it seems, because we need to be clear about what constitutes a "legislative act." First, we must distinguish measures that are binding (regulations, directives, and decisions) from those that are non-binding (e.g., recommendations). If we were to apply a broad definition of EU "action" that encompassed non-binding "soft" law then we could well conclude that an increased use of such measures is evidence of the effects of proportionality. In the present context, however, it is more appropriate to apply a narrow definition of EU "action" that is restricted to binding, "hard" measures. A second distinction must be made between those acts that are essentially legislative in character (regulations and directives) and those that are essentially administrative (decisions). Regulations and directives are legislative in that they are generally applicable; decisions are more akin to administrative orders in that they are binding only on the addressee. Third, we must distinguish those measures taken in areas of shared competence from those taken in areas of exclusive competence. The proper measure for the effectiveness of subsidiarity will be whether there has been a decrease in the number of measures that are binding, legislative in character, and in areas of shared competence.

Before turning to the record of enacted legislation, let us look again, this time in greater detail, at the measure the Commission cites, the volume of proposed legislation. A search of the database that tracks the European Union's legislative process indicates that the total number of proposals for regulations, directives, decisions, and recommendations has indeed declined over the period 1990-2004, though not as steeply as recorded in the *Better Lawmaking* reports (see Figure 12.1). What is most striking is the marked decline in the number of proposed regulations and the marked rise in the number of proposed decisions. If we exclude proposals for measures that are non-binding (recommendations) or administrative (decisions), then the data demonstrate that the number of proposals for new legislation (regulations and directives combined) fell steadily throughout the 1990s before levelling off in 2000-4. Such data present more convincing evidence for the effect of subsidiarity than that which is presented in the *Better Lawmaking* reports. There is some evidence, though less dramatic, for the influence of proportionality, in that although the number of proposed directives has not changed much over time, such directives rose incrementally as a

proportion of total proposals for new legislation over the period (16 percent of the total in the period 1990-4, 20 percent in 1995-9, and 22 percent
in 2000-4). Unfortunately, it is not possible to subdivide these proposed
measures into areas of shared and exclusive competence, so I will bracket
this distinction for now and return to it later.

The same general pattern holds true when we shift our focus from
proposed to enacted legislation. Figure 12.2 displays the total number of
binding acts (regulations, directives, and decisions) adopted each year between 1990 and 2004, including those measures no longer in force. The
figures here are much larger than those for legislative proposals because
they capture the vast number of largely technical measures that account
for the majority of binding acts adopted by the EU in a given year. Even
so, the same trends demonstrated in Figure 12.1 are discernable. The overall
number of binding acts adopted has declined, though not dramatically. But
when subdivided by type of act, the changes are more striking: the number
of adopted regulations, beginning from a high of over 1,500 in 1990, fell

**Figure 12.1: European Commission proposals for new legislative measures,
1990-2004**

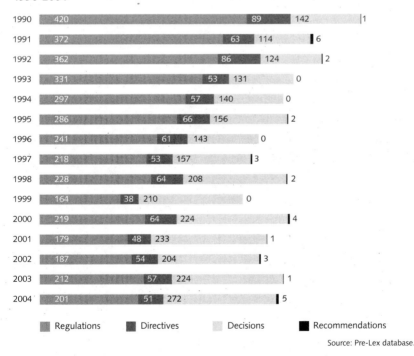

Source: Pre-Lex database.

steadily throughout the decade and levelled off at under 900 per year in 2000-4; the number of adopted directives changed little, hovering around 100 per year throughout the period; and the number of adopted decisions rose steadily, from an average of about 700 per year in the early 1990s to about 1,000 per year in 2000-4. To attest to the effects of proportionality, the number of directives (according to Celex) as a proportion of overall legislation (regulations and directives combined) rose over the same period (7 percent of the total in the period 1990-4, 8 percent in 1995-9, and 11 percent in 2000-4). Eur-Lex yields slightly different numbers, but the same overall trend (7, 9, and 12 percent, respectively).

What do these figures mean? There are two possible explanations. The first is predicated on the supposition that the drop in regulations and the rise in decisions are part of the same trend: in effect, the EU is "replacing" regulations with decisions. That is, when deciding which legislative instrument to employ in a particular circumstance, the EU is choosing decisions instead of regulations. If this explanation is true, then the general trend noted here would be more an instance of proportionality (because

Figure 12.2: Binding EU legislation adopted annually, 1990-2004

Year	Regulations	Directives	Decisions
1990	1518	95	525
1991	1463	103	639
1992	1516	122	617
1993	1381	118	741
1994	1263	79	945
1995	1147	72	765
1996	1043	95	789
1997	1030	81	971
1998	1025	100	934
1999	930	102	1030
2000	797	83	1049
2001	809	102	1197
2002	770	96	988
2003	845	126	981
2004	857	106	770

Regulations   Directives   Decisions

Source: Celex database.

decisions are less burdensome than regulations) than of subsidiarity (because the overall volume of "acts" has not declined significantly). By implication, this would invalidate the distinction I am making between legislative and administrative acts, because it would seem to indicate that regulations and decisions are interchangeable. In response, I should acknowledge that many regulations are indeed extremely technical and so narrowly targeted that they are indistinguishable from decisions. Yet the notion that decisions are "replacing" regulations may be refuted by an examination of adopted EU legislation subdivided by policy area. Other Eur-Lex data on regulations, directives, and decisions by type of instrument and policy area adopted annually between 1990 and 2004 (not reproduced here) show that the decline in regulations and the rise in decisions have, for the most part, been in quite different policy areas. While the number of regulations has declined most markedly in the fields of agriculture, external relations, and the customs union, the greatest increase in decisions is visible in the fields of competition policy and "general, financial, and institutional matters." For this reason, I favour a different explanation: the drop in regulations and the rise in decisions are two distinct but parallel trends. On the one hand, the legislative activity (regulations and directives) of the European. Union has decreased over time as the norm of subsidiarity has taken hold; on the other hand, administrative activity (e.g., decisions) has continued to increase with the expansion of regulatory responsibilities. These two distinct trends tend to be obscured by the fact that the number of binding acts adopted annually — comprising both legislative and administrative measures — has not declined dramatically since Maastricht.

The figures of adopted legislation cited thus far may be faulted because they necessarily include a large number of highly technical measures that should be categorized as administrative rather than legislative. This is even true of many regulations, which on paper are legislative acts. One way to eliminate this problem is to confine our searches to those measures adopted by the Council of Ministers, the main legislative institution of the EU. By doing so, the adopted acts number in the hundreds rather than the thousands and are more closely aligned with the numbers of legislative proposals cited above. Figure 12.3 displays the average number of regulations, directives, and decisions adopted each year between 1986 and 2005,[2] grouped into five-year blocks; it reveals the same general trends — regulations decreasing, decisions increasing, and directives holding steady. By this measure, the number of legislative acts (regulations and decisions) has indeed fallen precipitously over the period. In addition, directives make up an ever-increasing proportion of the total number of legislative acts (14 percent in 1986-90; 20 percent in 1991-5; 23 percent in 1996-2000; 31 percent in 2001-5), making a strong case for the effectiveness of proportionality over the period.

Figure 12.3: Binding acts adopted per year by the Council of Ministers, 1986-2005

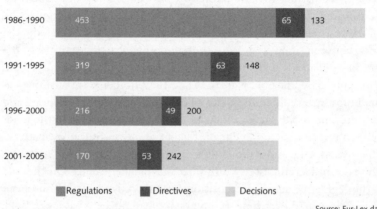

Source: Eur-Lex database.

Before we can be certain of the effect of subsidiarity, we must make one final calculation that will confine the analysis to legislative fields in which EU competence is non-exclusive. While proportionality applies in all fields, subsidiarity applies only in areas where the EU shares competence with the member states, according to the logic that the EU has no choice but to take action in areas where it has exclusive competence. The problem is that, as noted above, the Maastricht Treaty did not provide a catalogue of exclusive and shared competences. This omission sparked some academic debate. Some spoke for a maximalist definition of exclusive competence, arguing that all EU competences should be considered to be exclusive unless the relevant article of the treaty is drafted in a way that makes clear that member states retain competence (Toth 1994). Such a position would mean that many broad policy areas in which the European Union is very active, such as agriculture and the internal market, could be considered to be "exclusive," and that the member states may take action in these fields only insofar as competence has been "delegated back" to them by the EU. Others argued in favour of a more minimalist definition of exclusive competence that would limit such competence to a few fields (e.g., the customs union and external trade) (Dashwood 2004). This debate was tentatively resolved by the Convention on the Future of Europe, which produced a comprehensive catalogue of exclusive and shared competences that was eventually incorporated into the as-yet-unratified Constitutional Treaty (ibid.).[3] This document's list of exclusive competences is minimalist, confined to the following: customs union, competition, monetary policy for the Eurozone, fisheries conservation, common commercial policy, and the conclusion of certain international agreements (art. I-13, Treaty Establishing a Constitution for Europe).[4] With a reasonable degree of confidence, we can calculate the number of legislative acts adopted in areas of shared competence by subtracting measures taken in the above fields from the total.

The first section of Table 12.1 displays the average number of combined regulations and directives adopted per year by the Council of Ministers between 1986 and 2005, grouped in five-year blocks, subdivided by policy area, and then totalled. Those measures taken in areas of exclusive competence are listed in the second section of the table. Care has been taken to subdivide those categories that mix elements of exclusive and shared competence: for example, measures related specifically to fisheries conservation (Eur-Lex code 04.10.30), which is an area of exclusive competence, have been separated out from other measures related to fisheries, in which competence is shared. This table demonstrates that over this period there has been a decrease in the number of legislative acts passed in areas of exclusive competence, owing in particular to a precipitous drop in the number of customs union measures. This is an interesting fact, but it is not directly relevant for the calculation of the effects of subsidiarity. More to the point, when the number of acts in areas of exclusive competence is subtracted from the total, there is still a marked absolute decline in the remainder. The Council adopted on average, in areas of shared competence, 338 regulations and directives per year in the period 1986-90. This fell to 273 per year in the period 1991-5 and to 197 per year in the period 1996-2000, finally levelling off at about the same number, 196 per year, in the period 2001-5. These figures provide the most convincing evidence that subsidiarity has indeed brought about a decrease in the European Union's legislative output over this period.

One other question is addressed at the bottom of Table 12.1. Conventional wisdom remembers the late 1980s and early 1990s as a period of great legislative activity within the EU because of the effort to "complete" the internal market by 31 December 1992. Could the subsequent decrease in legislative output simply be explained by the completion of the 1992

Table 12.1: Average number of legislative acts (regulations and directives) adopted by the Council of Ministers annually, 1986-2005

Regulations and directives by policy area	1986-90	1991-5	1996-2000	2001-5
General, financial, and institutional matters	11	13	14	14
Customs union and free movement of goods	149	66	31	16
Agriculture	208	131	65	32
Fisheries	43	48	41	22
Freedom of movement for workers and social policy	7	8	7	9
Right of establishment and freedom to provide services	7	7	6	6
Transport policy	10	15	9	14
Competition policy	2	3	2	1
Taxation	2	5	3	6
Economic and monetary policy and free movement of capital	1	1	6	4
External relations	76	88	77	67
Energy	2	2	3	3
Industrial policy and internal market	24	23	20	24
Regional policy and coordination of structural instruments	2	4	3	3
Environment, consumers, and health protection	16	15	15	20
Science, information, education, and culture	1	2	1	2
Law relating to undertakings	2	2	2	5
Common foreign and security policy	0	2	6	9
Area of freedom, security, and justice	1	2	2	12
People's Europe	0	1	0	0
Total legislative acts	565	437	314	273
Acts in areas of exclusive competence				
Customs Union and free movement of goods	149	66	31	16
Competition policy	2	3	2	1
Monetary policy	0	0	1	0
Fisheries: conservation of resources	28	31	29	11
Common Commercial Policy	48	66	55	49
Total legislative acts in areas of exclusive competence	227	165	118	77
Total legislative acts in areas of shared competence	338	273	197	196
Internal market measures				
Freedom of movement for workers	0	1	0	0
Free movement of capital	1	0	2	2
Internal market: — approximation of laws	22	19	16	18
Internal market: — policy relating to undertakings	0	0	0	1
Total internal market	23	20	19	21
Total shared competence minus internal market	314	252	178	175

Source: Eur-Lex database.

program? An answer may be obtained by pulling out those measures specifically related to the internal market, adding them up and subtracting them from the total number of legislative acts in areas of shared competence. When this is done, it is immediately apparent that the number of measures adopted relating to the internal market has not, in fact, significantly declined since the early 1990s. Furthermore, the numbers are too small (about 20 per year) to have an impact on the overall trend. Thus, we can eliminate the completion of the internal market as an explanation for the overall decrease in EU legislation over this period.

The forgoing analysis leads to two broad conclusions. The overall annual legislative output of the European Union has declined significantly in the years since Maastricht; and the employment of less burdensome legislative instruments, in the form of directives as opposed to regulations, has risen over the same period. These trends provide convincing evidence that the principles of subsidiarity and proportionality have indeed had a substantial impact on the EU, causing it to govern in a manner that is increasingly respectful of the autonomy of its constituent member states. The broader implications of this change in EU governance are worth probing.

Conclusion

The question of how to maintain autonomy, however defined, in the face of globalization is increasingly urgent. It is particularly acute in the European Union, where, as we have seen, many critics have looked askance at supranational institutions possessing such broad law-making powers that they can whittle away at still-prized national autonomy. Indeed, many Europeans feel that there is now an inexorable tendency for decision-making authority to migrate "upwards" out of the hands of local and national communities and into the hands of "Europe," with unelected officials speaking in its name and personifying the impersonal "forces" of globalization.

The reason the principle of subsidiarity is so tantalizing is that it holds out the promise that a compromise solution between globalization and autonomy could be struck in a rational way. In this regard, a few prominent thinkers have given credence to the idea that subsidiarity could operate as a general principle by which global governance could be ordered (Carozza 2003; Slaughter 2004, 255-7; Wendt 2003, 506). Yet such musings are premature until it is definitively established whether subsidiarity has in fact "worked" in the European Union. But if it can be shown that member states of the EU have succeeded in maintaining their autonomy not through a blunt reassertion of sovereignty but through the more nuanced mechanism of subsidiarity, then that in itself is an indication that such a resolution is possible. Within Europe, the salience of this question will only increase in the future when — in an anticipated new procedure called the "early warning mechanism" — EU legislative proposals will also be scrutinized by national parliaments for their subsidiarity compliance (I. Cooper 2006).

Here we return to the moral dimension of subsidiarity. In essence, subsidiarity provides a particular way of thinking about legitimacy that judges central authority by its actions. Because local autonomy has inherent value, the actions of central authority are legitimate only if they remain within certain limits. What subsidiarity implies is that central authority will recognize local authority and govern within those limits. The leaders of the European Union, by promising to abide by the principle of subsidiarity, have in effect staked the legitimacy of the EU on its ability to govern within such limits. Recent events — such as the "no" votes against the Constitutional Treaty in France and the Netherlands — indicate that many voters are not convinced, and that they believe the EU has overstepped its bounds and invaded the autonomy of the member states. The empirical findings of this chapter suggest that these feelings are misplaced.

chapter 13

Institutions of Arctic Ordering: The Cases of Greenland and Nunavut

Natalia Loukacheva

> *As a region made up of peripheries with small human populations and limited*
> *resources, the Arctic is often overlooked in efforts to address the consequences*
> *of global environmental change and globalization. Yet the region is heavily*
> *impacted by these forces. What is needed to raise the voice of the Arctic in global*
> *forums is a strong coalition among local, subnational, and national actors com-*
> *mitted to speaking with one voice about Arctic concerns in a variety of settings.*
> — Oran Young, "Arctic Governance"

GLOBAL PRESSURES ARE BECOMING ever more obvious in the Arctic, even as local demands for legal and political autonomy increase in the region. This chapter looks at how the subnational governments of Greenland (Denmark) and Nunavut (Canada), each with local indigenous majorities and each with different degrees of autonomy within their larger states, are responding in institutional terms to the challenges of globalization. On the one hand, we see the growth of supraterritorial or transregional networks across the Arctic; this development suggests new roles for regional governing institutions mediating between diverse states as well as among diverse local political units. On the other hand, we see an escalation in the participation by the Inuit of Nunavut and Greenlanders in some aspects of international relations as they collectively assert their rights to autonomy. Institutional thickening is the result, as together the Inuit press claims for special representation at the international level, beyond the boundaries of the separate societies of which they continue to be a part.

The Arctic as a Distinct Region

The interdependence of the Circumpolar North and the necessity of coherent responses to global challenges have generated a diverse number of regional networks and multilateral regimes. Both networks and regimes have escalated substantive forms of cooperation and led to the integration of specific Northern policies in the European Union (EU) and in states claiming territory in the Arctic. This chapter inquires into what those regional networks and regimes mean both for global political ordering and for the strengthening of the collective autonomy of the indigenous peoples living in the region with respect to their respective states.

There are tensions between the devolution of powers to Greenland and Nunavut and the beginnings of the capacity of these entities to take independent positions in global arenas. These tensions can be observed in the framework of limited de jure and evolving de facto autonomy of these Arctic entities and the adaptive capacities of their governance systems to regional, national, and external policies. It is currently robust enough for governments in these two subnational units to aspire to be included in global negotiations and arrangements, despite the limited economic independence of Greenland and Nunavut and the uncertain prospects they face for sustainability in a context where both continue to face a high degree of dependence on financial support from their national governments. Tensions can also be seen in the clash between, on the one side, indigenous perspectives that view globalization as a continuation of the process of colonization and, on the other, the necessity for governance systems in Greenland and Nunavut to be responsive to and involved in global developments that affect their regions. Finally, tensions can be seen in the limited jurisdictional capabilities of both systems in foreign, defence, and security policies, which all have vast implications for present and future conditions in the region and which all suggest ultimate limits for the rising phenomenon of indigenous internationalism (Jull 1998, 1999).

In building Arctic institutional networks, the subnational units of Greenland and Nunavut in fact have been mostly dealing with regionalization within the Arctic rim, although they have addressed globalization to some extent especially through indigenous internationalism. However, in the face of serious economic and environmental challenges, both units must focus increasingly on problems posed by globalization. For both Greenland and Nunavut, the framework of Arctic regionalization will likely evolve incrementally. In the meantime, Nunavummiut are more likely to address global challenges in close partnership with the national government of Canada. In Greenland, depending on the result of anticipated changes in the constitutional status of the island in 2008-9, new arrangements for participation at the international level may be imminent.

The impact of globalization on the relationship between individual autonomy and collective autonomy within Greenland and Nunavut is complex. This chapter analyzes the struggle of both regions to gain a greater degree of political autonomy within their respective states. In both cases, this quest involves indigenous activism and supranational collaboration to build Arctic institutions. These processes reflect an assertion of the collective autonomy of indigenous groups through public governance or home rule. They give voice to the Inuit in global and Arctic politics, and they force the legal scope of collective autonomy in the region gradually to change. Regardless of the limitations caused by their evolving legal status, Greenland and Nunavut are creating a special relationship between themselves and other interested stakeholders through diplomatic activity in various institutions of global and Arctic governance. This is certainly one facet of globalization. Conversely, to the extent that globalization is interpreted as a continuation of colonization, it is perceived both to undermine the individual autonomy of local residents and constrain the quest for collective autonomy.

Nevertheless, despite their limited capabilities, the governments of Greenland and Nunavut aspire independently to influence global developments. Those aspirations are shaped by the traditional views and values of the Inuit majority in both regions. Thus, for example, *Inuit Qaujimajatuqangit* (IQ — traditional knowledge) became the core principle of the management of the Nunavut public government and is routinely evoked in addressing the pressing problem of climate change.

The practical possibilities of subnational governance in Greenland and Nunavut to steer developments in the region and more broadly are influenced by a number of factors. Among the most important of these factors are the following:

- the emergence of the Arctic as a recognized region (Keskitalo 2004), its growing global strategic importance, fundamental changes in its institutional structures, and increased collaboration between the eight

257

Arctic states — Canada, Denmark, Finland, Iceland, Norway, the Russian Federation, Sweden, and the United States — to advance Northern interests globally and within their respective societies

- complex linkages between Arctic eco-biological systems and global systems, which largely ensure the dependency of Arctic environmental issues on external forces (Pálsson 2004, 6)
- demographic, geopolitical, legal, social, economic, cultural, and historical changes effectively redefining current governance arrangements in Greenland and Nunavut and the legal scope of their autonomy
- the speed with which governance systems need to respond to or accommodate global challenges
- the expanding role of these substate units on the national scene in Denmark and Canada, the nature of their partnerships with national governments, and the general commitments of those governments to consider the needs and interests of their Northern lands in decision-making processes
- the particularities of the North with respect to geography, climate, remoteness, poor infrastructure, low population density, and high costs of communication
- high structural unemployment, widening disparities in incomes, limited prospects for economic growth, and continuing dependency on national transfers notwithstanding the expectations of citizens of Greenland and Nunavut to recover economic self-sufficiency
- the level of information, transformation, and dialogue among the Arctic nations and the global community in developing common strategies and understanding of the role of the North in dealing with challenges such as global warming and climate change (ACIA 2005), which make the Arctic a "health barometer for the planet" (Watt-Cloutier 2004)
- fluctuations in world market prices for renewable and non-renewable resources, which form the crux of growing economic activities in the region, and the character of corporate projects for the extraction of minerals, fresh water, and other resources
- legal limitations and bans on the global trade of traditional arts and crafts and wildlife (e.g., sealskin or whale) products, as well as hunting quotas on whales and other marine mammals
- the digital revolution and the challenge of harnessing innovative information and telecommunications technologies (Daléus 2002).

Governmental Adaptation to the Tension between Globalization and Autonomy

Politically, Greenland and Nunavut have limited capacity to shape the national policies of their respective states. This can be observed, for example, in these regions' tiny representation in their national parliaments, their capacity to foster their own interests in the national agendas of Denmark or Canada, and the diminishing value of Western electoral institutions among local residents (Bell 2004a).

Nunavut, because of the wide spectrum of Canada's federal structures that suggest the territory's participation as a relatively autonomous unit, is in a better position than Greenland to bring the voice of Northerners onto the national agenda. There are several dimensions of Nunavut's actual involvement in intergovernmental decision making. For example, when it signed a memorandum of understanding on climate change with Ottawa in 2003, Nunavut was the first Canadian territory or province to collaborate with the federal government's climate change program. In addition, Nunavut participates in a security group, consisting of representatives from federal and territorial government departments, including the Nunavut Tunngavik Incorporated (NTI), which is a watchdog organization for the implementation of the Nunavut Land Claims Agreement (NLCA) (J. George 2003). Another important intergovernmental institution is the annual Northern Premiers Forum. The prime minister meets regularly with provincial and territorial first ministers. Nunavut participates in the Council of the Federation and the Canada Health Council (Russell 2004, 228). Despite this extensive involvement in intergovernmental affairs within Canada, Nunavut, like Greenland, has a limited say in national institutional structures.

Is there any need for these subnational entities to become a more meaningful part of national or global governing mechanisms? If so, what would ensure greater legitimacy and authority for the voices of indigenous peoples represented therein?

Greenland and Nunavut function within different institutional, legal, and political settings, which result in distinct opportunities, constraints, and policies within Denmark and Canada, respectively. Despite these differences, the local economies of the regions share commonalities (e.g., limited infrastructure, technological difficulties and high costs associated with natural resource production, subsistence and transfer-based economies). These common challenges can be exacerbated by globalization in many ways. For example, the politics of whaling and the discourse within the International Whaling Commission (IWC), as noted by Rethmann in Chapter 6, have direct implications for indigenous autonomy and sustainable use of living resources. When the Greenland home rule government voluntarily reduced the IWC quota on fin whales from nineteen to ten animals in the hunting seasons of both 2006 and 2007, numerous small hunter communities that are highly dependent on whale resources suffered serious losses (Frederiksen 2005). Resource development in Nunavut could well attract outsiders, including foreigners, to supplement available workers in the territory. Such an outcome would challenge the territory's demographics and would require stronger affirmative action policies to protect Inuit culture and access to employment.

Of particular concern are issues that affect the North but that do not bring Northerners directly into the decision-making process: externally based changes in resource management, environmental programs, or economic development, and fiscal-transfer policies. The economic developments and sustainability in these subnational units are linked to current and evolving governance structures and to the resilience and cultural adaptation of indigenous and other Northern citizens.

The ability of Greenland and Nunavut to adapt to global changes is grounded partly in existing legal arrangements. Currently, both entities are constitutional hybrids (Eliasen 2004, 170; Harhoff 1993, 515). Autonomy in the form of public governance based on territorial principle, which speaks for non-Native residents as well, structures both subnational entities. It can be argued that the Inuit majority of Nunavut and their active participation in, and control of, the territorial government are turning a de jure territorial form of public government into a de facto indigenous one. It is "a public government with an Inuit face" (Nungaq 1999, 28). The territory of Nunavut was created as an integral part of a land claims settlement. Thus, the system of governance is linked to the Inuit use and management of their lands. Furthermore, the existence in Nunavut of the NTI, a powerful land-claims organization comprised only of Inuit, establishes what might be called a second level of corporate governance along with the public one.

Greenland's home rule system is not rooted in indigenous use or occupation of the land. At the time of its introduction in 1978, the Greenland Home Rule Act (HRA) reflected the relationship between an imperial power and its former colony, and it gave little consideration to Inuit rights. Over time, the Greenlandic system evolved into one that gives all inhabitants of the island a great deal of autonomy, and, in doing so at a functional rather than juridical level, it goes far towards meeting actual Inuit interests. Presently, Greenland evolved into a nation and the Inuit of Greenland act as national representatives of the country of Greenlanders. Thus, the existing home rule system and anticipated new legislation on Greenland's self-governance are oriented towards the rights of all Greenlanders and the Greenlandic nation, as opposed to the ethnic rights of the Inuit. After more than two decades of home rule, the Greenland system has attained a more advanced level of governance building than has Nunavut, where the process is rooted in Inuit nationalism and regionalism.

The Inuit of Nunavut are proud to be Canadian, and the future of the territory remains contingent on its developing closer cooperation and partnership with other parts of Canada. Greenland, on the other hand, may choose the path of independence (J. George 2004) or at least a new partnership agreement on self-governance within the Danish Kingdom, which would expand the legal scope of its autonomy in a number of areas (Commission on Self-Governance 2003). Even Greenland's probable future independence would still entail such an agreement, and autonomy under its terms can be regarded as a "transitional" stage in a more effective and self-reliant governance system. Because of the evolution of the Greenlandic system, the necessity of raising the island's profile in global developments, and challenges posed by globalization, Greenlanders are eager to accommodate their interests in changing global realities by acquiring more responsibilities than envisaged by the HRA. Therefore, Greenland's Commission on Self-Governance has agreed that Greenland should conduct its own affairs on an independent basis, including foreign policy that affects fishing, hunting, environment, tourism, transportation, trade, and security (ibid.).

Although it can be argued that Nunavut's aspirations to become a part of larger global governance processes are not as far reaching as Greenland's, Nunavut's current constitutional arrangement is nonetheless not sufficient to meet the needs of the Nunavummiut. Presently, the territory is in the process of negotiating a devolution agreement with the federal government. Nunavut is pushing for the transfer to it from Ottawa of province-like powers over waters, lands, and non-renewable resources (e.g., responsibility for the management of oil, gas, and mineral extraction on Crown lands and offshore), including jurisdiction over Canadian internal waters within the borders of the territory (Okalik 2006). Such a change would suggest a de facto evolution of a broader degree of autonomy.

Following Cooper's analysis in Chapter 12, it can be noted that even though the principle of subsidiarity is not entrenched in the federal model of Canada or the constitutional arrangement of Denmark, the idea of this principle would be applicable in dealing with an expanded version of autonomy for Greenland or Nunavut. It would allow multi-level governments of these Arctic jurisdictions to handle issues of regional concern in a more effective way. In line with Hedetoft's argument in Chapter 11, moreover, regional and global processes taking place in Greenland and Nunavut challenge Denmark's and Canada's sovereignty, as these subnational entities are expressing more interest in acquiring jurisdiction over "non-transferable" areas (e.g., foreign affairs and security). This partially reduces the collective autonomy of national states by enhancing the public governance of constitutional dependencies with an indigenous majority. The most important implications of changes for the autonomy of Greenland and Nunavut can be observed from an analysis of their international participation.

Legal Status and International Activity of Greenland and Nunavut

The growing importance of international involvement by Greenland and Nunavut directly affects their collective territorial autonomy and their relationships with their respective states. Currently, their legal capability as distinct international actors is limited. Although in practice Greenland and Nunavut may participate within a legal regime of "Arctic" international law — one that could cover spheres of Arctic sovereignty, environmental protection, and the law of the sea (Rothwell 1996, 161) — legally they remain a part of Denmark and Canada, respectively. Consequently, they do not have international legal capacity or an international legal personality, and they cannot be classified as subjects of international law. From a strict legal viewpoint, Greenlandic and Nunavut authorities cannot make independent decisions in the realm of foreign affairs, nor are they allowed to have diplomatic missions of their own or conclude unilateral agreements with foreign countries. Their jurisdiction in the international domain is limited by the priority of rights and obligations derived from treaties or other international documents signed by Denmark and Canada. Danish and Canadian authorities have exclusive priority in decision-making powers over foreign relations relating to their state interests, and Greenland and Nunavut cannot be independent members of international organizations that are made up of sovereign states.

Nevertheless, this situation is changing, particularly in Greenland's case.

Since the introduction in 2005 of the so-called Authorization Act (An Act concerning the Conclusion of Agreements under International Law by the Government of Greenland, no. 577, 24 June 2005), Greenlandic authorities were authorized to act in some areas of foreign affairs when these areas do not limit the constitutional responsibilities and powers of the Danish government related to the conclusion of agreements under international law. In other words, the government of Greenland was authorized to act on behalf of the kingdom in international affairs that relate solely to Greenland's jurisdiction. In practice, Greenland and Nunavut are involved in fostering international relationships, particularly with regard to their cultural, social, and economic interests.

The nascent institutional complex in the Arctic (Young 2005, 9) is marked by fragmentation and insufficient alliances among national, sub-national, and local constituencies. Challenges are many. First, this complex is shaped by a variety of actors attempting to address circumpolar issues. Second, it faces a shortage of resources and lack of coherence in existing institutions. Finally, there are overlapping as well as competing individual and global purposes and a proliferation of ambitious political groups. These factors make it difficult to achieve a common Arctic agenda and a strengthening of the Arctic voice transnationally. Despite these challenges, Greenland and Nunavut have particular interests in international coopera-tion; these interests define the priorities of these two entities and direct the forms of their international activity. The principle forms of participation include, but are not limited to, the following:

- *on a global level:* via the United Nations (e.g., the Permanent Forum on Indigenous Issues), United Nations Educational, Scientific and Cultural Organization, or International Labour Organization
- *on a regional level:* Arctic cooperation, for example, via the Arctic Council (for both Greenland and Nunavut); Nordic cooperation via the Nordic Council and the Nordic Council of Ministers (for Greenland); European cooperation via the European Union, and pos-sible Greenlandic membership in the Council of Europe (Commission on Self-Governance 2003); and cross-border cooperation between Greenland and Nunavut
- *by function:* interparliamentary cooperation (e.g., summits of parlia-mentarians of the Arctic region, the Nordic Council); Greenland's participation in the West Nordic Council, which focuses mainly on health, culture, hunting, infrastructure, and language issues;

intergovernmental cooperation (e.g., the Nordic Council of Ministers); supranational cooperation (e.g., Greenland and the EU); non-governmental cooperation (e.g., the International Arctic Science Committee); indigenous cooperation (e.g., the Inuit Circumpolar Council [ICC], the Indigenous Peoples' Secretariat)

- *by subject matter:* environmental cooperation (e.g., through the Arctic Council); fishery and hunting cooperation (e.g., the North Atlantic Salmon Conservation Organization, the Northeast Atlantic Fisheries Commission, the Northwest Atlantic Fisheries Organization, the IWC, the World Council of Whalers, the North Atlantic Marine Mammal Commission [Greenland only]); international trade cooperation (e.g., Greenland's Trade Council); cultural, educational, linguistic cooperation (e.g., participation of Greenland and Nunavut in the University of the Arctic programs); cooperation in defence and security matters (see Loukacheva 2007, chap. 5).

In many areas, Greenland and Nunavut have similar interests in international involvement as a result of their climatic, geographic, and economic similarities and their common challenges associated with the environment and globalization. However, as suggested by the preceding list, some fields are of particular interest to Greenland. It participates, for example, in forums for cooperation among Nordic countries, and it maintains special relationships with the EU. To be sure, Greenland's role in the pillars of Nordic collaboration such as the Nordic Council and the Nordic Council of Ministers is limited. But Greenland views its participation in these international forums as a chance to further its integration with other Nordic countries and to broadcast its "international" voice within the Nordic community.

Formal Nordic cooperation is challenged by the growth of the European Union's supranational institutions. The complexity of Greenland's relations with the EU is conditioned by two important factors. First, as part of Denmark, an EU member state, Greenland, which left the European Economic Community (EEC) in 1985, has to correlate its non-European features and home rule interests with EU policies. Second, Greenland has no direct role in the supranational institutions of the EU. Despite this, Greenland's "loose relation with Europe" has developed into closer forms of mutual cooperation and benefit.

Current Greenland-EU relations are subject to three regimes: Greenland as an Overseas Country or Territory within the EU; Greenland-EU fishery arrangements; and, since 1999, the Arctic Window within the EU's Northern Dimension policies. Fisheries issues constitute a cornerstone of Greenland-EEC/EU relations. Both parties have a mutual interest in managing the fisheries that contribute significantly to the Greenlandic and EU economies. At the same time, Greenland considers the Arctic Window a political space where Arctic nations and the EU share mutual interests, build closer ties between Arctic and other indigenous peoples, and enhance the Arctic–Northern Europe cooperative structures. In 2006, a new partnership between Greenland and the EU was affirmed in a number of documents. Greenland-EU collaboration was extended in areas other than fisheries, with particular focus on tourism, culture, food safety, energy, mineral resources, research, education, and training (Loukacheva 2007, chap. 5).

Although there is no direct link between Nunavut and the EU policies regarding the Arctic, policies implemented in Ottawa with respect to the North and the EU have significance for the territory. These include Ottawa's policy statement, *The Northern Dimension of Canada's Foreign Policy* (2000), as well as joint Canada-EU statements on Northern cooperation, defence, and security, and the EU-Canada Partnership Agenda (2004). These initiatives on the Northern Dimension and the strengthening of collaboration in the North at different levels and areas may permit Nunavut's greater participation in the implementation of Canada's foreign policy when it concerns the Arctic.

Common problems shared by Greenland and Nunavut are partially addressed by informal mechanisms of Arctic cooperation. The establishment of the Arctic Council in 1996 by the eight Arctic states is one example of such an informal arrangement (Young 2000, 125). The Inuit of Greenland and Nunavut exercise their mandate in the Arctic Council via the ICC, which, according to the 1996 Declaration on the Establishment of the Arctic Council, holds the status of permanent participant and partakes in activities and consultations with Arctic indigenous representatives within the council. Through the creation of the category of permanent participant, the Arctic Council considers the aspirations, needs, and opinions of Arctic indigenous residents in its work. This involvement should in the future bring about a new role for subnational entities' participation in Arctic international cooperation. In the meantime, active Inuit participation and support for the council's projects foster indigenous peoples' collaborative initiatives in the Circumpolar North.

The Inuit are involved in the activities of intra-state, intergovernmental, interparliamentary, and supranational forms of international cooperation through a variety of forums. Yet, this involvement continues to be challenged by the dominance of national states' doctrines and the limited legal capacity of subnational entities in international law. Representatives of these Arctic jurisdictions participate in international forums with an advisory mandate. The participation of Greenland and Nunavut in the institutional complex of the Arctic is not based on some legally binding regime but instead relies mainly on informal mechanisms. There are no adequate international or domestic regulatory provisions legalizing the international activity of Greenland and Nunavut (see Loukacheva 2007, chap. 5).

Global Implications and the Role of Greenland and Nunavut

There is not much room for non-state participants such as Greenland and Nunavut in global and regional forums to influence decision-making processes on issues that affect the Arctic. Moreover, globalization has boosted only to a limited degree the international activity of Greenland and Nunavut; on an institutional level, the Circumpolar North is more likely to be involved in the process of regionalization than that of globalization. Under these circumstances, should Greenland and Nunavut enhance their position and engagement in the framework of formal governing structures in the Arctic, or do they need to raise their voices and collaborate within a multi-level system of global governance?

Globalization affects Greenland and Nunavut in a number of ways. The economies of Greenland and Nunavut are intertwined with national economies and are sensitive to global trends, particularly in global resource management. Thus, fluctuations in the world natural resource markets, for example, can render unprofitable the already high cost of mining certain minerals. The globality of environmental issues as well as movements against seal and walrus hunting limit the possibilities of sealskin trade on world markets and cause further restrictions on subsistence hunting and whaling, on hunting rights with respect to marine mammals, and on land and resource management by indigenous populations. Nunavummiut and Greenlanders are inextricably connected to the global community and economy. For example, the seafood giant Royal Greenland, which is run by the home rule government and is the island's largest corporation and one of the world's leading seafood producers, recently considered importing qualified workers from eastern Europe to solve a labour shortage in its halibut-processing factory in Ilulissat (*Nunatsiaq News* 2004a). In a similar vein, to deal with the inadequate number of medical personnel in the territory's community health centres, Nunavut hired (under two-year contracts) about one hundred nurses from overseas, mostly from India and the Philippines (Minogue 2005).

In an effort to boost its economic self-sufficiency, Greenland is attempting to participate more fully in the global economy. Greenlanders are planning to sell fresh water and ice (*Nunatsiaq News* 2004b) and export icebergs to global markets (Greenland Home Rule Government 2004). Greenlandic entrepreneurs have started to brew beer using melted ice-cap water, and they intend to sell this unique brand in Europe and possibly the United States (J. George 2006). Greenlanders also hope to produce globally cheap hydro-electric power. In their desire to become a part of the global economy they hope to have agreements with Alcoa — the world's largest aluminium producer — and the Norwegian company Norsk Hydro to study the possibility of building an aluminium smelter and plant on the island (Greenland Home Rule Government 2006; *Copenhagen Post* 2007).

For its part, Nunavut hopes to develop a world-class tourism industry (Fotheringham 2004). Nunavut also has a successful innovative telemedicine program (Nunavut 2005a), which Greenland hopes to emulate (*Nunatsiaq News* 2006).

Because of climate change and the possible melting of ice in the Northwest Passage, the Artic region faces challenges connected with security (economic, environmental, food, and military) and potential year-round navigation and transportation. These challenges heighten the importance of Nunavut and Greenland in protecting the national sovereignty of their respective states, countering possible threats from global terrorism, and participating in the development of renewable and non-renewable resources by non-Native and foreign investors. As one observer notes, "the Arctic is a global barometer right now" (Bell 2004b). Given the potentially devastating effects of global warming and climate change on the region, it is important that Greenland and Nunavut, along with other Northern entities, have a say in policies to develop new approaches to environmental protection for wildlife and biodiversity loss (including the management of marine resources and the conservation of whales), to control persistent organic pollutants, to define new economic strategies, and to ensure cultural survival for particularly vulnerable communities dependent on a vanishing traditional way of life (ACIA 2005; Fenge 2001).

How might Greenland and Nunavut shape the consequences of globalization for themselves? Because of the indigenous majority of these jurisdictions, globalization presents a uniquely complex challenge for the development of Greenland's and Nunavut's governance systems. This majority demands that attention be paid to indigenous peoples' rights, concerns, and values. On the one hand, Greenland and Nunavut can try to develop their governance systems and continue to diversify and deepen their economies. Yet, despite the above examples of new economic prospects, the reality is that they have limited opportunities to compete in the global economy by developing new technologies or bringing new products to the global markets. On the other hand, Greenland and Nunavut can continue to work at the national and international levels for the protection of indigenous peoples' rights, traditional values, livelihood, and environment.

There are conceptual differences in approaches to globalization on the part of the Inuit and non-indigenous representatives of the territories. In the words of one Greenlandic authority, "globalization is nothing but another form of colonization. I state this fact because it is true as far as indigenous peoples are concerned ... It goes almost without saying that the notion of globalization is neither value-free nor clinical as we witness the shrinking of ancestral lands and territories worldwide" (Rasmussen 2004). At the same time, as Sheila Watt-Cloutier noted when she was chair of the ICC, "Inuit face many challenges in finding our place in the new world order of globalization ... Notwithstanding our struggles and our limited numbers, we Inuit do have a significant role to play globally" (Watt-Cloutier 2004). This aspiration to have a meaningful voice in global developments also puts on the agenda the issue of legalization of indigenous internationalism and indigenous peoples' rights in global governance.

Globalization enhances supraterritorial relations and international collaboration between indigenous peoples, which is developing at the level of non-governmental organizations. Such collaboration is closely connected with the phenomenon of "indigenous internationalism," "Inuitism" (a movement directed towards strengthening contacts among the Inuit in the Arctic) (Gulløv 1979, 137), or "Pan-Inuit" cooperation (Petersen 1984). Cross-border collaboration can be observed in the Memorandum of Understanding (MOU) on Cooperation signed by the Inuit of Greenland and Nunavut in 2000; an agreement to jointly manage polar bears (Nunavut 2005b); and a 2006 trade annex to the MOU with the goal of intensifying mutual growth in trade through private business initiatives and deeper cooperation among business councils and schools, networking organizations, trade unions, tourist councils, and other interested institutional structures in both territories. Cross-border collaboration has been signified by visits from premiers and other government officials, conferences, workshops, and other types of cultural, trade, and educational exchange between Greenland and Nunavut (Greenland Home Rule Government 2001, 169-73). Cross-border or multilateral cooperation is also evident in Inuit participation in indigenous peoples' and governmental/parliamentary organizations as well as non-governmental bodies (ibid., 174-5).

Notwithstanding a relatively weak institutional organization in the Arctic, non-state actors such as the ICC are able to influence and express their interests within intergovernmental settings, thus enhancing the Inuit's concerns in international forums. The ICC is a major non-governmental international collective voice for the Inuit. Despite its limited advisory status, the ICC has obtained a solid mandate for promoting Inuit/indigenous rights within the United Nations. Thus, it contributed to the establishment in 2000 of the UN Permanent Forum on Indigenous Issues, where the ICC participates as an observer (OHCHR 2001), and was involved in the development of the UN Declaration on the Rights of Indigenous Peoples (Sambo 1992) adopted by the UN General Assembly in 2007. Because of its non-governmental nature, the ICC is more effective than government bodies in lobbying for the ventures of national governments. Embracing the Inuit of Canada, Denmark, the United States, and the Russian Federation and based on the Inuit culture, the ICC is a unique NGO that is able to enhance a new diplomacy in the Circumpolar North and that brings Inuit perspectives on global matters to the attention of international and national authorities (Simon 2004). The work of the ICC shows that the indigenous "transnational" NGO is often ahead of national governments in meeting indigenous needs and the challenges in the Arctic caused by global changes.

The increased salience of changes occurring in the Arctic (e.g., climate change, contamination by PCBs and other pollutants) poses global dilemmas. Indeed, the Arctic Human Development Report (AHDR 2004) and the Arctic Climate Impact Assessment Report (ACIA 2005) of the Arctic Council reveal the connectivity and globality of environmental, human, socio-economic, cultural, geopolitical, and legal challenges that Northerners and their governments have to address. They demand that nations in the global village take responsibility when their activities affect vulnerable Arctic ecosystems. This demand is evident from the ICC's Petition to the Inter-American Commission on Human Rights (2005) against the United States for its failure to protect the environment and for the violation of the rights of people beyond its own borders, as the impact in the Arctic of human-induced climate change infringes Inuit human rights, and affects Inuit subsistence and their relationship with the environment.

Conclusion

Because of the growing significance of the North in global developments, within recent decades we have witnessed the emergence in the Arctic of a new institutional complex for governance. Among other things, it features the increased international involvement of subnational units and indigenous peoples in addressing regional cultural, educational, economic, linguistic, health, and environmental matters. However, because of the mostly informal nature of that institutional complex — that is, the grounding of many institutions in various declarations and reports, and a minor reliance on legally binding arrangements (e.g., treaties or international conventions) — there is ambiguity in classifying developing Arctic structures in conventional institutional terms. It is also difficult to define the roles of multi-level governance participants (e.g., member states in contrast to subnational, supranational, non-state actors like NGOs and indigenous peoples' organizations) in associated institutions of global ordering.

The international involvement of Greenland and Nunavut takes place in two dimensions: transnational cooperation mostly within the Arctic, and indigenous cooperation on the regional and global levels. Partially bolstered by globalization, the international activity of the Inuit of Greenland and Nunavut and their governments shows that these substate entities are gradually becoming de facto subjects of international law. Despite limitations in their legal capabilities, and their weak ability to respond adequately to the challenges posed by external forces, the evolving nature of Greenland's home rule system and the devolution of powers from Ottawa to Nunavut enhance these entities' demands for broader participation in international forums. These demands have also been enhanced by the need to have stronger representation of these entities in international bodies to defend against possible neglect and non-consideration by national states, including neglect in fulfilling international obligations (Espersen 2004, 10).

The most important implication is that such de facto developments gradually change the legal scope of autonomy for the citizens of Greenland and Nunavut. They demonstrate that jurisdiction in foreign affairs is transferable to some extent to the governments of Greenland and Nunavut when such transfers are crucial for addressing local matters. This jurisdiction becomes a part of the internal right to self-determination or autonomy. They do not, however, necessarily threaten the sovereignty of their respective states. Changes taking place within the Arctic raise the standing of Greenland and Nunavut within their home states, putting pressure on Denmark and Canada to deal more effectively with global problems, especially in environmental and security arenas. The impact of global matters on Greenland and Nunavut suggests that their authorities require more powers and more opportunities for developing strategies and legal mechanisms to address the effects of globalization.

Currently, Nunavut is less involved than Greenland in international forums. But owing to structural, financial, and legal limitations and constraints on the development of transnational indigenous activism and institutions of Nordic and Arctic cooperation, both Greenland and Nunavut have only limited opportunities to promote their interests within these settings. In practice, their potential for input on global issues is more significant when dealing with environmental problems (e.g., climate change or pollution). In future, issues of international trade will most likely become a higher priority for Greenland and Nunavut on the global scale.

Subnational governments such as Greenland and Nunavut can increase their participation in global governance through deeper partnerships with their national authorities. In addition, the Inuit of Nunavut and Greenland are working with their national governments by participating in the observation of climatic changes and assessing the status of migratory species and monitoring polar bears, which are crucial for the implementation of existing international agreements dealing with ecosystems and the management of wildlife resources.

The Arctic remains vulnerable to the impact of global changes, but the modest capabilities of Greenland and Nunavut in various transnational forums suggest there is a growing need for reconsideration of their future role in global decision making. At the same time, there seems to be an increased sensitivity in regard to indigenous people's rights, not just by the governments of Denmark and Canada, but on the global scale. Might the extended autonomy of Greenland and Nunavut (e.g., competence in non-transferable areas) help to address pressing global challenges? With further institutional changes on the regional, national, trans-Arctic, and supranational levels, Greenlandic and Nunavut authorities could gain more responsibility. There might be a shift towards a more innovative legal understanding of the jurisdictional capacities of subnational units. Denmark and Canada have different motivations for granting greater autonomy to Greenland and Nunavut. If these entities become more sustainable and financially independent from national grants and subsidies, they could be in a better position to tackle local and regional problems. In partnership with national and international decision makers, both governmental and non-governmental, Nunavut and Greenland would be more successful in raising the voice of the Arctic in global forums.

chapter 14   Conclusion: Institutions, Autonomy, and Complexity

Louis W. Pauly

THIS BOOK IS A collaborative work. Although its various chapters are richly textured and capable of being read on their own, they were drafted in dialogue with one another. Read together, they provide a lens that allows us to see important manifestations of the interaction among the imperatives, opportunities, and challenges of globalization with the persistent and complicated modern human will-to-autonomy. Each chapter focuses on particular institutions of governance, of social ordering. Each is rich in detail. It is too simple to conclude that together they depict the straightforward tensions and contradictions between globalization and autonomy. Instead, organized around the questions set out in the introductory chapter, they give a glimpse of the complex trajectories of institutional change and innovation in our contemporary and likely future world. That complexity seems a central feature of a modernity being reconstituted before our eyes, sometimes referred to as a second modernity.

Organizations like the United Nations and the World Trade Organization (WTO) have mandates or aspirations that far exceed their current capacities, while emerging private structures ostensibly delivering de facto regulation suffer from legitimacy deficits that reflect their simultaneous location in the space of places and the space of flows. Although some serious experimentation with new institutional forms is now underway, in the contemporary period it seems mainly to be limited to regional venues, the most innovative of which is Europe. But pressures both for effective problem solving and for maximum feasible degrees of autonomy have now evidently gone global. This theme cuts across the chapters of our book. The story of institutional development and change thus far suggests not only that human beings want to shape and live in a world that is prosperous, secure, and sustainable, but also that they insist on one that preserves in principle a high degree of autonomy for themselves and for the collectivities with which they identify. As the chapters together suggest, however, even if the former is imaginable, in practice the latter seems feasible only for some individuals and some collectivities. If the authors of this book could speak with one voice, they would likely predict that the path ahead in each of the institutional arenas examined will not be a straight one. Across all of those arenas — and surely in many others that would need to be included in any comprehensive study of our world's rapidly changing political, social, and cultural architecture — the key institutional feature is increasing complexity.

The building up and breaking down of key institutions for coordinating the actions of states is certainly part of the long story of internationalization, despite the often overly simplified functionalist logic and assumption of inevitability associated with much related analysis. In this regard, one thinks of the League of Nations, commercial unions, monetary standards, and federations that have come and gone. Even in cases where reform has actually been achieved, erosion and constant adaptation seem more common than stability. The trend is clearly evident in the institutions established by the victorious Allies after the Second World War. Globalization, however, promises deeper and more profound changes in the relationships that constitute institutions aspiring to authoritative social ordering, relationships between individuals, between large groups of individuals, and even between different species.

There is nothing inevitable about the creation of structures to sustain what is best in those relationships or to ameliorate their negative consequences. Reshaping old institutions and fostering new ones requires basic agreement on principles and norms and the willingness of leaders and followers to make trade-offs between those that are competing or contradictory. The transformative processes of globalization do not necessarily make it any easier to achieve such agreements or engineer such trade-offs. In fact, by making increasingly visible the multipolarity of the world, whether in terms of economic power, cultural systems, or social practices, they render more and more inconceivable a world where institutions are designed, adapted, and led by the United States and European states alone. In such a context, the multifaceted concept of autonomy and the question of whose autonomy is accommodated provide important metrics for setting achievable goals and defining realistic limits. Among the many books recently written on globalization, beyond the novelty of some of our case histories, our collaborative claim to originality lies precisely in setting out, grounding empirically, and exploring comparatively the utility of autonomy as such a metric.

Globalization and Autonomy in Institutional Perspective

The work of Simmel on the relationship between individual autonomy and the formation of new collectivities, cited in Chapter 1, originally helped establish the field of sociology. Nearly a century later, economic sociologists would note without controversy that modern market society has produced more prosperity for more people than any other social organization in history. As Fligstein (2001, 3), for example, observes, "It has done so by creating the conditions for social exchange between large groups of human beings, often separated across large geographic spaces." Those conditions include institutional foundations for such exchange that are stable, efficient, and perceived to be fair. Since the dawn of modernity, human beings separated from one another by space and time, as well as by more artificial boundaries, have reconstituted such institutional foundations repeatedly. In an irony Simmel would surely have appreciated, sometimes that reconstitution involves the curtailment of the very autonomy born of the collapse of medieval social systems.

To combine the language of economics and politics, the world's most prosperous societies have today only sometimes managed to combine economies of scale and scope with the defence of human autonomy, defined in both collective and individual terms. Although there is no single model of a perfectly balanced society, the various societies that constitute today's advanced industrial world, along with growing parts of the emerging industrial world, struggle constantly to attain and maintain a delicate balance. They seek stable points of equilibrium among the prosperity produced by a unified market, the legitimate social ordering created by a sense of collective belonging, and the fulfillment associated with the freedom both to escape wants and to make personal choices. Not all of their citizens can enjoy all three outcomes equally. Even for those coming close, the complex pressures of globalization repeatedly shake the ground under their feet. Even in many prosperous societies, women and members of visible minority groups clearly remain at a disadvantage when it comes to degrees of personal autonomy and sharing in the framing of modes of collective autonomy. If Charles Taylor (2004) is right, moreover, our current condition inescapably narrows, limits, and channels all human possibilities. Still, we have only to recall the tragic history of the twentieth century in much of the world to imagine that things could be worse. And we have only to neglect the various risks Beck (1999) now sees humanity running to fail to imagine that things could become very much worse for all societies now conjoined in a transforming system.

Reflecting the dynamic search for prosperity, belonging, and autonomy and the desire to sustain equilibria reached under the dynamic conditions of globalization are the social, cultural, and political institutions constructed mainly by the world's leading societies at the end of the Second World War. As noted in the opening chapter, we have long understood that the pressures of internationalization can disrupt such equilibria, especially but not only in poor societies less able to buffer themselves from exogenous changes or to export the consequences of internal disruptions. Globalization, in turn, can have similar effects, but its fundamentally transformative nature makes it less easy to predict the institutional implications, both internal to unique societies or external to them all. Its myriad processes open and at least potentially disrupt established institutions cutting across them, as the powers of the longer-standing leading societies are engaged by emerging centres of power. The implications also often seem to entail the necessity of constructing entirely new kinds of institutions of global ordering.

In the face of these pressures, the chapters of this book help bring the limits of institutional adaptation into view. While I give an optimistic reading of recent developments at the United Nations and between the UN and the Bretton Woods institutions, there is no doubt that they are all caught in a long, continuing series of crises in identity and confidence. The contradictory impulses coming from their memberships are readily observable. They remain inadequately empowered and resourced to handle the vast expectations routinely thrust upon them. Surprisingly, however, neither their leading members nor their weaker supporters and critics are seriously moving to abandon them. They are imperfect instruments, neither wholly effective nor wholly legitimate, but their persistence suggests the practical reality of their usefulness for various purposes and of the difficulty of designing alternative instruments. Close observers often suppose these uses to include the roles of scapegoat, crisis manager, epistemic community, supplemental resource provider, representative body, or legitimating mechanism. Occasional high-profile meetings like the summit held in Monterrey, Mexico, in 2002 seem to occur in the context of patterned social and political behaviour, a pattern that moves from crisis to hope to disappointment. If I am right, the distinctive feature of the post-1945 institutions of global ordering lies precisely in the continued rekindling of the hope they signify. It is a hope that reformed instruments established by states acting cooperatively can transcend narrow interests and solve pressing human problems posed initially by internationalization and increasingly by globalization.

That hope may not yet be robust, but more evidence justifying it is presented in the chapters by Gensey and Winham and by Coleman. Despite noting some backsliding in the years after the 1994 Final Act of the Uruguay Round of trade negotiations, Coleman is judicious in his contention that the Agreement on Agriculture included in the act — and its entrenchment in the WTO with its Dispute Settlement Understanding (DSU) — represented progress. The difficulty the members of the WTO confronted in following that agreement up in the subsequent Doha Round certainly justifies a cautious view. Still, the DSU mechanism discussed both by Gensey and Winham and by Coleman has had an observable effect in moving both developed and developing member states beyond the fragile intergovernmentalism of the past. At least in the important trade arena, it is becoming implausible to imagine states jettisoning their commitments to more open markets. In this light, the incipient movement of judicial authority to the global level of governance is noteworthy. More plausible is an interpretation of this movement as an early response to the political and legal dilemmas posed by globalization. A durable liberal trading order on the scale of the post-1994 system depends upon more than voluntaristic and easily reversible decisions by truly autonomous states.

That such orders are capable of being constructed at deeper and more local levels is suggested by Irr in her chapter on the United Nations Educational, Scientific and Cultural Organization (UNESCO), where we see an ostensibly quite weak intergovernmental organization at the centre of an evolving network that imagines and constructs the world's cultural "heritage." That network links states and non-state actors, which are coming to share a set of normative understandings on the worth of cultural creativity in all the world's societies. These understandings increasingly cast a clear shadow of illegitimacy around acts of cultural destruction that in earlier eras might have been passed off simply as the internal affairs of sovereign states. An imagined dialogue among the world's cultures becomes more manifest.

The idea that order implies the movement of regulatory authority beyond the local and the national is still quite tentative and episodic. The contestability of this very point comes out of a careful reading of Rethmann's chapter on the International Whaling Commission. Although Rethmann diagnoses a stubborn stalemate in the building of a regime that balances still quite divergent positions on the place of another species in a human-centred world order, the striking feature in the contemporary period is the expansion of a global environmental network that fits uneasily in the context of traditional interstate negotiations. The fact that network representatives have a place at the new negotiating table cannot be downplayed. The effects of cultural and even linguistic transformation are not hard to see. Where the older language of conservation, harvesting, and the sustainability of resource stocks once dominated and conditioned negotiations, we now hear the language of rights, including the rights inhering not only in the cultures of indigenous peoples but also in another living species, significantly a long-standing dimension of many indigenous cosmologies. This linguistic transformation and the prominence of the trans-state network of activists appear unlikely to be reversed. The notion that autonomy is reserved only for states already sounds illegitimate. Even frustrating and still open-ended negotiations, then, are plausibly interpreted as chapters in a dynamic story unlikely to end in a reversion to the internationalized world of the past.

Eaton and Porter as well as Cutler reach a similar conclusion in their chapters on evolving global regimes for accounting and legal services. Key elements in the understructure of a global economy, these regimes already appear to be enhancing the collective and individual autonomy of privileged private actors vis-à-vis the nation-states within which they remain physically based. To be sure, the legitimacy of the quasi-governing arrangements that have the consequence of reinforcing the autonomy of private actors remains highly questionable. But, again, it is becoming more difficult to imagine a reversion to the prior public-sector-led arrangements of an international economy than to imagine their continued adaptation to the requirements of a new global economy. As Eaton and Porter put it, when "globalized technical expertise becom[es] entangled with the power and interests of large multinational corporations," the outcome "may plausibly be labelled private global authority."

Lest the observer leap prematurely to an unambiguously cosmopolitan set of expectations for the future development of global institutions, the Webb and Sinclair chapter hoists a cautionary flag, reflecting upon the vital area of social policy. In the long run, it is inconceivable that the architecture of a global economy, a global culture, and a global polity can find firm footing upon the grounds of idiosyncratic, segmented, and truly autonomous societies. Certainly most comparative analysts expect and constantly seek evidence for a certain convergence of basic social policy norms. Increasingly, as Webb and Sinclair note, prominent non-governmental organizations operating across national boundaries are certainly pushing in just such a direction. As they also note, the traditional organs of the state, both at the local and the international levels, by virtue of the political legitimacy vested in them, retain the ability finally to determine the content of actual social policies. As in the cases covered in earlier chapters, however, the novel element in the social policy story is "NGO success in highlighting issues" transnationally. Even basic social policy, conditioned by unique nation-state histories and circumstances and still very political, is no longer made in hermetically sealed legislative, executive, or judicial chambers.

Our collaborative contention by virtue of the concluding chapters of this book is that the new perimeters around collective and individual autonomy are today most clearly being drawn and redrawn within regions and within federal unions. Those perimeters are now undoubtedly porous and often intentionally rendered opaque. On this theme, the Cooper and Hedetoft chapters provide nuanced analysis of the European Union (EU), where the limits of sovereignty as traditionally conceived have been breached, likely irrevocably, barring a cataclysm. Variation remains in the still-dynamic outcomes within contemporary Europe in terms of the reconstitution of the collectivities that constitute the EU. What is already certain is that the autonomy characteristic of any one of them is now attenuated. The effect is obvious in matters of internal policy. But even in the external realm, where the member states of the EU retain the full panoply of sovereign prerogatives, a complex collective identity seems in formation, not least when it confronts American unilateralism. As Hedetoft puts the core dilemma: "In conditions of globalization wedded to the concrete context of European integration, the dichotomy between real and formal sovereignty translates into a choice between abandoning sovereignty and retaining some measure of autonomy while gaining more external influence, or maintaining the constitutional and formal trappings of sovereignty but losing or conceding autonomy and influence" (224).

To some extent, Clarkson's chapter represents a contrasting case. The reconstitution of political autonomy occasioned by globalization processes within North America can certainly be depicted as a "zero-sum game" that the smaller states on the Continent cannot win. It remains true, nevertheless, that the economic, cultural, and social outcomes measured by the metric of autonomy are less clear-cut. Business elites across Canada, the United States, and Mexico appear freer, while organized and especially unorganized labour appears notably more constrained. The implications for external policy across those cases seem to vary as well. In this regard, Hedetoft's insight from the European experience seems equally compelling: "the answer to the key question of whether globalization is constraining or widening the space for manoeuvre and flexible adaptation of small states is: both, depending on political choices regarding [formal] sovereignty, on the nature and complexity of transnational alliance building, and on geopolitical positioning" (224).

As the Clarkson and Hedetoft chapters suggest, it is within formally discrete national communities that the pressures of globalization may be having their most profound institutional effects. Loukacheva gives us a nice example in the complex and still-tentative cases of building more autonomous governing institutions among the indigenous peoples of the vulnerable and environmentally fragile Arctic region. In both Greenland and Nunavut, she claims, we are witnessing an expansion and deepening of transboundary networks, which at least promise indigenous peoples more capacity to secure a greater degree of political autonomy. To some extent, moreover, the degree to which that promise can be met is being defined through intensified collaboration among the peoples of Greenland and Nunavut "as they collectively assert their rights to autonomy." The optimist will conclude that incipient and quite novel institutions of effective and legitimate Arctic governance are coming into sight. But even the optimist must be daunted by the enormity of the physical challenge to the region's ecosystem that is simultaneously becoming all too obvious, a challenge only a blind ideologue would deny as a consequence of globalization in its most obvious form. Global warming and the construction of serious regional institutions now appear to be inextricably interconnected processes.

Institutional Transformation in a More Complex Environment

In Chapter 1, we assert that "the denser the space of flows, and the greater the challenge of holding the allegiance of super-empowered elites, the more difficult it is to address problems of global order through existing institutions. At a certain point as globalization proceeds, institutional adaptation seems likely to be superseded by the necessity to create new kinds of institutions" (5). To be sure, the subsequent chapters portray partly contradictory demands for individual as well as collective autonomy inside processes of globalization. They depict often conflicting responses to the diverse claims of efficiency, justice, and stability at particular globalizing moments. The institutional picture sketched across the various case histories nevertheless reinforces the conviction expressed by Sen in the opening chapter: the image as well as the reality of supraterritoriality in the very processes that sustain — or endanger — life itself cannot help but force a re-imagining of the good society.

None of the collaborators in this book advocates the wholesale jettisoning of the structures of global ordering the current generation of human beings has inherited. Nor have they forgotten the historical and theoretical reasons for their original construction. None traces an inevitable process through which contemporary public authorities wither away. Indeed, those authorities clearly remain vital, even in arenas where the imperatives of private ordering are on the rise. But all of the authors of this book have opened the analytical room for deeper research on institutional transformation in a world made new and apparently more fragile by globalization. In this light, they have underlined the usefulness of focusing on tractable, observable, and differentiated changes in the relative autonomy of individuals and collectivities. Much work remains to be done, but there is no going back.

Abbreviations

AD	anti-dumping duties
AICPA	American Institute of Certified Public Accountants
AISI	American Iron and Steel Institute
ASBJ	Accounting Standards Board of Japan
BIT	bilateral investment agreement
BMD	Ballistic Missile Defense
BWU	blue whale unit
CAP	Common Agricultural Policy
CCALMR	Center for Coastal and Land-Margin Research
CMS	Convention on Migratory Species
CNC	Conseil National de la Comptabilité
CONGO	Conference of Non-Governmental Organizations
CPA	Certified Public Accountants
CUFTA	Canada-United States Free Trade Agreement
CVD	countervailing duties
CWB	Canadian Wheat Board
DESA	Department of Economic and Social Affairs (of the UN)
DSB	Dispute Settlement Body
DSU	Dispute Settlement Understanding
EC	European Community
ECJ	European Court of Justice
ECOSOC	Economic and Social Council (of the UN)
EDC	Export Development Canada

EEA	European Economic Area
EEC	European Economic Community
ENGO	environmental non-governmental organization
EU	European Union
FAIR	Federal Agriculture Improvement and Reform
FASB	Financial Accounting Standards Board
FfD	financing for development
FSF	Financial Stability Forum
FSRI	Farm Security and Rural Investment
FTC	Free Trade Commission
G77	Group of 77 (developing countries within UNCTAD)
GAAP	generally accepted accounting principles
GATT	General Agreement on Tariffs and Trade
GERIM	Groupe d'Études et de Recherches Interdisciplinaires sur la Méditerranée
GM	genetically modified
HRA	Home Rule Act
IAASB	International Auditing and Assurance Standards Board
IASB	International Accounting Standards Board
IBRD	International Bank for Reconstruction and Development
ICA	international commodity agreement
ICC	Inuit Circumpolar Council
ICC	International Chamber of Commerce
ICCROM	International Centre for the Preservation and Restoration of Cultural Property
ICITO	Interim Commission for the International Trade Organization
ICOMOS	International Centre for the Study and Preservation and Restoration of Cultural Property
ICRW	International Convention for the Regulation of Whaling
ICSW	International Council on Social Welfare
IDRC	International Development Research Centre
IFAC	International Federation of Accountants
IFAD	International Forum on Accountancy of Development
IFI	international financial institution
IFRS	International Financial Reporting Standards
IGO	intergovernmental organization
IIA	International Institute of Agriculture
IISD	International Institute of Sustainable Development

ILO	International Labour Organization
ILRF	International Labour Rights Fund
IMO	International Maritime Organization
IOSCO	International Organization of Securities Commissions
IP	intellectual property
ISA	International Standards on Auditing
ITO	International Trade Organization
IUCN	International Union for Conservation of Nature and Natural Resources (World Conservation Union)
IUCN	World Conservation Union
IWC	International Whaling Commission
JICPA	Japanese Institute of Certified Public Accountants
MCRI	Major Collaborative Research Initiative
MOF	Ministry of Finance
MOU	Memorandum of Understanding
NACEC	North American Commission for Environmental Cooperation
NACLC	North American Commission for Labor Cooperation
NAFTA	North American Free Trade Agreement
NAO	national administrative office
NATO	North Atlantic Treaty Organization
NGO	non-governmental organization
NLCA	Nunavut Land Claims Agreement
NMP	new management procedure
NTI	Nunavut Tunngavik Incorporated
ODA	official development assistance
OECD	Organisation for Economic Co-operation and Development
PCAOB	Public Company Accounting Oversight Board
RMP	revised management procedure
RMS	revised management scheme
SAP	structural adjustment program
SME	small and medium-sized enterprises
TEC	Treaty of European Communities
TEU	Treaty of European Union (1993)
TNC	transnational corporation
TRIPS	Trade-Related Aspects of Intellectual Property Rights
UNCITRAL	United Nations Commission on International Trade Law
UNCTAD	United Nations Conference on Trade and Development

UNDP	United Nations Development Programme
UNEP	United Nations Environmental Programme
UNESCO	United Nations Educational, Scientific and Cultural Organization
UNIDROIT	International Institute for the Unification of Private Law
USDA	United States Department of Agriculture
WEDO	Women's Environment and Development Organization
WHC	World Heritage Committee
WSSD	World Summit on Social Development
WTO	World Trade Organization
WWF	World Wildlife Fund

Notes and Acknowledgments

Chapter 2: The UN, the Bretton Woods Institutions, and the Reconstruction of a Multilateral Order

This chapter extends a program of research supported from the start by the Social Sciences and Humanities Research Council of Canada, both through its Major Collaborative Research Initiative and the Canada Research Chairs Program. It builds on my work in Grande and Pauly (2005) and Bernstein and Pauly (2007), and benefited greatly from discussions with Ngaire Woods and her colleagues in the Global Economic Governance Programme of University College, Oxford, and from the constructive criticism offered by William Coleman and two anonymous referees.

Chapter 4: Agricultural Trade and the World Trade Organization

I would like to thank Stefan Tangermann, John Weaver, and Robert Wolfe for their comments on an earlier version of this chapter.

1   The United Nations Food and Agriculture Organization (FAO) is the successor of the IIA and took over much of its information and statistics-gathering activities.
2   A more detailed description of the development of this epistemic community is available in Coleman (2001).

Chapter 6: Fantasies at the International Whaling Commission

1   The ICRW was preceded by the 1931 Geneva Convention for the Regulation of Whaling, the 1937 International Agreement for the Regulation of Whaling, and protocols adopted in 1938, 1944, and 1945 that proposed amendments to the 1937 international agreement.
2   The participants were Antigua and Barbuda, Argentina, Australia, Austria, Belgium, Belize, Benin, Brazil, Chile, China, Côte d'Ivoire, Denmark, Dominica, Finland, France, Gabon, Germany, Grenada, Guinea, Hungary, Iceland, India, Ireland, Italy, Japan,

Kenya, the Republic of Korea, Mauritania, Mexico, Monaco, Mongolia, Morocco, the Netherlands, New Zealand, Nicaragua, Norway, Oman, the Republic of Palau, Panama, Peru, Portugal, the Russian Federation, St. Kitts and Nevis, St. Lucia, St. Vincent and the Grenadines, San Marino, Senegal, the Solomon Islands, South Africa, Spain, Suriname, Sweden, Switzerland, Tuvalu, the United Kingdom, and the United States. In 2004, the Czech Republic joined this list of participants.

3   CMS (Convention on Migratory Species), CCALMR (Center for Coastal and Land-Margin Research), IMO (International Maritime Organization), IUCN (World Conservation Union), and UNEP (United Nations Environment Programme).

4   See http://www.worldwidewhale.com (accessed 27 June 2005).

5   Today the most contested form of Aboriginal whaling outside of the auspices of the IWC is the bowhead hunt in the Canadian Arctic. According to cetological research and statistics (Domning 1999; Whitehead, Reeves, and Tyack 2000), there are only five bowhead stocks left worldwide, and three almost certainly face extinction. With an estimated 8,000 individuals, bowhead main populations are concentrated in the Bering, Chukchi, and Beaufort Seas. By comparison, the estimates for the Nunavut stock in the Canadian Arctic range between 120 and 150 individuals, although there is some controversy around this number (Nunavut Wildlife Management Board 2000). Since the finalization of the Nunavut Land Claims Agreement in 1993, four bowhead whales have been harvested: in 1996 in Repulse Bay, 1998 in Pangnirtung, 2000 in Coral Harbour, and 2002 in Igloolik. At this point, the future of the hunt is uncertain.

6   See http://www.worldcouncilofwhalers.com (accessed 13 February 2003).

7   *ECO* is the environmental voice at the IWC. It is put together each evening by representatives of environmental NGOs and then distributed the next morning. It records votes by member nations and provides background and commentary from NGOs about the proceedings of the IWC. Its goal is to create a space for direct access to debates.

8   Cetologists, including Jim Darling, Linda Weilgart, Hale Whitehead, Kenneth Norris, Katherine Payne, Robert Payne, and Sidney Holt, have become particularly well known for their anti-whaling advocacy. Most credited with starting this movement is cetologist Paul Spong, who in the 1970s argued against capturing whales and for researching them "in the wild."

Chapter 8: Transnational Law and Privatized Governance

1   Examples of delocalized laws include the International Chamber of Commerce Uniform Customs and Practices for Documentary Credits and INCOTERMS 2000; delocalized dispute settlement rules and procedures include the International Chamber of Commerce and United Nations Commission on International Trade Law (UNCITRAL) Rules on International Commercial Arbitration and Conciliation (see Cutler 2003, 208-22).

2   It is known as the "poison pill" defence to a takeover because it involves special redemption or conversion rights for shareholders, which are triggered upon a hostile takeover, thus making the takeover an expensive one.

3   To provide a sense of the economic significance of transnational law firms, the ten largest law firms with global operations listed in the annual revenue survey undertaken by *American Lawyer* for 2006 have a combined revenue (approximately US$14.3 trillion) exceeding the GDP of many states, including Armenia, Chad, Laos, Rwanda, Jamaica, Zambia, Togo, Brunei, Benin, and Malta. The 2006 survey reveals that the top eleven

firms earned over $1 billion that year, with the top four earning over $1.5 billion. In comparison, the hundredth firm earned $268 million (see *American Lawyer* 2007).

4 Marx (1976, 873) noted that "primitive accumulation plays approximately the same role in political economy as original sin does in theology. Adam bit the apple, and thereupon sin fell on the human race." This gave rise to dominant, mythical understandings about two kinds of people: the "riotous living and the frugal elite." In political economy, similar processes of naturalizing the dispossession and appropriation of labour power gave rise to the dominant, and equally mythical, understanding that there are two kinds of workers: those who own the product of their labour and those who do not.

5 The leading ten transnational law firms include Clifford Chance (UK); Skadden, Arps, Slate, Meagher & Flom LLP & Affiliates (US); Freshfields, Bruckhaus, Deringer (UK); Linklaters (UK); Baker & McKenzie (US); Allen & Overy (UK); Jones Day (US); Latham & Watkins (US); Sidney Austin, Brown & Wood LLP (US); and Mayer, Brown, Row & Maw LLP (US).

Chapter 9: Transnational Actors and Global Social Welfare Policy

1 Our review of transnational non-governmental organization efforts at the WSSD is based on a reading of extensive conference documentation available on UN websites (see http://www.un.org/esa/socdev/wssd/index.html) and the detailed record of negotiations published by the International Institute for Sustainable Development (IISD) in its *Earth Negotiations Bulletin* (available at http://www.iisd.ca/wssd95.html), as well as other sources specifically cited.

2 Our characterization of the approaches taken by different actors is based on our reading of NGO, government, and IGO statements available at http://www.un.org/esa/socdev/wssd/statements/.

3 A small number of groups that favoured liberal perspectives participated in the WSSD (e.g., the International Chamber of Commerce and some right-wing think tanks), but they did not play a prominent role in the meetings and did not join collective NGO efforts like the Alternative Declaration. We do not address their roles in this chapter.

4 However, it did call for increased dialogue between the UN and the IFIs, and highlighted the role of ECOSOC in reviewing implementation of the WSSD commitments (United Nations 1995, 25-6).

5 On the impact of the Internet on international activism more generally, see Deibert (2000).

6 Individual CONGO NGOs like the ICSW already had well-developed internal mechanisms for formulating joint positions, but as already noted, the NGOs that were just beginning to participate in UN processes at the time of the WSSD were not satisfied with those traditional mechanisms. The work of the Development Caucus is discussed in detail in van Reisen (2000).

Chapter 10: Differentiated Autonomy

This chapter presents the main thrust of the argument of my next book, *Does North America Exist? Transborder Governance under NAFTA and the War on Terror*. It is the product of research done with students over the four-year period 2001-5. I would like to acknowledge in particular the assistance of Daniella Aburto, Mary Albino, Maria Banda, Stefanie Bowles, Kristen Brown, Christiane Buie, Ana Maria Cuenca, Sarah Davidson Ladly, Lanchanie Dias, Kate

Fischer, Zahra Habib, Ben Hutchinson, Ben Hyman, Dina Khorasanee, Christina Kish, Erick Lachapelle, Ian Macdonald, Regina Martyn, Alison McQueen, Megan Merwart, Jennifer Mullen, Chris Pigott, Roopa Rangaswami, Rick Russo, Jesse Sherrett, Michael Shloznikov, Anne Swift, Emily Tan, Carlton Thorne, Antonio Torres-Ruiz, and Mary Yu. The financial support of the Dean of the Faculty of Arts and Science at the University of Toronto made possible three research trips to Washington, DC, in the spring of 2002, 2003, and 2004 with two dozen of these students. The research has also been supported by various grants from the Social Sciences and Humanities Research Council of Canada.

Chapter 12: Subsidiarity and Autonomy in the European Union

1   This is based on research employing the various official databases of EU law (Eur-Lex, Celex, and Pre-Lex) detailed below. Despite some troubling inconsistencies and anomalies in the figures that these yield, they all provide consistent and robust support for the above conclusion.
2   The analysis extends to 30 June 2005. Averages have been adjusted to account for this.
3   I say "tentatively" because the Constitutional Treaty has not yet been fully ratified, and — at the time of writing — seems ever more unlikely to become so. Yet it provides us with the closest thing we have to an "official" catalogue of competences.
4   We may safely set aside the competence for the conclusion of international agreements, because these occupy a body of law separate from what we are examining here, which is internal legislation.

Works Cited

"A better world for all." 2000. Joint Statement by NGO Caucuses. Geneva, 28 June. http://www.earthsummit2002.org/wssd/wssd5/wssd5NGOs.htm (accessed 12 July 2006).

Abdelal, Rawi. 2007. *Capital rules.* Cambridge, MA: Harvard University Press.

Abel, R. 1994. Transnational law practice. *Case Western Reserve Law Review* 43 (2): 737-870.

ACIA. 2005. *Arctic Climate Impact Assessment.* Cambridge: Cambridge University Press.

AHDR. 2004. *Arctic human development report.* Akureyri: Stefansson Arctic Institute.

Alesina, Alberto, I. Angeloni, and L. Schuknecht. 2005. What does the European Union do? *Public Choice* 123 (3-4): 275-319.

Alston, Philip. 1997. The myopia of the handmaidens: International lawyers and globalization. *European Journal of International Law* 8 (3): 435-48.

Anderson, Kym. 2001. Developing country interests in agricultural trade reform: A Cairns Group perspective. In *Trade and agriculture: Negotiating a new agreement,* ed. Joseph A. McMahon, 89-120. London: Cameron May.

Andresen, Steinar. 1989. Science and politics in the international management of whales. *Marine Policy* 13 (2): 99-118.

—. 2001. The whaling regime: "Good" institutions but "bad" politics? In *Toward a sustainable whaling regime,* ed. Robert L. Friedheim, 235-69. Seattle: University of Washington Press.

Annisette, Marcia. 2002. Imperialism and the professions: The education and certification of accountants in Trinidad and Tobago. *Accounting, Organizations and Society* 25 (7): 631-59.

Appadurai, Arun. 1986. The social life of things: Commodities in a cultural perspective. Cambridge: Cambridge University Press.

—. 1996. *Modernity at large: Cultural dimensions of globalization.* Minneapolis: University of Minnesota Press.

—. 2002. Deep democracy: Urban governmentality and the horizon of politics. *Public Culture* 14 (1): 21-47.

Appiah, Anthony Kwame. 2005. *The ethics of identity.* Princeton, NJ: Princeton University Press.

Arnold, Patricia J., and Prem Sikka. 2001. Globalization and the state-profession relationship: The case [of] the Bank of Credit and Commerce International. *Accounting, Organizations and Society* 26 (6): 475-99.

Arrighi, Giovanni. 1997. Globalization, state sovereignty, and the "endless" accumulation of capital. Paper presented at Conference on States and Sovereignty in the World Economy. University of California, Irvine, 21-23 February.

Arthurs, Harry. 1997. Globalization of the mind: Canadian elites and the restructuring of legal fields. *Canadian Journal of Law and Society* 12 (2): 219-46.

—. 1999. A global code of ethics for the transnational legal field. *Legal Ethics* 2 (1): 21-31.

Arunachalam, Jaya. 1995. Statement on behalf of the National Union of Working Women (NGO), India, at the World Summit for Social Development, Copenhagen, Denmark, 8 March. http://www.un.org/documents/ga/conf166/ngo/950308114635.htm (accessed 6 July 2006).

Azzi, Giuseppe. 1998. Better lawmaking: The experience and view of the European Commission. *Columbia Journal of European Law* 4 (3): 617-28.

Bairoch, Paul. 1989. European trade policy, 1815-1914. In *The Cambridge economic history of Europe from the decline of the Roman Empire*. Vol. 8, *The industrial economies: The development of economic and social policies,* ed. Peter Pollard and Sidney Mathias, 1-160. Cambridge: Cambridge University Press.

Barnett, Michael, and Martha Finnemore. 2004. *Rules for the world: International organizations and global politics*. Ithaca, NY: Cornell University Press.

Bartelson, Jens. 1995. *A genealogy of sovereignty*. Cambridge: Cambridge University Press.

Bauman, Zygmunt. 1998. *Globalization: The human consequences*. Cambridge: Polity.

Baxter, James. 1999. Officials see silver lining in cloud of lost trade disputes: WTO is expected to rule against Canada on Auto Pact, drug patents, asbestos. *Ottawa Citizen,* 13 July, C1.

Bayly, C.A. 2004. *The birth of the modern world: 1780-1914, in Blackwell history of the world*. Oxford: Blackwell.

Beaverstock, J.V. 2001. Transnational elite communities in global cities: Connectivities, flows and networks. *GaWC Research Bulletin* 63 (Z), http://www.lboro.ac.uk/gawc/rb/rb63.html (accessed 16 August 2006).

Beaverstock, J.V., R.G. Smith, and P.J. Taylor. 1999. The long arm of the law: London's law firms in a globalizing world-economy. *Environment and Planning* 31 (10): 1857-76.

—. 2000. Geographies of globalization: US law firms in world cities. *Urban Geography* 21 (2): 95-120.

Beck, Ulrich. 1992. *Risk society: Towards a new modernity*. London: Sage.

—. 1999. *World risk society*. Cambridge: Polity.

—. 2002. The cosmopolitan society and its enemies. *Theory, Culture and Society* 19 (1-2): 17-44.

—. 2006. *Cosmopolitan vision*. London: Polity.

Bell, Jim. 2004a. The loudest voice of all. Editorial. *Nunatsiaq News,* 2 July.

—. 2004b. Have money, will travel: U.S. grant fund eyes Nunavut. *Nunatsiaq News,* 27 August.

Benton, Lauren. 2002. *Law and colonial cultures: Legal regimes in world history, 1400-1900*. Cambridge: Cambridge University Press.

Bermann, George. 1994. Taking subsidiarity seriously: Federalism in the European Community and the United States. *Columbia Law Review* 94 (2): 331-456.

Bernstein, Steven, and Louis W. Pauly, eds. 2007. *Global liberalism and political order: Toward a new grand compromise?* Albany: State University of New York Press.

Bernstein, Steven, and William D. Coleman, eds. Forthcoming. *Unsettled legitimacy: Political community, power, and authority in a global era*. Vancouver: UBC Press

Blustein, Paul. 2001. *The chastening*. New York: Public Affairs.

Bodenhorn, Barbara. 2003. Fall whaling in Barrow, Alaska: A consideration of strategic decision-making. In *Indigenous ways to the present: Native whaling in the Western Arctic*, ed. Allen P. McCartney, 277-305. Edmonton: Canadian Circumpolar Institute Press.

Bourdieu, Pierre. 1987. The force of law: Toward a sociology of the juridical field. *Hastings Law Journal* 38 (5): 814-53.

Bowley, Graham. 2005. In Europe, a shared foreign policy, too. *International Herald Tribune*, 19-20 February.

Brainard, Lael. 2003. Compassionate conservatism confronts global poverty. *Washington Quarterly* 26 (2): 149-69.

Brainard, Lael, Carol Graham, Nigel Purvis, Steven Radelet, and Gayle E. Smith. 2003. *The other war: Global poverty and the Millennium Challenge Account*. Washington, DC: Brookings Institution.

Branner, Hans. 1992. Danish European policy since 1945: The question of sovereignty. In *European integration and Denmark's participation,* ed. Morten Kelstrup, 297-327. Copenhagen: Copenhagen Political Studies Press.

Brewster, Mike. 2003. *Unaccountable: How the accounting profession forfeited a public trust*. Hoboken, NJ: Wiley.

Brodhead, Tim, and Brent Herbert-Copley. 1988. *Bridges of hope? Canadian voluntary agencies and the Third World*. Ottawa: North-South Institute.

Brodie, Janine. 2004. Globalization and the social question. In *Governing under stress: Middle powers and the challenge of globalization*, ed. Stephen Clarkson and Marjorie Griffin Cohen, 12-30. London and New York: Zed Books.

Brower, Harry. 2004. *The whales, they give themselves: Conversations with Harry Brower, Sr.* Fairbanks: University of Alaska Press.

Brown, Michael, and John May. 1991. *The Greenpeace story*. New York: Dorling Kindersley.

Brubaker, Rogers. 1996. *Nationalism reframed*. Cambridge: Cambridge University Press.

Buira, Ariel, and Jose Antonio Ocampo, eds. 2005. *Reforming the governance of the IMF and World Bank*. New York: Anthem.

Bull, Hedley. 1977. *The anarchical society: A study of order in world politics*. London: Macmillan.

Buzan, Barry, Charles Jones, and Richard Little. 1993. *The logic of anarchy*. New York: Columbia University Press.

Cain, Maureen, and B. Harrington, eds. 1994. *Lawyers in a postmodern world: Translation and transgression*. Buckingham, UK: Open University Press.

Camilleri, Joseph A., and Jim Falk. 1992. *The end of sovereignty: The politics of a shrinking and fragmenting world*. Aldershot, UK: Edward Elgar.

Campbell, John, John A. Hall, and Ove Kaj Pedersen, eds. 2006. *National identity and the varieties of capitalism: The Danish experience*. Montreal and Kingston: McGill-Queen's University Press.

Canada. 2005. Bill C-9: An Act to Amend the Patent Act and the Food and Drugs Act.

Caramanis, Constantinos. 2002. The interplay between professional groups, the state, and supranational agents: Pax Americana in the age of "globalization." *Accounting, Organizations and Society* 27 (4/5): 379-408.

Carozza, Paolo G. 2003. Subsidiarity as a structural principle of international human rights law. *American Journal of International Law* 97 (1): 38-79.

Carroll, Berenice A. 1972. Peace research: The cult of power. *Journal of Conflict Resolution* 16 (4): 585-616.

Castells, Manuel. 1996. *The rise of the network society.* Vol. 1, *The information age: Economy, society and culture.* Oxford: Blackwell.

Castoriadis, Cornelius. 1991. *Philosophy, politics, autonomy: Essays in political philosophy,* ed. David Ames Curtis. New York: Oxford University Press.

Charlton, Peter. 2004. The globalization of law. 5th Globalization and World Cities Study Group and Network Annual Lecture. http://www.lboro.ac.uk/gawc/rb/a15.html (accessed 16 August 2006).

Chase, Stephen. 2002. No bad blood with Ottawa over subsidies: Brazil. *Globe and Mail,* 22 January, B11.

Christiansen, Thomas, and Simona Piattoni, eds. 2004. *Informal governance in the European Union.* Aldershot, UK: Edward Elgar.

Claes, Dag Harald, and Bent Sofus Tranøy, eds. 1999. *Utenfor, Annerledes og Suveren? Norge under EØS-avtalen* [Outside, different, and sovereign? Norway under the EEA agreement]. Bergen: Fakbogsforslaget.

Clark, Ian. 2005. *Legitimacy in international society.* Oxford: Oxford University Press.

Clarkson, Stephen. 2002. *Uncle Sam and us: Globalization, neoconservatism, and the Canadian state.* Washington: Woodrow Wilson Press; Toronto: University of Toronto Press.

—. 2004. Global governance and the semi-peripheral state: The WTO and NAFTA as Canada's external constitution. In *Governing under stress: Middle powers and the challenge of globalization,* ed. Marjorie Griffin Cohen and Stephen Clarkson, 153-74. Black Point, NS: Fernwood Publishing.

Clarkson, Stephen, Sarah Davidson Ladly, Megan Merwart, and Carleton Thorne. 2005. The primitive realities of continental governance in North America. In *Complex sovereignty: Reconstituting political authority in the twenty-first century,* ed. Edgar Grande and Louis W. Pauly, 168-94. Toronto: University of Toronto Press.

Claude, Inis L., Jr. 1966. Collective legitimization as a political function of the United Nations. *International Organization* 20 (3): 367-79.

Clavin, Patricia. 2003. "Money talks": Competition and cooperation with the League of Nations, 1929-1940. In *Money doctors: The experience of international financial advising, 1850-2000,* ed. Marc Flandreau, 219-48. London: Routledge.

Coate, Roger A. 1988. *Unilateralism, ideology, and U.S. foreign policy: The United States in and out of UNESCO.* Boulder, CO: Lynne Reinner.

Coate, Roger, and Hans N. Weiler. 1986. Withdrawing from UNESCO: A decision in search of an argument. *Comparative Education Review* 30 (1): 132-9.

Coffey, W.J. and A.S. Bailly. 1992. Producer services and systems of flexible production. *Urban Studies* 29 (6): 857-68.

Cohen, Marjorie Griffin, and Stephen Clarkson, eds. 2004. *Governing under stress: Middle powers and the challenge of globalization.* London and New York: Zed Books.

Cohn, T. 1993. The changing role of the United States in the global agricultural trade regime. In *World Agriculture and the GATT,* ed. W. Avery, 17-38. Boulder, CO: Lynne Rienner.

Coleman, William D. 1998. From protected development to market liberalism: Paradigm change in agriculture. *Journal of European Public Policy* 5 (4): 632-51.

—. 2001. Policy networks, non-state actors and internationalized policy-making: A case study of agricultural trade. In *Non-state actors in world politics,* ed. Daphné Josselin and William Wallace, 93-112. Hound Mills, UK: Palgrave.

Coleman, William D., Wyn P. Grant, and Timothy E. Josling. 2004. *Agriculture in the new global economy*. Cheltenham, UK: Edward Elgar.

Colwell, Rita R. and David Pramer. 1994. Back to the future with UNESCO. *Science* 265 (5175): 1047-8.

Commission of the European Communities. 2005. *Better Lawmaking 2004 (Annex)*. SEC (2005) 364.

Commission on Self-Governance. 2003. *Report from the Commission on Self-governance,* trans. Marianne A. Stenbæk. http://www.nanoq.gl (accessed 3 October 2005).

Condliffe, J.B. 1941. *The reconstruction of world trade: A survey of international economic relations.* London: George Allen and Unwin.

Cook, Peter. 1999. The case against Canada and the EU. *Globe and Mail,* 10 March, B2.

Cooke, T.E., and M. Kikuya. 1992. *Financial reporting in Japan.* Oxford: Blackwell.

Cooper, Andrew F., John English, and Ramesh Thakur, eds. 2002. *Enhancing global governance.* Tokyo: United Nations University Press.

Cooper, David J., Royston Greenwood, Bob Hinings, and John L. Brown. 1998. Globalization and nationalism in a multinational accounting firm: The case of opening new markets in Eastern Europe. *Accounting, Organizations and Society* 23 (5/6): 531-48.

Cooper, Ian. 2006. The watchdogs of subsidiarity: National parliaments and the logic of arguing in the EU. *Journal of Common Market Studies* 44 (2): 281-304.

Copenhagen Post. 2007. Aluminium giant eyes Greenland: Alcoa could become Greenland's largest employer if plans to build a refinery on the island are pushed through, 15 February.

Cornish, Mary, and Crystal Stewart. 2005. Wal-Mart and the struggle for global labour justice. *Lawyers Weekly,* 22 July, 3.

Cosgrove, Dennis. 1994. Contested global visions: One-world, whole earth, and the Apollo space photographs. *Annals of the Association of American Geographers* 84 (2): 270-94.

Covaleski, Mark A., Mark W. Dirsmith, and Larry Rittenberg. 2003. Jurisdictional disputes over professional work: The institutionalization of the global knowledge expert. *Accounting, Organizations and Society* 28 (4): 323-55.

Cox, Robert. 1994. Rethinking the end of the Cold War. *Review of International Studies* 20 (2): 187-200.

Cox, Robert, with Timothy Sinclair. 1996. *Approaches to world order.* Cambridge: Cambridge University Press.

Cutler, A. Claire. 1991. The "Grotian tradition" in international relations. *Review of International Studies* 17 (1): 41-65.

—. 1997. Artifice, ideology, and paradox: The public/private distinction in international trade law. *Review of International Political Economy* 4 (2): 261-85.

—. 2003. *Private power and global authority: Transnational merchant law in the global political economy.* Cambridge: Cambridge University Press.

—. 2004. Critical globalization studies and international law under conditions of postmodernity and late capitalism. In *Critical globalization studies,* ed. Richard Appelbaum and William Robinson, 197-205. New York and London: Routledge.

—. 2005. Gramsci, law and the culture of global capitalism. *Critical Review of International Social and Political Philosophy* 8 (4): 527-42.

—. 2006. Transnational business civilization, corporations, and the privatization of global governance. In *Global Corporate Power,* ed. Christopher May, 199-225. Boulder, CO: Lynne Rienner.

Cutler, A. Claire, Virginia Haufler, and Tony Porter, eds. 1999. *Private authority in international affairs*. Albany: State University of New York Press.

Daléus, Lennart. 2002. *IT and the Arctic*. Report for the Fifth Conference of Parliamentarians of the Arctic Region. Tromsø, Norway, 11-13 August.

Darling, Jim. 1999. *Gray whales*. Stillwater, MN: Voyageur Press.

Dasgupta, P. 2003. Globalization of law and practices. *Legal Services India*, 6 March 2003. http://www.globalpolicy.org/globaliz/law/intlaw/2003/0306dasgupta.htm (accessed 26 June 2006).

Dashwood, Alan. 2004. The relationship between the member states and the European Union/European Community. *Common Market Law Review* 41 (2): 355-81.

Davey, William. 2005. The WTO dispute settlement system: The first ten years. *Journal of International Economic Law* 8 (1): 17-50.

Deacon, Bob, Minna Ilva, Meri Koivusalo, Eeva Ollila, and Paul Stubbs. 2005. Copenhagen Summit ten years on: The need for effective social policies nationally, regionally and globally. *Policy Brief* no. 6. Helsinki: Globalism and Social Policy Programme.

De Búrca, Grainne. 1998. The principle of subsidiarity and the Court of Justice as an institutional actor. *Journal of Common Market Studies* 36 (2): 217-35.

—. 1999. Reappraising subsidiarity's significance after Amsterdam. Harvard Jean Monnet Working Paper No. 7/99. http://www.jeanmonnetprogram.org/papers/99/990701.html (accessed 29 October 2007).

de Gorter, Harry, Lilian Ruiz, and Merlinda D. Ingco. 2004. Export competition policies. In *Agriculture and the WTO: Creating a trading system for development,* ed. Merlinda D. Ingco and John D. Nash, 43-60. Washington, DC: World Bank and Oxford University Press.

Deibert, Ronald J. 2000. International plug 'n play? Citizen activism, the Internet, and global public policy. *International Studies Perspectives* 1: 255-72.

della Porta, Donatella, and Sidney Tarrow. 2005. Transnational processes and social activism: An introduction. In *Transnational protest and global activism,* ed. Donatella della Porta and Sidney Tarrow, 1-17. Lanham, MD: Rowman and Littlefield.

DeSombre, Elizabeth. 2001. Distorting global governance: Membership, voting, and the IWC. In *Toward a sustainable whaling regime,* ed. Robert L. Friedheim, 183-200. Seattle: University of Washington Press.

Dezalay, Yves, and Bryant Garth. 1996. *Dealing in virtue: International commercial arbitration and the construction of a transnational legal order*. Chicago: University of Chicago Press.

Diebold, William, Jr. 1952. The end of the I.T.O. *Essays in International Finance*, No. 16 (October). Princeton, NJ: Department of Economics and Social Institutions.

Direct Marketing. 1997. US applauds ruling on Canada magazine laws. 60 (4): 9.

Dirlik, Arif. 2007. *Global modernity: Modernity in the age of global capitalism*. Boulder, CO: Paradigm Publishers.

Disney, Julian. 2000. Civil society, the Copenhagen Summit and international governance. In *Civil society, NGOs and global governance*. GASPP Occasional Paper No. 7/2000, 9-22.

Ditchburn, Jennifer. 1999. Trade representative heats up magazine dispute. *CBC Current Affairs Online*, 12 January. http://www.cbc.ca/news (accessed 3 July 2003).

Domning, Daryl P. 1999. Endangered species: The common denominator. In *Conservation and management of marine mammals,* ed. John R. Twiss Jr. and Randall R. Reeves, 332-42. Washington, DC: Smithsonian Institution Press.

Donovan, Greg P. 1982. *Aboriginal/subsistence whaling*. Cambridge, UK: International Whaling Commission.

Doyal, Len, and Ian Gough. 1991. *A theory of human need*. New York: Guilford Press.

Drache, Daniel. 2002. One world, one system? The diversity deficits in standard-setting, development and sovereignty at the WTO; A report card on trade and the social deficit. *Robarts Centre Research Reports*, York University, Toronto.

Drake, William, and Kalypso Nicolaides. 1992. Ideas, interests, and institutionalization: "Trade in services." and the Uruguay Round. *International Organization* 46 (1): 37-100.

Dunn, John. 2003. Autonomy's sources and the impact of globalization. In *Virtues of independence and dependence on virtues,* ed. Ludvig Beckman and Emil Uddhammar, 47-62. New Brunswick, NJ: Transaction Publishers.

Earth Negotiations Bulletin (ENB). Various issues. International Institute for Sustainable Development. http://www.iisd.ca/wssd95.html (accessed 24 February 2006).

ECIMD-G (European Commission Internal Market Director-General). 2004. Comment letter in response to "Identifying Issues for the IASC Foundation Constitution Review," 11 February. http://www.iasb.org (accessed 21 August 2006).

Economist. 2004. Fair's fair: A row over accounting for derivatives has huge consequences, 6 March.

—. 2005. Crime and punishment: Can the government afford to indict one of the Big Four accounting firms? 23 June.

—. 2006. A matter of oversight: The PCAOB. 18 February.

Edwards, Michael. 1999. *Future positive: International cooperation in the 21st century.* London: Earthscan Publications.

Electronic-Commons.Net. 2003. UN system and civil society: An inventory and analysis of practices. Background Paper for the Secretary-General's Panel of Eminent Persons on United Nations Relations with Civil Society. http://www.ecommons.net/stage/main.pht ml?css=default&section=publicaccess&show=background_paper (accessed 5 July 2005).

Eliasen, Bogi. 2004. The Faroes and Greenland in UN documents. In *The right to national self-determination: The Faroe Islands and Greenland,* ed. S. Skaale, 169-78. Leiden and Boston: Martinus Nijhoff Publishers.

Ellis, Richard. 1991. *Men and whales.* New York: Alfred A. Knopf.

Ellul, Jacques. 1967. *The technological society.* New York: Alfred A. Knopf.

Emmerij, Louis, Richard Jolly, and Thomas G. Weiss. 2001. *Ahead of the curve? UN ideas and global challenges.* Bloomington: Indiana University Press.

Espersen, Ole. 2004. Summary and main conclusions. In *The right to national self-determination: The Faroe Islands and Greenland,* ed. S. Skaale, 1-12. Leiden and Boston: Martinus Nijhoff Publishers.

Esping-Andersen, Gosta. 1990. *Three worlds of welfare capitalism.* Cambridge: Polity Press.

Estella, Antonio. 2002. *The EU principle of subsidiarity and its critique.* Oxford: Oxford University Press.

European Convention. 2004. *Draft treaty establishing a constitution for Europe.* http://europa. eu.int/futurum/constitution/table/index_en.htm (accessed 28 June 2006).

Falk, Richard. 2003. Globalization from below: An innovative politics of resistance. In *Civilizing globalization: A survival guide,* ed. Richard Sandbrook, 191-205. Albany: State University of New York Press.

Felice, William. 1997. The Copenhagen Summit: A victory for the World Bank. *Social Justice* 24 (1): 107-19.

Fenge, Terry. 2001. The Inuit and climate change. *Isuma* 2 (4): 79-85.

Ferry, Elizabeth. 2005. *Not ours alone: Patrimony, value, and collectivity in contemporary Mexico.* New York: Columbia University Press.

Finlayson, Jock A., and Mark W. Zacher. 1988. *Managing international markets: Developing countries and the commodity trade regime.* New York: Columbia University Press.

Fligstein, Neil. 2001. *The architecture of markets.* Princeton, NJ: Princeton University Press.

Føllesdal, Andreas. 1998. Survey article: Subsidiarity. *Journal of Political Philosophy* 6 (2): 190-218.

Fotheringham, W.G. 2004. Nunavut tourist industry needs outside investment. *Nunatsiaq News,* 2 January.

Frederiksen, Rasmus. 2005. Quota on fin whales are cut in half. 22 June. http://www.dk.nanoq.gl (accessed 21 September 2005).

Freeman, Milton M.R., and Urs P. Kreuter. 1994. Introduction. In *Elephants and whales: Resources for whom?* ed. Milton M.R. Freeman and Urs P. Kreuter, 1-16. Amsterdam: Gordon and Breach Science Publishers.

Friedheim, Robert L. 2001. Introduction: The IWC as a contested regime. In *Toward a sustainable whaling regime,* ed. by Robert L. Friedheim, 3-51. Seattle: University of Washington Press.

Friedman, Elisabeth Jay, Kathryn Hochstetler, and Ann Marie Clark. 2005. *Sovereignty, democracy, and global civil society: State-society relations at UN World Conferences.* Albany: State University of New York Press.

Friedman, Lawrence, M. Robert, W. Gordon, Sophie Pirie, and Edwin Whatley. 1988. Law, lawyers, and legal practice in the Silicon Valley: A preliminary report. *Indiana Law Journal* 64: 555-68.

Friedman, Marilyn. 2003. *Autonomy, gender, politics.* Oxford: Oxford University Press.

Gambell, Ray. 1999. The International Whaling Commission and the contemporary whaling debate. In *Conservation and management of marine mammals,* ed. John R. Twiss Jr. and Randall R. Reeves, 179-98. Washington, DC: Smithsonian Institution Press.

Genschel, Philipp. 2004. Globalization and the welfare state: A retrospective. *Journal of European Public Policy* 11 (4): 613-36.

George, Jane. 2003. Security group trains for Arctic ship disaster. *Nunatsiaq News,* 28 November.

—. 2004. Greenland pushes for complete self-reliance. *Nunatsiaq News,* 10 September.

—. 2006. Welcome to Beerland. *Nunatsiaq News,* 4 August.

George, Stephen. 1990. *An awkward partner.* Oxford: Oxford University Press.

Giddens, Anthony. 1984. *The constitution of society.* Berkeley and Los Angeles: University of California Press.

Gill, Stephen. 2000. Towards a postmodern prince? The Battle in Seattle as a moment in the new politics of globalization. *Millennium: Journal of International Studies* 29 (1): 131-40.

—. 2003. *Power and resistance in the new world order.* Houndsmill, UK: Palgrave Macmillan.

Gill, Stephen, and David Law. 1988. *The global political economy: Perspectives, problems and policies.* Baltimore, MD: Johns Hopkins University Press.

Globe and Mail. 2003. Wheat board math. Editorial, 5 August.

Goldmann, Kjell. 1994. *The logic of internationalism: Coercion and accommodation.* London: Routledge.

Goldstein, Judith, Milees Kahler, Robert Keohane, and Anne-Marie Slaughter. 2000. Introduction: Legalization and world politics. *International Organization* 54 (3): 385-99.

Goldstein, Judith, and Robert O. Keohane, eds. 1993. *Ideas and foreign policy.* Ithaca, NY: Cornell University Press.

Gough, Ian. 2003. *Lists and thresholds: Comparing the Doyal-Gough theory of human need with Nussbaum's capabilities approach.* Bath, UK: ESRC Research Group on Wellbeing in Developing Countries.

Grande, Edgar, and Louis W. Pauly, eds. 2005. *Complex sovereignty: Reconstituting political authority in the twenty-first century.* Toronto: University of Toronto Press.

Grande, Edgar, Heiko Prange, and Dieter Wolf. n.d. Perverse choices? State capacities in the age of globalization. Unpublished paper.

Greenland Home Rule Government. 2001. Tip of the iceberg: A summary of contacts, cooperation and agreements between Greenland and Canada. Nuuk: Greenland Home Rule Government Publication.

—. 2004. Statement regarding the government of Greenland's strategy for exporting ice and water. The Bureau of Minerals and Petroleum, the Government of Greenland. The Home Rule Parliament Act No. 7 of May 31st, 2001, on the exploitation of ice and water for exportation, http://www.bmp.gl (accessed 4 July 2005).

—. 2006. Preliminary studies on utilizing hydropower. The Ministry of Industry, Labour and Vocational Training has signed a joint action plan on preliminary studies with the aluminium company Alcoa. News Release, 17 July. http://www.nanoq.gl (accessed 21 July 2006).

Gulløv, Hans. 1979. Home Rule in Greenland. *Études/Inuit/Studies* 3 (1): 131-42.

Haas, Ernst B. 1971. The study of regional integration: Reflections on the joy and anguish of pre-theorizing. In *Regional integration: Theory and research*, ed. Leon N. Lindberg and Stuart A. Scheingold, 3-43. Cambridge, MA: Harvard University Press

—. 1990. *When knowledge is power.* Berkeley and Los Angeles: University of California Press.

Habermas, Jürgen. 1998. *Between facts and norms: Contributions to a discourse theory of law and democracy,* trans. William Rehg. Cambridge, MA: MIT Press.

Hall, Peter A., ed. 1989. *The political power of economic ideas.* Princeton, NJ: Princeton University Press.

Hall, Rodney Bruce, and Thomas Biersteker, eds. 2002. *The emergence of private authority in global governance.* Cambridge: Cambridge University Press.

Hannum, Hurst. 1990. *Autonomy, sovereignty, and self-determination: The accommodation of conflicting rights.* Philadelphia: University of Pennsylvania Press.

Hansen, John Mark. 1991. *Gaining access: Congress and the farm lobby, 1919-1981.* Chicago: University of Chicago Press.

Hardt, Michael, and Antonio Negri. 2000. *Empire.* Cambridge, MA: Harvard University Press.

Harhoff, Frederik. 1993. *Rigsfællesskabet: The community of the Danish realm.* English Summary. Århus: Forlaget Klim.

Harvey, David. 1990. *The condition of postmodernity: An enquiry into the origins of cultural change.* Cambridge, MA: Blackwell Publishers.

—. 2003. *The new imperialism.* Oxford: Oxford University Press.

Haworth, Lawrence. 1986. *Autonomy: An essay in philosophical psychology and ethics.* New Haven, CT: Yale University Press.

Hedegaard Rasmussen, Lise. 2002. *Suverænitet, integration og interdependens* [Sovereignty, integration, and interdependence]. Århus: Jean Monnet Center, University of Århus.

Hedetoft, Ulf. 1994. The state of sovereignty in Europe: Political concept or cultural self-image? In *National cultures and European integration: Exploratory essays on cultural diversity and common policies,* ed. Staffan Zetterholm, 13-48. Oxford: Berg.

—. 1998. Sovereignty and European integration from a Scandinavian perspective. In *Political symbols, symbolic politics: European identities in transformation,* ed. Ulf Hedetoft, 191-208. Aldershot, UK: Ashgate.

—. 2003a. *The global turn: National encounters with the world.* Aalborg: Aalborg University Press.

—. 2003b. The interplay between mass and elite attitudes to European integration in Denmark. In *Denmark's policy towards Europe after 1945*, ed. Hans Branner and Morten Kelstrup, 282-305. Odense: Odense University Press.

—. Forthcoming. Globalization and US empire: Moments in the forging of the global turn. In *Empires and Autonomy: Moments in the History of Globalization*, ed. Stephen M. Streeter, John C. Weaver, and William D. Coleman. Vancouver: UBC Press.

Held, David. 1995. *Democracy and the global order: From the modern state to cosmopolitan governance*. Stanford, CA: Stanford University Press.

Held, David, Anthony G. McGrew, David Goldblatt, and Jonathan Perraton. 1999. *Global transformations: Politics, economics and culture*. Stanford, CA: Stanford University Press.

Herman, Barry. 2002. Civil society and the financing for development initiative at the United Nations. In *Civil society and global finance*, ed. Jan Aart Scholte and Albrecht Schnabel, 162-78. Tokyo: United Nations University Press.

Herman, Barry, Frederica Pietracci, and Krishnan Sharma, eds. 2001. *Financing for development: Proposals from business and civil society*. Tokyo and New York: United Nations University Press.

Hessini, Leila, and Anita Nayar. 2000. *Social watch: A movement toward social justice. An evaluation report*. New York: Strategic Analysis for Gender Equity. http://www.socialwatch.org/en/acercaDe/evaluacion.htm (accessed 12 July 2006).

Hill, Martin. 1946. *The economic and financial organization of the League of Nations: A survey of twenty-five years' experience*. Washington, DC: Carnegie Endowment for International Peace.

—. 1978. *The United Nations system: Coordinating the economic and social work*. Cambridge: Cambridge University Press.

Hobsbawm, Eric. 1996. *The age of extremes: The short twentieth century, 1914-1991*. New York: Vintage.

Holsti, Kalevi. 2004. *Taming the sovereigns: Institutional change in international politics*. Cambridge: Cambridge University Press.

Hopkins, A.G. 2002a. The history of globalization — and the globalization of history? In *Globalization in world history*, ed. A.G. Hopkins, 11-46. London: Pimlico.

—. 2002b. Introduction: Globalization — An agenda for historians. In *Globalization in world history*, ed. A.G. Hopkins, 4-11. London: Pimlico.

Hoskin, Keith, and Richard Macve. 1994. Writing, examining, disciplining: The genesis of accounting's modern power. In *Accounting as social and institutional practice,* ed. Anthony G. Hopwood and Peter Miller, 67-97. Cambridge: Cambridge University Press.

Howe, Geoffrey. 1990. Sovereignty and interdependence: Britain's place in the world. *International Affairs* 66 (4): 675-95.

Howe, Stephen. 2003. *American empire: The history and future of an idea*. London: openDemocracy, 12 June. http://www.openDemocracy.net (accessed 28 June 2006).

Howse, Robert. 2003. How to think about the "democratic deficit" at the WTO. In *International economic governance and non-economic concerns: New challenges for the international legal order,* ed. S. Griller, 79-101. Vienna and New York: Springer-Verlag.

Hudec, Robert. 1970. The GATT legal system: A diplomat's jurisprudence. *Journal of World Trade Law* 4: 615-65.

—. 1991. *Enforcing international trade law: The evolution of the modern GATT legal system*. Salem, NH: Butterworth Legal Publishers.

Hunter, Robert. 1979. *Warriors of the rainbow: A chronicle of the Greenpeace movement*. New York: Holt, Rinehart, and Winston.

Hurd, Ian. 1999. Legitimacy and authority in international affairs. *International Organization* 53 (2): 379-403.

Hussey, Roger. 1999. Shame about standards. *Accountancy International.* http://www.ifac.org/ Library (accessed 21 August 2006).

IAASB (International Auditing and Assurance Standards Board). 2004. *Annual report.* http:// www.ifac.org (accessed 21 August 2006).

IMF, OECD, UN, and World Bank. 2000. *A better world for all: Progress towards the international development goals.* Washington, DC, Paris, and New York: Authors.

IWC. 1981. Chairman's report of the thirty-second annual meeting. *Report of the International Whaling Commission.*

Inayatullah, Naeem, and David L. Blaney. 1995. Realizing sovereignty. *Review of International Studies* 21 (1): 3-20.

Ingco, Merlinda D., and John D. Nash. 2004. What's at stake: Developing country interests in the Doha Development Round. In *Agriculture and the WTO: Creating a trading system for development,* ed. Merlinda D. Ingco and John D. Nash, 1-22. Washington, DC: World Bank and Oxford University Press.

International Trade Reporter. 2003. Canada blocks US request for WTO panel on Wheat Board. 20 March.

Irwin, Douglas A. 1996. *Against the tide: An intellectual history of free trade.* Princeton, NJ: Princeton University Press.

Iyer, Ram. 2001. A question of interpretation. *Accountancy* 127 (1289): 101-2.

Jack, Ian. 2001. Canada to appeal WTO dairy ruling. *National Post,* 7 July.

Jackson, John H. 1969. *World trade and the law of the GATT.* New York: Bobbs-Merrill.

—. 1997. *The world trading system: Law and policy of international economic relations.* Cambridge, MA: MIT Press.

—. 1998. *The World Trade Organization: Constitution and jurisprudence.* London: Pinter.

—. 2005. The changing fundamentals of international law and ten years of the WTO. *Journal of International Economic Law* 8 (1): 3-15.

James, Alan. 1999. The practice of sovereign statehood in contemporary international society. In *Sovereignty at the millennium,* ed. R. Jackson, 35-51. Oxford: Blackwell.

Jelved, Marianne. 2000. Det suveræne Danmark. *Politiken,* 29 April.

Jessop, Bob. 2002. *The future of the capitalist state.* Cambridge, UK: Polity Press.

Jolles, Carol Zane. 2002. *Faith, food, and family in a Yupik whaling community.* Seattle: University of Washington Press.

Jolly, Richard. 1995. *The UN and the Bretton Woods institutions.* London: Macmillan.

Josling, Timothy E., Stefan Tangermann, and T.K. Warley. 1996. *Agriculture in the GATT.* Basingstoke, UK: Macmillan.

Jull, Peter. 1998. "First world" indigenous internationalism after twenty-five years. *Indigenous Law Bulletin* 4(9): 8-11.

—. 1999. Indigenous internationalism: What should we do next? *Indigenous Affairs* 1: 12-17.

Kahler, Miles. 1995. *International institutions and the political economy of integration.* Washington, DC: Brookings Institution.

Kalland, Arne. 1993. Management by totemization: Whale symbolism and the anti-whaling campaign. *Arctic* 46 (2): 124-33.

—. 1994. Whose whale is that? Diverting the commodity path. In *Elephants and whales: Resources for whom?* ed. Milton M.R. Freeman and Urs P. Kreuter, 159-86. Amsterdam: Gordon and Breach Science Publishers.

Katzenstein, Peter. 1985. *Small states in world markets.* Ithaca: Cornell University Press.

—. 2005. *A world of regions: Asia and Europe in the American Imperium.* Ithaca, NY: Cornell University Press.

Kaufman, Robert R., and Alex Segura-Ubiergo. 2001. Globalization, domestic politics, and social spending in Latin America. *World Politics* 53 (4): 553-87.

Kennedy, David. 1997. New approaches to comparative law: Comparativism and global governance. *Utah Law Review* 1997 (2): 545-638.

Keohane, Robert O. 1984. *After hegemony.* Princeton, NJ: Princeton University Press.

—. 1994. Hobbes' dilemma and institutional change in world politics: Sovereignty in international society. In *Whose world order: Uneven globalization and the end of the Cold War,* ed. Hans-Henrik Holm amd Georg Sørensen, 165-86. Boulder, CO: Westview.

Keohane, Robert O., and Stanley Hoffmann. 1991. Institutional change in Europe in the 1980s. In *The new European community: Decision-making and institutional change,* ed. Robert O. Keohane and Stanley Hoffmann, 1-39. Boulder, CO: Westview.

Keskitalo, Eva C.H. 2004. *Negotiating the Arctic: The construction of an international region.* New York and London: Routledge.

Kindleberger, C.P. 1989. Commercial policy between the wars. In *The Cambridge economic history of Europe from the decline of the Roman Empire.* Vol. 8, *The industrial economies: The development of economic and social policies,* ed. Peter Pollard and Sidney Mathias, 161-96. Cambridge: Cambridge University Press.

Klein, Naomi. 2001. Reclaiming the Commons. *New Left Review* 9: 81-9.

Knauss, John A. 2001. Foreword. In *Toward a sustainable whaling regime,* ed. Robert L. Friedheim, vii-viii. Seattle: University of Washington Press.

Knight, W. Andy. 2000. *A changing United Nations: Multilateral evolution and the quest for global governance.* London: Macmillan.

—, ed. 2001. *Adapting the United Nations to a postmodern era.* London: Palgrave.

Knorr Cetina, Karin D. 1997. Sociality with objects: Social relations in postsocial knowledge societies. *Theory, Culture and Society* 14 (4): 1-30.

Krasner, Stephen D. 1985. *Structural conflict: The third world against global liberalism.* Berkeley and Los Angeles: University of California Press.

—. 1999. *Sovereignty: Organized hypocrisy.* Princeton, NJ: Princeton University Press.

—. 2001a. Problematic sovereignty. In *Problematic sovereignty: Contested rules and political possibilities,* ed. S.D. Krasner, 1-23. New York: Columbia University Press.

—. 2001b. Abiding Sovereignty. *International Political Science Review* 22 (3): 229-51.

Lake, David. 2003. The new sovereignty in international relations. *International Studies Review* 5 (3): 303-23.

Lanoszka, Anna. 2006. Autonomy and domination within the global trade system: Developing countries in quest for democratic WTO. *Globalization and Autonomy Online Compendium.* http://www.globalatuonomy.ca.

Latham, R., and S. Sassen. 2005. Digital formations: Constructing an object of study. In *Digital formations: IT and new architectures in the global realm,* ed. R. Latham and S. Sassen, 1-33. Princeton, NJ: Princeton University Press.

Lavelle, Louis. 2000. The Big Five's credibility gap is getting wider. *Business Week,* 30 October, 90-1.

Lavigne, David M., Victor B. Scheffer, and Stephen R. Kellert. 1999. The evolution of North American attitudes toward marine mammals. In *Conservation and management of marine mammals,* ed. John R. Twiss Jr. and Randall R. Reeves, 10-45. Washington, DC: Smithsonian Institution Press.

Lengyel, Peter. 1986. *International social science: The UNESCO experience.* New Brunswick, NJ: Transaction Books.

Lipschutz, Ronnie D. 1992. Reconstructing world politics: The emergence of global civil society. *Millennium: Journal of International Studies* 21 (3): 389-420.

Lipschutz, Ronnie D., with James K. Rowe. 2005. *Globalization, governmentality and global politics: Regulation for the rest of us?* London and New York: Routledge.

Litowitz, D. 2000. Gramsci, hegemony, and the law. *Brigham Young University Law Review* 2000 (2): 515-51.

Livingston, Robert Eric. 2001. Glocal knowledges: Agency and place in literary studies. *PMLA* 116 (1): 145-57.

Loukacheva, Natalia. 2007. *The Arctic promise: Legal and political autonomy of Greenland and Nunavut.* Toronto: University of Toronto Press.

Luhmann, Niklas. 1984. The self-description of society: Crisis fashion and sociological theory. *International Journal of Comparative Sociology* 25 (1/2): 59-72.

Macdonald, Ian. 2003. NAFTA and the emergence of continental labour co-operation. *American Review of Canadian Studies* 33(2): 29-52.

Mackenzie, Catriona, and Natalie Stoljar, eds. 2000. *Relational autonomy: Feminist perspectives on autonomy, agency, and the social self.* New York: Oxford University Press.

Mackintosh, N.A. 1965. *The stocks of whales.* London: Fishing News Books.

Maddison, Angus. 1995. *Monitoring the world economy, 1820-1992.* Paris: OECD.

—. 2001. *The world economy: A millennial perspective.* Paris: OECD.

Mann, Janet, Richard C. Connor, Peter C. Tyack, and Hal Whitehead. 2000. *Cetacean societies: Field studies of dolphins and whales.* Chicago: University of Chicago Press.

Marx, Karl. 1976. *Capital: A critique of political economy.* Vol 1, Trans. B. Fowkes. Harmondsworth, UK: Penguin Books.

Mayor, Federico, in collaboration with Jérome Bindé. 2001. *The world ahead: Our future in the making.* Paris: UNESCO.

McBarnet, Doreen. 1984. Law and capital: The role of legal form and legal actors. *International Journal of the Sociology of Law* 12 (3): 231-8.

McClure, Wallace. 1933. *World prosperity as sought through the economic work of the League of Nations.* New York: Macmillan.

McRae, Donald. 2000. The WTO in international law: Tradition continued or new frontier? *Journal of International Economic Law* 3 (1): 27-41.

Mehrotra, Santosh, and Richard Jolly, eds. 1997. *Development with a human face.* Oxford: Clarendon.

Merryman, John. 1986. Two ways of thinking about cultural property. *American Journal of International Law* 80 (4): 831-53.

Meyer, John W., J. Boli, G. Thomas, and F. Ramirez. 1997. World society and the nation-state. *American Journal of Sociology* 103 (1): 144-81.

Miller, Peter, and Ted O'Leary. 1994. Governing the calculable person. In *Accounting as social and institutional practice,* ed. Anthony G. Hopwood and Peter Miller, 98-115. Cambridge: Cambridge University Press.

Miller-Segarra, Tracy. 2002. Changes inevitable for audit-consulting relationships. *Accountants Media Group,* 30 October.

Millon-Delsol, C. 1992. *L'etat subsidiaire.* Paris: Presses Universitaires de France.

Minogue, Sara. 2005. Nunavut snags 36 nurses from overseas. *Nunatsiaq News,* 2 September.

Mittelman, James H. 2000. *The globalization syndrome: Transformation and resistance.* Princeton, NJ: Princeton University Press.

Milward, Alan. 1992. *The European rescue of the nation-state.* London: Routledge.

Morgan, G., and S. Quack. 2005. Institutional legacies and firm dynamics: The internation-alisation of British and German law firms. *Organization Studies* 26: 1765-86.

Morris-Suzuki, Tessa. 2000. For and against NGOs. *New Left Review* 2: 63-85.

Murphy, Craig. 1994. *International organization and industrial change*. New York: Oxford University Press.

—. 2006. *The United Nations Development Programme*. New York: Cambridge University Press.

Nedelsky, Jennifer. 2001. Judgment, diversity, and relational autonomy. In *Judgment, imagina-tion and politics*, ed. Ronnie Beiner and Jennifer Nedelsky, 103-20. Lanham, MD: Rowman and Littlefield.

NGO Forum. 1995. The Copenhagen Alternative Declaration, 8 March. http://www.un.org/documents/ga/conf166/ngo/950310124616.htm (accessed 23 February 2006).

Nobes, Christopher. 1992. *International classification of financial reporting*. 2nd ed. London and New York: Routledge.

Nordlinger, Eric A. 1981. *On the autonomy of the democratic state*. Cambridge, MA: Harvard University Press.

Nunatsiaq News. 2004a. Royal Greenland to seek foreign labour. 17 September.

—. 2004b. Greenland to sell water and ice. 23 April.

—. 2006. Greenland wants telemedicine. 25 August.

Nunavut. 2004. New fuel price reflects higher cost of world oil. News release, 26 July. http://www.gov.nu.ca (accessed 31 August 2006).

—. 2005a. Nunavut first in Canada to provide all its communities with Telehealth Units. News release, 1 February. http://www.gov.nu.ca (accessed 31 August 2006).

—. 2005b. Nunavut and Greenland agree to manage shared polar bear populations. News release, 28 April. http://www.gov.nu.ca (accessed 31 August 2006).

Nunavut Wildlife Management Board. 2000. Inuit bowhead knowledge study. http://www.nwmb.com/english/resources/bowhead_study.php (accessed 13 September 2006).

Nungaq, Zebedee. 1999. Zebedee Nungaq on Nunavut. *Inuktitut* 85: 19-32.

Nye, Joseph S. 2002. *The paradox of American power*. New York: Oxford University Press.

O'Brien, Robert, Anne Marie Goetz, Jan Aart Scholte, and Marc Williams. 2000. *Contesting global governance: Multilateral economic institutions and global social movements*. Cambridge: Cambridge University Press.

O'Brien, Susie, and Imre Szeman. 2001. Introduction: The globalization of fiction / the fic-tion of globalization. In Anglophone literatures and global culture. Special issue, *South Atlantic Quarterly* 100 (3): 603-26.

Obstfeld, Maurice, and Alan M. Taylor. 2004. *Global capital markets*. Cambridge: Cambridge University Press.

OECD (Organisation for Economic Co-operation and Development). Various years. *Development cooperation report: Statistical annex*. Paris: OECD.

—. 2001. Policy brief: Towards more liberal agricultural trade. *OECD Observer*. Paris: OECD.

—. 2002. *Agricultural policies in OECD countries: A positive reform agenda*. Paris: OECD.

OHCHR (Office of the United Nations High Commissioner for Human Rights). 2001. *United Nations guide for indigenous peoples*. Geneva: Office of the High Commissioner for Human Rights.

Okalik, Paul. 2006. Devolution and nation building in Canada's North. Speech to the Public Policy Forum Seminar on Economic Transformation North of 60. Ottawa, Ontario, 13 December. http://www.gov.nu.ca (accessed 14 February 2007).

Onuf, Nicholas, 1991. Sovereignty: Outline of a conceptual history. *Alternatives* 16 (1): 425-45.

Østerud, Øyvind, 2004. Globalization in Norwegian: Peculiarities at the European fringe. In *Governing under stress: Middle powers and the challenge of globalization*, ed. Stephen Clarkson and Marjorie Griffin Cohen, 34-50. London and New York: Zed Books.

Ostry, Sylvia. Forthcoming. The World Trade Organization: System under stress. In *Unsettled legitimacy: Political community, power, and authority in a global era*, ed. Steven Bernstein and William D. Coleman. Vancouver: UBC Press.

Pálsson, Gunnar. 2004. Statement of Ambassador Gunnar Pálsson, Chair of the Senior Arctic Officials at the Sixth Conference of Parliamentarians of the Arctic Region. Nuuk, 3-6 September.

Parsons, Talcott. 1971. *The system of modern societies.* Englewood Cliffs, NJ: Prentice-Hall.

Pasha, Mustapha Kamal, and David Blaney. 1998. Elusive paradise: The promise and peril of global civil society. *Alternatives* 23: 417-50.

Paul, Joel. 1988. The isolation of private international law. *Wisconsin International Law Journal* 7 (1): 149-78.

Pauly, Louis W. 1997. *Who elected the bankers? Surveillance and control in the world economy.* Ithaca, NY: Cornell University Press.

—. 2005. The political economy of international financial crises. In *Global political economy,* ed. John Ravenhill, 176-203. Oxford: Oxford University Press.

—. 2008. IMF surveillance and the legacy of Bretton Woods. In *Orderly change: International monetary relations since Bretton Woods*, ed. David Andrews. Ithaca, NY: Cornell University Press.

Pauwelyn, Joost. 2000. Enforcement and countermeasures in the WTO: Rules are rules. Toward a more collective approach. *American Journal of International Law* 94 (2): 335-47.

Payne, Roger. 1995. *Among whales.* New York: Scribner.

PCAOB (Public Company Accounting Oversight Board). 2003. *Annual report.* http://www.pcaobus.org (accessed 21 August 2006).

Petersen, Robert. 1984. The pan-Eskimo movement. In *Handbook of North American Indians.* Vol. 5, *Arctic,* ed. David Damas, 724-8. Washington: Smithsonian Institute.

Petersmann, Ernst-Ulrich. 1995. The transformation of the world trading system. *European Journal of International Law* 6 (2): 161-221.

Peterson, M.J. 1992. Whalers, cetologists, environmentalists, and the international management of whaling. *International Organization* 46 (1): 147-86.

Picciotto, Sol, and Ruth Mayne, eds. 1999. *Regulating international business: Beyond liberalization.* New York: St Martin's Press.

Pinter, Francis. 2001. Funding global civil society organizations. In *Global civil society 2001,* ed. Helmut Anheier, Marlies Glasius, and Mary Kaldor. London: Centre for the Study of Global Governance, London School of Economics and Political Science.

Pollack, Mark A. 2000. The end of creeping competence? EU policy-making since Maastricht. *Journal of Common Market Studies* 38 (3): 519-38.

Poulantzas, Nicos. 1974. *Political power and social classes.* London: New Left Books.

—. 1978. *State, power, socialism.* Trans. P. Camiller. London: Verso.

Powell, M.J. 1993. Professional innovation: Corporate lawyers and private lawmaking. *Law and Social Inquiry* 18 (3): 423-52.

Quack, Sigrid. 2004. Legal professions and transnational lawmaking: A case of distributed institutional entrepreneurship. Presented at a Conference on Global Governance and the Role of Non-State Actors at the London School of Economics, November 2004.

"The Quality Benchmark for the Social Summit". 1994. An NGO statement for the third session of the Preparatory Committee of the Social Summit (September). Unpublished document reproduced as Annex 5 in van Reisen (2000), 58-62.

Radelet, Steven. 2003. Bush and foreign aid. *Foreign Affairs* 82 (5): 104-17.

Radway, Janice. 1997. *A feeling for books: The Book-of-the-Month Club, literary taste and middle-class desire.* Chapel Hill: University of North Carolina Press.

Rasmussen, Henriette. 2004. On globalization and intangible cultural heritage. Keynote speech at the International Conference on Globalization and Intangible Cultural Heritage, Opportunities, Threats and Challenges. Tokyo, 26-27 August. http://www.nanoq.gl (accessed 9 November 2004).

Raustiala, Kal. 2003. Rethinking the sovereignty debate in international economic law. *Journal of International Economic Law* 6 (4): 841-78.

Redekop, John H. 1976. A reinterpretation of Canadian-American relations. *Canadian Journal of Political Science* 9 (2): 227-43.

Reich, Robert. 1991. *The work of nations.* New York: Knopf.

Reimann, Kim D. 2006. A view from the top: International politics, norms and the world-wide growth of NGOs. *International Studies Quarterly* 50 (1): 45-67.

Reus-Smit, Christian. 2004a. The politics of international law. In *The politics of international Law,* ed. Christian Reus-Smit, 14-44. Cambridge: Cambridge University Press.

—, ed. 2004b. *The politics of international Law.* Cambridge: Cambridge University Press.

Riddell-Dixon, Elizabeth. 2004. Democratizing Canadian foreign policy? NGO participation for the Copenhagen Summit for Social Development and the Beijing Conference on Women. *Canadian Foreign Policy* 11 (3): 99-118.

Robertson, Roland. 1992. *Globalization: Social theory and global culture.* London: Sage.

Robinson, William. 2004. *A theory of global capitalism: Production, class, and state in a transnational world.* Baltimore, MD: Johns Hopkins University Press.

Rosenau, James N. 1990. *Turbulence in world politics: A theory of change and continuity.* Princeton, NJ: Princeton University Press.

Rosenau, James N., and Ernst-Otto Czempiel, eds. 1992. *Governance without government: Order and change in world politics.* Cambridge: Cambridge University Press.

Rothwell, Donald R. 1996. *The polar regions and the development of international law.* Cambridge: Cambridge University Press.

Rudra, Nita. 2002. Globalization and the decline of the welfare state in less developed countries. *International Organization* 56 (2): 411-45.

Rudwick, Martin. 1992. *Scenes from deep time.* Chicago: University of Chicago Press.

Rupert, Mark. 2000. *Ideologies of globalization: Contending visions of world order.* London and New York: Routledge.

Russell, Peter H. 2004. *Constitutional odyssey: Can Canadians become a sovereign people?* 3rd ed. Toronto: University of Toronto Press.

Sambo, Dalee. 1992. Indigenous human rights: The role of Inuit at the United Nations Working Group on Indigenous Peoples. *Études/Inuit/Studies* 16 (1-2): 27-32.

Samuels, Amy, and Peter Tyack. 2000. Flukeprints: A history of studying cetacean societies. In *Cetacean societies: Field studies of dolphins and whales,* ed. Janet Mann, Richard C. Connor, Peter L. Tyack, and Hal Whitehead, 9-44. Chicago: University of Chicago Press.

Santos, B. 1987. Law: A map of misreading. Toward a postmodern conception of law. *Journal of Law and Society* 14 (3): 297-300.

—. 1995. *Towards a new common sense: Law, science and politics in the paradigmatic transition.* London: Routledge.

Sassen, Saskia. 1998. The state and the global city: Notes toward a conception of place-centered governance. In *Globalization and its discontents,* ed. Saskia Sassen, 195-218. New York: New Press.

—. 2002. Opening remarks: Producing the transnational in the national. In *Transnational legal processes: Globalization and power disparities,* ed. M. Likosky, 189-96. London: Butterworths.

—. 2004. Local actors in global politics. *Current Sociology* 52 (4): 649-70.

—. 2006. *Territory, authority, rights.* Princeton, NJ: Princeton University Press.

Schechter, Michael G., ed. 2001. *United Nations-sponsored world conferences.* Tokyo: United Nations University Press.

—. 2005. *United Nations global conferences.* London and New York: Routledge.

Schmitt, Carl. 1934/1996. *The concept of the political.* Trans. George Schwab. Chicago: Chicago University Press.

Schneiderman, David. 2000. Investment rules and the new constitutionalism: Interlinkages and disciplinary effects. *Law and Social Inquiry* 25: 757-87.

Scholte, Jan Aart. 1998. The IMF meets civil society. *Finance and Development* 35 (2): 42-5.

—. 2000. Global civil society. In *The political economy of globalization,* ed. Ngaire Woods, 173-201. New York: St Martin's Press.

—. 2002. Civil society and democracy in global governance. *Global Governance* 8 (3): 281-304.

—. 2005. *Globalization: A critical introduction.* 2nd ed. Basingstoke, UK: Macmillan.

Scoffield, Heather. 1998. Brazil slams Bombardier subsidies. *Globe and Mail,* 4 November.

Seck, Sara. 1999. Environmental harm in developing countries caused by subsidiaries of Canadian mining corporations: The interface of public and private international law. In *Canadian Yearbook of International Law.* Vol. 37, ed. Donald M. McRae, 139-223. Vancouver: UBC Press.

Sell, Susan. 1999. Multinational corporations as agents of change: The globalization of intellectual property rights. In *Private Authority and International Affairs,* ed. A. Claire Cutler, Virginia Haufler, and Tony Porter, 169-98. Albany: State University of New York Press.

—. 2003. *Private power, public law: The globalization of intellectual property rights.* Cambridge: Cambridge University Press.

Sen, Amartya Kumar. 1999. *Development as freedom.* New York: Random House.

Shell, G.R. 1995. Trade legalism and international relations theory: An analysis of the World Trade Organization. *Duke Law Journal* 44 (5): 829-927.

Shoyer, Andrew. 1998. The first three years of WTO dispute settlement: Observations and suggestions. *Journal of International Economic Law* 1 (2): 277-302.

Silver, Carole. 2000. Globalization and the US market in legal services: Shifting identities. *Law and Policy in International Business* 31 (4): 1093-151.

Simmel, Georg. 1971. *On individuality and social forms,* ed. Donald N. Levine. Chicago: University of Chicago Press.

Simon, Mary. 2004. The Arctic: A barometer of global change and a catalyst for global action. Speaking notes on behalf of ICC. New York, 26 April. http://www.inuitcircumpolar.com (accessed 12 October 2004).

Skogstad, Grace. 2003. Who governs? Who should govern? Political authority and legitimacy in Canada in the twenty-first century. *Canadian Journal of Political Science* 6 (5): 955-73.

Slaughter, Anne-Marie. 2004. *A new world order.* Princeton, NJ: Princeton University Press.

Slaughter, Anne-Marie, Andrew S. Tulumello, and Stepan Wood. 1998. International law and international relations theory: A new generation of interdisciplinary scholarship. *American Journal of International Law* 92 (3): 367-97.

Slijper, E.P. 1962. *Whales.* London: Hutchinson.

Smith, Adam. 1776/1991. *The wealth of nations.* New York: Everyman's Library.

Soros, George. 1998. *The crisis of global capitalism.* New York: Public Affairs.

Spanogle, J. 1991. The arrival of international private law. *George Washington Journal of International Law and Economics* 25: 477-522.

Spar, Debora. 1997. Lawyers abroad: The internationalization of legal practice. *California Management Review* 39 (3): 8-28.

Spruyt, Hendrik. 1994. *The sovereign state and its competitors.* Princeton, NJ: Princeton University Press.

Standish, Peter. 2000. *Developments in French accounting and auditing 2000.* http://www.experts-comptables.org/html/countries/gb/index.html (accessed 21 August 2006).

Steinhardt, R. 1991. The privatization of public international law. *George Washington Journal of International Law and Economics* 25 (2): 523-53.

Stewart, Frank, ed. 1995. *In the presence of whales: Contemporary writing on whales.* Anchorage: Alaska Northwest Books.

Stiglitz, Joseph. 2002. *Globalization and its discontents.* New York: Penguin.

Strange, Susan. 1954. The economic work of the United Nations. In *Yearbook of World Affairs,* 118-40. London: Stevens and Son.

Strati, Anastasia. 1991. Deep seabed cultural property and the common heritage of mankind. *International and Comparative Law Quarterly* 40 (4): 859-94.

Strayer, Joseph. 1970. *On the medieval origins of the modern state.* Princeton, NJ: Princeton University Press.

Stubbs, Paul. 2003. International non-state actors and social development policy. *Global Social Policy* 3 (3): 319-48.

Sullivan, Helena. 2002. Regional jet trade wars: Politics and compliance in WTO dispute resolution. *Minnesota Journal of Global Trade* 12 (1): 71-108.

Suzuki, Tomo. 2007. Accountics: Impacts of internationally standardized accounting on the Japanese socio-economy? *Accounting, Organizations and Society* 32: 263-301.

Sylvester, Christine. 1992. Feminists and realists view autonomy and obligation in international relations. In *Gendered states: Feminist (re)visions of international relations theory,* ed. V. Spike Peterson, 155-77. Boulder, CO: Lynne Rienner.

Tabb, William K. 2004. *Economic governance in the age of globalization.* New York: Columbia University Press.

Tarrow, Sidney. 2005. *The new transnational activism.* Cambridge: Cambridge University Press.

Task Force on the United Nations. 2005. *American interests and UN reform.* Washington: United States Institute of Peace.

Taylor, Charles. 1991. *The malaise of modernity.* Toronto: Anansi.

—. 2004. *Modern social imaginaries.* Durham, NC: Duke University Press.

Taylor, Paul. 2000. Managing the economic and social activities of the United Nations system: Developing the role of ECOSOC. In *The United Nations at the millennium,* ed. Paul Taylor and A.J.R. Groom. London: Continuum.

Tendler, Judith. 2004. Why social policy is condemned to a residual category of safety nets and what to do about it. In *Social policy in a development context,* ed. Thandika Mkandawire, 119-41. New York: Palgrave and UNRISD.

Teubner, Gunther. 2002. Breaking frames: Economic globalization and the emergence of *lex mercatoria. European Journal of Social Theory* 5 (2): 199-217.

Therien, Jean-Philippe. 1999. Beyond the North-South divide: The two tales of world poverty. *Third World Quarterly* 20 (4): 723-42.

Tomlinson, Brian. 2003. *An analysis of revenue trends, 1993-2000, for Canadian development cooperation civil society organizations.* Ottawa: Canadian Council on International Cooperation.

Tomlinson, John. 1999. *Globalization and culture.* Chicago: University of Chicago Press.

Toth, Akos. 1994. A legal analysis of subsidiarity. In *Legal issues of the Maastricht Treaty*, ed. David O'Keeffe and Patrick M. Twomey, 37-48. London and New York: Chancery Law Publishing.

Touron, Philippe. 2005. The adoption of US GAAP by French firms before the creation of the International Accounting Standards Committee: An institutional explanation. *Critical Perspectives on Accounting* 16: 851-73.

Toye, John, and Richard Toye. 2004. *The UN and global political economy.* Bloomington: Indiana University Press.

Trubeck, D., Yves Dezalay, S. Buchanan, and J. Davis. 1994. Global restructuring and the law: Studies in the internationalisation of the legal fields and transnational arenas. *Case Western Reserve Law Review* 44 (2): 407-98.

Tweedie, Sir David, and Thomas R. Seidenstein. 2005. Setting a global standard: The case for accounting convergence. *Northwestern Journal of International Law and Business* 25 (3): 589-608.

UNESCO. 2001. *Convention concerning the world cultural and natural heritage. Report of the rapporteur.* 25th session. Paris: Bureau of the World Heritage Committee.

UNGA (United Nations General Assembly). 2002. *Final outcome of the International Conference on Financing for Development.* UN Doc. A/CONF.198/1.

UN-HABITAT. 2004. *The state of the world's cities 2004/5: Globalization and urban culture.* London: Earthscan.

United Nations. 1995. *Report of the World Summit for Social Development.* A/CONF.166/9. 19 April. http://www.un.org/esa/socdev/wssd/ (accessed 6 June 2005).

—. 2004. *A more secure world: Our shared responsibility. A report of the Secretary General's High-level Panel on Threats, Challenges and Change.* New York: United Nations.

—. 2005. *In larger freedom: Towards development, security and human rights for all. Report of the Secretary General.* New York: United Nations, 21 March.

US GAO (US General Accounting Office). 2003. *Public accounting firms: Mandated study on consolidation and competition.* Report to the Senate Committee on Banking, Housing, and Urban Affairs and the House Committee on Financial Services, July.

Van Hacke, S. 2003. The principle of subsidiarity: Ten years of application in the European Union. *Regional and Federal Studies* 13 (1): 55-80.

Van Kersbergen, Kers, and Bertjan Verbeek. 1994. The politics of subsidiarity in the European Union. *Journal of Common Market Studies* 32 (4): 215-36.

—. 2004. Subsidiarity as a principle of governance in the European Union. *Comparative European Politics* 2 (2): 142-62.

van Reisen, Mirjam. 2000. The "prehistory" of Social Watch: The transformation of NGO networking in ongoing international negotiations. Report prepared for Social Watch. http://www.socialwatch.org/en/acercaDe/dientesDelLeon.htm (accessed 6 July 2006).

Vaubel, Roland. 1986. A public choice approach to international organization. *Public Choice* 51 (1): 39-57.

Vernon, Raymond. 1995. The World Trade Organization: A new stage in international trade and development. *Harvard International Law Journal* 36 (spring): 329-40.

Von Borries, R., and M. Hauschild. 1999. Implementing the subsidiarity principle. *Columbia Journal of European Law* 5 (3): 369-88.

Wæver, Ole. 1995. Identity, integration and security. Solving the sovereignty puzzle in EU studies. *Journal of International Affairs* 48 (2): 389-431.

Wai, Robert. 2001. Transnational liftoff and juridical touchdown: The regulatory function of private international law in an era of globalization. *Columbia Journal of Transnational Law* 40 (1): 209-74.

Walker, Robert B.J. 1993. *Inside/outside: International relations as political theory*. Cambridge: Cambridge University Press.

Walker, Robert B.J., and Saul Mendlovitz, eds. 1990. *Contending sovereignties: Redefining political community*. Boulder, CO: Lynne Rienner.

Wallerstein, Immanuel. 1995. *After liberalism*. New York: New Press.

Wapner, Paul. 1996. *Environmental activism and world civic politics*. Albany: State University of New York Press.

Watt-Cloutier, Sheila. 2004. Testimony of Sheila Watt-Cloutier, Chair of the Inuit Circumpolar Conference. Senate Committee on Commerce, Science and Transportation. Washington DC, 15 September. http://www.inuitcircumpolar.com (accessed 12 October 2004).

Webb, Michael C. 2004. Defining the boundaries of legitimate state practice: Norms, transnational actors and the OECD's project on harmful tax competition. *Review of International Political Economy* 11 (4): 787-827.

Wei-guo, Zhang. 1996. China's challenge: Building an accounting system. *Australian Accountant* 66 (7): 26.

Weiler, Joseph H. H. 1999. *The constitution of Europe: "Do the new clothes have an emperor?" and other essays*. Cambridge: Cambridge University Press.

—. 2001. The rule of lawyers and the ethos of diplomats: Reflections on the internal and external legitimacy of WTO dispute settlement. *Journal of World Trade* 35 (2): 191-207.

Weiss, Thomas G., Tatiana Carayannis, Louis Emmerij, and Richard Jolly. 2005. *UN voices*. Bloomington: Indiana University Press.

Weiss, Thomas G., David P. Forsythe, and Roger A. Coate. 2004. *The United Nations and changing global politics*. 4th ed. Boulder, CO: Westview Press.

Wendt, Alexander. 2003. Why a world state is inevitable. *European Journal of International Relations* 9 (4): 491-542.

Weyler, Rex. 2004. *Greenpeace*. Vancouver: Raincoast Books.

WHC (World Heritage Committee). 1977a. *Final Report*. 1st session. Paris.

—. 1977b. *Operational guidelines for the implementation of the World Heritage Convention*.

—. 1983. *Final report*. 7th session. Florence, Italy.

—. 1984. *Final report*. 8th session. Buenes Aires, Argentina.

—. 1986. *Report of the rapporteur*. 10th session. Paris.

—. 1990. *Report of the World Heritage Committee*. 14th session. Banff, Canada.

—. 1991. *Report of the World Heritage Committee*. 15th session. Carthage, Tunisia.

—. 1995. *Report of the rapporteur*. 19th session. Berlin.

—. 1999. *Report of the rapporteur*. 23rd session. Marrakesh, Morocco.

Whelan, Christopher J. 2001. Ethics beyond the horizon: Why regulate the global practice of law? *Vanderbilt Journal of Transnational Law* 34 (4): 931-52.

Whitehead, Hal, Randall R. Reeves, and Peter L. Tyack. 2000. Science and the conservation, protection, and management of wild cetaceans. In *Cetacean societies: Field studies of whales and dolphins,* ed. Janet Mann, Richard C. Connor, Peter L. Tyack, and Hal Whitehead, 308-33. Chicago: University of Chicago Press.

Willetts, Peter. 2000. From "consultative arrangements" to "partnerships": The changing status of NGOs in diplomacy at the UN. *Global Governance* 6 (2): 191-212.

Willoya, William, and Vinson Brown. 1963. *Warriors of the rainbow*. New York: Naturegraph Press.

Wilson, Edward O. 2003. *The future of life.* London: Abacus.

Winham, Gilbert. 1992. *The evolution of international trade agreements.* Toronto: University of Toronto Press.

—. 1998. The World Trade Organization: Institution-building in the multilateral trade system. *World Economy* 21 (3): 349-68.

—. 2005. An interpretative history of the Uruguay Round negotiation. In *Kluwer companion to the World Trade Organization,* ed. Arthur Appleton, Patrick McCrory, and Michael Plummer. Amsterdam: Springer.

Winner, Langdon. 1977. *Autonomous technology: Technics-out-of-control as a theme in political thought.* Cambridge, MA: MIT Press.

Wolfe, Robert. 1998. *Farm wars: The political economy of agriculture and the international trade regime.* Houndmills, UK: Macmillan.

—. 2005. See you in Geneva: Legal (mis)representations of the international trading system. *European Journal of International Relations* 11 (3): 339-65.

Woodmansee, Martha. 1994. *The author, art, and the market: Rereading the history of aesthetics.* New York: Columbia University Press.

Woods, Ngaire. 2001. Making the IMF and the World Bank more accountable. *International Affairs* 77 (1): 83-100.

—. 2006. *The globalizers: The IMF, the World Bank and their borrowers.* Ithaca, NY: Cornell University Press.

WTO (World Trade Organization). 1997. *Canada: Certain measures concerning periodicals.* Report of the panel, WT/DS31/R, 14 March. Geneva: World Trade Organization.

—. 1999. *Final reports on PROEX and Canadian Measures.* WTO panel report, WT/DS46/R, 12 March. Geneva: World Trade Organization.

—. 2004a. *United States: Subsidies on upland cotton.* Report of the Panel, WT/DS267/R. Geneva: World Trade Organization.

—. 2004b. *European Communities: Export subsidies on sugar.* Report of the Panel, WT/DS266/R. Geneva: World Trade Organization.

—. 2005a. *United States: Subsidies on upland cotton.* Report of the Appellate Body, WT/DS267/AB/R. Geneva: World Trade Organization.

—. 2005b. *European Communities: Export subsidies on sugar.* Report of the Appellate Body, WT/DS265/AB/R. Geneva: World Trade Organization.

Xiao, Jason Zezhong, Pauline Weetman, and Manli Sun. 2004. Political influence and co-existence of a uniform accounting system and accounting standards: Recent developments in China. *Abacus* 40 (2): 193-216.

Yablokov, Aleksei V. 1994. Validity of whaling data. *Nature* 367: 108.

Young, Oran R. 2000. The structure of Arctic cooperation: Solving problems/seizing opportunities. Conference report. *Fourth Conference of Parliamentarians of the Arctic Region,* 117-37. Helsinki: Edita.

—. 2002. Arctic governance: Preparing for the next phase. Article presented at the Arctic Parliamentary Conference. Tromsø, Norway, 11-13 August.

—. 2005. Governing the Arctic: From Cold War theater to mosaic of cooperation. *Global governance: A review of multilateralism and international organizations* 11 (1): 9-15.

Yúdice, George. 2003. *The expediency of culture: Uses of culture in the global era.* Durham, NC: Duke University Press.

Zahle, Henrik. 1998. *EU og den danske grundlov* [EU and the Danish constitution]. Copenhagen: Chr. Ejler.

Zeff, Stephen. 2002. "Political" lobbying on proposed standards: A challenge to the IASB. *Accounting Horizons* 16 (1): 43-54.

Zemsky, V.A., Y.A. Berzin, Y.A. Mikhalyev, and D.D. Tormosov. 1995. *Materials on whaling by Soviet Antarctic whaling fleets (1947-1972)*. Moscow: Center for Russian Environmental Policy.

Contributors

Diana Brydon is Canada Research Chair in Globalization and Cultural Studies at the University of Manitoba, where she directs the Centre for Globalization and Cultural Studies and teaches postcolonial literature and theory. Her current research investigates global imaginaries and critical literacies in the context of discourses of home.

Stephen Clarkson has taught political economy at the University of Toronto for four decades. His work has focused on aspects of the Canada-US relations and, since NAFTA was signed, on tri-national continental integration. He is currently finishing a large study, *Does North America Exist? Transborder Governance under NAFTA and the War on Terror.* Clarkson is a Fellow of the Royal Society of Canada and a Senior Fellow at the Centre for International Governance Innovation.

Ian Cooper is Assistant Professor of International Relations at Mount Allison University. He completed his PhD in Political Science at Yale University and has held post-doctoral fellowships at the University of Toronto and the Université catholique de Louvain, Belgium.

William D. Coleman is a Canada Research Chair on Global Governance and Public Policy. He is also Founder and Director of the Institute on Globalization and the Human Condition and Professor of Political Science at McMaster University. His research interests include theories of globalization, global dimensions of public policy, and the politics of agriculture and food.

A. Claire Cutler is a Professor of International Relations and International Law in the Political Science Department at the University of Victoria, Canada. She is author of *Private Power and Global Authority: Transnational Merchant Law in the Global Political Economy* and is presently working on a study of law and capitalism.

Sarah Eaton is a doctoral candidate in the Department of Political Science at the University of Toronto. She has published articles on international accounting standards and East Asian international political economy. She is currently researching changes in China's financial system.

Guy Gensey is Senior Trade Policy Advisor with the Ministry of Economic Development, Government of British Columbia. He taught political science for four years at Dalhousie University before taking up his current position in 2007. Gensey is presently writing an article on Canada's foreign equity limitations in the financial sector, as laid out in its international trade commitments.

Ulf Hedetoft is Professor of Nationality and Migration Studies, and Director of the SAXO Institute at the University of Copenhagen. He is also Director of the Academy for Migration Studies in Denmark (AMID).

Caren Irr teaches American literature and culture in the English department at Brandeis University. She is the author and/or editor of three books and numerous articles on cultural studies, US and Canadian writing, and the commons.

Natalia Loukacheva is a Research Associate at the Munk Centre for International Studies, University of Toronto. She is the author of *The Arctic Promise: Legal and Political Autonomy of Greenland and Nunavut*.

Louis W. Pauly holds the Canada Research Chair in Globalization and Governance and directs the Centre for International Studies at the University of Toronto. His previous books include *The Myth of the Global Corporation* and *Who Elected the Bankers? Surveillance and Control in the*

World Economy. With Emanuel Adler, he edits the journal *International Organization*.

Tony Porter is Professor of Political Science at McMaster University. His most recent book is *Globalization and Finance*.

Petra Rethmann is Associate Professor of Anthropology at McMaster University. She is the author of *Tundra Passages: Gender and History in the Russian Far East* and numerous articles on cultural identity, material culture, and history.

Emily Sinclair is a Master's candidate in the Faculty of Environmental Studies at York University. Her graduate research focuses on urban planning and the politics of social reproduction articulated around local and global food movements.

Michael Webb is Associate Professor of Political Science at the University of Victoria. He is author of *The Political Economy of Policy Coordination*. His recent publications on the Organisation for Economic Co-operation and Development and global tax governance examine the impact of non-state actors and norms on the revenue-raising side of social welfare policy.

Gilbert R. Winham is Professor Emeritus of Political Science and Adjunct Professor of Law at Dalhousie University. He is a Fellow of the Royal Society of Canada and a past Woodrow Wilson Fellow (2001/2). He has served frequently on NAFTA dispute settlement panels.

Index

PRINTED AND BOUND IN CANADA BY FRIESENS
SET IN BEMBO BY GEORGE KIRKPATRICK

Text design: GEORGE KIRKPATRICK
Copy editor: BARBARA TESSMAN
Proofreader: LESLEY ERICKSON
Indexer: ANNETTE LOREK